William Adamson

The Religious Anecdotes of Scotland

William Adamson

The Religious Anecdotes of Scotland

ISBN/EAN: 9783337325039

Printed in Europe, USA, Canada, Australia, Japan

Cover: Foto ©Lupo / pixelio.de

More available books at **www.hansebooks.com**

THE RELIGIOUS ANECDOTES

OF

SCOTLAND

Edited By

WILLIAM ADAMSON, D.D.

Edinburgh

Author of "Robert Milligan's Difficulties; or, Struggle and
Triumph: A Scotch Life Story,"
&c., &c

SECOND EDITION

LONDON: SIMPKIN, MARSHALL & CO
GLASGOW: THOMAS D. MORISON
1893

RESPECTFULLY DEDICATED

TO

Scotchmen and Scotchwomen

AT

HOME AND ABROAD

BY

A FELLOW COUNTRYMAN

The Compiler.

PREFACE.

There has been of late a great desire to enter upon the study, more or less minutely, of the particulars of individual lives. This has risen, in the main, from a motive worthy of all praise. It has been said that "the proper study of mankind is man," and in harmony with this idea, the desire has been developed, to know the details of the lives of those who have really lived, and who have made an impression on the minds of their contemporaries. Hence the numerous biographies, and volumes similar to the present, which have made their appearance.

It is somewhat difficult to define an Anecdote, and yet most people know it when it is placed before them. The word anecdote does not now bear its original significance, which was a secret history, something unedited and unpublished. On the contrary it means the reverse of this. It is not a story, nor a description, nor yet a connected series of stories. Taken, in its manifest and more correct form, as now understood, it is a particular, separated incident, of an interesting nature, which is a complete unity in itself. It thus presents a complete mental picture, and like pictures generally, is of a nature to arrest attention and instruct. Those who have a cultivated mind can at once discriminate an anecdote from what is like it, and will be able to appreciate what it makes known, while others do not trouble themselves about its nature, but seek to understand what it means. But all have a liking for the detached fact, which makes them feel that they can see deeper into the working of the human soul, and understand the emotions and motives which rule there. This gives the anecdote an attractive power, which culture does not destroy, but refine, and which is common to man as man.

PREFACE.

Scotch literature abounds with anecdotes of all kinds, and all degrees of excellency. This was to be expected from the strongly marked traits of Scotch character and the strength and massiveness of those who have made Scottish history. Especially, is this true of the religious side of Scottish history. That history is the record of struggle, severe contests, secessions, protests, sufferings, and progress. These gave rise to incidents of interest, which have a meaning, and these incidents have been cherished in the memory of the people. Thus the religious anecdotes of Scotland are, as it were, a minor history, which brings the noble of the past, close to those who live, that they may be inspired with their spirit and led to imitate their example. This is done in a pleasant manner by gaining a knowledge of the men of the past, their manner of life, their spirit, and the circumstances of their lot.

The present volume does not profess to cover the whole field of Scottish anecdote, not even of that which, in a broad sense, has to do with religion and religious matters. It contains what the title imports, "Religious Anecdotes" only, and these of a more serious character. There is an all but innumerable number of incidents of a humorous, pawky nature, about churches, ministers, elders, beadles, and others, which are purposely excluded from this collection. These can be found elsewhere, and especially in the pages of the famous Dean Ramsay. We have confined ourselves to anecdotes which are calculated to both interest and instruct. They are fitted to be read at the family table, the fireside, on Sabbaths as well as on other days, and can be used by public speakers "to point a moral or adorn a tale." They have been culled from a large number of sources, and in the most catholic spirit. Care has been taken that nothing which could offend the most refined taste should be inserted. All phases of religious movement and life have been reflected. In this manner the prominent traits of Scottish religious character have been exhibited. The volume is issued with the hope that it may deepen faith, inspire hope and courage, and promote Christian activity.

CONTENTS.

	PAGE
Lord Hailes discovering Hidden Treasures	17
Shirra of Kirkcaldy	19
Josephus Utilised at Peebles	20
Carlyle and his Mother	21
John Knox and Queen Mary	22
Samuel Rutherford's Last Words	24
Hearing the Word—Ebenezer Erskine	25
A Pedlar at Balmoral	26
The Marrow of Modern Divinity	27
The Good Bishop Leighton	28
A Swearer Reproved	30
A Prodigal's Return	31
Scruples of Conscience Overcome	33
The Upright Highlander	34
The Royal Mail Guard	35
Robert Macleod's Prayer	37
Lord Braxfield on the Sabbath Day	38
The Bible and the Criminal	40
Jenny Geddes and her Stool	43
"I will be with you alway."—The Rev. Robert Bruce ...	44
Shirra of Kirkcaldy on Liberty and Equality	45
The Missionary and the Infidel in Edinburgh	46
Rev. Dr. William Anderson and the Extortioner	48
Anecdotes of Peden the Prophet	49
The Men of St. Kilda cannot forget God	50
Patrick Hamilton at the Stake	51
Thomas Edwards; or, Independence and Industry ...	52
The Rev. Ebenezer Brown and Orderly Church Service ...	54
Dr. Guthrie's Gospel Bells	55
James Stirling, the Scientific Cobbler of Milngavie ...	57
The Power of Conscience	59
A Simpleton's Theology	61

CONTENTS.

	PAGE
The Rev. Dr. Beattie Teaching Natural Theology ...	62
Covenant Tent Preaching ...	63
The Rev. James Guthrie of Fenwick ...	65
Rob Roy—"The Ruling Passion strong in Death,"	66
In a Good Cause—Rev. Wm. Wilson, of Perth ...	67
The Sea Captain at the Northern Coasts of Scotland ...	68
A Christian Pilgrim ...	69
Archbishop Leighton—Anecdotes of ...	70
Self-Righteousness Exposed ...	71
Providential Deliverances experienced by the Rev. Henry Erskine ...	72
The Rev. Dr. Alex. Macleod and the Wrong Way ...	73
The Conversion of the Haldanes ...	74
Rev. Dr. M'Crie and the Publisher ...	75
Rev. Dr. James Morison—"There's nae Chirtin' in Heaven"	76
A Mistake Improved; or, how the Evil One may be Shot...	76
Dundonald and the Minister ...	78
A Scottish Old Time Revival ...	79
Dr. Eadie's Sermon to Shepherds ...	81
Rabbi Duncan on Angels ...	82
Dr. Chalmers—A Lost Opportunity ...	84
Sir Andrew Agnew's Loyalty to Conviction...	85
The Rev. Hector M'Phail and his Faithful Wife ...	87
An Earnest Scotch Methodist ...	88
Professor John Wilson and the Unkind Carter ...	90
Wishart as an Evangelist...	91
The Biggar Bellman's Son ...	92
Help in Time of Need ...	94
The Rev. John Angel James at Perth...	95
David Hume and the Child ...	96
Sorrow and Genius—The Grave of Burns ...	98
A Fifty Years Communicant ...	98
Rev. George Gilfillan Preaching his own Funeral Sermon	100
"A Soft Answer Turneth Away Wrath" ...	101
Bishop Cowper's Death ...	102
A Very Young Disciple ...	103
Change in Preacher and Preaching, and its Results ...	104
Coupar Justice ...	106
Just Lippen to Him—Dr. Chalmers ...	107

CONTENTS.

	PAGE
Duncan Matheson and the Power of Sacred Song ...	108
Welsh of Irongray	109
Theological Discussion in Ayrshire	111
The Chieftain Starting Too Late	111
A Blasphemer's Prayer Answered	112
A Gospel Minister Declining Praise	113
Dr. John Duncan—The Logic of Salvation...	114
John Brown of Haddington	117
Cowie of Huntly...	118
M'Cheyne and an Old Woman...	119
Dr. John Brown—Play with and Pray for Children ...	121
Dr. Chalmers' Daughter	122
John Brown of Priesthill	122
Acting Death Leading to Life...	124
The Rev. John Jamieson's Letters	126
Carlyle and the Seceder Elder...	127
Rev. Ebenezer Brown and the Carters	128
Robert Burns's Reflections	129
Rev. George Gilfillan's Generosity	130
Archbishop Usher and the Eleventh Commandment ...	131
Highland Respect for the Sabbath	132
Dr. Begg on how to Treat Opponents...	133
John Brown, the Exemplary Gravedigger	134
Rev. Dr. W. L. Alexander—A Gentle Effective Rebuke ...	135
George Wishart, An Anecdote of	136
Sir Walter Scott's Last Days	137
William Gilbert Carpenter Brought to Decision ...	139
Dr. Chalmers—Needed and Unexpected Encouragement ...	141
Saint Columba and his Horse	142
A Saintly Highland Elder's Assurance of Salvation ...	143
Dr. Chalmers on Hyper-Criticism	145
Thumbing the Promises...	146
Edward Irving and the Shoemaker	148
The Rev. William Dunn of Cadder	149
An Honest Executioner	151
Adam Scott, Shepherd in Upper Dalgliesh	151
A Novel Way of Finding out Christians	152
A Covenanter and his Dreams...	153
The Erskines as Preachers	155

CONTENTS.

	PAGE
The Rev. Dr. M'Crie and Professor Dugald Stewart	156
James Guthrie's Courage and Death	157
A Soldier at Fort-George	159
Walter Mill, the Last Popish Victim in Scotland	162
Dr. Balmer—A Boy Theologian	163
Robert Flockhart and the Bible	164
A Merry Gentleman's Advice	166
Bread upon the Waters	166
Dr. Chalmers' Astronomical Discourses	167
Sir David Brewster Disgusted	169
The Rev. Dr. M'Crie's Sincerity	170
The Queen's Table at Balmoral	171
Mary Campbell and the Gift of Tongues	171
Mary Campbell's Belief in Miraculous Healing Power	172
St. Andrew and Scotland	173
Brownlow North's Sudden Awakening	174
Norman Macleod and a Waif	175
Dr. Lawson and the Captious Church Member	177
Ebenezer Erskine and the Murderer	178
Dr. Jamieson and the Suggested Text	179
Seeking for God in the Scottish Highlands	180
The Rev. Robert Bruce of Edinburgh	181
Saint Columba Receiving a Lesson in Charity	183
The General Assembly and Foreign Missions in 1796	184
Christian Charity overcoming Unbelief	185
Irving and the Scoffer	187
An Antique Scottish Matron	188
Dr. John Brown's Early Experiences	189
A Fruitful Sermon of the Rev. Dr. Chalmers	191
Life through Death	192
Three Remarkable Parishioners at Arbirlot	194
The Friends, or Quakers, in Scotland	195
Lord Brougham's Decision of Character in Early Life	196
The Humanity of Burns	197
Dr. Guthrie—Drink and Death at Blairgowrie	197
Dr. Wm. Anderson and the Cameronian Elder	199
The Father of the Rev. Dr. Wardlaw	202
Joy in Tears	203
The Sabbath Market	203

CONTENTS.   xiii

	PAGE
David Hume and Principal Robertson	204
Lord Haddo's Spiritual Change	205
The Old Ferryman on the Frith of Forth	206
A Thief Outdone...	207
Sir J. Y. Simpson's Superstitious Forefathers	208
In a Cleft of the Garrick Fells...	210
The Wigton Martyrs	211
King Robert Bruce and the Spider	212
An Old Style of Preaching	213
A Muscular Christian	214
Brownlow North and the Colonel	216
Richard Cameron's Suffering and Death	217
Donald Cargill kept from Suicide	218
M'Cheyne as a Preacher...	220
Trial of the Duke of Argyll	221
Norman Macleod's First Sermon before the Queen...	222
Martyrs at Perth	224
A Methodist Minister in Orkney	225
Dr. Guthrie and "a Beautiful Field in Edinburgh"	226
The Importance of Decision	228
Returning Good for Evil	229
The Anniversary of a Deliverance at Haddington...	231
Dr. Chalmers' Integrity	232
Chalmers and Tholuck...	233
Brownlow North Turning a Letter to Account	234
Knox's Prayer for Scotland	235
Flockhart's Important School-Lesson...	236
Livingstone's Modesty...	237
An Old-Fashioned Saint	238
Rev. William Wilson and the Soldier...	240
"If ye Kenned how I love Him"	241
Good Seed Strangely Sown	244
A Lamb of Christ's Flock—Rev. Mr. M'Cheyne	244
His Word is at Stake	245
Thomas Campbell Closing his Life	246
A Character at West Linton	247
The Duke of Buccleuch and the Herd-Boy	248
An Explanation...	249
The Last Martyr of the Covenant	250

	PAGE
Dr. Henry and the Wearisome Minister	252
Major-General Burn's Dream	253
A Mistake of the Intellect	255
Dr. William Anderson on Ministers' Stipends	255
Dr. Norman Macleod's Last Hours	256
The Simplicity of Faith	258
Resignation to the Divine Will—A Highland Tale	258
Hugh M'Kail—His Last Hours	260
Rev. Dr. Macleod and the Poor Woman	262
The Rev. Dr. Ritchie and the Swearer	264
Burns in Paisley	265
The Duke of Gordon and the Farmer	266
Rev. Dr. Lawson giving a Wise Answer	267
Ebenezer Erskine and the Blasphemers	268
St. Columba and the Robber	269
Study and Study	270
Invitation to Public Worship	271
Moderatism: its Fascination and Evil Influence	272
George Buchanan's Truthfulness and Humility	274
Professor Wodrow Measuring his Grave	275
Patronage and Popular Preachers	276
Preaching Seventy Years ago	277
The Rev. Dr. M'Gavin and the Deserted Climbing Boy	279
Dr. Wardlaw—The Outer and Inner Man	281
Edward Irving's Dying Hours	282
Two Kings and two Kingdoms in Scotland	284
The Disruption	285
John Welsh and his Wife	286
The Rev. Robert Morison and the Artist	289
Hume's Scepticism and Grief	291
The Rev. Dr. Ferguson's Hymn—"He loved Me"	292
Carlyle and Emerson	294
Rev. John Patison Preaching the Word	294
The Boy who became a Captain	295
Dr. Guthrie—A Special Providence at Arbirlot	297
Benevolence and Fidelity Rewarded at Ochiltree	298
Lady Glencairn appointing a Minister	299
Montagu Stanley, the Actor	301
Dickson's Hymn, "Jerusalem, my Happy Home"	303

CONTENTS.

	PAGE
Rev. John Milne's Earnestness	304
An Old Hearer at the Cromarty Frith	306
Seed Early Sown in the Highlands	306
Dr. Muir illustrating the Influence of a Floating Chapel	308
Torture and Conscience at Edinburgh	309
The Religious Influence of Mountains	311
Scotch Itinerating Preachers	311
Carlyle in Sorrow	312
Dr. Chalmers—An Edinburgh Boarding School Anecdote	314
Firmness and Love in Ragged School Work	315
A Lily among Thorns in Dundee	317
Moffat's First Sermon to the Heathen	319
The Highland Widow and her Son	320
"Give me a Bairn's Hymn,"	322
Bad Drink for a Child	323
A St. Monance Fisherman's Triumph in Death	324
Healing by Faith and Prayer	326
Rev. Donald Campbell and Satan	328
Priestly Cursing; its Effects	329
The Prevailing Argument	330
Michael Bruce and the Paraphrases	331
The Wife of the Rev. James Fraser, of Alness	332
Martyrdom in Glasgow	334
A Filial Prayer Answered in Aberdeen	335
The Duke of Argyll and Mr. Darwin	336
St. Kentigern and King Morken	338
An Awful Providence at Kirriemuir	339
Patrick Simson and King James	340
Provost Drummond's Benevolence	341
A Sensible Advice to a Minister	342
Rev. Dr. Andrew Thomson's Silent Sermon	343
The Pious Highland Soldier in America	344
John Mack, Soldier and Minister	345
Simple-minded Answers	346
The Rev. Dr. Guthrie and the Irishman	347
The Rev. Dr. Begg and the Radicals	348
The Rev. Dr. Macdonald and the Preaching Cure	349
Robert Pollok's First Public Sermon	350
Duncan Matheson's Conversion	352

CONTENTS.

	PAGE
A Prayer Wonderfully Answered	353
The Rev. William Lindsay of Letham, and the Apprentice	354
Thomas Lermont and his Prophecy	355
Scotchmen an Argument for the Bible	357
Lord Hailes and an Infidel	358
The Rev. John Martin's Trust in the Lord	359
Robert Annan, the Christian Swimmer	360
The Repentant Publican; or, no Terms with God	361
Rev. Thomas Hog's Marvellous Restoration to Health	362
An Argyllshire Minister's Dream	364
Seeing and Believing	365
A Swearer Reproved in Huntly	367
A Second Jenny Geddes and the Chartist	368
John Knox's Vocation	369
Knox Closing his Life	370
"Our Bairn that's Deein'"	371
Dr. William Ritchie and his Violin	372
True to Conscience	373
Benevolence Stimulated in Glasgow	375
Dr. Erskine Moderating a Call	377
The Gospels of St. Margaret	378
Peden's Prevailing Prayer	379
An Old Tar Sweeping Out Darkness	380
The Mother of the Erskines	382
A Pretended Miracle Exposed	383
Burns on True Manhood	384
An Honest Street Arab in Edinburgh	385
God never Dies—a Widow's Faith	387
Hugh Miller Publicly Catechised	387
The Covenanter's Bible	389
A Conversion in Ayr Prison	390
An Old Sermon Re-delivered with Effect	391
M'Phail and the Judge	392
A Glasgow Infidel's Death-Bed	393
A Boy's Faith and Love	394
Dr. Chalmers and the Drover	395
No Strife in Heaven	397
Hector M'Phail and the Kitchen Maid	398
Guthrie the Martyr's Little Willie	399

THE RELIGIOUS ANECDOTES OF SCOTLAND.

LORD HAILES
DISCOVERING HIDDEN TREASURES.

THERE is an interesting anecdote, which was related by the late Rev. Dr. Walter Buchanan, with reference to one of the means which seems to have been provided in order to secure the New Testament, either from interpolation or corruption.

"I was dining," said Dr. Buchanan, "some time ago with a literary party, at old Mr. Abercromby's, of Tullibody (the father of Sir Ralph Abercromby, who was slain in Egypt), and we spent the evening together. A gentleman present put a question, which puzzled the whole company. It was this: 'Supposing all the New Testaments in the world had been destroyed at the end of the third century, would their contents have been recovered from the writings of the three first centuries?' The question was novel to all, and no one even hazarded a guess in answer to the inquiry.

"About two months after this meeting, I received an invitation to breakfast with Lord Hailes (Sir David Dalrymple) next morning. He had been of the party. During breakfast, he asked me if I recollected the curious question about the possibility of recovering the contents of the New Testament, from the writings of the three first centuries. I replied, 'I remember it well, and have often thought of it without being able to form any opinion or conjecture on the subject.'

"'Well, said Lord Hailes, 'that question quite accorded with the taste of my antiquarian mind. On returning home, as I knew I had all the writers of those centuries, I began immediately to collect them, that I might set to work on the arduous task as soon as possible.' Pointing to a table covered with papers, he said, 'There have I been busy for these two months, searching for chapters, half-chapters, and sentences of the New Testament, and have marked down what I found, and where I have found it, so that any person may examine and see for himself. I have actually discovered the whole New Testament, except seven or eleven verses (I forget which), which satisfies me that I could discover them also. Now,' said he, 'here was a way in which God concealed or hid the treasures of his Word, that Julian, the apostate emperor, and other enemies of Christ, who wished to extirpate the Gospel from the world, never would have thought of; and though they had, they never could have effected their destruction.'"

SHIRRA OF KIRKCALDY.

THE REV. ROBERT SHIRRA of Kirkcaldy was a popular preacher in his day, and was marked by many peculiarities of style which, however, did not mar his influence, nor prevent him from being a faithful minister of the Word. From his ministrations, the common people derived much good, and his short comments on Scripture texts were quaint and suggestive. Having had occasion to quote the saying of the Psalmist, "I said in my haste all men are liars," he remarked, "It would seem, David, that in saying this you were hasty or ill-advised, and you seem to think your saying it calls for an apology; had you lived in our day, you might have said it at your leisure, and made no apology about it." Quoting, on another occasion, these words from the 119th Psalm, "I will run the way of thy commandments, when thou shalt enlarge my heart," he said, "Well, David, what is your first resolution? '*I will run.*' Run away, David, who hinders you? What is your next? 'I will run *the way of thy commandments.'* Better run yet, David; what is your next? 'I will run the way of thy commandments, *when thou shalt enlarge my heart.'* No thanks to you, David; we could run as well as you, with such help." At another time, Mr. Shirra, having had occasion to quote Philippians iv. 11, "I have learned, in whatsoever state I am, therewith to be content," he said, "Aye, Paul, ye have learned well, ye have got far on; but let us be thankful we're at the schule."

At Kinghorn, as at the other ferries on the Forth, a hundred years ago, it was the practice of the boatmen whose turn it was to sail, to call the loungers and passengers, by bawling from one end of the town to the other, "The boat, aho!—to Leith, aho!" Mr. Shirra was preaching from the tent of the Associate Congregation at Kinghorn on a fast-day, and observing "lang Tam Gallawa" with several boatmen and passengers, in the bustle of passing down to Pettycur, he paused in his discourse, and addressed them as follows, with an energy and seriousness peculiar to himself—"Boatmen, aho!" The boatmen and passengers instantly stopped to listen. He proceeded—"Boatmen, you cry, 'The boat aho!—to Leith, aho!' We cry, 'Salvation, aho!—to heaven, aho!' You sail under Skipper Gallawa there; we sail aneath Jesus Christ. We ha'e Christ for our skipper, the Holy Spirit for our pilot, and God himself at the helm. Your boat, let me tell you, is but a fir deal frae Norawa; the keel of our boat was laid at Bethlehem, built in Judea, rigged in Jerusalem, launched in Calvary. We ha'e the cross o' Christ for a helm, a cedar of Lebanon for a mast, and the redemption of mankind for freight. Your voyage under an earthly skipper, short as it is, may end in shipwreck and disaster; but our voyage, lang as it may be, wi' Christ for our skipper, will end in everlasting joy and glory unspeakable. Slip awa' noo, for 'time and tide will nae man bide;' but mind what I've said t'ye—dinna swear, nor tak' the holy name o' God in vain, as ye wont to do, and I'll pray for ye." In such lowly phrase and with such persuasiveness did this earnest man commend the gospel of the Lord Jesus Christ. In doing so, he not unfrequently evoked a smile, but the state of mind produced was in many cases like the opening of the earth to receive the seed of the kingdom.

JOSEPHUS UTILISED AT PEEBLES.

Dr. William Chambers, in writing the memoirs of his brother Robert, says that "among a considerable part of the population of Peebles, who lived down closes, and in old thatched cottages, news circulated at third or fourth hand, or was merged in conversation on religious and other topics. My brother and I derived much enjoyment, not to say instruction, from the singing of old ballads, and the telling of legendary stories, by a kind, old female relative, the wife of a decayed tradesman, who dwelt in one of the ancient closes. At her humble fireside, under the canopy of a huge chimney, where her half-blind and superannuated husband sat dozing in a chair, the battle of Corunna and other prevailing news was strangely mingled with disquisitions on the Jewish wars. The source of this interesting conversation was a well-worn copy of L'Estrange's translation of Josephus, a small folio, of date 1720.

"The envied possessor of the work was Tam Fleck, 'a flichty chield,' as he was considered, who, not particularly steady at his legitimate employment, struck out a sort of profession by going about in the evenings with his Josephus, which he read as the current news; the only light he had for doing so being usually that imparted by the flickering blaze of a piece of parrot coal. It was his practice not to read more than from two to three pages at a time, interlarded with sagacious remarks of his own, by way of foot-notes, and in this way he sustained an extraordinary interest in the narrative. Retailing the matter with great equability in different households, Tam kept all at the same point of information, and wound them up with a corresponding anxiety as to the issue of some moving event in Hebrew annals. Although in this way he went through a course of

Josephus yearly, the novelty somehow never seemed to wear off.

'Weel, Tam, what's the news the nicht?' would old Geordie Murray say, as Tam entered with Josephus under his arm, and seated himself at the family fireside.

'Bad news, bad news,' replied Tam; 'Titus has begun to besiege Jerusalem!—it's gaun to be a terrible business;' and then he opened his budget of intelligence, to which all paid the most reverential attention. The protracted and severe famine which was endured by the besieged Jews, was a theme which kept several families in a state of agony for a week; and when Tam in his readings came to the final conflict and destruction of the city by the Roman general, there was a perfect paroxysm of horror. At such *seances* my brother and I were delighted listeners. All honour to the memory of Tam Fleck."

CARLYLE AND HIS MOTHER.

CARLYLE stood in awe of his stern father, concerning whom, he says, "We had all to complain that we could not freely love. His heart seemed as if walled in;" but in his relation to his mother, the love was so perfect that it cast out fear. She taught herself to write that she might have the joy of writing to him. She subscribed herself, "Your old Minnie." When he sent her a present, she called it "my son's venison." When a young man she sent him such motherly words as these,—"Oh Tom, mind the golden season of youth, and remember your 'Creator in the days of your youth.' 'Seek God while he may be found, call upon him while he is near.' We hear that the 'world by wisdom knew not God.' Pray for his presence with you, and his counsel to guide you. Have you got through your bible yet? If you have, read it again. I hope you will not be weary, and may the Lord open your understanding. . . . Good-night, Tom, for it is a stormy night, and I must away to the byre to milk." Ere she lays the pen down, she adds,— "Now, Tom, be sure to tell me about your chapters." Very motherly and tender is all this, and of a nature which the son would understand and remember. Her love, care, and interest continued on to the end. When most needed were most given.

How faithfully the son returned that love! He was never weary of sounding the praises of the father who had been so sternly faithful; and when he mentioned his mother's name, even when he was a grey old man of more than fourscore, his tones melted with tender emotion. One day in London, when he was within a few months of eighty, Carlyle was walking in company with an American stranger, who had that day called to see him. They approached a street-crossing. When half way over, Carlyle suddenly stopped, and, stooping down, kicked something out of the mud at the risk of being run over by one of the many carriages that were rushing past. With his bare hands he brushed the mud off, and placed the white substance in a clean spot on the curbstone. "That," said he, in a tone as sweet and in words as beautiful as his companion had ever heard, "is only a crust of bread. Yet I was taught by my mother never to waste, and, above all, bread, more precious than gold, the substance that is the same to the body that the truth is to the soul. I am sure the little sparrows, or a hungry dog, will get nourishment from that bit of bread." Thus did he bear in his heart till his last days on earth the homeliest lesson he had learnt from the lips of his mother.

JOHN KNOX AND QUEEN MARY.

THE Reformer Knox had many interviews with Mary Queen of Scots, and these brought out the character of both parties. In a sermon in St. Giles's Church, when the Queen's marriage was talked about, he said,—"Now, my Lords, to put an end to all, I hear of the Queen's marriage. . . . Whensoever the nobility of Scotland professing the Lord Jesus consent that an infidel (and all Papists are infidels) shall be head to your sovereign, you do so far as in you lieth to banish Christ Jesus from this realm."

Mary as well as Knox knew that this was the hinge of the whole question, and the preacher was instantly sent for to the palace. On his appearance the Queen burst into a passion of tears. Never had Prince been handled as she was—she had borne with him, had listened to him, and had sought his favour—"and yet I cannot be quit of you. I vow to God, I shall be once revenged." Knox stood unmoved, and then calmly reasoned that in the pulpit, and as preacher, he was not his own master, and was bound to instruct his hearers in their duty. "But what have you to do with my marriage?" said Mary. Knox began to point out the importance of her marriage to the commonwealth; but the Queen impatiently repeated the question, and added, "What are *you* in this commonwealth?" "Madam," answered Knox, "a subject born within the same. And albeit I be neither earl, lord, nor baron in it, yet God has made me (how abject that ever I be in your eyes) a profitable member within the same." And thereupon he repeated to her the same very practical doctrine which he had given in the pulpit two hours before. Mary again had recourse to tears, and her indignation that the Reformer remained unmoved under them, was not diminished by his quaint protest that he was really a tender-hearted man, and could scarcely bear to see his own children weep when corrected for their faults. Ordered to depart from her presence, he found himself in the ante-room, shunned by the nobles, but near the "Queen's Maries," or other ladies of the Court, in their rich dresses. Knox felt lonely, and records himself how he "procured the company of women" in this interval. "Oh, fair ladies," said he "how pleasing were this life of yours, if it should ever abide, and then in the end we might pass to heaven with all this gay gear! But fie upon that knave Death, that will come, whether we will or not!" These grim pleasantries led to conversation which lasted till the Royal permission came for him to go home. "And so that storm quieted in appearance," but in December of the same year Knox again stood at the bar, and on this occasion no man stood by him. The

Queen was sure of her victory. "That man," she said, looking around, "made me weep, and never shed a tear himself; I will see if I can make him weep." This rash exultation was checked by the constant bearing of the accused, who, through a long examination, maintained his right to caution his countrymen against "the pestilent Papists, who have inflamed your grace against those poor men." "You forget yourself," said the Chancellor, "you are not now in the pulpit." "I am in the place," he answered, "where I am demanded of conscience to speak the truth, and therefore the truth I speak, impugn it whoso list." The Lords of the Council, who at first frowned upon Knox, before the day closed, pronounced him innocent by a majority. The Queen came back into the room, and the vote was taken in her presence over again; but with the same result. "That night was neither dancing nor fiddling in the Court;" and the firmness of Knox maintained the freedom of the Protestant cause.

SAMUEL RUTHERFORD'S LAST WORDS.

SAMUEL RUTHERFORD was born about 1600, and lived till he was over sixty years of age. His letters, especially, have been much appreciated and extensively read. "These," says Dr. Grosart, "have long been a Christian classic in Scotland, and in Holland, and Germany, and in the United States of America and Canada, and our Colonies. One still comes across the book, well thumbed, and not unseldom tear-blurred—the white tears of joy—in lowland cottages and shepherd-huts and farm-steads of the North. Not long since, a travelling friend met with two editions among the forsaken towns of Zuyder Zee. It went to my heart to meet with a copy under the shadow of Mount Hermon. In the back-woods of the Far West, the book lies side by side with the *Pilgrim's Progress*. In Cumberland, Westmoreland, and Durham, and in the North of Ireland, it is in living demand. Originally published in the lowliest guise, it has passed through innumerable, or at least, unnumbered editions. Mr. Rutherford was characterised by devoutness and spirituality of mind, and those elements of character manifested themselves at the closing scenes of his life, as his words on his dying-bed show.

Some of his words are these: "I shall shine; I shall see Him as he is, and all the fair company with him, and shall have my large share. It is no easy thing to be a Christian; but as for me, I have got the victory, and Christ is holding forth his arms to embrace me. I have had my fears and faintings, as another sinful man, to be carried through creditably; but as sure as ever he spake to me in his Word, his Spirit witnessed to my heart, saying, 'Fear not;' he has accepted my suffering, and the out-gate should not be matter of prayer, but of praise." He said also, "Thy Word was found, and I did eat it, and it was to me the joy and rejoicing of my heart;" and a little before his death, after some fainting, he saith, "Now I feel, I believe, I enjoy, I rejoice;" and turning to Mr. Blair, then present, he said, "I feed on manna, I have angel's food; my eyes shall see my Redeemer; I know that he shall stand at the latter day on the earth, and I shall be caught up in the clouds to meet him in the air;" and afterwards he uttered these words, "I sleep in Christ, and when I awake, I shall be satisfied with his likeness. Oh! for arms to embrace him!" And to one speaking anent his painfulness in the ministry, he crieth out, "I disclaim all; the port I would be in at, is redemption and forgiveness of sins through his blood:" and thus, full of the Spirit, yea, as it were overcome with sensible enjoyment, he breathes out his soul, his last words being, "Glory, glory dwelleth in Immanuel's land!"

HEARING THE WORD.
An Anecdote of Ebenezer Erskine.

A LADY who was present at the dispensation of the Lord's Supper, where the Rev. Ebenezer Erskine was assisting, was much impressed by his discourse. Having been informed who he was, she went next Sabbath to his own place of worship to hear him. But she felt none of those strong impressions she experienced on the former occasion. Wondering at this, she called on Mr. Erskine, and, stating the case, asked what might be the reason of such a difference in her feelings. He replied, "Madam, the reason is this: last Sabbath you went to hear Jesus Christ, but to-day you have come to hear Ebenezer Erskine."

A PEDLAR AT BALMORAL.

A GREAT drunkard in the Highlands of Inverness-shire was led to attend a lecture on Temperance, and was induced to become a member of a temperance society. For months the craving of his appetite for strong-drink was excessive; but true to his resolution, he set his face like a flint against every temptation. The marsh of his heart being thus drained of one poison, he next received the seed of the Word into its soil. It was hid there until quickened by the Sun of Righteousness, and nourished by the rains and dews of the Spirit, when it brought forth fruit in Christian life and character. Having no settled occupation, he yet could not be idle; and having, by the kindness of a few friends, managed to stock a little box with trinkets, and other cheap ware, he set out as a pedlar.

In the course of his peregrinations, he found himself at Balmoral, and thinking that if he could get the patronage of the Queen, it would help him greatly, he resolved to make the attempt. There was something in his look and manner which at once commended him to the favour of some of the household officials, who had it in their power to bring him under the notice of the Earl of Carlisle, then attending the Court as a Minister of State. The noble, with his usual frankness and goodness of heart, sympathised with Donald, and promised to recommend his case to the Queen. When her Majesty came to know it, Donald was commanded to appear in the Royal presence, and met with a most gracious reception. Not only did the Queen purchase his wares, but gave him permission to wear the royal arms as the Queen's pedlar, and sent Donald away with a lighter heart and a heavier purse than he had when he entered the royal chamber. On leaving, the Earl of Carlisle took him to his room, and there Donald was presented with a glass of wine with which to drink the Queen's health. Looking at it, he felt at first a kind of trembling, but then, lifting his heart in prayer for Divine aid, he said, "Your lordship will excuse me; I cannot drink the Queen's health in wine, but I will drink it in water." The noble earl asked his reasons.

"My lord," said Donald, "I was a drunkard; I became an abstainer, and I trust by God's grace I have become a Christian; but I know that if I were to taste intoxicating drink, it would at once revive an appetite which is not dead but dying, and I should most likely go the whole length of the drunkard again. God has only promised to support me in the path of duty, and that path, in my case, is plainly to abstain."

The noble earl at once commended Donald for his frankness and honesty, and, in taking leave, assured him that it would afford her Majesty the highest satisfaction to know that she had amongst her loyal and devoted subjects one who, in the midst of such strong temptations, could maintain his principles with integrity and honour. Donald left, rejoicing to think that he had been enabled to "drink" to the glory of God.

THE MARROW OF MODERN DIVINITY.

ONE day, Thomas Boston, when visiting in the house of one of his people at Simprin, found a little old book above the window-head, which he took down and began to read. It was a book that has become famous in Scotland, "The Marrow of Modern Divinity." It had been brought from England many years before, in the Commonwealth wars, and it had lain like a hidden seed in that quiet corner. The book had been written—or, rather, compiled—by one Edward Fisher, the son of an English knight, and a Master of Arts of Oxford. It gave, in the form of a dialogue the opinions of the leading Reformers,

Luther and Calvin, and of such English divines as Hall and Hooker, on the doctrines of grace and the offer of the gospel.

The object of the book was to clear away the barriers which are so often raised between the sinner and Christ, in the shape of certain conditions, such as repentance, or some degree of outward or inward reformation, and to present him immediately with the words, "Whosoever will, let him come," assured that in heartily receiving Christ, full repentance and a new life will follow. The system of Neonomianism, as it was called, which changed the gospel into a modified and easier kind of law, had grown up in Scotland, as elsewhere, and this little book became the instrument of a revival of clearer and fuller gospel-preaching. It did what the discovery of "Luther on the Galatians," in the house of a country schoolmaster, has done for Sweden of late years, or, to use a Scripture figure, what the bones of Elisha did for the body of the man cast into his sepulchre, when "he revived and stood up on his feet." Such remarkable instances of the vitality of truth over the graves of prophets and preachers occur ever and again in the history of the Church.

Boston tells us that he "rejoiced in the book as a light which the Lord had seasonably struck up to him in his darkness; that he digested its doctrine, and began to preach it." Through him it found its way into the hands of James Hogg, of Carnock, who republished it with a recommendation in 1717.

THE GOOD BISHOP LEIGHTON.

LEIGHTON'S memory is blessed in Dunblane to this day, as it is wherever his name is known, and worth and usefulness of the highest order are appreciated. The very walk by the side of the river Allan, which he used so much for study and exercise that it was called the "Bishop's Walk," seems to have still lingering about it an atmosphere of sanctity and devotion. His writings praise him in the gates. After the lapse of nearly two centuries they still deservedly hold a high place in the Christian literature of Britain. His "Commentary on St. Peter" is a very great favourite; has been reprinted times without number, and one may confidently predict that it will hold its place while the English language continues to be one of the languages of the Christian world.

"The good Bishop" is the honourable designation by which Leighton used to be distinguished. He "was good" in the largest and noblest sense of the epithet. He was "good" in the sense of being benevolent. The world has not been blessed with many finer copies of Him who was Love incarnate, and who went about doing good. Good-doing was emphatically the work of Leighton's life, and the delight of his heart. On one occasion his generous kindness was rather amusingly misconstrued, which revealed in him a power of humour that his habitual gravity kept much in the shade. A poor lady — a young widow — the relict of a minister cut off in early life, received from the Bishop many tokens of his compassionate interest in her and her children. These excited her grateful surprise. By and bye she set herself to account for them; but she could light on no satisfactory explanation of them except by supposing that the Bishop, who was a bachelor, had fallen in love with her; she did what she could to cherish the latent flame in his bosom, and waited with earnest expectation for his declaring himself. His delay in doing so she fondly ascribed to his modesty, making him shy to "pop the question," as the same cause, according to the bride, had made her bridegroom "senselessly civil" in their courtship. At length, when her patience was worn out, she resolved to help him over his difficulty. He was one day in his favourite resort—the Bishop's Walk—on which the community, by common consent, shunned to intrude, for fear of disturbing him. The widow ventured to break in on his solitude, and presented herself before him. Apprehending that some new and sudden disaster had overtaken her, Leighton inquired with more than his usual earnestness for her children. She replied that they "were all well, but she had been unable to rest till she disclosed to his Lordship a *revelation* which had been made to her." "A revelation made to you," answered the astonished dignitary. "Yes, my Lord," said the widow; it was revealed to me that your Lordship and I were about to be married." "Indeed!" rejoined his Lordship, "no such revelation, however, has been made to me, and if we are to be married by revelation, the marriage cannot take place, you know, until it be revealed to both parties."

A SWEARER REPROVED.

A GENERAL who was in early life much addicted to profane oaths, dates his reformation from a memorable check he received from a Scottish clergyman. When he was a lieutenant, and stationed at Newcastle, he got involved in a brawl with some of the lowest class in the public street; and the altercation was carried on, by both parties, with abundance of impious language. The clergyman, passing by, was shocked with the profanity, and stepping into the crowd with his cane uplifted, thus addressed one of the leaders of the rabble,—" Oh, John, John! what is this I hear? you only a poor collier boy, and swearing like any lord in all the land. Oh, John! have you no fear of what will become of you? It may do very well for this gallant gentleman (pointing to the lieutenant) to bang and swear as he pleases; but you—but you, John! it is not for you, or the like of you, to take in vain the name of Him in whom ye live and have your being." Then turning to the lieutenant, he continued, "Ye'll excuse the poor man, sir, for swearing, he is an ignorant body, and kens no better." The young officer slunk away in confusion, unable to make any reply. Next day he made it his business to wait on the minister, and thanked him sincerely for his well-timed reproof, and has ever since been an example of the strictest purity of language.

A PRODIGAL'S RETURN.

A WRITER, whose name for obvious reasons is withheld, says—"I was standing by the side of my mother, under the spacious porch of Dr. Beattie's Church, Glasgow, awaiting the hour for afternoon service, when I observed two young men turn a corner, and walk towards the church. They were dressed in their working clothes, unshaven and dirty, and slightly intoxicated. As they passed the church-door, they assumed a swaggering, irreverent gait, laughed, and finally commenced singing a profane song. My mother turned to me, and said, 'Follow those two men, and invite them to a seat in our pew.'

"I soon overtook them, and delivered my mother's message. One laughed scornfully, and began to swear; the other paused and pondered; he was evidently struck with the nature of the invitation. His companion again swore, and was about to drag him away; but he still paused. I repeated the invitation, and in a few seconds he looked in my face and said, 'When I was a boy like you, I went to church every Sunday. I have not been inside a church for three years. *I don't feel right.* I believe I will go with you.' I seized his hand, and led him back to the house of God in spite of the remonstrances and oaths of his companion. An excellent sermon was preached from Eccles. xi. 1, 'Cast thy bread upon the waters; for thou shalt find it after many days.' The young man was attentive, and seemed abashed and downcast.

"At the conclusion of the service, my mother kindly said to him, 'Have you a Bible, young man?' 'No, ma'am; but I can get one,' was his reply. 'You can read, of course?' she said. 'Yes, ma'am.' 'Well, take my son's Bible until you can procure one of your own, and come to church again next Lord's-day; I will always be happy to accommodate you with a seat.'

"He put the Bible in his pocket and hurried away. At family-worship that evening, my mother prayed fervently for the conversion of that young man.

"Next Sunday came, and the next, but the stranger did not appear. My mother frequently spoke of him, and appeared grieved at his absence. He had doubtless been the subject of her closet devotions. On the third Sabbath morning, while the congregation were singing the first psalm, the young man again entered our pew. He was now dressed genteelly, and appeared thin and pale, as if from recent sickness. Immediately after the benediction, the stranger laid my Bible on the desk, and left the church, without giving my mother an opportunity she much desired of conversing with him. On one of the blank leaves of the Bible, we found some writing in pencil, signed 'W. C.' He asked to be remembered in my mother's prayers. Time rolled on; my mother passed to her heavenly rest; I grew up to manhood, and the stranger was forgotten.

"Many years afterwards, the ship St. George, of which I was the medical officer, anchored in Table Bay. On the next day being Sunday, after morning service, a gentleman, seated behind me, asked to look at my Bible. In a few minutes he returned it, and I walked into the street. I had arranged to dine at 'The George,' and was mounting the steps in front of that hotel, when the gentleman who had examined my Bible laid his hand on my shoulder, and begged to have a few minutes' conversation. We were shown into a private apartment. As soon as we were seated, he examined my countenance with great attention, and then began to sob; tears rolled down his cheeks; he was evidently labouring under some intense emotion. He asked me several questions— my name, age, occupation, birth-place, etc. He then inquired if I had not, when a boy, many years ago, invited a drunken Sabbath-breaker to a seat in Dr. Beattie's Church. I was astonished; the subject of my mother's anxiety and prayers was before me. Mutual explanations and congratulations followed, after which he gave me a short history of his life.

"He was born in the town of Leeds, of highly respectable and religious parents, who gave him a good education, and trained him up in the way of righteousness. When about fifteen years of age, his father died, and his mother's straitened circumstances obliged her to take him from school, and put him to learn a trade. In his new situation he imbibed all manner of evil, became incorrigibly vicious, and broke his mother's heart. Freed now from all parental restraint, he left his employers, and travelled to Scotland. In the city of Glasgow he had lived and sinned for two years, when he was arrested in his career through my mother's instrumentality. On the first Sabbath of our strange interview, he confessed that after he left the church, he was seized with pains of unutterable remorse. The sight of a mother and son worshipping God together recalled the happy days of his own boyhood, when he went to church and Sunday-school, and when he also had a mother—a mother whose latter days he had embittered, and whose grey hairs he had brought with sorrow to the grave. His mental suffering threw him on a bed of sickness, from which he arose a changed man. He returned to England, and cast himself at the feet of his maternal uncle, and asked and obtained forgiveness. With his uncle's consent, he studied for the ministry; and, on being ordained, he entered the missionary field, and had been labouring for several years in Southern Africa.

"'The moment I saw your Bible this morning,' he said, 'I recognised it. And now, do you know who was my companion on the memorable Sabbath you invited me to church? He was the notorious Jack Hill, who was hanged about a year afterwards for highway robbery. I was dragged from the very brink of infamy and destruction, and saved as a brand from the burning. You remember Dr. Beattie's text on the day of my salvation, "Cast thy bread upon the waters, for thou shalt find it after many days."'"

SCRUPLES OF CONSCIENCE OVERCOME.
An Anecdote of the Rev. Adam Wadderstone.

THE REV. ADAM WADDERSTONE, minister of the parish of Bathgate, who died in 1780, was a most excellent man, and took a deep interest in the temporal as well as spiritual welfare of his flock. His popularity in his parish and his influence among all classes were enhanced by the fact that he was an enthusiastic curler, and almost always headed his parishioners in their encounters on the ice with the curlers of the neighbouring parishes. A like-minded member of his session, "a true son of the besom," John Clarkson by name, having very late one Saturday evening received from the people of Shotts a challenge to the curlers of Bathgate to meet them early on the following Monday, was at a loss how to communicate the pleasing intelligence to his minister. After many qualms of conscience and some hours of sleepless anxiety, he made up his mind to tell him the news on Sunday morning before he entered the pulpit. Mr. Wadderstone no sooner entered the session-house than John said to him in a low tone,—"Sir, I've something to tell ye: there's to be a parish play wi' the Shotts folk the morn at ——." "Whist, man, whist!" was the rejoinder. "Oh, fie shame, John! fie shame! nae speaking to-day about warldly recreations." But the ruling passion proved too strong for the worthy clergyman's scruples of conscience, for just as he was about to enter the inner door of the church he suddenly wheeled round, and returning to the elder, who was now standing at the *plate* in the lobby, he whispered in his ear, "But whan's the hour, John? I'll be sure and be there."

THE UPRIGHT HIGHLANDER.
An Anecdote of Scotch Honesty.

It will be seen that trust begets trust Only by the same principle can true **friendship exist.** When human beings distrust and suspect each other, then good-bye to honourable friendships. There's an end to the confidence and love attached to this beautiful silken tie that binds man to man, family to family, nation to nation. Two centuries ago it was thought an insult in the Highlands to ask a note from a debtor. It was considered the same thing as saying, "I doubt your honour." If parties had business matters to transact they stepped into the open air, fixed their eyes on the heavens, and each repeated his obligation with no mortal witness. A mark was carved upon some rock or tree near by as a remembrance of the compact. Such a thing as a breach of contract was rarely met with, so highly did the people regard their honour. When the march of improvement brought the new mode of doing business, they were often pained by those innovations.

An anecdote is handed down by a farmer who had been in the Lowlands, and learnt worldly wisdom. On returning to his native parish he had need of a sum of money, and made bold to ask from a gentleman of means named Stewart. This was kindly granted, and Mr. Stewart counted out the money. This done, the farmer wrote out a receipt and offered it to Mr. Stewart. "What is this, man?" cried Mr. Stewart, eyeing the slip of paper. "It is a receipt, sir, binding me to give ye back yer gold at the right time," replied Sandy. "Binding ye! Well, my man, if ye canna trust yersel, I'm sure I'll no trust ye; ye canna have my gold!" And, gathering it up, he put it back in his desk, and turned the key on it. "But," sir, "I might die," replied the canny Scotchman, bringing up an argument in favour of his new wisdom, "and perhaps my sons may refuse it ye, but the bit o' paper would compel them." "Compel them to sustain a dead father's honour!" cried the Celt; "they'll need compelling to do right; if this is the road ye're leading them ye can gang elsewhere for the money, but ye'll find nane in the parish that'll put more faith in a bit o' paper than in a neighbour's word of honour and his fear o' God."

THE ROYAL MAIL GUARD.

Anecdote of the Dumfries Mail.

"ONE guard, I remember well—M'George," writes the author of "Rab and his Friends." "He had been in the army, and was a gentleman—stern, and not given to speak; even with his companion, the driver, he would let a whole day pass in silence—a handsome, firm, keen face. I remember well, too, when I had gone day after day to meet the mail, to be taken into Edinburgh to school after my vacation among the hills, and to my rapture the mail was full, and we came back rejoicing at the respite. 'Is she full?' asked again my grave and dear old uncle, six feet and more on his soles. 'Yes,' said M'George, with a gentle grin, and looking me in the face; 'she's full o' emptiness!' whereupon the High School boy was bundled inside, and left to his meditations. Our guard, I must say, came and looked in upon me at each stage, comforting me greatly with some jargonelle pears, the smell and relish of which I can feel now. I fell asleep, of course, and when we stopped at the 'Black Bull,' found myself snug in the potentate's great-coat. All this impressed me the more, when I heard of his death many years after.

"It was a snow-storm—a night of wild drift in midwinter—nothing like it for years. The mail from Dumfries was late, and the tradespeople of Moffat had gathered at Mrs. Cranstoun's inn, waiting for it. Up it came. They crowded round M'George, entreating him not to proceed. 'At Tweedshaws it'll be awful;' but he put them aside. 'They (meaning the Post-office authorities) blamed me once, they'll never blame me again.' And saddling the two strongest horses, he and the driver mounted and took their way into the night, stumbling dumbly up the street. The driver returned, having at the 'Beef-Tub'—a wild hollow in the hills, five miles out of Moffat—given it up in despair, and in time; M'George plunging on, and not to be spoken to. The riderless horse came back at midnight. Next morning at daybreak—the wind hushed, the whole country silent and white—a shepherd saw on the heights at Tweedshaws something bright like a flame. He made his way to it —it was the morning sun shining on the brass-plate of the post-bags, hung up on a bit of paling: we have seen the very stake—and out of the snow stretched a hand, as if pointing to the bags: M'George dead, and as the shepherd said, 'wi' a kind o' a pleesure on his face.'"

ROBERT MACLEOD'S PRAYER.
An Anecdote of Ross-shire.

ROBERT MACLEOD was an honest and ardent Christian, and lived in Killearnan, Ross-shire, and was much given to prayer. The story of his first prayer in Donald Macpherson's family is worthy of repeating. To Robert's bewilderment, his host abruptly asked him to pray at family worship, during a visit which he paid him. He dare not refuse; so turning on his knees, and addressing his Creator, he said—"Thou knowest that though I have bent my knees to pray to Thee, I am much more under the fear of Donald Macpherson than under the fear of Thyself." Not, perhaps, a bad beginning. It was at once earnest and honest.

A remarkable instance of Robert's warm love to the brethren, and of his nearness to God in prayer, has been often repeated, and is undoubtedly true. The case of the godly John Grant was pressed closely on his spirit, along with an impression of his being in temporal want. He was strongly moved to plead with God for "daily bread," for His child, and so constantly was he thinking of him for three days, that at mid-day of the fourth, he resolved to set out for John's house, and he gave himself little rest till he reached it. Full of the impression that stirred him from home, he arrived at the house, and entering it, went at once to the place where the meal-chest used to be, and to his astonishment, found it nearly full.

"This is a strange way, Robert, of coming into a friend's house," John said, as he advanced to salute him; "were you afraid I had no food to give you, if you should remain with me to-night?" "No," was Robert's answer, "but that meal-chest gave me no small trouble for the last few days; but if I had known it was so far from being empty, as I find it is, you had not seen me here to-day." "When did you begin to think of it?" John inquired. Robert mentioned the day and the hour when his anxiety about his friend began. "Well, Robert," John said, "the meal-chest was then as empty as it could be; but how long were you praying that it might be filled?" "For three days and a half I could scarcely think of anything else," Robert answered. "O what a pity," his friend said, "you did not complete the prayers of the fourth day; for on the first I got a boll of meal, another on the second, and a third on the following; but, on the fourth day, only half a boll arrived, but now you are come yourself, and I count you better than them all." Then, rejoicing in each other's love, and in the love of their Father in heaven, who heareth the cry of the needy, they warmly embraced each other.

REMEMBER THE SABBATH DAY.
Anecdote of Lord Braxfield, of the Court of Session.

A FEW years before the death of the late Lord Braxfield, one of the Lords of Session, when he and another of the judges were on the autumnal circuit, the court met on a Saturday at one of the country towns, where the assizes are usually held. After going through the customary forms, and doing some business of no great importance, they adjourned till Monday. At the close of the meeting, one of the jurymen, a gentleman of large fortune, earnestly requested the judges to permit him to go home. The only answer he received was a pressing invitation to dine with them, which he promised to do, adding, that he hoped they would have the goodness to allow him to leave town in the evening. The company at dinner was very numerous. The two judges sat at the head of the table. Several lawyers, and many gentlemen, besides the magistrates of the burgh, were present. Not long after dinner, the gentleman above mentioned, renewed his request, and very earnestly begged their lordships would give him leave to go home.

"What is all your hurry to get home," said Lord Braxfield; "why should not you remain here as well as the others, and do your duty to your country?" "My Lord," replied the gentleman, "I shall tell you": This year I am a great farmer; a good deal of my corn is cut down, and, owing to the bad weather which we have had for some time past, I fear that much of it is in a sad condition. Yesterday and to-day the weather has been much better, and I daresay by to-morrow some of it will be ready to take in." "Surely," said Lord Braxfield, "you do not mean to make your servants take in corn on Sunday?" "I do, my Lord," answered the gentleman; "and I don't think they can be better employed than in saving the fruits of the earth, for the use of man and beast. I am persuaded that God Almighty will be better pleased to see them employed in that useful work, than attending any church whatever; and it is my decided opinion, that at this season, especially in such broken weather as we have had for some time past, the country people should be enjoined, instead of going to church, to improve every Sabbath, when the weather is good, in removing to the barn-yard all the corn that is fit for taking in." Before he had finished this last sentence, Lord Braxfield drew himself forward on his chair with considerable agitation; and looking at him in a manner that showed he was not pleased, he said, with an elevated tone, that produced a complete silence in the company, and in that broad Scottish accent which his Lordship commonly used, and which sometimes gave a particular emphasis to what he said—" Sir! you are surely not thinking what you are saying. Were you to do what you propose, it would, in the first place, be such an outrage, such a gross violation of the laws of your country, as should not be suffered to pass unpunished; and if any of his Majesty's justices of the peace near you, did not lay your feet fast, they would not do their duty. In the second place, sir, it would be a most gross violation of the commandments of Almighty God; and it is absurd to say, He will be better pleased to see us and our servants breaking his commandments than keeping them. Besides, sir, in the third place, your conduct would discover such a distrust in the Providence of God, as a man that calls himself a Christian should at least think shame to own. Sit still, sir, where you are, for you shall not get away till the business of the court is over in this place." As his Lordship said this, his colleague (the late Sir Thomas Miller, afterwards President of the Court of Session), laying his hand on Lord Braxfield's shoulder, and smiling, said to him, "My Lord, I always knew that your Lordship was a great lawyer, but I did not know before that you were so great a divine." "As long as I live," resumed Lord Braxfield, in his warm, animated tone, "I shall think it my duty to set my face against all unnecessary working on the Sabbath-day. Works of real necessity must be done. If a flood come down, and your grain is in danger of being carried away and lost, certainly your people cannot be better employed than in saving it. It is their duty, then, to work, rather than go to church; but for people to lead in corn on Sunday, when there is no urgent necessity for it, is what I hope will never be tolerated in a Christian country."

THE BIBLE AND THE CRIMINAL,
Or the Influence of the Gospel.

A FEW years ago (says the Rev. William Gilchrist, M.A.) a wild and savage youth, who had wrought as a collier, was committed to prison for housebreaking. He was tried and sentenced to banishment for life. I (says Mr. Gilchrist) watched to do him good, and sought to reach his mind. An opportunity occurred sooner than was expected. The first time I saw him after his return to Bridewell, which was on the day following his trial, he appeared to be glad he was still in the land of the living. He had been astonished and horror-struck at the predicament in which he found himself, when at the bar of the Justiciary Court. These feelings had not altogether subsided; and respecting his narrow escape, he said, with considerable emotion, "They were for hanging me! Were it not for some folk, who spoke them fair, I wad ha'e been hanged!" Every time it was alluded to, he trembled at the imminent danger he had been in. A point upon which he was assailable was now at last discovered. I instantly availed myself of it, and reminded him of his thinking that there was little or nothing wrong with his conduct. He acknowledged that he did so think; "but," it was replied, "there must surely have been something dreadfully bad in what was within so little of costing you your life." "Surely," said he, "surely, there must."

After he was convinced that he had done wrong in this material instance, I proceeded to show him that he was chargeable with many other things, which were not right, and that he was indeed under a sentence of death on account of them—that all sinners were doomed to die. This subject, with which other people are so well acquainted, was new to him; he felt deeply interested in it and concerned. When he was told of the awful and everlasting destruction from which we were delivered—of the kindness and mercy of Him who descended from heaven to earth to deliver us, and of what He did and suffered on our behalf—it exceeds my power to describe the pitch of interest and anxiety to which his mind was raised. He exclaimed, "Is all that in The Book?" "Yes, and a great deal more than I have been able to tell you." With an intenseness of feeling and alacrity, which brooked no delay, he pressed the Bible into my hands. "There," said he, "read it to me." I had formerly endeavoured to inculcate the doctrines of the Bible on him in vain; now he was no careless hearer. The passages quoted in conversation regarding the Lamb of God who taketh away the sins of the world; regarding the love of God, who sent his only and well-beloved Son into our world, that whosoever believeth in him should not *perish*, but have everlasting life—were read to him. He looked like one who had received a treasure richer than of gold.

Thenceforward this poor creature seemed greatly changed. Under the influence of instruction, he evinced a degree of intellect and energy of mind that appeared not in him before; and all his thoughts were bent on learning to peruse the Scripture himself.

He remained in Bridewell three or four weeks after this interview; and so intent was he in being taught, that, not satisfied with all the attention I could pay him, the Governor, in waying his daily rounds through the house, was at different times insisted on *to wait and give him a lesson.* His progress was astonishing; and very little more learning would have enabled him to read the Bible.

The brief story of this miserable convict is striking and melancholy. I gathered from him that he was the son of a wild and ill-behaved woman, who was of a respectable family, but, nevertheless, could not be kept at home, or persuaded to conduct herself in a becoming manner. She had had divers other illegitimate children. When he was only a fortnight old, she was prevented from throwing him into a coal-pit by a stranger female. The kind creature who rescued, afterwards nursed him; and though poor, gave him food and shelter till he could provide for himself. He had never received any instruction. He said, he only once saw his father (a man in good business, in a thriving village), who gave him *sixpence,* and sent him about his business. As soon as he could do anything, he began to work in a coal-mine. One anecdote he told respecting himself illustrates the working of his mind after it was set a-thinking. On a certain occasion, the roof of the mine fell in, and a large fragment of rock, which had been over his head, came down above him. The one end of it, however, struck the floor, and the other against the wall of the mine, and he, then being but a little boy, sat as safely under it as though nothing had happened. "Now," he added, looking inquisitively into my face, "I suppose it was God who preserved *me* then?" I was not prepared for this question; and as soon as I recovered the power of articulation, he was told that there could be no doubt of it whatever—he was then and there preserved by the good providence of God from being dashed in pieces. He was in raptures at recieving this information. It was a new and joyful light to his mind. And it evidently afforded him happiness to think that, though few or none seemed to care for his welfare, there was an all-seeing eye which watched over him, and an almighty arm stretched forth, and ready to help and save him.

JENNY GEDDES AND HER STOOL.

An order was given by the King to introduce a new Service Book into the churches of Scotland, and this was to be done on the 23rd of July, 1637. On that day a great concourse of people, including the Lord Chancellor and the Archbishop of St. Andrews, along with several members of the Privy Council, the Judges of the Supreme Court, the Magistrates of the City, and a great multitude of the citizens, assembled in the church of St. Giles, then called the "Great Church," to witness the ceremony. In the morning the usual prayers had been read from the old Book of Common Order. The Dean of Edinburgh, in his surplice, was to read the new service, and the Bishop of Edinburgh was to preach. As soon as the Dean took his place in the reading-desk, and opened the obnoxious volume, a murmur arose in the congregation, and on his proceeding to announce the collect for the day, an old woman, named Janet Geddes, who kept a greengrocer's stall in the High Street, is said to have exclaimed,—"Deil colick the wame o' thee, thou fause thief! Dost thou say mass at my lug [ear]?" and to have flung at the Dean's head the stool on which she had been sitting. A scene of uproar and confusion immediately ensued. A crowd, consisting principally of women, rushed to the desk with loud menaces, and the Dean, in great alarm, threw off his surplice and fled. The Bishop of Edinburgh then ascended the pulpit and attempted to restore order, but without effect. A volley of sticks and other missiles was hurled at him, accompanied with cries of "A pope! a pope! Stone him! stone him!" so that he could not be heard. "The gentleman," says a contemporary writer, "did fall a-tearing [weeping], and crying that the mass was entered amongst them, and Baal in the church. There was a gentleman who was standing behind a pew and answering 'amen' to what the Dean was reading. A she-zealot, hearing him, starts up in choler. 'Traitor,' says she, 'does thou say mass at my ear?' and with that struck him in the face with her bible in great indignation and fury." The rioters were at length expelled from the church, and the doors having been bolted, the Dean emerged from his hiding-place, and resumed the service. It was rendered almost inaudible, however, by the shouts of the mob without, who battered at the door, and shouted, "A pope! a pope! Antichrist! Pull him down!" and other exclamations of the same sort. At the close of the service, the Dean made his escape unnoticed; but the Bishop of Edinburgh, who was very unpopular, was threatened and assailed by the populace, and was with difficulty rescued from their hands.

"I WILL BE WITH YOU ALWAY."
An Anecdote of the Rev. Robert Bruce.

THE REV. ROBERT BRUCE, an eminent minister in Scotland, having to preach on a solemn occasion, was late in coming to the congregation. Some of the people beginning to be weary, and others wondering at his stay, the bells having been rung long, and the time far spent, the beadle was desired to go and inquire the reason, who, coming to his house, and finding his chamber-door shut, and hearing a sound, drew near, and listening, overheard Mr. Bruce often, and with much seriousness, say, "I protest I will not go except thou go with me." Whereupon the man, supposing that some person was in company with him, withdrew without knock at the door. On being asked, at his return, the cause of Mr. Bruce's delay, he answered he could not tell; but supposed that some person was with him, who was unwilling to come to church, and he was engaged in pressing him to come peremptorily, declaring he would not go without him. Mr. Bruce soon after came, accompanied with no man, but he came in the fulness of the blessings of the Gospel of Christ; and his speech and his preaching were with such evidence and demonstration of the Spirit, that it was easy for the hearers to perceive he had been in the mount with God, and that he enjoyed the presence of his Divine Master.

LIBERTY AND EQUALITY.

MANY years ago, when the revolutionary mania first began to affect the heads of the operatives in our large manufacturing towns, and when it was seriously proposed amongst them to overturn all existing institutions, and establish liberty and equality on the French model, the Rev. Mr. Shirra, of Kirkcaldy, was waited upon by some of the members of his congregation who wished to know his opinion on the subject. Mr. Shirra told them he could not answer them off-hand that day, but he would take the matter into serious consideration, and on the following Sabbath would give his sentiments publicly from the pulpit. It was immediately buzzed about that Mr. Shirra was to preach on liberty and equality, and a great multitude accordingly flocked to his meeting-house. On the congregation assembling, Mr. Shirra went on with the usual services, without making any allusion to the matter, until, at the close, he expressed himself somewhat as follows:—" My friends, I had a call from some of you the other day, wanting to know my opinion about liberty and equality, when I told you if you came here to-day I would let you know it. Now, since that time I have travelled in the spirit all over the world, and I shall just tell you what I have seen in my travels. I have travelled over the earth, its frozen and burning zones, mountains, and valleys, moist places and dry, fertile lands and deserts; and I have found grown men and children, big and little, strong and weak, wise and ignorant, good and bad, powerful and helpless, rich and poor—no equality there. I have travelled through the sea—its deeps and shoals, rocks and sandbanks, whirlpools and eddies, and I have found monsters and worms, whales and herrings, sharks and shrimps, mackerels and sprats, the strong devouring the weak, and the big swallowing the little—no equality there. I have ascended to heaven, with its greater and lesser lights, its planets and comets, suns and satellites—and I have found thrones and dominions, principalities and powers, angels, cherubim and seraphim—no equality there. I have descended to hell, and there I found Beelzebub the prince of the devils, and his grim councillors, Moloch and Belial, tyrannizing over the other devils, and all of them over wicked men's souls—no equality there. This is what I have found in my travels, and I think I have travelled far enough; but if any of you are not satisfied with what I have told you, and wish to go in search of liberty and equality yourselves, you may find them if you travel somewhere that I have not visited. You need not travel the same road that I have done. I can tell you positively you will never find them on the earth, neither in the sea, nor in heaven, nor hell. If you can think of anywhere else, you may try. Meanwhile, I have given you all the information I can. It rests with you to make a proper use of it."

THE MISSIONARY AND THE INFIDEL IN EDINBURGH.

Mr. Alexander Paterson, Missionary of Kilmany, as he was called, had a sphere of work in Edinburgh. The following is an account of how he dealt with those he visited:—

"Your husband, I understand, is very ill," he said, as he knocked at a door in Holyrood Street, where he had heard a professed infidel was sick; "I am anxious to see him." Shutting the door with great violence, the woman hastened to a neighbour's house. Mr. Paterson, however, went in. The man he found in bed reading the newspapers. "What do you want?" said he, in a surly and somewhat sneering tone. "You and I are strangers," replied Mr. Paterson, mildly, "but I hope we'll not be long so. I'm a missionary; and as I was just going through the neighbours, I heard you were in distress, and I came in to see you." "I don't want you," he said, gruffly. "But I want you." "And what do you want with me?" "I want you to come to Jesus, the Saviour of sinners; and he wants you to come to him. Let me tell you it's a serious thing to die." "Oh! I've made up my mind to that, so you need say no more to me about it;" and taking up the newspapers, he resumed his reading. "What have you made up your mind to?" "Oh! to die, to be sure, there's nothing for me but death." "Well, and how is it to be with you after death? You know that after death comes the judgment." "Oh! I want to know no more of you. God is merciful, and I've no fear of him damning me; He never made man to damn him." "I know that; it is man that damns himself. The Lord says, 'You have destroyed yourselves;' and he adds, 'in Me is your help.' 'Look to me,' says Jesus, 'and be ye saved.'" "Oh! I've plenty of you; I want none of your talk." Finding he could make nothing of him, he said, "Will you allow me to pray for you?" "Oh, if you like. I don't much care about your prayer."

The missionary prayed, but the moment he began, the man took up his paper, and read. "I'll come back and see you," said Mr. Paterson, when he had finished praying. "You may, if you like," rejoined the man; "but I don't care about your coming." Two other visits proved equally ineffectual to rouse the man to any concern about the future; but, not despairing, Paterson returned to the house a fourth time. "I'll pray for you once more," he said. And as he began, the poor man resumed his newspaper. But before he had prayed a few minutes, the paper fell from his hand. When the prayer was concluded, he was bathed in tears, and so also was his wife. "Oh!" he said, with a faltering voice, and grasping the missionary by the hand, "will you come back and see me?" "I will, with all my heart." And he left them both in tears. Returning the next day, he found the man poring over his Bible. "I'm glad to see that book in your hands," said he. "What has led you to lay aside the newspaper, and turn to that?" "Oh! sir, it was your last prayer. I felt my heart melted; and ever since I've felt myself to be in an awful state. Oh! what a sinner I've been. All that you've said of me as a sinner was true." "Well, I've said just what that blessed book says of myself, and of everyone who is out of Christ. But Christ died for the chief of sinners; his blood was shed for you and me. Hear what he says: 'If we confess our sins, he is faithful and just to forgive us our sins, and to cleanse us from all unrighteousness.'" At parting, the man, now all humble and anxious for the pardon of his sins, earnestly entreated the missionary to return and to pray for him. On a subsequent visit Mr. Paterson found him weaker, but happier, trusting in the Saviour who had died for him, and blessing the Bible for the sweet promises which he now found to be his comfort in his affliction; and he died in the hope and consolation of the Gospel.

THE REV. DR. WILLIAM ANDERSON AND THE EXTORTIONER.

THE Rev. Dr. William Anderson, of Glasgow, was a bold man, and had the courage of his opinions. On one occasion he was expounding the words, "He that putteth not out his money to usury." "Does that mean," he said, "asking ten per cent. or more? Not entirely. It means also the spirit in which the per cent. is taken. There was once in this church a poor widow, and she wanted twenty pounds to begin a small shop. Having no friends, she came to me, her minister; and I happened to know a man, not of this church, who could advance the money to the poor widow. So we went to this man, the widow and I, and the man said he would be happy to help the widow; and he drew out a bill for twenty pounds, and the widow signed it, and I signed it too. Then he put the signed paper in his desk, and took out the money and gave it to the widow; but, counting it, she said, 'Sir, there are only fifteen pounds here.' 'It is all right,' said the man, 'that is the interest I charge.' And, as we had no redress we came away. But the widow prospered; and she brought the twenty pounds to me, and I took it myself to the office of the man who lent it, and I said to him, 'Sir, there are the twenty pounds from the widow;' and he said, 'There is the paper you signed, and if you know any other poor widow, I will be happy to help her in the same way.' I replied, '*You* help the widow, sir! you have robbed this widow, and, if you do not repent, you will be damned!' And, my friends, I kept my eye on that man, and before six months was over, God smote him, and he died."

An acquaintance in Edinburgh adds to this story the following:—"And when his will was produced and read, it appeared that on the very day I had spoken to him, he put to it a codicil, leaving fifty pounds to the poor. Poor deluded mortal, to think his soul's salvation could be bought for fifty pounds!"

ANECDOTES OF PEDEN THE PROPHET.

ONE thing which strikes us in the life of Peden is the authority with which he spake. The bold and awakened tenor of his address, both to private individuals, and before a public auditory, remind us of Elijah or John the Baptist, speaking in tones of astonishment and alarm in the ears of their impenitent countrymen. When he was prisoner in the Bass Rock, one Sabbath morning, being engaged in the private worship of God, a young woman came to the chamber-door, mocking with loud laughter. He said, "Poor thing, thou mockest and laughest at the worship of God; but, ere long, God will work such a sudden, surprising judgment on thee that shall stay thy laughing, and thou shalt not escape it." Very shortly thereafter, as she was walking upon the rock, there came a blast of wind that swept her into the sea, and she was lost. Another day, while he was walking upon the rock, some soldiers passing by him, one of them cried, "The devil take him." He said, "Fie, fie, poor man; thou knowest not what thou art saying; but thou wilt repent that." At which words the soldier stood astonished, and went to the guard distracted, crying aloud for Mr. Peden, saying the devil would immediately take him. Peden came and spoke to him, and prayed with him. The next morning, again visiting him, he found him in his right mind, under deep convictions of great guilt. The guards being to change, they desired him to go to his arms. He refused, and said—"I will lift no arms against Jesus Christ's cause, nor persecute His people; I have done that too long." The governor threatened him with death the next day, at ten o'clock: he confidently said three times, "Though you should tear all my body to pieces, I will never lift up arms that way." About three days after, he was put out of the garrison by the governor, who sent him ashore. Having a wife and children, he took a house in East Lothian, where he became an eminent Christian.

THE MEN OF ST. KILDA CANNOT FORGET GOD.

NATURE has an unconscious influence on the mind of man. This is illustrated in the following facts which Dr. Macleod related at a meeting, held in reference to the establishment of schools in the Highlands and Islands of Scotland:—A friend of mine happened to be in a boat, by which a poor, simple-hearted man, from the island of St. Kilda was advancing, for the first time in his life, from his native rock to visit the world; and as he advanced towards the island of Mull—a world in itself in the estimation of the poor St. Kilda man—the boatmen commenced telling him the wonders he was so soon to see. They asked him about St. Kilda; they questioned him regarding all the peculiarities of that wonderful place; and rallied him not a little on his ignorance of all those great and magnificent things which were to be seen in Mull.

He parried them off with great coolness and good humour. At length a person in the boat asked him if he ever heard of God in St. Kilda. Immediately he became grave and collected. "To what land do you belong?" said he; "describe it to me." "I," said the other, "come from a place very different from your barren rock; I come from the land of flood and field, the land of wheat and barley, where Nature spreads her beauty in abundance and luxuriance before us." "Is that," said the St. Kilda man, "the kind of land you come from? Ah, then, you may forget God, but a St. Kilda man never can. Elevated on his rock, suspended over a precipice, tossed on the wild ocean, he never can forget his God—he hangs continually on his arm." All were silent in the boat, and not a word more was asked him regarding his religion. They felt that he had a depth of religion, and a sublimer faith than they possessed. God had spoken to his soul in the tempest and the flood, and made known his love and power in the ocean-girt home where he and his people dwelt.

PATRICK HAMILTON AT THE STAKE.

ARCHBISHOP BEATON being afraid to proceed openly against Hamilton, advised that he should be decoyed to St. Andrews, on the pretext of a friendly conference with him about his doctrine. The open-hearted young man eagerly embraced the proposal, and fell into the snare. It is needless to dwell on the revolting consequences. He was easily induced by some insidious priests to declare his sentiments. At the dead hour of night he was dragged from his bed, taken to the castle, and, after confessing his faith before the Archbishop, was condemned to be burned at the stake as an obstinate heretic. On the afternoon of Friday, February 28, 1528, this gentle and gracious youth was led to the place of execution, where a stake was fastened, with wood, coals, powder, and other inflammable materials piled round it. When he came to the place, he stripped himself of his gown, coat, and bonnet, and gave them to a favourite servant. "These," said he, "will not profit in the fire; they will profit thee. After this, of me thou can'st receive no commodity except the example of death, which I pray thee to bear in mind; for albeit it be bitter to the flesh, yet is it the entrance into eternal life, which none shall possess that deny Christ before this wicked generation." When bound to the stake, he exhibited no symptom of fear, but commended his soul to God, and kept his eyes stedfastly directed towards heaven. The executioner set fire to the train of powder, which, however, did not kindle the pile, but severely scorched the side of the martyr. In this situation he remained unmoved, till a new supply of powder was brought from the castle.

Meanwhile, the friars who stood around him, cruelly molested him, crying out, "Convert, heretic, call upon our Lady—say *Salve regina.*" "Depart and trouble me not," he said, "ye messengers of Satan." One of them in parcular, called Friar Campbell, rendered himself conspicuous for his rudeness in disturbing the last moments of the martyr. "Thou wicked man," said Hamilton, addressing him, "thou knowest that I am not a heretic, and that it is the truth of God for which I now suffer; so much didst thou confess unto me in private—and thereupon I appeal unto thee to answer before the judgment-seat of Christ." At length the fire was kindled, and, amidst the fire and fury of the flames, he was distinctly heard pronouncing these last words—"How long, O Lord, shall darkness cover this realm? How long wilt thou suffer this tyranny of men? Lord Jesus, receive my spirit."

THOMAS EDWARDS, THE SCOTCH NATURALIST;
Or, Independence and Industry.

THOMAS EDWARDS, the Scotch Naturalist, was of humble birth, and wrought while pursuing his studies as a country shoemaker. With his own hands he gathered a remarkable collection of natural objects, which he brought from Banff, where he lived, to Aberdeen to exhibit. When in the granite city, Dr. Cadenhead, one of the principal physicians, and oculists of the city, visited the collection. Going directly up to Edwards, he asked, "Well, how are you getting on?" "Very poorly," was the answer. "And no wonder," said the visitor. "How?" "How!" he almost shouted, "because the people here don't believe in such a thing. I am sure of it from what I know and have heard." "But," responded Edwards, "if they would only come!" "Come!" said Dr. Cadenhead," that's the very thing. It seems they'll not come; and, although they did, what satisfactory evidence is there that what they see is the result of your own unaided and individual labour? You are quite a stranger here. You should have had some persons of high-standing in the city to take you under their patronage—say, the Professors of both Colleges, or the Provost and Town Council. Oh! you needn't stroke your head and look on the floor. It would have been much better." "I never considered myself in a position," said Edwards, "to seek such a favour." "Then you'll not succeed here unless you do something of the sort." "In that case, then," said Edward, "I'll be plain enough to tell you that I never will succeed." "You are too stiff, too unbending," said the Doctor. "Then you know very well that you have nobody in Aberdeen to confirm your extraordinary statement. You say the whole collection is entirely the work of your own hands, and that it is your own exclusive property?" "Yes; I bought the game birds; and, as regards the others, I procured the whole of them myself—preserved them, and cased them, just as you see them." "And had you to work for your living all that time?" "Yes; and for the living of my family, too." "Then you have a wife and a family?" "Yes, I have five children." "But do you mean to say that you have maintained your wife and family, by working at your trade, all the while that you have been making this collection?" "Yes." "Oh, nonsense! How is it possible that you could have done that?" "By never losing a single minute, nor any part of a minute, that I could by any means improve." "Did you ever hear of any one else who had ever done the like before?" "No; but thousands might have done it, and much more too. I never thought that I was doing anything meritorious; but if I have, as a journeyman shoemaker, done anything worthy of praise, then I must say that there is not a working man on the face of the earth that could not have done much more than I have done; for of all the occupations known, that of shoemaking is surely the worst. Too often, however, working-men do not go into the fields to drink the sweets of Nature, but rush unthinkingly into the portals of hell, and drown their sorrows in whisky. In this way they beggar themselves, and pauperise their families."

In concluding the conversation, Edwards said, "My

chief school was the Earth; and my principal teacher was Nature. What I have been able to do, has been done by economising every farthing of money, and every moment of time." The secret of his life is found in the words he delivered to boys, "In searching for the living things, my desire was not to destroy for destruction's sake, but simply that I might learn all I could concerning the beautiful and wonderful works of God." Concerning Edwards it may be said, "Seest thou a man diligent in his business? he shall stand before Kings." He has been recognised by the Queen, and by the learned and great of the earth, and, in the evening of his life, there has been light.

THE REV. EBENEZER BROWN AND ORDERLY CHURCH SERVICE.

THE REV. EBENEZER BROWN, of Inverkeithing, was a godly man, was very refined in his feelings, and elevated in his tastes. He went on one occasion to London in order to be present at a large missionary meeting; and being there on the Sabbath, he had an opportunity of preaching in the metropolis, and of witnessing London manners. A journey from Scotland to the great city at that period was of a much rarer occurrence than it is now, and would have been regarded as an important event in one's lifetime. Mr. Brown felt it so, and as he had an opportunity of seeing many things not commonly known at home, he resolved to give his people the benefit of his experience. On the first Sunday after his return, he took occasion to state, in the course of his forenoon sermon: "My friends, I have three wonders to tell you of to-day which I saw when in London," and then went on with his discourse without further reference to the matter, finished the sermon, and concluded the service by prayer and praise and the benediction in the usual way. On leaving the church, many looks were cast at the worthy minister, as much as to say, "you have forgotten to tell us the three wonderful things." The news got wind in the village in the interval, and there was a large turnout in the afternoon, the church being completely filled by the time Mr. Brown made his appearance. All was expectation, and the people were not doomed to disappointment a second time. After concluding the public worship, Mr. Brown said,—" Well, my friends, I have now to tell you the three wonders I saw in London." With that all the people sat down in breathless attention and silence. "The first wonder I have to tell I saw in London is, when I came into the pulpit in the morning the folks were waiting on me; I didna need to wait for them; and I never saw the like o' that in Inverkeithing. The second wonder I have to tell you I saw in London is, that when I was drawing the prayer to a conclusion, there was no jostling and making a noise, and sitting down; they a' stood till I said Amen; and I never saw the like o' that in Inverkeithing. And the third wonder I have to tell you I saw in London is, that there was nae reaching for hats, and a bundling up o' bibles when the last psalm was a-singing, and no a' coming down the stairs when the blessing was being pronounced; but they a' waited till the Amen, and then they sat down a wee; and I never saw the like o' that in Inverkeithing till this afternoon." This practical discourse had its effect, and is bearing fruit still. It is needed in the nineteenth as well as it was required at the end of the eighteenth century.

DR. GUTHRIE'S GOSPEL BELLS.

A Scotch lady, when in Edinburgh, noticed a very lofty attic in the High Street, in the neighbourhood of Dr. Guthrie's Church. The thought struck her that there might be some poor lonely creature living in one of those upper storeys, whom no one visited or cared for; so, lifting up her heart to God for guidance and blessing, she began her investigation. After ascending the almost innumerable stairs in the building, she reached the top storey, where the poorest people lived. Knocking at one of the doors, she was answered by an old woman, who, opening it cautiously, asked the stranger what she wanted. "I want to see you?" replied the lady. "No one ever comes here, or wants to see me," said the old woman, in no inviting tones. "Well," rejoined the kind visitor, "that is just the reason why I wish to see you." Then the cautious old woman opened the door, and let the lady into her little room, which only contained enough furniture for the bare necessities of its aged inmate. The only seats were a rocking-chair and a stool, and the visitor, taking the stool, made the old woman seat herself near the fire in her rocking-chair. After a few kind words, which opened the poor woman's heart, the lady visitor said, "I am not going to ask you, my friend, if you know the Lord; but I should like to hear if you can tell me anything to show me that the Lord knows you, and has found you out in your little lonely room?" The old woman's face brightened up at once. "Yes, I can," she answered; "and I will tell you all about it, though I have never told any one before. If He had not known me and sought me, I should never have known Him; for I lived like a heathen in this room. I have had many troubles, and lost my all; and not having a friend, or any one to love, I shut myself up in my own misery, and did not want to know my neighbours. Week-days and Sundays were all alike and dark to me. I never went anywhere. I lived just as if I had no soul; and thus I should have lived and died had not the Lord had mercy upon me." "And how did He awaken you from your state of spiritual death?" "By Dr. Guthrie's bells," replied the old woman; "when they rang on Sundays, I use to wish they would leave off. They troubled me; they seemed calling to me—till at last I could bear it no longer; so one day I put on my shawl, and went to church just to get peace, as it were, from the bells." "Well, and how did you like what you heard?" "Not at all. I came home very angry with Dr. Guthrie; for as I stood in the crowded aisle, he preached all his sermon about me, and I determined never to go and hear him again. But when the next Sunday came, the bells tormented me more than ever. I was forced to go; and again I came home feeling what a sinner I was. Thus I continued from week to week; and then I had a dream which cut down all my hopes. I seemed to be in a square place, where a number of flowers in pots were standing, and in the middle of them I saw Dr. Guthrie with a watering-pot. He went round and watered every pot and plant until he came to one which I thought meant me; and then he stood still and said, in a solemn voice, ' It is no good watering this, for it has no roots,' and he passed me by. And when I awoke, I felt what a dreadful state I was in." And thus the arrow of conviction entered this poor sinner's heart, till the Lord who had wounded her in love was pleased to heal her wounds with the atoning blood of Jesus Christ.

THE SCIENTIFIC COBBLER OF MILNGAVIE.

JAMES STIRLING of Milngavie, sometimes called the "scientific cobbler," was in his early days, and till advanced in life, a victim to strong drink. After having suffered severely, he was brought seriously to reflect on the course he was pursuing, by the following touching incident:—One night on his return home, after having spent a whole day in the public-house, he found his wife engaged, as usual, in reading a chapter of the New Testament to the children. The portion of Scripture read was the twenty-fifth of Matthew's Gospel, in which these words occur—" When the Son of Man shall come in his glory, and all the holy angels with him, then shall he sit on the throne of his glory; and before him shall be gathered all nations; and he shall separate them one from another, as a shepherd divideth his sheep from the goats; and he shall set the sheep on his right hand, but the goats on the left." His youngest boy, then about four years of age, was lying with his head on his mother's lap, and just when she had read those striking words, he looked up earnestly in her face and asked—" Will father be a goat, then, mother?" "This," says Stirling himself, "was too strong to be resisted. The earnest, innocent look of the child, the bewilderment of the poor mother, and, above all, the question itself, smote me to the heart's core. I spent a sleepless, awfully miserable night, wishing rather to die than live such a life. I was ashamed to go to church on the following Sabbath. I stopped at home, and read the "Six Sermons on Intemperance," by Beecher, which had found their way into the house; but how, I never knew. But so it was, that when looking about the house for some suitable book to read on Sabbath, I laid my hands on them, and they seemed as if written and printed, and sent there for me alone. I was now decided. My resolution was taken, as it had never been before. All the men on earth could not tempt me to drink ale or beer, thick or thin."

Shortly after this a temperance meeting was held, at which Stirling attended, and put his name to the pledge. As soon as he had publicly enrolled his name, one of his sons, then a boy, who was present, ran home as fast as a pair of the nimblest feet in the village could carry him, to tell his mother, who was lying unwell, the glad news. "Mother! mother!" he cried out in eager haste, as the door flew open, and he rushed to the bedside, "father has just put down his name, and the minister has put down his, and they're all putting down their names." "Thank God!" ejaculated the broken-hearted wife, who had passed through a long night of weeping, and on whom light was now breaking at last. "Thank God!" But she could say no more till she found relief in tears. And such tears! It was the first time in her married life that tears had started from the long-sealed fount of joy. "Thank God!" she said, after a pause; "if he has signed he'll keep it. Yes, he'll keep it. Yes, he'll keep it," she added, with still greater emphasis, and her pale face flushed, as it had not been for many years, with the pride of early love. "Thank God! he has signed it, and I'll sign it too, and ye must all sign it, for oh! surely the time, the set time, to favour us, and many poor families, has come at last." From that evening till the day of his death, Stirling devoted himself to promote the cause of temperance and religion, and thousands were blessed by his works and words.

THE POWER OF CONSCIENCE.
Illustrated by an Incident in Glasgow.

FARQUHAR MACKAY was born in the north of Scotland, and at an early period was deprived of both his parents. When his sixteenth summer closed, he was apprenticed to a saddler at some distance from his birthplace, and left his relatives with other feelings than those of regret. Beyond the reach of his aunt's solemn entreaties, and the gentle reproofs of a sister, who by this time had embraced the Saviour, he now desecrated the Sabbath, contracted intemperate habits, and wrought all manner of evil with greediness. During his stay from home a solemn providence befel him, and one well fitted, if improved, to give his thoughts a new direction. One fine Sabbath morning, he and four other young lads resolved on a sailing excursion. Having departed in all safety, they spent the greater part of the day over their cups in a house of refreshment. Two hours before sunset they were on their way back, when a sudden tempest arose, and their frail bark, under management far from good, upset. Ere succour came, his four companions had disappeared, and he alone was rescued from a watery grave. Impending death in his own case, actual death in the case of his companions, made but a momentary impression—his fears fled with the tempest that gave them birth; and for all this, "he sinned yet more, and hardened his heart." At length, impatient of restraint, and smarting under the rebukes of a master whose confidence he had lost, he abandoned his trade, and proceeded to Glasgow. Here he remained for some time in the most destitute condition. Every spare article of clothing was sold to meet the cravings of hunger, and often, in the depth of his distress, was he tempted to cast himself into the river. Friendless and penniless, this poor prodigal wandered the streets from morn to eve, courting the meanest drudgery to keep soul and body together, and cursing the day of his birth. After a time, burglars became his companions. He took their oath, learned their tactics, and in robbery soon equalled the most daring among them. Two years had been spent in this dangerous and disgraceful course, when a circumstance occurred which made his slumbering conscience ill at ease, and led him to alter his plans. He and his companions, after surveying the ground in the guise of pedlars, had arranged to enter and plunder the house of a widow lady resident in the suburbs. Midnight found this ruffian band silently surrounding the house, and endeavouring, for some time to no purpose, to effect an entrance. By dint of ingenuity and labour, a back window was thrown open, and in they rushed to steal, and mayhap to destroy. It fell to our youth's lot to enter the lady's bed-chamber. Startled by the lantern-glare and the sound of footsteps, the sleeping invalid awoke, and screamed aloud for aid. Presently a murderous weapon was raised, a horrid threat uttered, and the keys demanded by the robber. These were at once given up. The owner saw her desk opened, and a considerable sum of money extracted. The keys were coolly returned, and the masked thief was preparing to withdraw, when the terror-stricken witness of the theft, summoning up all her courage, and heedless of consequences, exclaimed, "Knowest thou that for all this God will bring thee into judgment!" He smiled, and hurried away. Arrived at his den in the city he speedily found he had brought with him something else than spoil. An accusing conscience sat enthroned within, marshalling all its terrors, and giving birth to

> "Pangs that rack the anxious mind."

"Judgment" (the widow's closing word) rose up before the eye of his mind, and covered him with confusion. This "fire shut up in his bones"—this scorching thought, he strove earnestly to get rid of, but still it glowed. For two whole weeks it was unquenchable. Wretched man! what would he not have given for some spiritual drug; for a cup of Lethe's waters—for a balm-application to his open wounds! Oh! to erase "Judgment" from the tablet of memory. In the midst of such mental torture as this, he addressed to the widow a penitential letter, enclosing the money he had taken from her desk; and then, having abandoned for ever his burglar associates, set sail for America. At the end of his days he was an honoured and respected man, and left behind him many tokens of his good-doing.

A SIMPLETON'S THEOLOGY.
An Incident in the Parish of Crawfordjohn.

THE following fact occurred at the farm of Abingdon, in the parish of Crawfordjohn, at the distance of well nigh a century from the present day. It was then, as it is in greater or less degree still, the practice among the farmers to lodge the wayfaring poor; and as the farmer's room is often but small, and the character of such random guests sometimes doubtful, they are furnished with blankets and straw in some of the out-houses, where, however, they are comfortably sheltered. It was in the practice of this generous hospitality, that the character of the humble subject of it was revealed to view.

Says the narrator to his brother—"I remember an anecdote of my mother, which Sir Walter Scott would have valued. A poor wandering simpleton, or idiot, came to her father's house one winter evening, and sat by the fire. It was soon noticed that he was very unwell, and being asked what ailed him, his reply was, 'I'm unco cauld.' After giving him warm gruel, he was put to a warm bed in the kiln. At a late hour one of the maid-servants came in, saying, 'that the poor thing in the kiln was aye muttering and speaking to himself.' My mother and others went to listen, when they distinctly overheard him speaking over and over again the following bit of rhyme—

"'Three o' ane, and ane o' three,
And ane o' three will save me.'

The next morning dawned, but the soul of the poor wanderer had gone to the bosom of that 'Ane o' Three,' on whose mercy he relied. My mother," the narrator adds, "could not relate the anecdote with dry eyes. Is there not, in the simple language of this poor wanderer, the distinct recognition of the doctrine of the Trinity, and of the mediatorial work of the Saviour, together with his Divinity, as that 'Ane o' Three,' to whom the simple soul committed itself, in full confidence that, in his own appropriating language, 'He will save me'? It reminds us of the Saviour's striking language, 'I thank thee, O Father, Lord of heaven and earth, because thou hast hid these things from the wise and prudent, and hast revealed them unto babes, even so, Father, for so it seems good in thy sight.'"

REV. DR. BEATTIE TEACHING NATURAL THEOLOGY

THE late Dr. Beattie, of Aberdeen, wishing to impress on the mind of his son, a little boy about six years of age the important truth that God made him, used the following method:—"In the corner of a little garden," says the Doctor, "without informing any person of the circumstance, I wrote in the mould, with my finger, the three initial letters of his name, and sowing garden cresses in the furrows, covered up the seed and smoothed the ground. Ten days after this, he came running to me, and, with astonishment in his countenance, told me that his name was growing in the garden. I laughed at the report, and seemed inclined to disregard it, but he insisted on my going to see what had happened. 'Yes,' said I, carelessly, on coming to the place, 'I see it is so; but what is there in this worth notice? is it not mere chance?' and I went away. He followed me, and taking hold of my coat, said with some earnestness, 'It cannot have happened by chance,—somebody must have contrived matters so as to produce it.' 'So you think,' said I, that what appears as the letters of your name, cannot be by chance?' 'Yes,' said he, with firmness, 'I think so.' 'Look at yourself,' I replied, 'and consider your hands and fingers, your legs and feet, and other limbs; are they not regular in their appearance, and useful to you?' He said they were. 'Came you then hither,' said I, 'by chance?' 'No,' he answered, 'that cannot be;

something must have made me.' 'And who is that something?' I asked. He said, 'I do not know.' I had now gained the point I aimed at, and saw that his reason taught him (though he could not express it) that what begins to be must have a cause; and that what is formed with regularity must have an *intelligent* cause. I therefore told him the name of the GREAT BEING who made him, and all the world; concerning whose adorable nature, I gave him such information as I thought he could in some measure comprehend. The lesson affected him greatly, and he never forgot either it or the circumstance that introduced it."

COVENANT TENT PREACHING.

IT is a Sabbath-day among the mountains, and a company of the Persecuted have assembled. Around, is a mighty chasm of cliffs, called the Cartland Crags, where Wallace used to take refuge, through which a river is flowing, at present so low, owing to the heat of summer, that men could walk all but dry-shod up its channel. A hundred Covenanters — men, women, and children included — assembled to hear a minister, who stands up in a pulpit stone, and having a birch tree waving over his head. Between him and the congregation is a clear, deep pool, formed by the diminished stream, and there, after the sermon is over, a row of young maidens come gliding over the stream, to give away a number of infants who are to be baptized. The baptismal water is lying in the hollow of a large stone beside the brink of the pool. How beautiful to look down, as you see the boys doing, into the clear water and see the whole scene, from the maidens, the parents and the minister, up to the topmost peaks of the sky-striking summits, reflected there over the purest of mirrors. The minister baptizes seven infants in the name of the Father, the Son, and the Holy Ghost, and gives out a psalm, with the words,—

> " Lo, children are God's heritage,
> The womb's fruit his reward,
> The sons of youth, like arrows, are
> For strong men's hands prepared."

The psalm is reverberated like musical thunder from the surrounding crags, and all again is silent. Suddenly, a large stone falls from the rock above their heads into the pool; a voice is heard from the summit, and when they look up, there is a shepherd's plaid waving in the air in the hand of the watchman stationed above. It is the signal of instant danger, and immediately the whole congregation vanish into caves and hidden recesses, known only to themselves. They vanish almost in a moment; but they have been seen by a party of soldiers who have reached the top of the rock, and who exclaim when they see them, "They are delivered into our hands—they are caught in this nook as in a net; let us down, and they are our own. Halloo, boys! halloo! Remember Drumclog, and let the blasted whigs perish!" They leave their horses, and rush down a cleft in the crags, and arrive at the spot. But, to their utter astonishment, nothing is to be seen; nothing but a bonnet that had fallen from one of the Covenanters' heads, and the Bible the minister had been using, and which they spurn into the pool. They are utterly unable to discover where their enemies have fled, and awful are the curses and the threats which they utter. But, louder than these curses and threats, hark! a sound like a distant muttering thunder far up the stream. It comes rolling, and warring, and deepening, as it descends. "What can it be?" The crags shake as if to the sound and stamp of earthquake. "Lord! have mercy on us!" cried the soldiers, falling down on their knees and looking a hundred ways in their consternation, with pale faces and white lips. Meanwhile, the minister comes out of the cave where Wallace had long ago found refuge, and exclaims, "The Lord God Omnipotent reigneth. It is a powerful voice that comes from the Lord Most High." What is it?—what can it be? It is a water-spout which has burst among the hills, and there the river raging in flood is coming down in its irresistible power. The whole hollow of the cliffs is filled with the waters. An army must have been swept away by that raging torrent. The soldiers perish in a few minutes, swept down by the flood;

but far up in the cliffs are the Covenanters, now emerged from their hiding-places, and, with clasped hands and streaming eyes, uttering prayers to the Almighty, and some of them exclaiming,—"We will sing unto the Lord, for He hath triumphed gloriously; the horse and his rider He hath cast in the depth of the waters."

GUTHRIE OF FENWICK.

This most worthy minister of the gospel, cousin of James Guthrie the martyr, took a great interest in his flock and all others who would receive him. He took all the means he could think of, to win men's hearts and lead their thoughts to eternal things. One man whom he urged to have family worship pled as an excuse that he could not pray. "Try it," insisted the minister. At last the man, in perplexity exclaimed,—"Oh, Lord! thou knowest that this man will have me to pray, but I cannot." "Stop," interrupted Guthrie, "You have done enough," and then prayed himself so fervently, that, when he had finished, the woman said to her husband, "Surely this must be the minister." He was one evening travelling home very late. Having lost his way in a moor, he laid the reins on the neck of his horse, and committed himself to the direction of Providence. After long travelling over fields and ditches, the horse brought him to a farmer's house, into which he went, and requested permission to sit by the fire till morning, which was granted. A Popish priest was administering extreme unction to the mistress of the house, who was dying. Mr. Guthrie said nothing till the priest had retired; then he went forward to the dying woman, and asked her if she enjoyed peace in the prospect of death in consequence of what the priest had said and done to her. She answered that she did not; on which he spoke to her of salvation through the atoning blood of the Redeemer. She understood and believed the message of mercy, as it fell from his lips, and she died actually triumphing in Jesus Christ her Saviour. After witnessing this astonishing scene, Mr. Guthrie mounted his horse, and rode home to Fenwick. On his arrival, he told Mrs. Guthrie that he had seen a great wonder during the night. "I came," said he, "to a farm-house, where I found a woman in a state of nature; I saw her in a state of grace, and left her in a state of glory."

ROB ROY MACGREGOR.
"The Ruling Passion Strong in Death."

ROB ROY was born a Protestant and a Presbyterian; but he latterly became a Papist. He did so, more in compliment to the pervert Earl of Perth, than for any other reason that could be assigned. He had never been a very decided or fervent religionist; neither did he become so. After he had lapsed into Popery, he did not disguise that he was not by any means enamoured with all its principles and practices. On this head Sir Walter Scott has said, in one brief paragraph, all that can be said—"In his latter years, he embraced the Roman Catholic faith, perhaps on Mrs. Cole's principle, that it was a comfortable religion for one of his calling. He is said to have alleged as the cause of his conversion, a desire to gratify the noble family of Perth, who were then strict Catholics. Having, as he observed, assumed the name of the Duke of Argyle, his first protector, he could pay no compliment worth the Earl of Perth's acceptance, save complying with his mode of religion. Rob did not pretend, when pressed closely on the subject, to justify all the tenets of Catholicism, and acknowledged that extreme unction always appeared to him a great waste of ulzie, or oil."

Notwithstanding his predatory and perilous "calling"—notwithstanding the many and powerful enemies who hunted for his life—notwithstanding his outlawry by the Government, and the prize of £1000 set upon his head, Rob Roy, after many hairbreadth escapes, died, as is known, in his own house at the head of Loch Voil, in a good old age; and he sustained to the last the character which he had borne all his life long. Learning on his death-bed that one of his enemies wished to visit him, "Raise me from my bed," said he; "throw my plaid around me, and bring me my claymore, dirk, and pistols—it shall never be said that a foeman saw Rob Roy Macgregor defenceless and unarmed." During the brief interview, Rob "maintained a cold, haughty civility," and when the foeman left, "Now," said he, "all is over, let the piper play, 'Ha til mi tulidh' ('We Return no more')," and he is said to have expired before the dirge was finished. Thus did Rob Roy die as he had lived—a brave, and self-willed, and godless man.

IN A GOOD CAUSE.
An Anecdote of the Rev. William Wilson, of Perth.

THE Rev. William Wilson, of the West Church, Perth, one of the founders of the Secession Church, was put out of the Kirk of Scotland because of his sympathy with the Erskines, and on the following Sabbath he was refused admittance into his own church. He thereafter went and preached in the Glover's Yard to a vast concourse of people. Mr. Wilson's father had lain hid for a season in the Mearns' Moor, in the days of former persecutions, and a young girl carried his food to his place of retreat. She seems to have become an inmate of the family, and she was treated with peculiar and tender deference, in Mr. Wilson's household at Perth. On the morning of this trying Sabbath, this aged domestic was somewhat apprehensive and uneasy. Her busy memory brought back the scenes of her youth, when she glided away stealthily, morning and evening, to the wild and gloomy morass where her master was concealed. The privations of the father made her anxious for the welfare of the son. And as the tide of these sad recollections filled her heart, she could not help looking wistfully in her master's face, as he was leaving his home on his way to the church, and saying to him, "Tak' tent, Mr. William, tak' tent what ye're doing, for I fear, if things gang on in this way, I'll get yer meat to carry to the moor, as I did yer guid faither afore ye." When Mr. Wilson returned from the service of the day, he retired at once to his chamber. Many thoughts must have pressed upon him, and he sought quiet, uninterrupted meditation.

His eldest daughter, a girl of about twelve years of age, had witnessed with natural curiosity the strange proceedings, had seen her father seek admission to his own church, and had heard the gruff refusal which the magistrates gave him. She had also been in the Glover's Yard, and had beheld thousands of faces looking up to her sire with intense excitement. But she was sorely puzzled to understand these novelties. Her natural wish was to hear them explained by her father. The matter appeared to her young mind so solemn, that she was afraid to ask what she coveted. But with restless anxiety she hung about the door of the study, anxious to obtain at least a glimpse of his countenance. Her father at last observed her, and reading her wishes in her features, called her to him, and, patting her kindly on the head, said to her, "Bell, this has indeed been a day of trial; but we have reason—great reason to be thankful that it has not been a day of shame. If anybody asks you, Bell, why your papa lost his kirk, you may just say, as good Mr. Guthrie, before his execution bade my mother say of him, if any one asked her why he lost his head—'It was in a good cause.'"

THE SEA CAPTAIN AT THE NORTHERN COASTS OF SCOTLAND.

"OH for a sight of the sun!" the skipper of a Scotch vessel cried as he scanned with anxious eye the fog around. The ship was bound for home, but Cape Wrath, on the north-west extremity of Scotland, must be passed first, and the Pentland Skerries and the Pentland Frith were dangers to be dreaded in such a fog as then enveloped the vessel. They had not seen the sun for several days, and without his aid the captain dare not proceed at full speed, consequently many hours were lost. "There he is!" shouted the mate, as a sudden break in the clouds revealed the welcome orb; and the captain raising to his eye a triangular instrument called a sextant, looked through its glasses towards the sun and took a sight. A minute or two passed, and then the skipper, with brow cleared of anxiety, and with a cheery look, went below into his cabin to work out a problem and consult the charts. He knew now exactly the position of the vessel, and "full speed" was the gladdening command. It was that sight of the sun which sent the ship onward on its course. Men are on a troubled sea, and the mists of sin, ignorance, and error, hide the face of the moral Sun of the universe. Like the Scotch captain, they should look to the Sun of Righteousness by the eye of faith, and the clouds would depart, and the darkness would pass away.

A CHRISTIAN PILGRIM AT HUNTLY.

A REAL Christian pilgrim was Isobel Chrystie, of Huntly, who was upwards of ninety years of age. "Come awa, my son David," said Isobel to the missionary one day as he entered her humble cot. "Perhaps," was his reply, "the hands are the hands of Esau, but the voice is Jacob's. How do you know that I am not a hypocrite?" "Ah," said she, "d'ye think I dinna ken the breath o' a true Christian?" The Rose of Sharon may lie hid in the believer's bosom, but its fragrance cannot be concealed from others. "We ocht to lay down our lives for the brithren, an' hoo' could we dee for them if we dinna ken them?" So thought Isobel Chrystie. When in the course of conversation allusion was made to the salvation of the dying thief, she rattled her little staff on the floor and said,—"That was a gey trophy to gang throu' the gowden gates o' heaven. I'm thinkin' there was a gey steer amo' the angels, but nane o' them would try to pit him oot. Na, na; Christ brocht him ben." When Isobel lay dying, she was unable to recognise minister, missionary, friend, or neighbour. To each inquiry she still replied,—"I dinna ken you." At last the question was put to her, "Isobel, d'ye ken Christ?" The countenance of the dying saint brightened at the sound of her Saviour's name. Looking up with a smile, she promptly replied,—

"That I do, but nae sae muckle as I would like, and will do by an' bye." That night the aged believer went to be with Him whom she remembered and knew when all others were forgotten and unknown.

ANECDOTES OF ARCHBISHOP LEIGHTON.

ARCHBISHOP LEIGHTON has been called the Fenelon of Scotland, and was one of those pious men who commend their religion by their spirit, walk, and conversation. He entered the ministry in 1641, and was ordained minister of Newbottle. Contentions about different modes of church government, and similar matters, were then at their height; but it was Leighton's great aim to win souls to Christ, and not to make them proselytes of a party. He seldom mixed with those who attended Presbyteries, and condemned their practice of introducing those topics so prominently in the pulpit. They, on the other hand, were ill-pleased with his silence on these matters; and in a Synod he was publicly reprimanded for not "preaching up to the times." "Who," he asked, "does preach up to the times?" It was answered that "all the brethren did." "Then," said Leighton, "if all of you preach up to the times, you may surely allow one poor brother to preach up Christ Jesus and eternity." "I would rather," said he on another occasion, "convince a man that he has a soul to save, and induce him to live up to that belief, than bring him over to my opinion in whatever else beside." He seemed to live continually as if he realised the presence and protecting hand of God.

During the civil wars, he was anxious to visit his brother, who was engaged in the Royalist army, before an expected engagement should take place. Whilst proceeding to the camp, he lost his way in a vast thicket, and night came on before he could find an outlet in any direction. Almost spent with hunger and fatigue, he began to think his situation desperate, and, dismounting, spread his cloak upon the ground, and knelt down to pray. With implicit devotion he resigned his soul to God, entreating, however, that if it were not the Divine pleasure for him to conclude his days, some way of deliverance might be opened up for his safety. Then mounting his horse, he threw the reins upon its neck, and the animal, left to itself—or, rather, conducted by Almighty Providence—made straight into the high road, threading all the mazes of the wood with reasoning certainty. In this manner the good man lived, and all parties were constrained to say regarding him, "Behold a man who serves the Master in love and in truth."

SELF-RIGHTEOUSNESS EXPOSED.
Anecdote of Mr. Hay Macdowall Grant.

Mr. HAY MACDOWALL GRANT was an adept in dealing with those who had religious difficulties, or who trusted to their own goodness. He once came into contact with a particularly self-righteous man, who remarked, "Well, sir, I have got my own way of getting to heaven." "What is it?" "Well, I expect to get to heaven by keeping God's commandments." "Certainly," said Mr. Grant; "that is an excellent way, provided you keep them." "Well," replied the man, "that is just what I am doing." "Do you keep all God's commandments?" "Certainly I do." There was a pause in the conversation, when Mr. Grant suddenly asked him what time it was? "Two o'clock," replied the man, "When did you get up this morning?" inquired Mr. Grant. "At six o'clock, sir." "Six to two; that means eight hours. You don't remember how long you spent in prayer this morning?" The man coloured up to the roots of his hair, and then stammered out, "Well, perhaps ten minutes"—and then, knowing that he had grossly exaggerated—"or perhaps five minutes; or somewhere thereabouts." "Well," said Mr. Grant, "we will set it down at five minutes. Eight hours of to-day have passed away, and you have spent five minutes with your God. Do you remember what comes first in the great commandment, 'Thou shalt love the Lord thy God with all thy heart, and with all thy soul, and with all thy strength, and with all thy mind'? Is that the way you treat a God whom you love?" The man's head hung down, and he said no more about keeping God's commandments.

An old woman whom he visited had a name all over the country side for being one of the most pious old bodies that could be met with, but he found her perfectly built up in her own self-righteousness, and trusting to that for salvation. He went into the subject fully, pointing out to her that she was just making the same mistake that the Jews did of old; and as the force of the Scriptural statements which he adduced began to make itself felt, he said it was most touching to witness the conflict. With tears rolling down her cheeks, and a piteous look upon her face, she exclaimed, 'Eh, sir, do you mean to tell me that it maun a' gang for naething?" "Well," said Mr. Grant, "you have to choose between your own righteousness and Christ's; you cannot rest on both." There was a silence for a time, during which Mr. Grant was engaged in prayer for her, as he saw the terrible struggle that was passing within her. At last she lifted up her face, with a look of resolution upon it, and cried aloud, "O God, it shall a' gang for naething!" and there and then she accepted Christ as her all.

PROVIDENTIAL DELIVERANCES EXPERIENCED BY THE REV. HENRY ERSKINE.

THE Rev. Henry Erskine was often in great straits and difficulties. Once when he and his family had supped at night, there remained neither bread, meal, flesh, nor money in the house. In the morning, the young children cried for their breakfast, and their father endeavoured to divert them, and did what he could at the same time to encourage himself and wife, to depend upon that Providence that hears the young ravens when they cry. While thus engaged, a countryman knocked hard at the door, and called for some one to help him off with his load. Being asked whence he came, and what he would have, he told them he came from Lady Raeburn with some provisions for Mr. Erskine. They told him he must be mistaken, and that it was more likely to be for another Mr.

Erskine in the same town. He replied, "No;" he knew what he said; he was sent to Mr. Henry Erskine; and cried, "Come, help me off with my load, or else I will throw it down at the door." Whereupon they took the sack from him, and, on opening it, found it well stored with fish and meat. At another time, being in Edinburgh, he was so reduced that he had but three-halfpence in his pocket. When he was walking about the streets, not knowing what course to steer, one came to him in a countryman's habit, presented him with a letter, in which were enclosed several Scotch "ducatoons," with these words written, "Sir, receive this from a sympathising friend. Farewell." Mr. Erskine never could find out whence the money came. At another time, being on a journey on foot, his money failed, and he was in danger of being reduced to distress. Having occasion to fix his walking-stick in some marshy ground among the rushes, he heard something tinkle at the end of it. It proved to be two half-crowns, which greatly assisted in bearing his charges home. In days of persecution and poverty, God wonderfully interposes for his people.

THE WRONG WAY.

I WAS sitting—Rev. Dr. Alex. Macleod tells us—one day in a railway carriage, which I expected to take me to the town of Newburgh on the banks of the Tay. We came to a parting of the ways called the Ladybank Junction. At this point, as I learned afterwards, the train divided, and one portion went on to Dundee, the other to Newburgh and Perth. I heard the guard cry out quite plainly, "Change here for Dundee;" but I did not hear, "Change for Newburgh and Perth." I said to a gentleman beside me, "Are we right?" "All right, sir; I am going your way, too;" and the train moved on. The next station on the right road should have been Collessie. The station we actually stopped at was called Springfield. "This is Collessie," I said to my fellow-passenger, the man who was going my way too. "Oh, it's all right, Springfield and Collessie are two names for the same place," said he.

After Collessie we should have come to Newburgh, the little town at which I was due. Instead of that, I saw a great, spreading town, with towers and church-spires rising above the roofs. The man beside me was now fairly roused, and he cried, in a very loud voice, "We're wrong, sir—we're in the wrong train!—we should have changed carriages at Ladybank. This is Cupar, on the road to Dundee." And here I was within an hour or so of the time I should have been at Newburgh a good twelve miles away from it, and no train back for three hours to come. While I lounged about the station, and sat in the waiting-room, I began to think of mistakes on journeys, of wrong roads, of the hardships and losses of taking wrong roads, and of the need there is of looking well after the right road. I remembered the Bible proverb which says, "There is a way which seemeth right unto a man; but the end thereof are the ways of death." I thought of the great journey of life, and of the roads on that journey which seem to be right, but are wrong. These are many, and should all be avoided.

THE CONVERSION OF THE HALDANES.

JAMES HALDANE, Esq., pastor of one of the Baptist churches in Edinburgh, was a junior member of a highly respectable family. In his youth he joined the British navy, and rose to the post of captain in one of his Majesty's war ships. On one occasion, being engaged in a warmly-contested battle, he saw the whole of his men on deck swept off by a tremendous broadside from the enemy. He ordered another company to be "piped up" from below, to take the place of their lost companions. On coming up, they saw the mangled remains strewn upon the deck, and were seized with a sudden and irresistible panic. On seeing this, the captain jumped up, and swore a horrid oath, imprecating the vengeance of Almighty God upon the whole of them, and wishing that they might all sink to hell. An old marine, who was a pious man, stepped up to him, and respectfully touching his hat, said—"Captain, I believe God hears prayer; and if God had heard your prayer just now, what would have become of us?"

Having spoken this, he made a respectful bow, and retired to his place. After the engagement, the captain calmly reflected upon the words of the old marine, and was so deeply affected by them, that he devoted his attention to the claims of religion, and was subsequently converted to God. Of course he informed his brother Robert of what had taken place; but instead of being gratified by it, his brother was greatly offended, and requested him never to enter his house till he had changed his views. "Very well, Robert," said James, "but I have one comfort in the case, and that is, you cannot prevent my praying for you;" and holding out his hand, he bade him good bye. His brother Robert was much affected by this; he could not get rid of the idea that his brother was constantly praying for him. He saw the error of his ways, and after much investigation and reflection, became a decided Christian. The brothers Haldane united in good work at home and abroad. By their sacrifices and labours they gave an impetus to evangelical religion in Scotland. They became the fathers of churches, and preachers of the gospel to the poor and those who stood in need of hearing the glad tidings of great joy.

THE REV. DR. M'CRIE AND THE PUBLISHER.

THE REV. DR. M'CRIE was a man of great ability and of nobility of character. He was a writer of eminence and spirit, and was far above all selfish and mercenary motives into his literary engagements. On this ground he refused many an application made to him by booksellers who were anxious to employ his pen. Nothing was more sure to defeat their object, than to commence their solicitations by an offer of money. On one occasion in particular, Mr. Constable, the publisher, who was eager to engage him in writing some short and popular lives of the Reformers for his Miscellany, waited upon him, and enlarging his offer to a thousand guineas for three volumes of no great size, he said—"I am going to Abbotsford to-morrow, and wish to have to say to Sir Walter Scott that you have consented." "Mr. Constable," was the reply, "I should be sorry if you had it to say to Sir Walter, that a descendant of the old Covenanters could be bribed with money to do a thing he was not inclined to do." And so they parted.

"THERE'S NAE CHIRTIN IN HEAVEN."
An Anecdote of the Rev. James Morison, D.D.

The Rev. A. M. Wilson, preaching at Bathgate (the birthplace of the Rev. Dr. Morison) on the words, "Yet there is room," related the following incident: One day, about sixty years ago, there was considerable commotion in one of the junior classes of the parish school in Bathgate, arising from a struggle among the boys to find room on the form which they occupied. The master called up one of the boys, and asked what all the noise was about. "Please, sir," replied the urchin, "it's Jamie Morison, and he's swearing." Young Morison was then called up and examined as to this grave accusation, to which he at once gave a most emphatic denial. Upon the question being put to the accuser, "What did Morison say?" the answer was, "He said *there's nae chirtin in heaven.*" Coming events cast their shadows before them. The whole after-life of Principal James Morison has been devoted to the proclamation and enforcement of that declaration of his childhood.

A MISTAKE IMPROVED;
Or, how the Evil One may be Shot.

In times gone by, a worthy elder of the Kirk, who had spent the day on the hills in shooting, was belated; and on his way home, considerably after elders' hours, as he passed Carlie Crag, Logie, Perthshire, he espied on it an object which arrested his attention. So far as he could judge in the dark, it seemed a dog of the mastiff species. But was it not very like the Evil One, in the appearances he had been represented by the minister, and as the elder had often heard them described? A moment's reflection satisfied him that the suspicion was well founded. What was he to do? What did it become one of his standing in the kirk to do? He knew that the enemy was invulnerable by common shot. But fortunately, he had a silver coin in his pocket. This coin he quietly slipped into his gun, a trusty musket, which had been found on Sheriffmuir. Having thus charged, he kneeled, breathed a prayer, levelled his piece and fired, and down tumbled his victim to the foot of the crag. He could not wait to inspect it; he was at once too overjoyed and too eerie to do that. He betook himself to the manse as fast as his feet would carry him, and reported to the minister the matchless feat he had done. Early next morning they went together to the Crag to examine the carcase of the fallen foe, and to consider how it was to be disposed of, when lo! instead of his remains, there lay the lifeless body of Nannie, the bonnie pet goat of a poor old woman who resided in the neighbourhood. The disappointment and grief of the elder knew no bounds. Even the minister shared his mortification, and could not refrain from shedding tears with him. The innocent goat was shot, and lay dead there as a stone, and the bad dog was still alive! But there was one consolation—the elder had meant well, and had displayed most heroic valour. The minister, too, who had the faculty of "finding good in everything," improved the event of the week in his pulpit work on the following Sabbath. Choosing for his theme the duty of resisting the devil, he discoursed, to the manifest relief and comfort of the elder, and to the edification of the whole congregation, on the various shapes and forms which that personage may assume. If he went about as a roaring lion, why might he not appear also, when it better suited his purpose to do so, as a collie, or a mastiff, and as sleek or shaggy? After dilating in this strain at great length, he concluded very sagely, pertinently, and practically, in this wise:—" But whatever form he may assume, he cannot be overcome or destroyed by powder and shot. There is a gun, however, that will shoot him, and it is this,—the Bible. Shoot him, then, every one of you with this Bible, and he shall be shot."

DUNDONALD AND THE MINISTER;
Or, Trusting to Chance, and leaving all to the Last.

ON the occasion of a bonspeil between two rival parish clubs in Ayrshire, the one side was headed by the Earl of Dundonald, the other by the minister of the parish. The players were well matched, the ice was in excellent condition, and the play first-rate. The match was between seven rinks a-side. The result of the contest rested with the seventh rink, the skips of which were Lord Dundonald and the minister. The players had counted shot about all day, and at last stood thirty. There remained only the Earl and the minister to play their last shots. The stone at the tee belonged to the rink of the latter, and seemed impregnably guarded. The Earl however, threw his stone on chance with such force that it rolled over the mass of guards huddled together in front, and lighted on the tee a "pat-lid," apparently placed beyond the possibility of ejection, protected as it was by the guard of his adversary's stones. Such a shot had never been seen before by the oldest curler present, and it was hailed with deafening cheers as decisive of the contest.

The minister had still to play, but he was told it was no use trying. "Let him try my shot," said the Earl, ironically. "Dinna halloo till ye're oot o' the wud," exclaimed the minister's skip. "I'll no allow him to throw awa' his stane on sic a chance shot as your Lordship took. But I'll see what he can do, an' if he jist plays his auld ordinar', I think the odd shot an' the game will be oor ain yet. Ye see this stane, sir, aff the ice?" addressing the minister, "it's twa yards on this side o' the tee; ye used tae like an inwick weel, an' I've seen ye tak' mony sic an ane—mind it's oor ain stane, sae I carena whether ye inwick or ootwick it. Clear the ice, my lads; soop clean, and gie us fair play for the last shot. Tak' time and jist play, sir, as ye've dune a' day, an' I'm sure ye'll come toddling in here," pointing to the tee. The minister did as he was directed, his stone took the inwick, removed the winner from the tee, and lay game shot. The Earl, mortified and crestfallen at such an unexpected result, exclaimed with a round oath, "What the world brought the body here to-day? I wish he had been in his study, for he has played the very mischief with us all day." "What's that, my Lord, ye're sayin' o' me?" inquired the minister, who had overheard the profane exclamation. "I was just saying," replied the Earl, "that it would have been better for us if ye had been at your books preparing for the morn." "I didna come here to-day, my Lord, unprepared for the morn," rejoined the sturdy clergyman, "for I hope I'm no like mony o' the great folks o' this world, that *trust to chance, and leave a' to the last day.*"

A SCOTTISH OLD TIME REVIVAL;
Or, Cambuslang in Whitefield's Time.

MORE than a hundred years ago—in the year 1742—there was an extraordinary religious awakening in the West of Scotland. It began in Cambuslang, a parish on the Clyde, near Glasgow. There were not over nine hundred souls in the parish, yet out of that number about five hundred were, it was believed, converted. The awakening in Cambuslang was preceded by a year's faithful preaching of regeneration and the atonement by the pastor, Rev. John M'Culloch. Then for twelve weeks came daily preaching—generally out-door or in tents. Whitefield (then in the zenith of his power and popularity) came to Cambuslang, and delivered a dozen discourses. Boanerges never stayed long in one spot; he used to say, "More than two weeks in one place kills me as dead as a door-nail." But his two visits to the rural parish near Glasgow were inundations of blessings to the thirsting multitudes. Mighty audiences from Glasgow and Western Scotland thronged to hear him. He frequently addressed 20,000 souls in a day!

At the first communion season after his visit, no less than seventeen hundred persons sat down to the tables, which were spread under tents. A few weeks after, the Lord's Supper was dispensed again; and probably it was the most extraordinary communion service ever witnessed on earth. No less than forty thousand people gathered to witness the solemnities. Preaching went on for several days previous under Whitefield and others; but on the second Sabbath in August, the Pentecostal scene culminated. The day was mild and genial, the air fragrant with the breath of new-mown hay, and the fields yellow with the wheat-harvest. At half-past eight on that memorable Sabbath morning, the "action sermon" was preached. Then came the "fencing the tables;" then, immediately after this, the table was spread, and the first company passed into the Lord's Supper. During the whole day the sacred service went forward; no less than twenty-four companies of over one hundred, each sitting down in rotation! The whole number who partook of the sacred emblems was about three thousand. The soft twilight was stealing over the "braes" when the last group left the communion tent, and there was only light enough left to read four lines of a psalm as a doxology. A grey-haired pastor turning homeward from the hallowed place, exclaimed, in the fulness of his grateful heart, "Lord! now lettest Thou, Thy servant, depart in peace; for mine eyes have seen Thy salvation." Such a revival could not be without abiding fruits. Accordingly, we are told that after the close of the extraordinary meetings, the morals of the whole neighbourhood were changed. Profanity became almost unknown. God's day was honoured in every dwelling. Nearly every house became a house of prayer. Evil speaking ceased. Old enmities and family feuds were forgotten. Every father was a kinder parent; every child more dutiful. Religion went into men's daily business as a controlling principle; sceptics owned its power, and scoffers were silenced before the beauty and majesty of daily godliness. May He who holdeth the seven stars in His right hand renew such a period!

DR. EADIE'S SERMON TO SHEPHERDS.

THE late Professor Eadie was in the summer of 1860, along with some other ministers, on a visit to St. Mary's Loch, and the famous hostelry of the famous Tibby Shiels. Under her management, the neighbouring shepherds were summoned to hear a sermon from the Professor on Sunday afternoon. The sermon was a great event in the district. How it got so well advertised in so short a space of time could not be quite understood; but, certainly, when the hour came, the hills and dells seemed to have sent their last man to the little chapel, all aware of the name and fame of the expected preacher. There they were, shaggily but decently homespun in aspect and attire, "maud" on shoulder, and crook in hand, with weather-beaten but sagacious faces—a congregation of shepherds; and the "dowgs" seemed as numerous as their masters, and were equally well-behaved. When Dr. Eadie lounged in through the little side-door, and heaved himself into the pulpit, and brushing the elf-locks from his brow, looked round him, with his peering, half-humorous glance, as he proceeded to give out the psalm, the impression produced upon his audience was evidently mingled, half-expectant, half-doubtful. He was not exactly clerical-looking, and his manner was anything but conventional; but there was a homely dignity about him, and indisputable weight, and soon both gravity and unction began to show themselves.

When he announced his text—"How much, then, is a man better than a sheep?"—perplexity struggled with a wondering interest in the upturned faces which dared not smile. Was the speaker quizzing them, or needlessly coming down to them? or would he justify after all his singular choice of a subject, and give them a sober, but fresh original discourse? They were not held long in suspense. As Eadie went on, following a line of thought familiar to him, but lighting it up with numerous illustrations drawn from the surrounding scenery, and the occupation of his hearers, attention grew deeply fixed.

The dignity and worth of man was his theme—as made in the image of God; as endowed with reason, with conscience, with immortality; as redeemed by the great Son of Man from the sin into which he had fallen; as destined to everlasting glory. And as he pressed their human responsibilities on the men before him, and urged them to seek through Christ the true end of their being, every eye was bent on him, and every countenance glowed with intelligent admiration. The closing psalm was sung with Scottish solemnity and fervour; and when the congregation was dismissed, the hearty comments heard on every side from groups which lingered for a little together, before they broke up to scatter among the hills attested how thoroughly the service had been enjoyed

RABBI DUNCAN ON ANGELS.

"On a Sabbath," says the Rev. James Robertson, of Newington U. P. Church, "when I had been preaching one of a series of discourses on 'Angels in their revealed connexion with the work of Christ,' Dr. Duncan came into the vestry and said, 'Will you be so kind as to let me know when you are going to take up the case of my favourite angel?' 'But who is he, Doctor?' 'Ah, guess that.' 'Well, it would not be difficult to enumerate all those whose names are given us.' 'But I can't tell you his name; he is an anonymous angel, mine—guess him—eh?' 'Well, I think I must give it up, Doctor.' 'Then I'll have to tell you. It's the one who came down in Gethsemane, and "strengthened" my Lord to go through His agony for me, that He might get forward to the cross and finish my redemption there. I have an extraordinary love for that one, and I often wonder what I would say to him when I meet him first.' This was a thought Dr. Duncan never wearied of repeating, in varied forms, whenever the subject of angels turned up in conversation.

"A day or two after this the following conversation took place between him and Miss R——: April 21, 1864. *Dr. Duncan*—'I went last Sabbath and heard

Mr. Robertson preach one of a course of sermons on the angels.' *Miss R.*—'I think one sermon might have exhausted them.' *Dr. Duncan*—'Oh no, it is a very wide subject—do you think about the angels?' *Miss R.*—'Not much.' *Dr. Duncan*—'Do you hope you are an heir of salvation, and so have your own special ministering angels? Do you think you have "come unto Mount Zion"? Well, what have you come to? To "an innumerable company of angels," and yet you don't think much about the angels! The angels sang "Glory to God in the highest, on earth peace, good-will to men"—God, earth, men; the angels care for *men*—and you don't think much about the angels! The angels of heaven sang, "Glory in the highest, peace in *heaven.*" Have you and I some hope that God has granted to us repentance unto life? Then there was joy over us in the presence of the angels of God. And do we need daily repentance? Then doubtless the joy of the angels over us continues—and you don't think much about the angels! The Lord Jesus shall come "in the glory of his Father and of the holy angels;" and you will be taken quite by surprise that day, because you have never thought much about the angels!' *Miss R.*—'I may be off the earth before that.' *Dr. Duncan*—'Oh, and you will have time between death and the resurrection to get acquainted with the angels, so as you will not be surprised.' *Miss R.*—'But there is a great deal of sentimentality in much that is said about angels.' *Dr. Duncan*—'Oh, because there is a great deal of nonsense in other books about them, you will not attend to what the Word of God says about them! just as some persons, because the Papists worship the Virgin Mary, will not call her "the blessed Virgin," although it was said, "All generations shall call me blessed." I don't say that *fancy* will make anything of it. Fancy draws a bonny man with a pair of wings! but can faith not make something of it? and "faith cometh by hearing, and hearing by the Word of God."' *Miss R.*—'But I think the angels cannot do good to our souls, only outward good, Ps. xci. 11, 12.' *Dr. Duncan*—'I don't see why holy angels may not have as much power to do our souls good as the devil has power to do them ill. I take that passage to mean, thou shalt not *even* dash thy foot against a stone—they shall take charge of thee even down to that; it was more than that to the Head—and so also, I take it, it is to the members. I have my favourite angel, though I do not know his name. It is not Gabriel, who announced the birth of my Lord. It is that angel who, when our hope was staggering, and when twice He fell, appeared from heaven, and strengthened Him. If I get to heaven, and meet that one, I will say to him, "Art thou the angel who strengthened my Lord in His agony?" Did that angel do you no good? and though it is a less thing than strengthening the Head, did the angel who let Peter out of prison do you no good? —did Peter do you no good after he came out of jail?"

A LOST OPPORTUNITY.
An Anecdote of the Rev. Dr. Chalmers.

DR. CHALMERS on his return from England, lodged in the house of a nobleman near Peebles. The Doctor was known to excel in conversation as well as in the pulpit. He was the life and soul of the conversation at the nobleman's fireside. The subject was pauperism, its causes and cure. Among the gentlemen present there was a venerable old Highland chieftain, who kept his eyes fastened on Dr. Chalmers, and listened with intense interest to his communication. The conversation was kept up to a late hour. When the company broke up, they were shown into their apartments. The apartment of the Doctor was directly opposite to that of the old chieftain, who had already retired with his attendant. As the talented divine was undressing himself, he heard an unusual noise in the chieftain's room; the noise was succeeded by a heavy groan! He hastened into the apartment, which was in a few moments filled with the company, who all rushed in to the relief of the old gentleman. It was a melancholy sight which met their eyes. The venerable white-headed chieftain had fallen into the hands of his attendant. It was evidently apoplexy. He breathed for a few seconds and expired. Dr. Chalmers stood in silence, with both hands stretched out, and, bending over the deceased, he was the very picture of distress. He was the first to break silence. "Never in my life," said he in a tremulous voice, "did I see, or did I feel, till this moment, the meaning of that text, 'Preach the word; be instant in season, and out of season; reprove, rebuke, exhort, with all long-suffering and doctrine.' Had I known that my venerable old friend was within a few moments of eternity, I would not have dwelt upon that subject which formed the topic of this evening's conversation. I would have addressed myself earnestly to him. I would have preached unto him and you Jesus Christ and him crucified. I would have urged him and you, with all earnestness befitting the subject, to prepare for eternity. You would have thought it, and you would have pronounced it, out of season. But ah! it would have been in season, both as it respects him and as it respects you."

SIR ANDREW AGNEW'S LOYALTY TO CONVICTION.

Sir Andrew Agnew, M.P., was an earnest Christian who, for long, took an active part in the movement on behalf of the due observance of the Sabbath. Sir Andrew, and an intimate friend, were speaking one day of the difficulty of confessing Christ before the world. It was affecting to hear him acknowledge this difficulty, who had borne Christ's reproach so manfully and so meekly in all places. He observed that, when he first began to take up the cause of the Sabbath, there were many worldly men who disliked him so much, that they seemed anxious to stare him out of their company, and that he had felt this particularly at the new club. One hon. baronet, not satisfied with this species of annoyance, when he saw that Sir Andrew had courage enough to despise it, and to frequent the club regularly every day notwithstanding, began speaking to him, and acting as rudely as he well could towards him. One morning Sir Andrew was waiting for his breakfast at the club, when the baronet, to whom I allude, came in, apparently in great agitation. Sir Andrew, perceiving this, asked him if anything was wrong; to which he replied that his lady had last night had an attack of paralysis, and that she was dangerously ill. Sir Andrew said he felt for him sincerely, and expressed his sympathy warmly. Next evening he met him again with his two sons, who had come to see their mother, and he asked for the baronet's lady with much interest. The answer was that he had been sitting up with her all night, and that she was no better. Ultimately, however, she did recover; and on one occasion afterwards, the hon. baronet referred to came up to Sir Andrew, and, with feeling that did him great honour, said, " Sir Andrew, there are many people who like to laugh at you and abuse you, because of your Sabbath principles, and I confess that I have been among the number: but I trust I shall never so far forget myself again. A man gets a very different view of these subjects when standing beside what he thinks the dying-bed of his wife." Sir Andrew was much affected by this frank acknowledgment, and replied, "I understand you perfectly, for I have experienced all the same feelings myself. I, too, was once opposed to religion. When I first proposed to bring my Sabbath Bill into Parliament, I felt the difficulty I had to encounter; and, after having given notice of the Bill, I thought I should never have courage to proceed with it. The day was drawing near on which my motion was to come on. Every day I felt my courage growing less and less when, just a day or two before, a messenger arrived from the country with intelligence that my mother had had a stroke of apoplexy, and I must hurry down to see her. I went accordingly, and it was when watching beside the bed of my dying mother that I got grace and strength to bring in my Sabbath Bill." The conversation touched the feelings of both parties, and they ever afterwards entertained much respect for each other. Christian feeling and action had their appropriate effect, and love once more was the conqueror.

THE REV. HECTOR M'PHAIL AND HIS FAITHFUL WIFE.

The Rev. Hector M'Phail, of Resolis, was a minister for several years before his conversion. He had married a daughter of the godly Mr. Balfour, minister of Nigg. She had been one of Mr. Porteous's hearers, and had profited greatly by his preaching. Feeling painfully the difference between her husband's doctrine and that to which she had been accustomed, she told him, on a Sabbath morning soon after their marriage, that her soul was starving, and that, as all must give place to her care for its welfare, she had resolved to go on that day across to Kilmuir. He offered no opposition; he even accompanied her to the ferry. It was a sad journey the pious wife took that day to Kilmuir. Arriving at the manse before the hour for beginning the service in church, Mr. Porteous was not a little surprised to see her, and, on meeting her, asked very anxiously why she had come. She told him that as her soul was famished at Resolis, she was compelled to come for the bread of life to the place where she had been wont to receive it. Mr. Porteous retired to his study, and on rejoining her, said,—"If I am not greatly deceived you will not long have the same reason for leaving Resolis, for I expect that the Lord will soon give you, by the hand of your husband, the very finest of the wheat." His expectation was not disappointed. After parting with his wife on that morning, the fact of her desertion of his ministry made a deep impression on Mr. M'Phail's mind. Conscience testified that she was right; a deep sense of his unfitness for the work of the ministry was produced, and a process of conviction then began that extended over several years. At last he resolved to demit his charge, and to declare his resolution of doing so publicly before his congregation. With this view he sent for Mr. Fraser, of Alness, to preach on a week-day in his church, and to intimate, after sermon, his resignation of his charge. Mr. Fraser came and preached, but with no intention of giving the required intimation. During the sermon delivered on that day Mr. M'Phail's bonds were loosed, and, before the service was over, he was in no mood to turn his back on the work of preaching Christ to sinners. Full of hope and gladness he escorted Mr. Fraser next day to the Alness Ferry, and, on his way back, he called at the house of one of his elders, who had spent many an hour wrestling with the Lord for his minister. "What news, to-day, Mr. M'Phail?" the elder asked. "Good news, Hector M'Phail is not to preach any more," his minister replied, "but the Spirit of the Lord is to preach to you through him." "Oh! that is good news, indeed," cried the elder in an ecstacy of joy. From that day till his death, Mr. M'Phail was one of the most faithful, fervent, prayerful, and successful of ministers.

AN EARNEST SCOTCH METHODIST.

MR. ALEXANDER PATRICK, called the "Wallacetown Reformer," became an earnest Methodist, and was much blessed in his work. The following anecdote will illustrate his way of dealing with souls. Being one night at a private tea-party in Glasgow, where the guests were principally Wesleyans, Mr. Patrick, whose habits of prayer were to him the chief source of enjoyment, contrived to turn the party into a social prayer meeting. One of the company, a backslider from God, arose between the exercises and confessed his condition to be one of darkness and danger; that he was, in fact, at present an alien from God. The whole party immediately united in strong prayer to the Lord to restore his soul, and, in a very short time, they found an answer. The man was enabled to resume his former faith in a crucified Saviour; his joys were renewed, and his rejoicing diffused over the company the gladness of angels, who are represented as rejoicing over returning sinners.

> "My Jesus to know, and feel his blood flow,
> 'Tis life everlasting, 'tis heaven below!"

This exciting scene was made instrumental by the good Spirit in awakening another person then present, who had attended the ministry of the Methodists fourteen years, and had, till this period, remained a stranger to the renewing grace of God. Unable to conceal the distress he felt, from a deep conviction of his unsafe state, he arose, and earnestly invited the company to meet at his house the following evening. This was readily agreed to, in hope that God would answer prayer in this case also. At the hour fixed the friends assembled, and found that Mr. Patrick had not awaited the appointed time, but had spent the whole forenoon labouring with him for his deliverance. God had already shed on the seeking sinner the light of his countenance, and made him glad in the enjoyment of salvation. This person had long rested in mere dogmas and theory, which had left his heart unchanged, and the act of personal faith had been to him unintelligible. To point out this duty, and encourage him to perform it, was the task of Mr. Alex. Patrick. Putting his hand into his pocket, and drawing out a shilling, he said,—" Weel, noo, brother, were I to say, I'll give ye this shilling, wad ye believe me?" " Yes, I would, for ye're no trifler, Sandy." " And what, then, wad ye dae, if ye thocht me in earnest?" " Why, I'd reach out my hand and take it." " Very weel, God has in like manner gien his Son Jesus Christ for you and to you, and if ye wad believe, ye maun jist *tak'* him, and *trust* in him." " Oh! but I have been such a sinner." " Ah, weel, but God disna reject sinners because they hae sinned, but because they winna believe on and *lippen* tae his Son." " Well," replied his friend, with animation, " Do you say so, Sandy? If God will not send me to hell for my sin only, he shall not for unbelief. I will believe, I do believe, I believe just now; O, Jesus, thou art my Lord and my God!" At the moment he was accepting and trusting in the Saviour, the token of divine acceptance was instantly afforded:

"His chains fell off,
His heart was free."

The Spirit witnessed to his spirit that he was a child of God. The assembled friends who came to pray remained only to rejoice, because God had made known so fully and clearly his readiness to pardon. This person, after proving for some years the genuineness of his conversion, has lately been called home to God, dying in the faith.

PROFESSOR JOHN WILSON AND THE UNKIND CARTER.

PROFESSOR JOHN WILSON, "Christopher North," had a great love for animals, which he often exhibited in a practical way. For example:—One summer afternoon, as a lady who stayed in Moray Place, Edinburgh, was about to sit down to dinner, her servant requested her to look out of the window to see a man cruelly beating his horse. The sight not being a very gratifying one, she declined, and proceeded to take her seat at table. It was quite evident that the servant had discovered something more than the ill-usage of the horse to divert his attention, for he kept his eyes fixed on the window; again suggesting to his mistress that she ought to look out. Her interest was at last excited, and she rose to see what was going on. In front of her house stood a cart of coals, which the poor victim of the carter was unable to drag along. He had been beating the beast most unmercifully, when at that moment Professor Wilson, walking past, saw the outrage, and immediately interfered. The lady said, that from the expression of his face, and vehemence of his manner, the man was evidently "getting it," though she was unable to hear what was said. The carter, exasperated at this interference, took up his whip in a threatening manner, as if with intent to strike the Professor. In an instant, that well-nerved hand twisted it from the coarse fist of the man, as if it had been a straw, and, walking quietly up to the cart, he unfastened its *trams*, and hurled the whole weight of coals into the street. The rapidity with which this was done left the driver of the cart speechless. Meanwhile, poor Rosinante, freed from its burden, crept slowly away, and the Professor, still clutching the whip in one hand,

and leading the horse by the other, proceeded through Moray Place, to deposit the wretched animal in better keeping than that of its driver.

WISHART AS AN EVANGELIST.

In 1543, George Wishart, brother of the Laird of Pitarrow, in the Mearns, devoted himself to the work of an evangelist; he had for some time kept a school in Montrose, and taught his scholars to read the New Testament in the original language. To escape the persecution to which this offence exposed him, he fled abroad; but, returning to Scotland in 1543, he began his ministry in Dundee, lecturing on the Epistle to the Romans. Crowds of all ranks and classes attended his earnest ministrations, and many through his instrumentality were brought to the knowledge of Christ. The clergy were alarmed, and one of the chief men of Dundee, a friend of Cardinal Beaton, commanded him to leave the town, to whom Wishart made answer, and his words proved prophetic, "God is my witness that I never minded your trouble, but your comfort, yea, your trouble is more grievous to me than it is to yourselves; but I am sure, that to reject the Word of God, and to drive away his messenger, is not the way to save you from trouble, but to bring you into it. If it be long well with you, then you may believe that I am not led by the Spirit of Truth; and if unexpected trouble befall you, remember this is the *cause*, and turn to God by repentance, for He is merciful."

Wishart then left the town, but by and bye tidings reached him that the plague had broken out in Dundee. Though driven from it, his heart yearned over its miserable inhabitants, and he hastened back there to speak to the people the words of eternal life, as well as to minister temporal relief to the afflicted and dying. Reckless of the danger to which he exposed himself by labours so exhausting, he counted not his life dear to him. On one occasion he preached at the East Gate of the Cowgate. Without the gate were the booths which had been erected for the reception of the plague-smitten, at the spot which has since borne the name of the Sickman's Yards. The gate being shut, made a separation between the healthy and the infected. Wishart took his stand on the top of it, and preached such a sermon as only such a man could have preached in the circumstances. His text was, "He sent His word and healed them, and delivered them from destruction."

THE BIGGAR BELLMAN'S SON.

ROBERT FORSYTH, Advocate, was a strong-brained man, whose huge frame and head were well-known many years ago in the Parliament House, Edinburgh. His father was Robert Forsyth, bellman and gravedigger, and his mother's name was Marion Pairman. This worthy couple were united in marriage in 1764, and their only child, Robert, was born on the 18th January, 1766. Their condition in life was very humble, and they had to struggle with all the disadvantages and sorrows of extreme poverty; but they resolved to give their son, who early showed an aptitude for learning, a good education, in order to qualify him for the work of the ministry. He was sent early to the parish school but being the son of a poor man, he was treated with marked neglect, and made small progress. He soon, however, became extremely fond of reading. He borrowed such books as his neighbours could supply, and read them in the winter nights to his parents, to Robert Rennie, shoemaker, and others, who commended him highly for his industry and ability, and thus encouraged him to renewed exertions.

It is remembered at Biggar, that one evening he was busily engaged in reading aloud the poems of Sir David Lindsay, by the blaze of a piece of Auchenheath coal, after his mother had gone to bed, when that worthy matron said, "O, Robie man, steek the boords o' Davie Lindsay, and gie's a blad o' the chapter buik (the Bible), or I'll no fa' asleep the nicht." As he made slow progress in his classical studies at the parish school of Biggar, he was sent in his twelfth or thirteenth year to the burgh school of Lanark, then taught by Mr. Robert Thomson, a brother-in-law of the author of the Seasons. Forsyth then studied four years at the University of Glasgow, and manfully struggled with all the obstructions arising from the *res augusta domi*. During one of these years, a severe and protracted storm of frost and snow occurred, and prevented all communication from place to place by means of carts. The Biggar carrier was consequently unable to pay his usual visits to Glasgow for several weeks.

Old Forsyth was thrown into great distress regarding the state in which he knew his son would be placed from want of his ordinary supply of provisions. He therefore procured a quantity of oatmeal, and carried it on his back along the rough tracks on the top of the snow all the way to Glasgow, a distance of thirty-five miles, and just arrived when young Forsyth had been reduced to his last meal. He studied for the Church; but having no influence, though an eloquent preacher, he failed to get a pastoral charge to his mind, and so gave up the ministry, and took to the bar. At that time the men of the Parliament House were more exclusive than they are at present. They cared little for a new adherent to their ranks unless he came recommended by his connection with some aristocratic family. The idea of a sticket minister, and the son of a gravedigger, obtaining admission into their dignified order, was intolerable to the Dundases, the Forbeses, the Wedderburns, the Erskines, and others who, in those days, stood highest in the Parliament House. One of their number connected with the Biggar district, but never distinguished for obtaining any great amount of practice or ability, was specially opposed to Forsyth, and one day had the audacity to say, "Who are you, sir, that would thrust yourself into the Faculty? Are ye not the poor bellman's son of Biggar?" "I am so," said Forsyth coolly but sarcastically, "and I have a strong suspicion that, had you been a bellman's son, you would have been your father's successor." A retort well deserved, and most likely true.

HELP IN TIME OF NEED.
An Anecdote of the North of Scotland.

A FEW years after the victory of the Duke of Cumberland over Prince Charles Stuart at Culloden, in 1746, a poor but pious peasant dwelt in an out-of-the-way part of Scotland, bordering on the Highlands. He and his God-fearing wife had a numerous family; and there being few inhabitants in the district, work was often scarce, and income scanty. To get the two ends to meet was at times a very hard task; but prayer and pains had hitherto carried them through every difficulty. A season more trying than any, since their married life began, came at length upon them. There was no demand, at the end of autumn, for labour such as the peasant could do. Provisions were very dear, and speedily the little savings of the pious couple were entirely spent. No food remained in the poor cottage where they lived. Dinnerless and supperless the children had to be put to bed, and there they cried themselves to sleep. The parents bowed together before the throne of grace, asking for food for their offspring and themselves; and then the husband, worn out with fruitless search for work, and utterly cast down, retired to bed.

His wife, however, resolved to spend the night in secret prayer and meditation on the promises of her Father in heaven. Just when she was about to open her Bible, and was lifting up her heart with a desire for guidance and blessing, there darted into her mind these words of the fiftieth Psalm—"Every beast of the forest is mine, and the cattle upon a thousand hills." She did not think them suitable for meditation at the moment, and tried to forget them; but read where she might, and pray as she did with all the earnestness which her family's sad circumstances gave her, the words still came uppermost which had been first suggested to her. Five o'clock next morning found her wrestling with God for help in their time of need, when suddenly a loud knocking at the door of her cottage led her to inquire, "Who's there?" "A friend," was the reply. On her again asking who it was, the person outside said, "I'm a cattle dealer, and need help. Come quick, mistress." Opening the door, she saw to her surprise a large drove of cattle from the Highlands, on the road a little way above her dwelling. One of the cattle had fallen over a precipice at an unprotected part of the path, and broken one of its legs. The drover had assisted it up as best he could, and got it along to the peasant's cottage; but there it had fallen, and could not rise again even with help. The drover was sadly puzzled. It would detain him too long in that poor country district to try and find a purchaser. He must needs push on with the rest of his herd; and this he did after telling the peasant's wife that he had to beg her acceptance of the beast which lay at her door.

The husband speedily appeared on the scene, and could not but rejoice with the mother of his children over the abundant supply of flesh thus bestowed upon them. Their need of bread was also quickly met. Within an hour from the time when the drover's knock was heard, a man on horseback appeared, bearing a large sack of oatmeal. His mistress was a lady of title, residing some miles away, in whose household the peasant's wife had acted as a servant for years, to the great satisfaction of her employer. Knowing the trials of the poor at that season, the lady's thoughts had been turned during the previous evening to the possibility that her former maid and her family might be in want. Without delaying, the lady had ordered the sack of meal to be conveyed to the cottagers, and thus a bountiful supply of bread, as well as beef, relieved them from all anxieties regarding the future.

"Truly God is good to Israel;" and well, therefore, might the poet-king declare, "I have been young, and now am old, yet have I not seen the righteous forsaken, nor his seed begging bread."

THE REV. JOHN ANGEL JAMES AT PERTH.

"HAVING occasion," says the Rev. John Angel James, "to visit some friends at Perth, I was asked to call on a good woman in the humbler walks of life, who was represented to me as a very lively Christian; she was known by the familiar name of 'Kitty Lowrie.' On being introduced to her, I found that she had been for a considerable time confined to bed, and, from the nature of her complaint, was not likely to be long an inhabitant of this world. I found her speaking of death, not only without alarm, but with a manifest expression in her countenance of sacred joy; and she observed that a pious friend of hers at the Bridge-end was lately very ill, and, some time ago, she thought she would get away before her; but latterly she understood she was rather better, adding, with a remarkable cheerful expression of countenance, 'I now think I'll get the start of her yet. I just thought we were like two children taking a race home, to see who would be first at their father's door.' I then remarked to her that I had met with many Christians, who, though they had well-grounded hope, in looking forward to death, and were even satisfied in regard to the issue of it, felt often uneasiness in the prospect of the act of dying. It was a new, untried situation, and as it was often accompanied with much bodily distress, they felt, on this account, no small apprehension in contemplating its approach. To this she replied with uncommon cheerfulness,—I would rather say, with a holy joy lighting up her countenance —'I do not know what it may be when it comes, but I can only say I have never been feared for it [afraid of it] yet; there are just two things which make me quite easy on that subject—the first is, that whatever I may be called to suffer, I know I am in the hands of a reconciled Father, and he will do all things well; and, secondly, that whatever my bodily afflictions may be, I am sure it is well worth the suffering for the glory that is to follow.' We often hear of the moral sublime; we have here a specimen of the spiritual sublime, and that of the highest order."

DAVID HUME AND THE CHILD.

DAVID HUME, the celebrated infidel philosopher, and author of a History of England, was once dining at the house of an intimate friend. After dinner the ladies withdrew; and in the course of conversation, Hume made some assertion which caused a gentleman present to observe to him, "If you can advance such sentiments as those, you certainly are what the world gives you credit for being, an infidel." A little girl, whom the philosopher had often noticed, and with whom he had become a favourite, by bringing her little presents of toys and sweetmeats, happened to be playing about the room unnoticed; she, however, listened to the conversation, and, on hearing the above expression, left the room, went to her mother, and asked her, "Mamma, what is an infidel?" "An infidel, my dear," replied the mother; "why should you ask such a question? An infidel is so awful a character, that I scarcely know how to answer you." "O, do tell me, mamma," returned the child, "I must know what an infidel is." Struck with her eagerness, her mother at length replied, "An infidel is one who believes that there is no God, no heaven, no hell, no hereafter."

Some days afterwards Hume again visited the house of his friend. On being introduced to the parlour, he found no one there but his favourite little girl; he went to her, and attempted to take her up in his arms and kiss her, as he had been used to do; but the child shrunk with horror from his touch. "My dear," said he, "what is the matter?—do I hurt you?" "No," she replied, "you do not hurt me; but I cannot kiss you, I cannot play with you." "Why not, my dear?" "Because you are an infidel!" "An infidel!—what is that?" "One who believes there is no God, no heaven, no hell, no hereafter." "And are you not very sorry for me, my child?" asked the astonished philosopher. "Yes, indeed, I am sorry!" returned the child, with solemnity; "and I pray to God for you." "Do you, indeed, and what do you say?" "I say, O God, teach this man what Thou art!" A striking illustration of the words of sacred writ, "Out of the mouths of babes and sucklings thou hast ordained strength, because of thine enemies, that thou mightest still the enemy and avenger."

7

SORROW AND GENIUS.
An Anecdote of the Grave of Robert Burns.

In the spring after Burns died, Thomas Nimmo, a native of Carnwath, having received his discharge from the army in England, was travelling home with a comrade. Passing through Dumfries they inquired the way to St. Michael's churchyard to visit the poet's grave. Following a foot-path through the wilderness of ornaments which deck Death in that famous burying-ground, they looked around for a stone, to tell them where he slept. Not finding anything of the sort, they made up to a female in deep mourning, who was sitting on the ground a little farther on. Nimmo thus addressed her: "Mistress, we are strangers, and would feel obliged if you could show us the grave of Burns." Pointing to the narrow mound at her feet, and bursting into tears, she said: "That, soldiers, is his grave, and I am his widow." The poor fellows felt hurt at having intruded on her in such circumstances, apologised for their abruptness, tendered their simple, but heartfelt condolence, and went on their way. This would have been a good subject for a painter: Jean Armour at the grave of Burns, while yet no monument marked the spot; and it might have been called Sorrow weeping over Genius, which had been consigned to an early and too premature grave.

A FIFTY YEARS COMMUNICANT AT EDINBURGH.

On a cold, snowy winter's night some years ago writes a missionary, I accompanied a friend to visit an old woman in one of the closes that run off the High Street of Edinburgh. We ascended a stair, and found in a small room the old woman lying on her bed. No one could look on her features without seeing that death was very near. From our friend we learned that she was full eighty years of age; and she had made a kind of profession of religion for fifty years; had been a member of one of the most privileged congregations in Edinburgh; but that, alas! there was no reason to believe she knew anything of religion but the mere empty form. She had enjoyed the services of a faithful ministry, and had regularly sat down at the communion table, and now her ordinances were all over for ever. We went up to her bedside and said, "So you are very ill—death is very near—the doctor says you cannot live above a few hours: what is your hope for eternity?" "Oh," she said, "nobody can say a single word against me. I was a member of a church for fifty years, 'a regular joined member.' I was never absent from the sacrament once that I can remember." "If you are trusting for salvation to that," we said, "you are hiding in a refuge of lies, and death will sweep all your hope away." "Oh, but," she said, "I was always a decent woman; nobody can say anything against me." We quoted the passage from God's Word, "He that believeth shall be saved; he that believeth not, shall be damned." But she began again about what she called her "privileges" for fifty years, and her soul seemed so hardened and blunted by her life-long form of godliness, that the arrows of God's Word seemed to make no mark on her conscience. Here was a solemn lesson, to show what privileges unblessed can do. They had not been without effect, but the effect was but to sear and harden. They seemed, alas! to have been but the savour of death unto death. We thought of the fifty years' Sabbaths, and communion Sabbaths, under the ministry of men of God who had been blessed to the conversion of many sinners, and the refreshing of many of Zion's children. All these precious means of grace had been no means of grace to this poor dying sinner. They had been but weaving together the rag of self-righteousness which she was now clasping around her so closely. And now her feet were soon to stumble on the dark mountains. Suddenly she moved her hand, as if she wished to say something to us. We came very close to her, for her voice was growing feeble, and we hoped to hear some inquiry after Jesus. No; she had quarrelled with one of her neighbours about some trifle, and she wished us to take her part. Thus was she spending her dying breath. Her soul seemed silent against the warnings or threatenings that so often make a sinner tremble. The door of her heart seemed double-locked against the Lord knocking; a thick veil of formality was upon her heart—the growth of fifty years of dry, lifeless, fruitless profession; and now she was going before her Maker and Judge, with a miserable lie in her right hand. She died about two hours after; her light went out in darkness. We often read of shipwrecks; and often do we picture to ourselves that fearful moment when the perishing one discovers he is lost. But there is a still more terrible scene—the shipwreck of a soul. What an awful moment that must be, when a soul that has slept on secure in sin, with a name to live, discovers that all is lost—all hope gone for ever!—the false peace shivered to pieces, and the sinner now beyond the reach of mercy; remembered Sabbaths—remembered communions and professions—all crowding up to the agonised view of the lost. Let us give diligence to make our calling and election sure.

THE REV. GEORGE GILFILLAN PREACHING HIS OWN FUNERAL SERMON.

THE REV. Mr. BORWICK, Rathmillet, says that a good many years ago, he was assisting the late Mr. Marshall, Lochee, at the communion, and the Rev. George Gilfillan attended the Monday service. Mr. Borwick was at the time in very delicate health, and this could be easily seen by those who saw him. His text that day led him to speak for a time upon the subject of our departure from this world to the next, and the needed preparations for the change. On returning from the church to the manse, Mr. Gilfillan said to him, "I have been sitting somewhat in misery. Why did you take that text? Ministers so often preach their own funeral sermons." This remark was fully illustrated in his own case.

On the Sabbath preceding his death, which took place suddenly on Tuesday morning, 13th August, 1878, Mr. Gilfillan went into his own pulpit, as if he had known it was the last time he should stand there. All the hymns were of an impressive, solemn character, and bearing upon death. He chose as his text, Job xiv. 2, "Man cometh forth as a flower and is cut down; he fleeth like a shadow, and continueth not." The burden of his discourse was a vindication of God in relation to sudden deaths, some cases of which he mentioned as having recently taken place. His last words were—"Let us be ready when death comes—whether it comes swiftly or slowly—to adjust our mantle ere we fall, and say, with the blessed Saviour, 'Father, into Thy hands I commend my Spirit. Amen.'" He thus preached his own funeral sermon, and it is affecting to think that, at the close, he left his church never to return to it, with the notes of the "Dead March in Saul" sounding in his ears.

"A SOFT ANSWER TURNETH AWAY WRATH."

An Anecdote of the Rev. Dr. Jamieson's Congregation, Forfar.

THE wife of a respectable farmer, a very pious woman, having become a member of the Rev. Dr. Jamieson's congregation, Forfar, the husband was exceedingly angry, and felt scandalised that his wife should belong to a sect that was everywhere spoken against. He remonstrated with her on the subject, and even threatened that, if she persisted in going to that place, her conduct would make it necessary for him to expel her from his house. She heard him patiently and meekly, and, with a smile, intimated that he would not be so severe as he said. Matters came to a crisis on the Sabbath morning of the communion. The farmer got very excited, addressed his wife in a loud and menacing tone, forbade her to go to the church, and declared most solemnly that if she did so, she need not again return to his house, for he had made up his mind not to receive her. The only reply was, "William, you will not be so hard as you say."

The good woman dressed herself and set out. William was confounded. "This," said he to himself, "is most amazing. That wife of mine is as docile, obedient, and dutiful a woman as ever man had, in everything except in this point. There must be something uncommon about that church and minister. I'll go too." The church was at some distance; and as the farmer knew the road his wife was accustomed to take, he went by another, and was in church before her. "And what, sir," said he (when afterwards recounting the story), "do you think that I was doing all the time of the action sermon, and the serving of the tables? I was going to have a *roup* in a few weeks, and I was busy calculating what this field would bring, and what that lot of cattle would sell at." This unhallowed exercise continued till Dr. Jamieson went up to the pulpit to give directions after the communion was over. His attention was then arrested, and the arrow of conviction entered his soul. It was the moment of his merciful visitation; the day-spring from on high shone upon his mind, and he left the church a heart-stricken, humbled, and sincere penitent, who could find no rest till he had embraced the Saviour, and cast in his lot with those whom he had so cordially despised.

BISHOP COWPER'S DEATH.

In the year 1619, William Cowper, Bishop of Galloway, died. He would have been a very good man, if he had not been corrupted with superior powers and worldly cares of a bishopric, and other things. Owing to the position he occupied, he became involved in various polemical controversies, and among others with the wives of Edinburgh. One of the latter in her contention with the Bishop went so far as to charge him with apostacy, and summoned him to prepare an answer shortly to the Judge of all the world, at a time when it would appear that the health of the Bishop was indifferent. Within a day or two, after being at his pastime-game, golf, on the Links of Leith, he was terrified with a vision, or an apprehension; for he said to his playfellows, after he had in an affrighted and concerned way cast away his play-instruments, the clubs—"I vow to be about with those two men who have come upon me with drawn swords." When his playfellows replied, "My lord, it is a dream; we saw no such thing," he was silent, went home trembling, took to bed instantly, and died.

A VERY YOUNG DISCIPLE.

Some instances of very early piety are exceedingly touching and instructive. Such a case was that of Willie Greig, who was the son of a respectable tradesman. He was a most wonderful boy from his earliest years, and had ways of life and a manner of speech far beyond his experience. On Sabbath morning, when he reached the age of eight, he would go away to the church himself, and endeavour to understand as much of the sermon as possible, and repeat what struck him to his parents when he went home. Sometimes he would say, "The minister was not very good to-day; I did not know what he said." At other times he would be full of joy, and would begin his story by saying, "The minister looked at me, and spoke to me this morning," and then go on to make known what he remembered of the discourse, and other parts of the service. On Thursdays, he used to slip out of his home, and return after an hour or so with a tract in his hand. This he did for weeks without it being known where he went, and his mother at last discovered that he attended a mother's meeting, and seemed to delight in the service.

When ten years of age, Willie was laid up with scarlet fever, and passed through its various stages with ease and comparative comfort. The doctor was pleased with the progress toward betterness he made, and did not anticipate any danger. One Saturday, when Willie was in good spirits at the thought he would now be able to run about again, his father came home for dinner, and took it at the bedside to please his son. Willie, feeling his appetite returning, asked a piece of the meat the father was eating, and, without anticipating evil consequences, the father gave him a little piece. This, however, proved almost on the instant fatal. Reaction set in, and the symptoms were of the most alarming character. The doctor was sent for, pronounced the case hopeless, and that death would ensue in a few hours. The parents were overwhelmed with sorrow; and the father wept and refused to be comforted. Willie was the only one who could utter words of comfort and consolation. He wanted to be lifted on the knee of his mother, which request was granted. He then said, "Do not weep; look at those words hanging up there," pointing to a card that hung above the fire-place, on which were the words, "Suffer little children to come unto me, and forbid them not, for of such is the kingdom of heaven." "Jesus said that," he continued, "and I am going away to him, to heaven, and I will meet you all there. I am not afraid to die, for Jesus will be with me;" and throwing his arms round his mother's neck, he said, with great animation, "O mother! will ye no die with me, too, and we will all be in heaven, and happy together?" Gradually he sank in body, but rose in spirit, and, ere six hours passed, little Willie Greig passed in among the angels without his mother, but not alone—His angel does always behold the face of our Father which is in heaven.

CHANGE IN PREACHER AND PREACHING AND ITS RESULTS.

Dr. CHALMERS was minister of the parish of Kilmany, Fife, and preached what was called the liberal, or moderate, system for twelve years, but without producing the moral and spiritual effects he desired to produce. "For the greater part of that time," he said, "I would expatiate on the meanness of dishonesty; on the villainy of falsehood; on the despicable arts of calumny—in a word, upon all those deformities of character which awaken the natural indignation of the human heart against the pests and disturbers of human society. Even at this time, I certainly did press the reformations of honour and truth and integrity among my people; but I never once heard of any such reformations having been effected amongst them. If there was anything at all brought about in this way, it was more than ever I got any account of. I am not sensible that all the vehemence with which I urged the virtues and proprieties of social life had the weight of a feather on the morals of my parishioners."

At this period Sir James Craig, then residing at Dundee, one day met a Kilmany man on the road, with whom he entered into conversation. The man said to him, "You are well off at Dundee, sir, for ministers." Sir James remarked, knowing Chalmers's talents, "You are better off at Kilmany." The peasant replied, "As for Chalmers, sir, he is nae minister ava."

This indicates that though men of education saw and appreciated his natural powers, the common people did not hear him gladly as they did his Master, nor value him highly as a gospel minister. But a change came over the preaching and the preacher. He had been led to study the evidence and the nature of Christianity, and this led to a deeper and more personal faith in Christ as the Saviour. Having become personally alive to the gospel, he became as a preacher like a giant refreshed with wine. His discourses were powerful and impressive, and crowds flocked on the Sabbaths to the quiet and sequestered church of Kilmany, to hear the man whose lips and heart had been touched with a live coal from off the altar of God. The change was decided, and the fruits were unto salvation. In after days, Dr. Chalmers declared, "It was not until I got impressed by the utter alienation of the heart in all its desires and affections from God; it was not till reconciliation to Him became the distinct and prominent object of my ministerial efforts; it was not till the free offer of forgiveness through the blood of Christ was urged upon their acceptance, and the Holy Ghost given through the channel of Christ's mediatorship to all who ask Him, was set before them as the unceasing object of their dependence and prayers, that I ever heard of any of those subordinate reformations which aforetime made the earnest and zealous, but, I am afraid at the same time, the ultimate object of my earlier administrations."

The people knew and felt the change in their experience. Before Chalmers left the parish, on its being remarked to one of his simple-minded hearers, that their minister was like the Apostle Paul—"Paul," said he, "Paul wasna fit to haud the can'le to him!"—a remark which evinces how enthusiastically they valued the servant of Christ, who proclaimed to them the glad-tidings of great joy.

COUPAR JUSTICE.

What was called "Coupar Justice" was not always bad, but sometimes leaned heavily to mercy's side. We are confirmed in this view when we think that the famous Bailie John himself, stern judge as he was, knew how to be humane and compassionate. The best known tradition concerning him, shows a fine blending of justice and mercy in his administration. On the morning of a Court-day, as he lounged about the back of Beechhill, looking down on the Isla moving sluggishly on in its serpentine course, a Highlander appeared trudging into the town along the public road. The Bailie accosted him, and betrayed some anxiety to know the errand that had brought him to the Lowlands. He soon learned that Donald was one of the culprits who were to be arraigned that very day at his dread tribunal.

"Are you guilty?" the Bailie asked, quite mildly. "Ou, ay, she's guilty," replied the Highlander, shrugging his shoulders; "but there's nae proof." "What," said the Bailie, "will you give a false oath?" "Ay, an' that she will," answered the Celt, "there's mercy wi' God Almighty, but there's nane wi' Bailie Shon."

With this they parted; but, by and bye, Donald found to his utter dismay, his wayside friend on the bench transformed into his implacable judge. "Will you swear now that you are not guilty?" said the Bailie, in a rough, stentorian voice. For a moment the culprit was quite paralysed; but, quickly recovering himself, he answered firmly and roundly, "Yes, she'll swore." The Bailie looked a good deal nonplussed, but, after a silent pause, in which he gave the reason Donald had in the morning assigned for swearing due weight, he dismissed him thus: "Go home, you rascal, and never let me see your face again; and tell your friends in Kirkmichael that there is some mercy in Bailie John as well as in God Almighty."

JUST LIPPEN TO HIM.
An Anecdote of the Rev. Dr. Chalmers.

FREQUENTLY has it been my privilege, says Dr. W. L. Alexander, to follow Dr. Chalmers to some country district, and hear him, in language which he laboured to reduce as much as possible to the standard of "the common people," announce to them the way of salvation and the path to heaven. Sometimes, also, it was my lot to be his companion to some wretched hovel, where I have seen him take his seat by the side of some poor child of want and weakness, and patiently, affectionately, and earnestly strive to convey into his darkened mind some ray of truth that might guide him to safety and to God. On such occasions it was marvellous to observe with what simplicity of speech that great mind would utter truth. One instance of this I must be allowed to mention.

The scene was a low, dirty hovel, over whose damp and uneven floor it was difficult to walk without stumbling, and into which a small window, coated with dust, admitted hardly enough of light to enable an eye unaccustomed to the gloom to discern a single object. A poor old woman, bed-ridden, and almost blind, who occupied a miserable bed opposite the fire-place, was the object of the doctor's visit. Seating himself by her side, he entered at once, after a few general inquiries as to her health, etc., in religious conversation with her. Alas! it seemed all in vain. The mind which he strove to enlighten had been so long closed and dark that it appeared impossible to thrust into it a single ray of light. Still, on the part of the woman, there was an evident anxiety to lay hold upon something of what he was telling her; and encouraged by this he persevered, plying her, to use his own expression, with the efforts of the gospel, and urging her to trust in Christ. At length she said,—"Ah! sir, I would fain do as you bid me, but I dinna ken how. How can I trust in Christ?" "Oh, woman," was his expressive answer, in the dialect of the district, "just lippen to him." "Eh! sir," was the reply, "and is that a'?" "Yes, yes," was his gratified response, "just lippen to him and lean on him, and you'll never perish."

To some, perhaps, this language may be obscure, but to that poor dying woman it was as light from heaven; it guided her to the knowledge of the Saviour, and there is good reason to believe it was the instrument of ultimately conducting her to heaven. It is not easy to give an English equivalent for the word "lippen." It expresses the condition of a person who, entirely unable to support or protect himself, commits his interests or his life to the safe keeping of some person or object. Thus, a man crossing a chasm on a plank lippens to the plank; if it give way he can do nothing for himself. The term implies entire dependence under circumstances of risk and helplessness.

DUNCAN MATHESON AND THE POWER OF SACRED SONG.

ONE night, weary and sad, Duncan Matheson, when a missionary to the soldiers in the Crimea, was returning from Sebastopol to his poor lodgings in the old stable at Balaclava. He had laboured all day with unflagging energy, and now his strength was gone. He was sickened with the sights he had seen, and was depressed with the thought that the siege was no nearer an end than ever. As he trudged along in the mud, knee-deep, he happened to look up, and noticed the stars shining calmly in the clear sky. Instinctively, his weary heart mounted heavenward, in sweet thoughts of the "rest that remaineth for the people of God," and he began to sing aloud the well-known Scriptural verses,—

> "How bright these glorious spirits shine!
> Whence all their white array?
> How came they to the blissful seats
> Of everlasting day?
> Lo! these are they from suff'rings great,
> Who came to realms of light,
> And in the blood of Christ have wash'd
> Those robes which shine so bright."

Next day was wet and stormy, and when he went out to see what course to take, he came upon a soldier standing for shelter below the verandah of an old house. The poor fellow was in rags, and all that remained of shoes upon his feet were utterly insufficient to keep his naked toes from the mud. Altogether, he looked miserable enough. The kind-hearted missionary spoke words of encouragement to the soldier, and gave him at the same half-a-sovereign with which to purchase shoes, suggesting that he might be supplied by those who were burying the dead.

The soldier offered his warmest thanks, and then said,—"I am not what I was yesterday. Last night, as I was thinking of our miserable condition, I grew tired of life, and said to myself, Here we are not a bit nearer taking that place than when we sat down before it. I can bear this no longer, and may as well try and put an end to it. So I took my musket, and went down yonder in a desperate state about eleven o'clock; but as I got round the point, I heard some person singing the old tune,—'How bright these glorious spirits shine,' and I remembered the old tune and the Sabbath-school where we used to sing it. I felt ashamed of being so cowardly, and said, Here is some one as badly off as myself, and yet he is not giving in. I felt he had something to make him happy of which I was ignorant, and I began to hope I too might get the same happiness. I returned to my tent, and to-day I am resolved to seek the one thing." "Do you know who the singer was?" asked the missionary. "No," was the reply. "Well," said the other, "it was I;" on which the tears rushed into the soldier's eyes, and he requested the Scripture-reader to take back the half-sovereign, saying, "Never, sir, can I take it from you after what you have been the means of doing for me."

WELSH OF IRONGRAY.

THIS Mr. Welsh was grandson of the famous John Welsh of Ayr. Kirkton says in his history, that "he was a godly, meek, humble, man, and a good preacher, but the boldest undertaker that ever I knew a minister in Christ's Church, old or late; for, notwithstanding all the threatenings of the State, the great price of £500 set upon his head, the spite of bishops, the diligence of all bloodhounds, he maintained his difficult task of preaching upon the mountains of Scotland, many times to many thousands for nearly twenty years, and yet was kept always out of the enemy's hand. It is well known that bloody Claverhouse, upon intelligence that he was lurking in some secret place, would ride forty miles in a winter's night; yet when he came to the place he always missed his prey. I have known Mr. Welsh ride three days and two nights without sleep, and preach upon a mountain at midnight on one of the nights. He had for some time a dwelling-house near Tweedside; and sometimes, when the Tweed was strongly frozen, he preached in the midst of the river, that either he might shun the offence of both nations, or that two kingdoms might dispute his crime. He was eminently useful on the Borders. He used to say to his friends, who counselled him to be more wary, that he believed God would preserve him as long as he continued among dangers, but whenever he betook himself to safety, then his time should come; which accordingly came to pass after Bothwell, in 1679; when all forsook field-meetings, he went to London, and there died on the 9th of January, 1681.

"Being pursued with unrelenting rigour, he was one time quite at a loss where to go; but depending on Scottish hospitality, and especially on the providence of God, he in the evening called at the house of a gentleman of known hospitality to field-preachers and to himself. He was kindly received. In the course of conversation, Welsh was mentioned, and the difficulty of getting hold of him. The stranger says, 'I know where he is to preach to-morrow, and I will give you him by the hand.' At this the gentleman was exceedingly glad, and engaged the company of his guest with great cordiality. They set off next morning. When they arrived at the congregation, they made way for the minister, and also for his host. He desired the gentleman to sit down on a chair where he stood and preached. During the sermon, the gentleman appeared much affected. At the close, Mr. Welsh gave him his hand, which he cheerfully received, and said, 'Ye said you was sent to apprehend rebels, and I, a rebellious sinner, have been apprehended this day.'"

THEOLOGICAL DISCUSSION IN AYRSHIRE.

AYRSHIRE was at one time a place where theology was keenly discussed. This was not only indulged in by the learned and professional members of society, but by all classes and all characters as well. At Lochwinnoch, a man, whose life had not been at all consistent with that of a genuine Christian profession, was one of those who delighted to speculate in doctrines of divinity. When laid on a bed of severe illness, and in the prospect of death, he was wont even then to perplex and puzzle himself and his visitors with knotty questions about the doctrines of the Bible, and especially the decrees of God. One day, Thomas Orr—a person of a very different character—was sitting at his bedside, endeavouring to turn his attention to what more immediately concerned his duty and condition before God. He was met with a series of difficulties in the old style, when he said, "Ah, William, *this* is the decree you have at present to do with—'He that believeth shall be saved, and he that believeth not shall be condemned,'" after which William remained silent and thoughtful.

THE CHIEFTAIN STARTING TOO LATE.

To be too late by an hour is as bad as to be late by a year, and an opportunity once lost is gone forever. During the time when there was an insurrection in the North of Scotland, William III. issued a proclamation to the effect that all who laid down their arms, and came and took the oath of allegiance by the 31st of December, should be pardoned. Maclean, a chieftain of a prominent clan, resolved to return with the rest of the rebels, but had some pride in being the very last one that should take the oath. He postponed starting for this purpose until two days before the expiration of the term. A snow-storm impeded his way, and before he got up to take the oath, and receive a pardon from the throne, the time was up and past. While the others were set free, Maclean was miserably put to death. He started too late, and arrived too late. In like manner, some are in prospect of losing forever the amnesty of the gospel. Many are going to be forever too late. Remember the irreparable mistake of Maclean.

A BLASPHEMER'S PRAYER ANSWERED.

DURING the Crimean War, an officer of the army was residing with one of his friends who had a beautiful mansion in Forfarshire, on the banks of a fine river, where salmon are to be had in great abundance. The officer referred to was very much addicted to swearing, almost every sentence being preceded by an oath. He was also very fond of fishing, and often employed himself in the pursuit of the "gentle art."

One day he got the keeper to join him in a fishing excursion. In the course of conversation, he told the keeper that he had received orders to join his regiment, and added with an oath, that as he had not been very successful in his take of late, he hoped to be more successful this time, being his last trial. So away they rowed, and very soon he was all eagerness in the sport. He had, after patient perseverance, hooked a large fish, and as it was struggling, he got up to his feet. In his excitement he placed one foot on the edge of the boat, and made it give a lurch to one side, nearly upsetting it.

Thinking that he had lost his fish, with a terrible oath he called upon God to blast his foot. The keeper, who was a godly man, stood horrified at the words. Shortly after returning to the house, he having got ready to go away, mounted his horse, and proceeded to the railway station. He had not gone far, when the horse stumbled and fell—the cursed foot was caught below the horse, and was very much bruised. After the horse regained his feet, the officer found himself unable to walk, and required to be assisted to the house, where he lay for a considerable time. During his solitary confinement he was led to the Saviour, and to pardon, through his blood.

By and bye he joined his regiment, but remained a cripple for life. He soon found that the campaign was too much for him, and soon after he returned home and died, rejoicing, that though God had answered his prayer in cursing his foot, he had in mercy blessed his soul.

A GOSPEL MINISTER DECLINING PRAISE.

"My first meeting with Dr. M'Crie," says Mr. William Muir, Schoolmaster of Dysart, "was somewhat singular. It was in a steam-boat on the Clyde in 1823, if I mistake not. A reverend looking gentleman asked me some questions respecting places on the banks of the river, which my familiarity with the scene enabled me to answer. As we conversed, I summoned courage, or something worse, to ask him if he was a clergyman. He replied that he was. Like a true Scotchman, I pushed my inquiry, remarking that he would be from England. The stranger with a laugh, answered, 'Ah, no; not so far south as that—I come from Edinburgh.' 'From Edinburgh?' I eagerly said. Do you know, then, what Dr. M'Crie is doing? We have had no work from him for some time; is he not going to write the life of Alexander Henderson?' 'I do not think,' said he, 'that the doctor is engaged in any particular work at present.' I then spoke of the doctor's works and his abilities to execute a task of that kind, in a strain which I will not now repeat. I observed a slight flush come on the gentleman's face as I spoke; but were I to state the thought that this gave rise to in my mind, it would be a strong proof how distant were my suspicions from the idea that I was conversing with the person of whom I was speaking. He interrupted me with the question, 'Have you ever seen Dr. M'Crie?' Often have I wished that I had answered this question with more caution. I might have enjoyed, at an earlier period, something of his acquaintance. I replied that I had several years ago heard him preach, and that I thought as much of him as a preacher as a historian. The stranger here abruptly left me. The historian could hear his works praised—the minister could not. As a servant of the Lord Jesus, he could not receive praise from men."

THE LOGIC OF SALVATION.

Dr. JOHN DUNCAN, known by the title, "Rabbi," after passing through the darkness of doubt, almost approaching to Atheism, came to rest in the peace of the gospel. In the year 1862 he described his experience in these words:—" In this softened state of mind I went next day to meet Mr. Malan, who, my friend told me, was in Aberdeen. He was there, here, and everywhere, working his syllogism—'Whosoever believeth that Jesus is the Christ is born of God,' by which I believe he did much good, and some harm. But, for him I have to thank God. Malan that day greatly attracted me; his face beamed with happiness and love. You know he is overstrained, but his dogmatism did me good. I felt as if all the Christians around me were sceptics like myself;—here was a man who could say, 'I know, and am sure.' He was the first gentlemanly, intellectual, and altogether pleasant dogmatist I had met, and I was greatly attracted to him. The conversation turned on religious conversation. I quoted a Jewish word,—'When two sons of Israel meet and no words of the law pass between them, they make the Shechinah to depart from Israel.'

"Later in the evening he came and touched me on the shoulder, and said, 'They tell me you are a very learned man. What do you know?' I answered, rather petulantly, 'I know nothing.' 'Well,' said he, 'I believe that is not exactly what a Christian says. He does not say absolutely, I know nothing. I know Him that is *true*.' And so we talked, going away from the company, till late into the night, and going over many things. I fought against his syllogism. 'I believe Jesus is the Christ, but I don't believe that I am born of God.' At last, in our talk, I happened to be quoting a text. He started forward, and said,—'See! you have the word of God in your mouth.' It passed through me like electricity—the great thought that God *meant* man to know *His* mind: God—His Word—in my very mouth. It was, I believe, the seed of, perhaps, all I have, if I have anything, to this hour. Seminally, it was, perhaps, all there—though I cannot even now unfold it, much less then. Before leaving, I said, 'Will you pray with me?' He said, 'No, I cannot pray with unbelievers.' I said, in simplicity, 'You do not understand our language. When I ask you to pray with me, I mean to pray for me in my presence, permitting me to kneel beside you.' And he said, 'O yes, I will do that.' I went home and wrote a prayer, which I wish I had preserved. 'O God, my God, my God, because Thou hast made me, *teach me what is the meaning of being the Christ the Son of God*, that I may believe on Him.' It was defective, but it was not false, it was true so far. Then I sat down and wrought out a series of syllogisms. Thus—

"*Major*—He that believeth that Jesus is the Christ is born of God—*God*.

"*Minor*—But I believe that Jesus is the Christ—*John Duncan*.

"Therefore I am born of God.

"Then I said, No conclusion can be stronger than the weakest of the premises. These syllogisms were favourable to me, with this caveat. But those relating to the Spirit were unfavourable. Thus—

"*Major*—If any man have not the Spirit of Christ he is none of His—*God*.

"*Minor*—But I have not the Spirit of Christ—*John Duncan*.

"Therefore I am none of His.

"Then I took down Brown's Bible, and spread it before me, and I prayed—'I have been speculating about Thy Word: I know nothing; teach thou me.' And so my philosophical pride got a stroke which it has never recovered, though it sometimes troubles me yet. I then went to bed and there prayed, 'O God, I do not know what is the meaning of "the Christ," and if I should die before morning I should be lost. But thou knowest that I can study no more to-night. Let me not die before morning.' Whereupon, as one who had committed his case to God, I fell, with a certain sorrowful tranquillity, soon asleep."

Next morning Duncan appeared at the breakfast table with a page of syllogisms, wishing Mr. Malan's opinion of their soundness.

"*Major*—Ezek. xxxiii. 11: 'As I live saith the Lord God, I have no pleasure in the death of the wicked'—God.

"*Minor*—But I, John Duncan, am one of the wicked.

"Therefore the Lord God has no pleasure in my death. Is that right?" "Right," answered Malan.

"'But that the wicked turn from his way and live.' Therefore God will have pleasure if I turn from my way, and I shall live.

"'Right?' 'Right.'

"*Major*—John iii. 16: 'God so loved the world, that he gave his only begotten Son'—*Jesus Christ.*

"*Minor*—But I, John Duncan, am one of that world.

"Therefore God so loved me that He gave His only begotten Son—His love to me was what moved Him to give His Son. 'Can that be said?' 'It can—nothing is more certain: "That whosoever believeth on him should not perish, but have everlasting life."'

"Therefore God's express design in giving His Son, out of love to the world, was, that I, believing on Him, might not perish, but have everlasting life. 'Is that a safe conclusion?' 'It is, dear friend; only hold that fast, and it will deliver you out of all your misgivings, and set your feet upon a rock.'

"Well, next day, as I sat down to study, and took my pen in my hand, I became suddenly the passive recipient of all the truths which I had heard and been taught in my childhood. I sat there, unmoving for hours, and *they came and preached themselves to me*. There was now no investigation such as I had desired; but presentation of the truth to me passive. And I felt, sitting there, as if in that hour I had got matter for sermons for a lifetime. Now the temptation to daily sin was gone. I had not even to fight with it. And I was in an almost infantile state of mind—so that when I mislaid a paper in my study, I would kneel down and pray to find, and then go to seek it."

In fact, night after night he laid himself down to rest with the infant's prayer on his lips:—

"This night when I lie down to sleep,
I give my soul to Christ to keep,
If I should die before I wake,
I pray the Lord my soul to take."

JOHN BROWN OF HADDINGTON.

THE author of "Rab and his Friends," in a letter says—For the "heroic" old man of Haddington, my father [Rev. Dr. John Brown, Broughton Church, Edinburgh] had a peculiar reverence—as, indeed, we all have, as well we may. He was our king, the founder of our dynasty; we dated from him, and he was "hedged" accordingly by a certain sacredness or "divinity." I well remember with what surprise and pride I found myself asked by a blacksmith's wife, in a remote hamlet among the hop-gardens of Kent, if I was "the son of the Self-Interpreting Bible." I possess as an heirloom the New Testament which my father fondly regarded as the one his grandfather when a herd laddie got from the Professor who heard him ask for it, and promised it if he could read a verse. He had now acquired so much of Greek as encouraged him to hope that he might at length be prepared to reap the richest of all rewards which classical learning could confer on him, the capacity of reading in the original tongue the blessed New Testament of our Lord and Saviour. Full of this hope, he became anxious to possess a copy of the invaluable volume. One night, having committed the charge of his sheep to a companion, he set out on a midnight journey to St. Andrews, a distance of twenty-four miles. He reached his destination in the morning, and went to the bookseller's shop, asking for a copy of the Greek New Testament. The master of the shop, surprised at such a request from a shepherd boy, was disposed to make game of him. Some of the professors coming into the shop questioned the lad about his employment and studies. After hearing his tale, one of them desired the bookseller to bring the volume. He did so, and throwing it down, said, "Boy, read this, and you shall have it for nothing!" The boy did so, acquitted himself to the admiration of his judges, and carried off his Testament, and, when the evening arrived, was studying it in the midst of his flock on the braes of Abernethy.

COWIE OF HUNTLY.

At the end of last century, a notable preacher, of the name of George Cowie, exercised his gifts in the town and neighbourhood of Huntly. This faithful servant of God was consumed with zeal. He was sometimes so overpowered with a sense of the value of souls, that he needed to be supported by the elders as he went from the vestry to the pulpit. When speaking of preaching, he used to say, "Go direct to conscience, and in every sermon take your hearers to the judgment-seat." One day a preacher, who occupied his place, spoke as if the Holy Spirit was not needed by either saint or sinner. At the close of the service, Cowie stood up on the pulpit-steps, and solemnly said, "Sir, haud in wi' yer auld frien' the Holy Ghost; for if ye ance grieve Him awa', ye'll nae get Him back sae easy." He exhibited fine tact in dealing with men. One of his attached hearers was the wife of a wealthy farmer, who, after weeping and praying in vain for her ungodly husband, brought her grief before her pastor, whose preaching she could by no persuasion induce him to hear.

After listening to the case, which seemed quite inaccessible, he inquired, "Is there anything your guidman has a liking to?" "He heeds for naething in the world," was her reply, "forbye his beasts, his siller, an' it be na his fiddle." The hint was enough; the minister soon found his way to the farmhouse, where, after a dry reception, and kindly inquiries about cattle and corn, he awoke the farmer's feelings on the subject of his favourite pastime. The fiddle was produced, and the man of earth was astonished and charmed with the sweet music it gave forth in the hands of the feared and hated man of God. The minister next induced him to promise him to return his call, by the offered treat of a finer instrument in his own house, where he was delighted with the swelling tones of a large violin, and needed then but slight persuasion from his wife to accompany her to hear his friend preach. The word took effect in conviction and salvation, and the grovelling farmer was transformed into a son of God and heir of glory.

AN OLD WOMAN AND M'CHEYNE.

An old woman said that a sermon she heard Mr. M'Cheyne preach from the Song of Solomon was the means of her conversion. It was in the second chapter, from the 8th to the 17th verse, beginning with, "The voice of my beloved," etc. She said she thought herself all right—she had a good moral character, she went to church as often as her many duties would allow her; but that sermon stript her of her self-righteousness, and made her cry out —"What shall I do to be saved?" Her husband was a freethinker, and a great cause of sorrow to her. Then they were in the depths of poverty, for the family was large, and her husband's wages were very small. Still, the trouble at home was nothing, compared to the agony of mind she suffered from the horror of her sinful condition. One of the elders who chanced to see her told Mr. M'Cheyne of her state, who went to visit her. When she opened the door in answer to his knock, and saw him, she was frightened; but he soon put her at her ease by saying kindly, "Never mind me, I am a poor creature like yourself, and, in the sight of a great and holy God, we stand on the same platform; the only difference in the Lord's sight, in this world, is the difference between the righteous and the wicked: the prince and the peasant are equal in his eyes." He often, she said, came to see her after that, and she added, " Baith purse an' prayer were ready." One day when he came she was washing, and her house was very untidy, for which she was making excuses, when he interrupted her by saying, " Do you not know me better by this time, than to understand that it is not to see your house I come here, but only to talk with yourself?"

He would often say to her, when she told him of her troubles, " Ah! could we get an insight into the workings of God, we would see his principal work is training and pruning the vines in His vineyard." When asked if her husband ever saw the error of his ways, she said, " Yes, thank God; and, thank God that every one of my children, man and woman of them, who have grown up, have had cares enough—aye, and sins enough, too; but they all know and acknowledge God to be the true God, the Creator of heaven and earth; and, oh! that to me is everything." She then went on to say that her life, when her husband brought people of his own creed about him, had been most miserable—indeed, her horror of freethinkers was very great, no poverty, no hardship seemed to weigh with her, when compared to what a life of care spent amongst such people would be. She is very old now, and blind and poor; but God has not forgotten her, and she says her song is now, " I am poor and needy, but the Lord thinketh upon me."

This old woman told of the death of one of her children, about that revival time in Dundee. She said he was the " best laddie she ever knew," his dread of sin was so great, and his love of God and God's people was very deep and tender. When he was just dying, he said to her, " Mother, meet me in heaven. But I needna say this, for I ken ye will; but my father—oh! tell him to forsake that bad company, and come too." He then added, " Oh, mother! what bonnie!" " What is bonnie?" she asked, seeing such a heavenly look on his face. He smiled sweetly, and answered, " Ye couldna see them, mither; but I can "—and then, stretching out his hands, he said, " Guid nicht, mither! Come! Lord Jesus," and died. His father from that hour renounced his free-thinking notions, and she hoped became a follower of Him to whom her son had gone.

PLAY WITH AND PRAY FOR CHILDREN.

Dr. John Brown, in his lay sermons on Health, advises parents to play with and pray for their children. He says, "There is no such good plaything for grown-up children as *weans*—wee ones. It is wonderful what you can get them to do with a little coaxing and fun. Here is a pleasant little story out of an old book: A gentleman having led a company of children beyond their usual journey, they began to get weary, and all cried to him to carry them on his back, but because of their multitude he could not do this. 'But,' says he, 'I'll get horses for us all.' Then he cut little wands out of the hedge as ponies for them, and a great stake as charger for himself. This put mettle in their little legs, and they rode cheerily home. One thing, however poor you are, you can give your children, and that is your prayers, and they are, if real and humble, worth more than silver or gold—more than food and clothing, and have often brought from our Father who is in heaven, and hears our prayers, both money and meat and clothes, and all worldly things. You may always teach them to pray. Some weeks ago, I was taken out to see the mother of a little child. She was very dangerously ill, and the nurse had left the child to come and help me. I went up to the nursery to get some hot water, and in the child's bed I saw something raised up. This was the little fellow under the bed-clothes kneeling. I said, 'What are you doing?' 'I am praying God to make mamma better,' said he. God likes these little prayers and these little people—for of such is the kingdom of heaven. These are his little ones—his lambs—and he hears their cry; and it is enough if they only lisp his prayers. 'Abba, Father,' that is all he needs, and our prayers are never so truly prayers as when they are most like children's in simplicity, in directness, in perfect fulness of reliance. 'They pray right up,' as the pious negro said."

DR. CHALMERS'S DAUGHTER.

In one of the alleys running off from Fountain-Bridge, Edinburgh, a street crowded with drunkenness and pollution, is the low-roofed building in which this good woman is spending her life to help men and women out of their miseries. Her chief work is with drunkards, their wives and daughters. Some of the poor women of the neighbourhood who have sober husbands, complain against her, saying, "Why do you pass us? Because our husbands are good, you do not care for us. If we had married some worthless sot, you would then have taken care of us in our poverty!" In the winter, when the nights are long and cold, you may see Dr. Chalmers's daughter, with her lantern, going through the lanes of the city, hunting up the depraved, and bringing them to her reform meetings. Insult her, do they? Never! They would as soon think of pelting an angel of God. Fearless and strong in the righteousness of her work, she goes up to a group of intoxicated men, shakes hands with them, and takes them along to hear the Thursday night speech on temperance. One night, as she was standing in a low tenement, talking with the intemperate father, and persuading him to a better life, a man kept walking up and down the room, as though interested in what was said; but finally, in his intoxication, staggered up to her and remarked, "I shall get to heaven as easy as you will; do you think so?" Helen answered not a word, but opened her Bible and pointed to the passage, "No drunkard shall inherit the kingdom of God." The arrow struck between the joints of the harness, and that little piece of Christian stratagem ended in the man's reformation.

BROWN OF PRIESTHILL.

John Brown lived in a house called Priesthill, in the parish of Muirkirk, in the days of the Covenant. He was an amiable and blameless man, and had taken no part in the risings or public testifyings of the times. Nevertheless, his hour at last arrived. It was the 30th

of April, 1685. John Brown had been at home, and
unmolested for some time; he had risen early, and had
performed family worship. The psalm sung was the
twenty-seventh, and the chapter read the sixteenth of
John, which closes with the remarkable words, "In the
world ye shall have tribulation; but be of good cheer, I
have overcome the world." His prayer was, as usual,
powerful and fervent, for although he stuttered, in
prayer he could not but speak fluently in the dialect
of heaven. He then went away alone to the hill to
prepare some peat-ground. Meanwhile, Claverhouse
had come in late at night to Lesmahagow, where a
garrison was posted, had heard of John; had risen still
earlier than his victim, and by six on that grey April
morning, had tracked him to the moss; had surrounded
him with three troops of dragoons, and led him down
to the door of his own house. With the dignity of
Cincinnatus, leaving his plough in mid-furrow, John
dropped his spade, and walked down, it is said, "rather
like a leader than a captive." His wife was warned of
their approach, and, with more than the heroism of an
ancient Roman matron, with one boy in her arms, with
a girl in her hand, and, alas! with a child within her,
Isabel Weir came calmly out to play her part in this
frightful tragedy. Claverhouse was no trifler. Short
and sharp was he always in his brutal trade. He asked
John at once why he did not attend the curate, and if
he would pray for the king. John stated, in one distinct
sentence, the usual Covenanting reasons. On hearing it,
Claverhouse exclaimed, "Go to your knees, for you shall
immediately die!" John complied without remonstrance, and proceeded to pray, in terms so melting, and
with such earnest supplication for his wife and their
born and unborn children, that Claverhouse saw the
hard eyes of his dragoons beginning to moisten, and
their hands to tremble, and thrice interrupted him with
volleys of blasphemy.

When the prayer was ended, John turned round to
his wife, reminded her that this was the day come, of
which he had foretold her when he proposed marriage,

and asked if she was willing to part with him. "Heartily willing," was her reply. "This," he said, "is all I desire. I have nothing more now to do but to die." He then kissed her and the children, and said, "May all purchased and promised blessings be multiplied unto you." "No more of this," roared out the savage, whose own iron heart this scene was threatening to move. "You six dragoons, there, fire on the fanatic." They stood motionless, the prayer had quelled them. Fearing a mutiny, both among his soldiers and in his own breast, he snatched a pistol from his belt and shot the good man through the head. He fell, his brains spurted out, and his brave wife caught the shattered head in her lap. "What do you think of your husband, now?" howled the ruffian. "I aye thocht muckle o' him, sir, but never sae muckle as I do this day." "I would think little to lay thee beside him," he answered. "If you were permitted, I doubt not you would; but how are ye to answer for this morning's wark?" "To men, I can be answerable, and, as for God, I will take him in my own hands." And, with these desperate words, he struck spurs to his horse and led his dragoons away from the inglorious field. Meekly and calmly did this heroic and Christian woman tie up her husband's head in a napkin, compose his body, cover it with her plaid—and not till these duties were discharged did she permit the pent up current of her mighty grief to burst out, as she sat down beside the corpse and wept bitterly.

ACTING DEATH LEADING TO LIFE.

ONE evening, says the Rev. Dr. J. H. Wilson, when I was sitting in the gallery of the Independent Church, Cullen, the minister, in applying the text of his sermon, "Thou God seest me," said, with intense earnestness, "Sailors, write it on your binnacles; merchants, on your counters; carters, on your carts, 'Thou God seest me;'" and then turning to the gallery, where I was sitting, he seemed to fix his eyes on me, while he said, "Young man, write it on thy heart, 'Thou God seest me.'" That was all he said. But it was an arrow from God's quiver. I went home wretched, and could not tell why. Days and weeks passed away, and I was unhappy. I read, I prayed, and I wept and laughed, and laughed and wept, like a maniac, and father and mother thought I was going mad. Oh! the remembrance of those days. I cannot account for such feelings. All about me were *religious*, but none were *pious* except my dear mother, and her piety was not of the demonstrative cast. I had no sins of a glaring character to mourn over. Ours had been a family of love and obedience, and yet I was not happy. In this state I continued to hear the good minister, but to no profit. At length the way to peace seemed to open up. I was walking down the principal street of our little town one day, when I met an acquaintance, who stopped me, and said,—"Come, now, I want you very much. We are going to act the play of the 'Heart of Midlothian' for the benefit of the poor, and Mr. Mullender of the Theatre Royal is to help us. You will make a capital Madge Wildfire. What do you say?" The passage, "charity covereth a multitude of sins," rushed into my mind. "I will," was the response, and then with all my heart and energy I committed to memory, and practised for performance, this character. It suited my romantic nature. Madge was a religious maniac, and I could enter into all her griefs and sorrows and joys with zest. But Madge had to die. On the stage this scene troubled me. "I am mocking death," said I to myself, when prostrate on the boards. "What if God take me in this act of solemn mockery?" At that moment a flash of lightning seemed to come across the stage, and with it the words,—"Thou God seest me." I could stand it no longer. Rushing behind the scenes, and spoiling the whole play, I put on my daily dress, ran home, went into a summer house in the garden, wept and prayed, and prayed and wept, for a whole night, and until day came in the morning. Shortly after that, rest was found in Jesus, and a new life, with new aims, hopes, joys, and aspirations, began.

THE REV. JOHN JAMIESON'S LETTERS.

THE REV. JOHN JAMIESON, of Methven, who died in 1837, was celebrated as a letter-writer. His letters were written without the most distant prospect of publication, but they have run through several editions. Gilfillan says of them:—"Some of them, we hesitate not to say, are equal to any letters in the English language—nay, Cowper alone has equalled their *naïveté*, pathos, and occasional humour." Though mostly addressed to those requiring consolation, there are in several of them some rich pieces of worldly wisdom. He writes thus to his son Alexander, on "application to business":—

"In these times it is a great mercy to get a place, a greater to be kept in it, and, the greatest of all, to be accounted worthy of holding it. Do your diligence to repay his kindness by being everything, in the work committed to your charge, that such a man could desire. An Englishman's forte is superiority of execution. Though it were but the cleaning of a pair of shoes, never rest satisfied till you can do it better than any other man that puts his hand to the brush. Throw your whole soul into your work. Recollect that you can never claim a better place in advance, unless you fill the place well which you presently occupy; and that now-a-days it requires a man to be anything and everything in order to be something. 'Seest thou a man diligent in business? he shall stand before kings, he shall not stand before mean men;' keep a sharp eye a ready hand, a courteous manner, and a proud heart, that will not bow to meanness nor to mischief. Say little and do much; be every man's servant, and no man's debtor. Seek God in everything; trust and honour Him, and God will honour you. 'I love them that love me,' is His promise. A little self-denial for the present is the best security against trouble and vexation for the future. Be very careful of your clothes: they will keep their face the longer; and make a point never to sport a new suit till you are clear with the tailor. It is by such attention that we secure our own self-respect; and until we respect ourselves, we never can claim respect from others. Your salary cannot, in the first instance, be great. Make it do, however; you will thereby learn how to turn it to the best account when it becomes greater. A fool's income never keeps him; a wise man's always covers his demands. It is the blessing of God which maketh rich; but God evidently helps those who help themselves. To expect otherwise is to mock God."

If these quaint and wise sayings were attended to in the start of life, a bright and successful future would be experienced.

CARLYLE AND THE SECEDER ELDER.

CARLYLE, in his own nervous style, speaks thus of the Seceder Church he attended, and of one of its members:—"That poor temple of my childhood is more sacred to me than the biggest cathedral then extant could have been; rude, rustic, bare, no temple in the world more so; but there were sacred lambencies, tongues of authentic flame, which kindled what was best in one, and what has not yet gone out. Strangely vivid are some twelve or twenty of those old faces whom I used to see every Sunday, whose names, employments, or precise dwelling-places, I never knew, but whose portraits are yet clear to me as in a mirror. One of these was old David Hope, tall, straight, very clean always, brown as mahogany, with a beard as white as snow. He lived on a little farm, close by the Solway shore, a mile or two east of Annan—a wet country, with late harvests, which are sometimes incredibly difficult to save—ten days continuously pouring; then a day, perhaps two days, of drought, part of them, it may be, of high roaring wind; during which the moments were golden for you, and perhaps you had better work all night, as presently there will be deluges again. David's stuff, one such morning, was all standing dry, ready to be saved still, if he stood to it, which was very much his intention. Breakfast, wholesome hasty porridge, was soon over, and next in course came family worship, what they call 'takin the book,' *i.e.*, taking your Bible, psalm and chapter always part of the service. David was putting on his spectacles when somebody rushed in. 'Such a raging wind risen will drive the stooks into the sea if let alone.' 'Wind!' answered David, ' wind canna get ae straw that has been appointed mine. Sit doun an' let us worship God.'"

EBENEZER BROWN AND THE CARTERS.

"ONE story of him I must give," says Dr. John Brown. "My father, who heard it not long before his own death, was delighted with it, and for some days repeated it to every one. Uncle Ebenezer, with all his mildness and general complaisance, was, like most of the Browns, *tenax propositi*, firm to obstinacy. He had established a weekday sermon at the North Ferry, about two miles from his own town, Inverkeithing. It was, I think, held on the Tuesdays. It was winter, and a wild, drifting, and dangerous day; his daughters—his wife was dead—besought him not to go; he smiled vaguely, but continued getting into his big-coat. Nothing would stay him, and away he and the pony stumbled through the dumb and blinding snow. He was half-way on his journey, and had got in thought into the sermon he was going to preach, and was utterly insensible to the outward storm: his pony getting its feet *balled*, staggered about, and at last upset his master and himself into the ditch at the roadside. The feeble, heedless, rapt old man might have perished there, had not some carters, bringing up whisky-casks from the Ferry, seen the catastrophe, and rushed up, raising him and *dichtin'* him, with much commiseration and blunt speech, 'Puir auld m'n, what brocht ye here on sic a day?' There they were, a rough crew, surrounding the saintly man, some putting on his hat, sorting and cheering him, and others knocking the balls off the pony's feet, and stuffing them with grease.

"He was most polite and grateful, and one of these cordial rustics having pierced a cask, brought him a horn of whisky, and said, 'Tak' that, it'll hearten ye.' He took the horn, and, bowing to them, said, 'Sirs, let us give thanks!' and there by the roadside in the drift and storm, with these wild fellows, he asked a blessing on it, and for his kind deliverers, and took a tasting of the horn. The men cried like children. They lifted him on his pony, one going with him, and when the rest arrived at Inverkeithing, they repeated the story to everybody, and broke down in tears whenever they came to the blessing. 'An' to think o' askin' a blessin' on a tass o' whisky!' Next Presbytery day, after the ordinary business was over, he rose up—he seldom spoke—and said, 'Moderator, I have something personal to myself to say. I have often said, that real kindness belongs only to true Christians, but—' and then he told the story of these men; 'but more true kindness I never experienced than from these lads. They may have had the grace of God, I don't know; but I never mean again to be so *positive* in speaking of this matter.'"

ROBERT BURNS'S REFLECTIONS.

ROBERT BURNS had his seasons when he was led to think of the nature of man and the solemnity of existence. One of these seasons was the beginning of a new year. As the year 1789 was being ushered in, he wrote an affectionate letter to his brother, in which he says:—"I have just finished my New Year's Day breakfast in the usual form, which naturally makes me call to mind the days of former years, and the society in which we used to begin them; and when I look at our family vicissitudes, 'through the dark postern of time long elapsed,' I cannot help remarking to you, my dear brother, how good the God of seasons is to us, and that, however some clouds may seem to lower over the portion of time before us, we have great reason to hope that all will turn out well."

In another letter written on the same day he says, "I own myself so little a Presbyterian, that I approve set times and seasons of more than ordinary acts of devotion, for breaking in on that habituated routine of life and thought, which is so apt to reduce our existence to a kind of instinct, or even sometimes, and with some minds, to a state very little superior to mere machinery. This day—the first Sunday of May—a breezy, blue-skied noon; about the beginning of spring, and a hoary morning and calm sunny day about the end of autumn—these, time out of mind, have been with me a kind of holiday. We know nothing, or next to nothing, of the substance or structure of our souls, so cannot account for those seeming caprices in them, that we should be particularly pleased with this thing, or struck with that, which on minds of a different cast, make no extraordinary impression. I have some favourite flowers in spring, among which are the mountain-daisy, the hare-bell, the fox-glove, the wild-brier rose, the budding birch, and the hoary hawthorn, that I view and hang over with particular delight. I never hear the loud, solitary whistle of the curlew in a summer nook, or the wild, mixing cadence of a troop of grey plovers in an autumnal morning, without feeling an elevation of soul like the enthusiasm of devotion or poetry. Tell me, my dear friend, to what can this be owing? Are we a piece of machinery which, like the Æolian harp, passive, takes the impression of the passing accident? Or do these workings argue something within us above the trodden clod? I own myself partial to such proofs of those awful and important realities—as that God made all things—man's immaterial and immortal nature—and a world of weal or woe beyond death and the grave."

THE REV. GEORGE GILFILLAN'S GENEROSITY.

THE REV. GEORGE GILFILLAN was distinguished for his largeness of heart and his generosity. Many a poor man did he help with the good things of this life, and to many a student did he lend a helping hand when in difficulty. To the poor of his flock he was a true brother and pastor. On a melancholy occasion he had to meet one of the members of his church who had been called upon to follow one near to him to the grave. After the usual condolence, Mr. Gilfillan said to the bereaved, "I have missed you in the church, for a long time. What is wrong?" "O yes," said the poor man, "it is true, for I did not like to come with a coat I am ashamed of—it is so bare." The minister showing the nobility of his character, immediately disrobed himself of his coat, and handed it to the distressed one, saying,

There, my man, let me see my coat every Sunday until t becomes bare, and then call back." After so delivering himself, the divine retired to his studies in his shirt sleeves, and being observed by his worthy spouse, she says, "George, what have you done with your coat?" His answer was, "Never mind, my dear, I have just given it to God."

THE ELEVENTH COMMANDMENT.
An Anecdote of Archbishop Usher in Scotland.

At one time Archbishop Usher visited Scotland, and hearing much of the piety of the Rev. Samuel Rutherford, resolved on being a witness of it. Disguised as a pauper, on a Saturday evening, he solicited lodging for the night. Mr. Rutherford took him in, and directed him to be seated in the kitchen. Mrs. Rutherford catechised the servants, as a preparation for the Sabbath; and having asked the stranger the number of the Divine commandments, he answered eleven. The good woman hastily concluded him ignorant, and said, "What a shame it is for you, a man with grey hairs, in a Christian country, not to know how many commandments there are! There is not a child six years old, in this parish, but could answer the question properly." Lamenting his condition, she ordered his supper, and directed a servant to show him a bed in the garret. Mr. Rutherford having heard him at prayer, and finding out who he was, prevailed on the Archbishop to preach for him, which he agreed to do, on condition that he should not be made known. Early in the morning, Mr. Rutherford changed his clothes, suffered him to depart, and afterwards introduced him to breakfast as a minister on a journey. When in the pulpit, he announced his text—"A new commandment I give unto you, that ye love one another;"

and remarked that this might be reckoned the eleventh commandment. Mrs. Rutherford, remembering the answer she had received the night before from the stranger, was astonished, and looking at the preacher, almost imagined he might be the pitied traveller. The two holy men spent the evening in delightful conversation, and the Archbishop departed undiscovered, early on the following day.

HIGHLAND RESPECT FOR THE SABBATH.

ONE of the most peculiar, and, at the same time, pleasing features of the Highland character, is the respect universally paid to the Sabbath-day. A curious illustration of this was found at Banavie, a very comfortable inn at the western entrance of the Caledonian Canal. A large party, including the Rev. Dr. J. H. Wilson, of London, who tells the story, were there at dinner one Monday afternoon, a gentleman from England, resident for a time, and fishing salmon, being in the chair. In serving out a fine salmon, he expatiated on the fine quality of the fish, and concluded by saying,—"I know he is fresh and sweet, for he was all alive yesterday, and a hard struggle I had before I got him out of the water." A tall Highland farmer, of the name of Paterson, was supplied with a fine piece, and was about to dig into the portion which had been placed before him, when he instantly dropped the fish-knife, and, turning to the chairman, said, "Yesterday, sir, was the Sabbath-day, you would have been better employed in going to the church than in catching salmon on the Lord's Day." "I don't think so," replied the Englishman, "for if I may judge from what I saw yesterday evening on the hill-sides here, I think 'going to the kirk,' as you call it, did the people little good." "What do you mean?" inquired Paterson. "I mean this, that after being all day at the church in-doors, singing and preaching, and roaring, if I may call some of it by its right name, they came and squatted themselves on the hill-side, sat and drank whisky till they got drunk; then some of them fought, and one poor fellow lies in the hotel now in a very bad state." For a moment Paterson was thoughtful, and having recollected himself, he said,—"O yes, I understand it, sir, I see it; yesterday was the *sacrament Sunday.*"

DR. BEGG ON HOW TO TREAT OPPONENTS.

THE REV. DR. BEGG was a man of determination and activity. He took an active part in many public movements, and was a member of various committees and boards. He had also the courage of his opinions, and was a powerful debater in ecclesiastical courts and elsewhere. When a member of the Edinburgh School Board he had an earnest and animated discussion on one occasion on the subject of temperance, in which he contended, in opposition to another member, that alcohol was not poison, but a good creature of God. The contention was a little sharp on both sides, and feelings were considerably aroused. When the meeting was over, the Doctor left the room with his opponent, and they had not gone far when they were overtaken by a heavy shower of rain. They sought shelter in a passage at hand, and were enjoying a quiet crack when a lady member of the Board made her appearance. When she saw the two former disputants in cheery converse, she held up her hands in astonishment, and said,—"If it had been two ladies who had differed as much as you two did an hour ago, they would not have spoken to each other for years." "Ah," said the Doctor, "that would have been far wrong. I never allow feelings of a personal kind to enter into my public life, when I know others are as honest as myself. Fifty years ago, and more, my father said to me, 'Now, James, you are going into the world to mingle with men who have as good a right to have their opinion as you have. When they differ from you treat them with respect, and after the discussion is over, let the whole be ended. Act on this principle, James, and you will prevent much mischief and much pain to yourself.' I have always endeavoured to act thus, and I have found it a good plan." Dr. Begg then hailed a cab, and the two went home together.

JOHN BROWN, THE EXEMPLARY GRAVEDIGGER.

When the Rev. Henry Gray was minister of the parish of Hamilton, John Brown was gravedigger. He had his own ways, and one of his peculiar habits was to attend especially to the graves of children, and he invariably sowed them with white clover. Mr. Gray had not been long minister of the parish till he noticed the odd practice of the gravedigger; and one day, when he came upon John smoothing and trimming the lonely bed of a child which had been buried a few days before, he asked him why he was so particular in dressing and keeping the graves of the children. John paused for a moment at his work, and looking up, not at the minister, but at the sky, said,—" Of such is the kingdom of heaven."

"And on this account you tend and adorn them with so much care?" remarked the minister, who was greatly struck with the reply. "Surely, sir," answered John, "I canna make over-braw and fine the bed-coverin' of a little innocent sleeper that is waiting there till it is God's time to wauken it, and cover it with the white robe, and waft it away to glory. When sic grandeur is awaitin' it yonder, it's fit it should be decked out here. I think the Saviour that counts its dust sae precious will like to see the *white clover sheet spread abune it;* dae ye no think sae tae, sir?" "But why not thus cover larger graves?" asked the minister, hardly able to suppress his emotion. "The dust of all his saints is precious in the Saviour's sight." "Very true, sir," responded John, with great solemnity, "but I canna be sure wha are his saints and wha are no. I hope there are mony o' them lying in this kirkyard, but it wad be great presumption in me to mark them oot. There are some that I'm gey sure aboot, and I keep their graves as nate and snod as I can, and plant a bit flower here and there as a sign o' my hope, but I daurna gie them the white sheet. It's clean different, though, wi' the bairns. We hae His ain Word for their up-going, and sae I canna mak' an error there. Some folk, I believe, are bauld enough to say that it's only the infants o' the guid that will be saved." "And do you adhere to that doctrine?" inquired Mr. Gray. John answered by pointing to a little patch a few paces off, which was thickly covered with clover, "That ane," he said, "is the bairn o' Tam Sutton, the collier. Ye ken Tam, sir."

Mr. Gray did indeed know Tam, for he was the most notorious swearer, liar, and drunkard, in the parish, and John did not require to say any more to show that he disbelieved in the condemnation of infants.

"It's no only cruel and blasphemous," he answered, in a dry sarcastic way, "but it's quite absurd. Jist tak' that bairn o' Tam's as an example. According to their belief, it's lost; because we may, without any breach o' charity, say that Tam is at present a reprobate. But he is still in the place of hope, sir, and it is quite possible that he may be converted. What comes o' the bairn, then? Na, na," he added, looking reverently upward, "God is merciful, and Jesus died, and it was him that said, 'Of such is the kingdom of heaven.'" The minister took John's hand and silently pressed it. He had got the key to his deeper nature, and was thrilled by its unexpected richness.

A GENTLE EFFECTIVE REBUKE.

In the old coaching days, there were many disputes and contentions among the passengers, and these were indulged in for various reasons, and issued in different results. An incident of a rather instructive character happened to the late Rev. Dr. W. Lindsay Alexander when he was a young man. He had been appointed to go with the celebrated missionary, Richard Knill, as a deputation to the churches in the North of Scotland on behalf of the London Missionary Society, and had arranged to meet Mr. Knill at Blair-Athole. They met some stages in advance, but did not personally know each other. Richard Knill had met with a sceptic on the coach, and they had entered upon an argument regarding religion. For a good part of the way the missionary was engaged combating the infidel arguments used by his fellow-passenger, and had rather a tough job in hand. When the coach stopped at the hotel where the passengers were to dine, Dr. Alexander said,—"If I mistake not, you are Richard Knill?" "I am." "And I am Lindsay Alexander, appointed to accompany you to the churches in the north." Richard looked at him for a moment silently, and then said, "I am ashamed of you, sir." "Why?" "Why? because you sat all the time by my side when I was defending your Master, and you had not a word to say on his behalf." The young minister quietly received the gentle rebuke, and never forgot his first introduction to Richard Knill.

AN ANECDOTE OF GEORGE WISHART.

GEORGE WISHART, one of the first Scottish martyrs at the time of the Reformation, being desired to preach on the Lord's Day in the church of Mauchline, went thither with that design, but the Sheriff of Ayrshire had in the night-time put a garrison of soldiers into the church to keep him out. Hugh Campbell, of Kinzeanclough, and others in the parish, were exceedingly offended at this impiety, and would have entered the church by force, but Wishart would not suffer it, saying, "Brethren, it is the word of peace which I preach unto you; the blood of no man shall be shed for it this day. Jesus Christ is as mighty in the fields as in the church, and He Himself, while He lived in the flesh, preached oftener in the desert and on the sea-side than in the Temple of Jerusalem." Upon this the people were appeased, and went with him to the edge of a moor on the south-west of Mauchline, where, having placed himself upon a mound of earth, he preached to a great multitude. He continued speaking for more than three hours, God working wondrously by him, insomuch that Laurence Ranken, the Laird of Shield, a very profane person, was converted by his discourse. The tears ran from his eyes, to the astonishment of all present, and the whole of his after life witnessed that his profession was without hypocrisy.

SIR WALTER SCOTT'S LAST DAYS.

In the month of September, 1830, Sir Walter set out for London, on the way to the Continent. At Malta and Naples he received every attention, awakening sad surprise among those who had known him but a few years before, by his altered appearance. He visited Pompeii, murmuring, as he was carried among the disentombed ruins, "The city of the dead! The city of the dead!" He desired to return by the Tyrol and Germany, principally that he might meet the mighty Goethe. But on the 2nd of March that tower of German genius fell, and the melancholy tidings sounded through the heart of Scott as the hollow echo of the tomb. He exclaimed, "Alas! for Goethe; but he at least died at home. Let us to Abbotsford." In April he began the homeward journey. Arrived in Rome, the city of the Cæsars could awaken but little interest. But it was in the Eternal City that he gave utterance to one of the noblest sentences ever heard from human lips. He had been speaking of Goethe, and deploring the moral influence of some of his novels, and he added, "I am drawing near the close of my career; I am fast shuffling off the stage. I have been perhaps the most voluminous author of the day, and it is a comfort to me to think that I have tried to unsettle no man's faith, to corrupt no man's principle, and that I have written nothing which on my deathbed I should wish blotted."

In May he left Rome, and hastened with growing impatience to look once more upon the dear old land where he wished to lie in the near repose of death. Hurrying through Florence he crossed the Apennines, on through Bologna and Ferrara to Venice. Here he tarried a few days, then entered the Tyrol, but not to stay. On a leaf in the book of guests, an after-traveller found registered in Scott's own handwriting his name thus, "Sir Walter Scott, *for Scotland*." On he pushed through Munich and Heidelberg to Frankfort, where he embarked on the Rhine boat, and on June the 11th he as lifted into an English steamer at Rotterdam. On the 13th he reached London. Here many friends and all his family gathered around him. His children he blessed, but was unable to converse with them. Physicians came, but medical aid was unavailing. Outside, the great city was moved as though a king were about to die. Allan Cunningham, walking home late one night, saw several working-men at the corner of Jermyn Street, near the hotel where Scott lay; and one of them eagerly asked him, "Do you know, sir, if this is the street where he is lying?" Innumerable messages were sent daily, including inquiries from every member of the royal family. And when reports were current that his funds were exhausted, the Government offered whatever was needed from the public treasury.

But Abbotsford was the spot where the brave man desired to rest. He therefore proceeded thither on July 7th. Edinburgh was reached in a state of unconsciousness, and left for ever two days afterwards. As Abbotsford came in sight he was himself again; and, catching a view of the cherished dream of his early life, which now came back to cheer his closing eyes, he uttered a cry of delight. Hardly could he be kept in the carriage till the door of the dear abode was reached. Then, carried into the dining-room, he sat down bewildered. His faithful dogs bounded in, fawned on their honoured master, and licked his hands in token of their mute welcome home. Now he smiled and now sobbed, till his exhausted nature sank into sleep. When the next morning dawned he was perfectly conscious that he was really in Abbotsford; and, as his grandchildren wheeled him round the garden, he smiled his blessing on the children, the dogs, the blooming roses, and on all besides. "Nothing like my ain house in all my travels. Just one turn more." Next day he was wheeled round again and then taken into the library, where he could look out upon the silvery Tweed. He wished Lockhart to read to him, and when his son-in-law asked from what book, the quick reply was, "Need you ask? There is but one." This man had read the most of the books in the literature of his own country, and of other lands; he had written himself hundreds of volumes; he was surrounded at that moment by a vast library of books in all languages; and yet now in his dying hour there was but one book he thought worth listening to. Lockhart read him the 14th chapter of John.

On Tuesday, the 17th, he tried to write, but the pen dropped from his helpless hand; and, with tears flowing down his cheek, he fell back upon the pillow. The right hand of the Northern Wizard had for ever lost its cunning. Day after day he lingered in a state of delirium till the 17th of September, when he awoke conscious and calm. To his son-in-law he uttered these memorable last words, "Lockhart, I may have but a minute to speak to you. My dear, be a good man; be virtuous; be religious; be a good man. Nothing else will give you any comfort when you come to lie here." Deep sleep then supervened, and on the 21st of September, 1832, in the presence of all his children, with the sinking sun shining softly in through the open casement, and the silvery Tweed outside the window creeping along in mournful monody, the spirit of Sir Walter Scott ascended to the saints' everlasting rest. His eldest son closed and kissed his eyes, and the sadly sublime tragedy was all over. The curtain has fallen; let us withdraw. Brave man! he died free of debt; every bond cancelled, every engagement cleared. Amid the sobs of a great multitude, he was laid down to rest in his narrow bed, in certain hope of a blessed resurrection. With Carlyle's beautiful words we close: "Adieu, Sir Walter, pride of all Scotchmen, take our proud and sad farewell!"

WILLIAM GILBERT CARPENTER BROUGHT TO DECISION.

IN the Life of Hay Macdowall Grant, an interesting case of religious experience is given. William Gilbert Carpenter, Craigellachie, was a most respectable, and, nominally, religious man; an office-bearer in the church. On the morning of Mr. Aitken's last Sunday at Arndilly, he was debating whether he should go to his own church or attend the English minister's service at the Barn. He wished to do what was right, and felt some scruple about leaving his regular place of worship, but it seemed as if a voice said to him,—"Go, and thou shalt hear words whereby thou mayest be saved." During the discourse he was much affected, but on his way home his impressions began to wear off, as he joined in the criticisms of his neighbours; when suddenly, just as he was entering his own door, the thought flashed across his mind, "You have not heard the words whereby you were to be saved." Upon this he became intensely miserable, and began to turn the sermon over in his mind; this time, not with a view to criticism. Then he seemed to hear these words, "Did not the preacher tell you that there was one little word upon which eternal life might be said to depend, and that word was *until*. That we must 'ask *until* we receive, and seek *until* we find'?"

Smitten to the heart, he cried, "Oh, my God, I have often sought, but not until I found; and knocked, but not until the door opened; now, by God's help, I shall be no longer guilty of this fearful trifling with God and my own soul." He went into the workshop and bolted the door, with the full determination that, by God's help, he would not leave the spot until he had found the salvation for which he had so often prayed. Then he spent a night of agonizing prayer; sometimes he knelt, sometimes he paced up and down in the restlessness of his anguish; sometimes he lay prostrate on the floor, weeping and groaning in helpless anguish before the Lord. As the morning began to dawn upon him, the terrible thought took possession of his mind,—that he had so long trifled with the truth, that there was no salvation for him. While he was thus sinking into the very depths of despair, it seemed as if the same voice, which had spoken to him twice before, whispered in his ear,—"What was the Lord's first miracle?" and he cried aloud,—"Oh, my merciful Saviour, thou didst turn the water into wine, do the same to me, for the pots are, indeed, full to the brim with the water of tears!" Then it was that, quick as a flash of lightning, his sorrow was turned into joy; the thought of the all-sufficiency of the blood of Christ to atone for his sins filled him with joy and peace, and his lips were filled with praise. When he re-entered his house he opened his Bible, and his eyes fell on the words, "One thing I know, whereas I was blind, now I see."

NEEDED AND UNEXPECTED ENCOURAGEMENT.
An Anecdote of Dr. Chalmers.

Dr. CHALMERS, says Mr. J. Wright, had been preaching in the Barony Church, Glasgow, for the venerable Dr. Burns, on the Monday after the Communion, which was, in the suburban districts, about two months after the time of its celebration in the town churches. As was customary on such occasions, Dr. Burns invited the ministers who had assisted him, and some of his elders and friends, to dinner on the Monday. I was on that day one of the party, and I was exceedingly disappointed to see that Dr. Chalmers, who, in ordinary times, poured a fascinating influence over every company where he was, seemed extremely dull, nay, I may say, dejected. When he arose, about nine o'clock, to go away, as our tract homeward lay for some distance in the same direction, I left the company along with him. When we had got together, I said to the Doctor, "Are you well enough to-day, Doctor? for I noticed you have not to-day been in your usual tune." "Oh, yes," he said, "I am quite in good health, but I am not comfortable. I am grieved in my mind." Seeing that he so frankly communicated to me the general cause of his unusual appearance, I used the freedom to say, "Well, Doctor, is this a matter that I may be made acquainted with, as if it is not, I have no wish to pry into any thing of a private nature?" "Oh, yes!" he replied, "you may perfectly know it, for it is a matter that presses very grievously upon me. In short, the truth is," said he, in his own emphatic manner, "I have mistaken the way of my duty to God, in at all coming to your city. I am doing no good. God has not blessed, and is not blessing my ministry here."

On hearing this, I replied, "Well, Doctor, it is a very remarkable circumstance that, in the providence of God, you should have been sent with your complaint to me on this point, because I have it in my power, at any rate, to mention one instance in which your ministry has been made instrumental in bringing a soul from darkness to the marvellous light of the gospel of salvation." "Can you?" said he, "then you will give me the best news I have heard since I came among you." Mr. Wright then told him how that his own minister, Dr. Balfour, of the Outer High Church, had recently, in reading over the name of an applicant for membership, said,—"By the bye, I must tell you something about this young man, for his history is somewhat interesting and singular. He sat for nearly twenty years under my ministry, but when my worthy friend, Dr. Chalmers" (for that was the almost uniform designation he gave him when he had occasion to speak of him), "came to Glasgow, he was attracted to him by his splendid talents, and sat under his ministry for about two years, and then it pleased the Lord to come to him in the day of his power; and I have every reason to think him a truly converted young man. And now that he wishes to become a member of the church, he wishes to return to us. But," added Dr. Balfour, with a truly sublime humility, "it was not under my ministry that he was turned to the Lord, though he sat for the greater part of his lifetime in the Outer Church, but it was under the preaching of Dr. Chalmers." At this needed, though unexpected word of encouragement, Dr. Chalmers exclaimed,—"Ah! Mr. Wright, what blessed, what comforting news you give me. I knew it not; but it strengthens me." This timeous news was as water to the thirsty, and food to the perishing.

SAINT COLUMBA AND HIS HORSE.

SAINT COLUMBA was a man who was full of compassion, and he exercised it not only to his own species, but to every creature under heaven. A person had the presumption to ask him to bless his dagger. "God grant it then," said the Saint, "it may never shed a drop of blood of either man or beast." On the day of his death he had been to see and to bless the provisions of his monks, from whom he was to be taken away. On his return to the monastery, he sat down on the way to rest him. His old white horse, which used to carry the milk vessels betwixt the monastery and the fold, observed him, came where he was, reclined his head upon his breast, and, as if sensible of his master's near departure, began to express his grief by groans, and even tears. Dermit, his servant, offered to turn him away, but the Saint forbade: "Let him alone," said he, "let him alone, for he loves me, and I will not hinder him on this occasion to drop his tears in my bosom, and show the bitterness of his grief. To thee God hath given reason; but see, he hath planted affection even in brutes; and in this, even something like a prescience of my departure. Now, my faithful and affectionate friend, begone, and may you be kindly cared for by Him who made you!"

A SAINTLY HIGHLAND ELDER'S ASSURANCE OF SALVATION.

Mr. HUGH MACKENZIE was born in Kilmuir Easter, in 1728; in after years he left Ross-shire, and removed to Sutherlandshire. An eminent minister, who had often met him, was struck with his habitual assurance, and, that he might know the foundation of it, he went to visit him, a distance of thirty miles. To draw him out, he said to him: "Mr. Mackenzie, you are a man to be envied; you know nothing of doubts and fears; you always enjoy the full assurance of hope." The old man replied at once,—"Yes, yes, I understand you. Many a man speaks of my strong faith that does not know all it has to struggle with. But I shall tell you what my faith is. I am the emptiest, vilest, poorest sinner I know on the face of the earth. I feel myself to be so. But I read in His own word that He heareth the cry of the poor, and I believe Him, and I cry to Him, and He always hears me, and that is all the faith or assurance I have got." The venerable minister on telling me the incident, made the remark,—"If I know anything of true faith, Mr. Mackenzie's faith is a most scriptural and a most rational one."

Some years before his death, I happened to be at his son's house when the Lord's Supper was dispensed in the parish. On Monday, Mr. Mackenzie went to the tent to hear an old minister with whom he had been long intimate, and the text was, "He will speak peace to His people, and to His saints." The wind happened to be high, and when the sermon was over, the minister said to him,—"I fear Mr. Mackenzie, you were not hearing well." "Yes," was the answer, "I was hearing all day, and believing too." In the evening I accompanied his sons to call upon the old man. When the question was put, "How do you feel, to-night?" His answer was, "My case is more easily felt than described. You read that there is a 'peace of God which passeth all understanding,' and a 'joy unspeakable and full of glory,' and that is just my case to-night." When further questioned, he remarked: "I got into this state of mind whilst hearing that precious sermon, to-day;" and then, addressing his sons, he said, "Don't think that I despise your preaching. You preach the gospel, and I bless God for it; but you have not the experience of the old minister. The preaching we had to-day about the 'peace,' is what suits my soul." In 1829 he began to sink, and his son was sent for. On being asked by his son what his views were now as to the things of eternity, he answered, with beautiful simplicity, "I leave it all in His own hands. I am not able to think much, but I know He won't send me to hell." When his end was evidently near, and when asked how he felt, he was able to whisper,—"He has been entertaining me with a promise," and, soon after, he breathed his last in the one hundred and first year of his age.

DR. CHALMERS ON HYPER-CRITICISM.

Dr. Chalmers, says one of his friends, had preached for a missionary society in Dundee, a sermon which was published at the request of those who heard it, and an acquaintance of mine, a student of divinity in the Secession denomination, had written a critique on what he considered the solecisms of its composition. This critique, which he showed to me, I thought quite hypercritical; and on his expressing an intention of sending it to the Doctor, I said, that to pounce upon a few trivial slips in so excellent a discourse would show a very captious and illiberal disposition. He, however, sent it to the Doctor, alleging, as his reason, that the Established Church ministers looked upon those of the Dissenters as far inferior to them in learning, and he wanted to show that the latter were not afraid to enter the lists with the former, in so far, at least, as related to the art of composition. A few days afterwards I was surprised at being told by an acquaintance from Kilmany that I had given much offence to the Doctor's friends by sending him a communication condemnatory of his discourse.

Feeling hurt at being considered the writer of an article of which I had disapproved, I introduced the subject to the Doctor at our next meeting, and asked him if it were true that I was suspected of having written the article in question. "Everybody," he replied, "who has heard anything about the matter believes it to have proceeded from your pen." I said that I never could have acted so disingenuous a part as to write anonymously to him on any subject, to whom I had so many opportunities of expressing what I wanted to communicate *viva voce;* that my only connection with the critique was having seen it and disapproving of it. "Then you, perhaps, know," said the Doctor, "who the writer is?" I said I did, and had obtained his permission to tell his name should it be asked. "Who is he?" inquired the Doctor. "He is," I replied, "a Mr. S., a teacher, and expects shortly to become a licentiate in the Secession

Church." "Since he has not found," said the Doctor, "the sentiments of the discourse assailable, he might have spared the diction, though he had not found it altogether invulnerable; but it is not, I think, doing him any injustice to say, that his remarks are hypercritical, and afford much less evidence of critical ability than of an ambition to be thought possessed of it—an infirmity, alas! too common, and one against which the wisest and best among us would need to be on our guard."

THUMBING THE PROMISES AT DUNFERMLINE.

SOME years ago a number of Christians met together around a social board, near the town of Dunfermline, on a Christmas evening. They enjoyed themselves in a rational Christian way, and there was a full flow of sweet feeling, and much sweet and brotherly intercourse. The good things of this life had also been enjoyed, and all the more so that they were looked upon as good and perfect gifts from the great Giver. As the shades of evening were deepening into darkness, one of the party said, "We have really had a pleasant time of it since we met together, and I was just wondering if there were no poor persons near that we might make happier by way of practically showing our gratitude to God." Addressing the eldest daughter of the family, he said, "Jane, do you know any person near who might be in want this evening of some earthly comfort which we could give?" "Yes," said the young girl addressed, "there is Nancy in the cottage, who depends on what the Lord sends her by means of those who take an interest in the poor. She has no relative to care for her. Her husband is dead long ago. Her children are all gone, and she is now left alone. She would be thankful for anything that you might give her." "Well, Jane, if you think that she is one of those whom Jesus meant when he said, '*The poor ye have always with you*,' let us raise a contribution for this widow, and you and I will go and give it to her."

No sooner was the proposal made than it was carried into execution. A considerable sum of money was given by those assembled, and Jane and her companion set out to find Nancy's humble home. It did not lie far away. When they reached the door Jane lifted the latch without any ceremony, as was her wont, and went into the place where the poor widow sat. It was now dark, and the only light in the dwelling was that which came from the few embers on the fire. Before the fire old Nancy sat with her head bent over an old book, whose words she sought to make out by the little light which the fire emitted. She did not hear them as they entered, nor did she know that there was any person in her home till the gentleman looked over her shoulder and said, "Well, Nancy, we have come to see you; what is this you are so eager in reading?" Raising her head, and looking calmly up in the stranger's face, she replied, "Well, sir, this is the Bible, and I have just been thumbing the promises, sir—I have just been thumbing the promises; and they are all true, sir—they are all true." "And what promise of God have you been meditating on?" he asked further. "I have been thumbing," she said, "that precious one in which God says, '*His bread shall be given him, his water shall be sure.*'" (Isa. xxxiii. 16.) "It has stood me in dark days that are past, and it will not fail me even in darker days to come."

The gentleman was not a little astonished at this, and inquired, "What do you mean by thumbing this promise?" "I mean," she answered, "by putting my thumb on it to remind God that he has made such a promise, and that I believe that he has done so, and look for its fulfilment." "Great is your faith, my good woman," said the gentleman, "and according to your faith so will it be done unto you, for there is the promise," pointing to the Bible, "and here is the fulfilment of it in this sum of money which has come straight from God, though it is given by man." "To His name be all the praise!" exclaimed the aged saint, as tears of gratitude streamed down her withered cheeks. "He has never disappointed me yet. His promises are all yea and amen in Christ Jesus." She then entered into a statement of her past history and present circumstances, and dwelt upon the fact that the

Lord had never left her, that she had found Him true to His word, and that she had never thumbed the promises in vain.

EDWARD IRVING AND THE SHOEMAKER.

WHEN Edward Irving was in Glasgow, he visited the families in his parish, and won their confidence and took some of them captive by innocent wiles and premeditation. A certain shoemaker, radical and infidel, was among the number of those under Irving's special care, a home workman, of course, always present, silent, with his back turned upon the visitors, and refusing any communication except a sullen *humph* of implied criticism, while his trembling wife made her deprecating curtsey in the foreground. The way in which this intractable individual was finally won over, is attributed by some tellers of the story to a sudden happy inspiration on Irving's part, but by others, to plot and intention. Approaching the bench one day, the visitor took up a piece of patent leather, then a recent invention, and remarked upon it in somewhat skilled terms. The shoemaker went on with redoubled industry at his work; but at last, roused and exasperated by the speech and pretence of knowledge, demanded, in great contempt, but without raising his eyes, "What do *ye* ken about leather?" This was just the opportunity his assailant wanted; for Irving, though a minister and a scholar, was a tanner's son, and could discourse learnedly upon that material.

Gradually interested and mollified, the cobbler slackened work, and listened while his visitor described some process of making shoes by machinery, which he had carefully got up for the purpose. At last the shoemaker so far forgot his caution as to suspend his work altogether, and lift his eyes to the great figure stooping over his bench. This conversation went on with increased vigour after this, till finally the recusant threw down his arms—"Od, you're a decent kind o' fellow!—do *you* preach?" said the vanquished, curious to know more of his victor. The advantage was discreetly, but not too

hotly pursued; and on the following Sunday the rebel
made a defiant, shy appearance at church. Next day
Irving encountered him in the savoury Gallowgate, and
hailed him as a friend. Walking beside him in natural
talk, the tall probationer laid his hand upon the shirt-
sleeve of the shrunken sedentary workman, and marched
by his side along the well-frequented street. By the
time they had reached the end of their mutual way, not
a spark of resistance was left in the shoemaker. His
children henceforth went to school; his deprecating wife
went to the kirk in peace. He himself acquired that
suit of Sunday "blacks" so dear to the heart of the poor
Scotchman, and became a church-goer and respectable
member of society; while his acknowledgment of his
conqueror was conveyed with characteristic reticence,
and concealment of all deeper feeling in the self-excusing
pretence—"He's a sensible man, yon; he kens about
leather."

THE REV. WILLIAM DUNN OF CADDER.

THE REV. WILLIAM DUNN was minister of the parish of
Cadder, at the end of last century. Well, this quiet,
decent, unoffending country minister, in the neighbourhood of Glasgow, happened to be the Moderator, for the
time being, of the Presbytery of the bounds, and as such,
it fell to his lot, or it came to be his sacred duty, to preach
a sermon before the Synod of Glasgow and Ayr, in the
city of Glasgow. This sermon, when delivered, was
relished, and was reckoned to be a very able one, and
there were some sprinklings of lofty liberality about it,
rare of its kind, which gratified the hearts of some of the
lay members of the Synod, who heard it circumspectly
in the Old Tron. They, indeed, became so prepossessed
with the manner and the matter of the sermon, that they
desired to have it printed and published at their expense.
In this laudable fervour of ecclesiastical love towards Mr.
Dunn, it happened that the Secretary of the Glasgow
Reform Association was also specially directed to write
to him a letter, conveying to him the most respectful

thanks of that association for his very excellent sermon, as they were also pleased to call it. This, at the time, naturally afforded some gratification to the worthy minister in his own quiet manse at Cadder.

Not very long after the above event, or this true history of the sermon, the beagles of the law, instructed by the Sheriff of the county of Lanark, and commanded by the then Lord Advocate, Dundas, went to Cadder to search for "*seditious* papers." The minister, some how or other, got a hint that they were coming to him at the manse, and when they rapped at his front door, he scratched his head, and began to think that the only paper he was possessed of, smacking in the least degree of "sedition," was the aforesaid letter of thanks about his relished sermon; so he ran up stairs to his old mahogany drawers, turned up that original and till then treasured letter, and threw it into the smouldering peat-fire of his own kitchen. He then made his obeisance, and frankly told the officers of the law what he had just done. Will it be credited? he was soon afterwards actually seized by the cuff of the neck, on a petition and complaint of the Lord Advocate of Scotland, for falsely and fraudulently destroying or putting away seditious letters or papers, and, on that positive complaint, he was dragged to the bar of the High Court of Justiciary in Edinburgh! He repeated to their Lordships the veritable statement as here given. He did more, he threw himself "on the *clemency* of the Court," and respectfully besought them to pardon him if he had done anything wrong.

Their Lordships, after delivering their unanimous opinions "on the *criminality* of the act of which he stood charged," solemnly declared "that if he (the Rev. Mr. Dunn) had been served with an indictment, instead of a petition and complaint, they must have inflicted on him *the highest arbitrary punishment*." As it was, and seeing he had humbly thrown himself on the clemency of the Court, they just decerned and "ordained him to be imprisoned in the Tolbooth of Edinburgh for the space of three months."

AN HONEST EXECUTIONER IN AYRSHIRE.

During the "killing time," there were so many executions in some parts of Scotland, as to make them common. So convinced were all classes of the innocence and moral worth of those who suffered, that no executioner could be prevailed upon to carry the sentence into effect. At last one of the prisoners, bribed and dragged into service, executed his companions, but soon afterwards died himself in despair. In Irvine, the hangman, a poor simple Highlander, named William Sutherland, peremptorily refused to execute the good men merely for opposing the bishops, whom he said "he had never liked since he knew how to read his Bible." Solicitations, promises, and threats, were all used with him, but in vain. They threatened him with the *boots*. "You may bring your boots and the spurs too," said William, "you shall not prevail." They swore they would pour melted lead on him—they would roll him in a barrel full of spikes; but the Highlander stood firm. They then put him in the stocks, and the soldiers having charged their pieces, and blind-folding him, rushed upon him with fearful shouts and imprecations; but all in vain. Confounded at his fortitude, they declared "that the devil was surely in him." "If the devil be in me," said William, "he is an unnatural devil, for if he were like the rest, he would bid me take as many lives as I could; but the Spirit that is in me will not suffer me to take good men's lives." "Tell me," said one of the judges, "who put these words into your mouth?" "Even He who made Balaam's ass to speak and reprove the madness of the prophet," replied William. At length, finding that they could make nothing more of him, they allowed him to escape.

ADAM SCOTT, SHEPHERD IN UPPER DALGLIESH.

Hogg tells of a shepherd of the name of Adam Scott, who lived in Upper Dalgliesh, who had a remarkable gift of prayer. He says—I had an uncle who herded with him, from whom I heard many quotations from Scott's prayers, a few of which are as follows:—

"We particular thank Thee for Thy great goodness to Meg, and that ever it came into your head to take any thought of sic an useless baw-waw as her." (This was a little girl that had been somewhat miraculously saved from drowning.)

"For Thy mercy's sake—for the sake of Thy poor sinfu' servants that are now addressing Thee in their ain shilly-shally way, and for the sake o' mair than we dare weel name to Thee, hae mercy on Rab. Ye ken yoursel he is a wild, mischievous callant, and thinks nae mair o' committing sin than a dog does o' licking a dish; but put Thy hook in his nose, and Thy bridle in his gab, and gar him come back to Thee wi' a jerk that he'll no forget the langest day he has to leeve."

"Dinna forget poor Jamie, wha's far awa' frae amang us the nicht. Keep Thy arm o' power about him, and oh! I wish ye wad endow him wi' a like spunk and smeddum to act for himsel. For if ye dinna, he'll be but a bauchle in the world, and a back-sitter in the neist."

"We're a' like snails, we're a' like slogie riddles; like hawks to do evil, like snails to do good, and like slogie riddles, that let through a' the good and keep the bad."

"Bring down the tyrant and his lang neb, for he has done muckle ill the year, and gie him a cup o' Thy wraith, and gin he winna take that, give him kelty."

Kelty signifies double, or two cups. This was an occasional petition, for one season only, and my uncle never could comprehend what it meant. The general character of Scott was one of decision and activity; constant in the duties of religion, but not over-strict with regard to some of its moral precepts.

A NOVEL WAY OF FINDING OUT CHRISTIANS.

DUNCAN MATHESON, the evangelist, in the course of his itineracy, once found himself in a strange out-of-the-way region, without a friend, without lodging, and without means. It was drawing towards night, and he knew not where to go. Seeing a boy crossing a field, he called to him, and said, "Are there any godly people here about?" "Na, na," replied the lad, "there is nae sic fouk in this parish." "Are there any believers?" asked the Evangelist. "Bleevers!" exclaimed the boy; "I never heerd o' sic things." "Any religious people, then?" "I dinna ken ony o' that kind; I doot they dinna come this road at a'." "Well, then," said the missionary, "making a last attempt, "Are there any who keep family worship?" "Family worship," replied the lad, with a bewildered look; "fat's that?" The boy having taken his last stare at the curious stranger, was about to go. Matheson was at his wit's end, when a happy thought struck him. "Stop," he cried; "Are there any hypocrites hereabout?" "Ou, aye," replied the youth, brightening into intelligence; "the fouk say that ———'s wife is the greatest hypocrite in a' the pairish." "Where is her house?" "Yonner by," said the lad, pointing to a house about a mile distant. Having rewarded his guide with a penny, the last he had, he made his way to the dwelling of "the greatest hypocrite in the parish," and knocked at the door as the shades of night were falling. The door was opened by a tidy, cheerful, middle-aged matron, to whom the stranger thus addressed himself,—"Will you receive a prophet in the name of a prophet, and you'll not lose your reward?" She smiled, and bade him welcome. The hospitalities of that Christian home were heaped upon him, and he spent a delightful evening in fellowship. In this way a lasting friendship began, and, what was better, a door of usefulness was opened to him.

A COVENANTER AND HIS DREAMS.

JAMES HOWIE was not a native of Lochgoin. He belonged to the Mearns branch of the family, but he was married to Isobel, eldest daughter of John Howie, with whom he resided after his marriage, at Lochgoin. The old man, the father-in-law, who was infirm, and much afflicted with asthma, had one night a dream of rather a striking nature. After the disaster at Pentland, a number of those concerned in that rising found refuge in the wilds in the vicinity of Lochgoin, and the residence of the Howie's became in a manner their headquarters. It was the place in the lonely waste to which they resorted for prayer and social intercourse, and the humble roof often sheltered many a hungry and weary wanderer.

One night, when a number of refugees met in his house, the aged man dreamed that he was at the Cross of Kilmarnock, and distinctly heard General Dalziel give orders to a party of his dragoons to repair to Lochgoin, the which, as it was situated in the heart of the moors, was by no means easy of access, especially to horsemen. When the party had advanced about two miles on their way, he imagined that one of the soldiers used him rudely, on which he awoke and found it was a dream.

In a little he fell asleep again, and dreamed that he met with the troopers a second time, whom he accompanied on their march till they came to a stream which they had to pass, when one of the sturdy dragoons seized him by the shoulders, and pushed him forcibly into the torrent till it reached his knees, and the sudden chill of the cold water broke his slumbers, and he began to be a little thoughtful.

He fell asleep for the third time, and once more met with the soldiers, and went along with them till they came to the bottom of the rising ground on which his dwelling stood, when, being maltreated by them as formerly, he started from his bed, and cried to the persons in concealment to look out on the moor and see if danger was approaching. One of the company ran to the little turfen eminence that was reared a few yards from the house for the purpose of observation—and which stands to this day—and saw, to his astonishment, in the grey of the morning, the muskets and points of the bayonets of a party of military just at hand. He hastened back to make the announcement, and the company within instantly made their escape, and hid themselves in the hollow of a brook behind a moss, which afforded them a retreat from the vigilance of their enemies. The worthy

old man, whose dream was the means of saving the
fugitives, hastily left his bed, and, wrapping his cloak
about him, went out and stationed himself at the end of
the house. When the party advanced, John was leaning
against the wall, and, apparently, panting for breath.
The troopers, astonished at seeing the worthy in this
position at so early an hour, cried out, taking the Divine
name in vain in a profane manner,—"What have we
here?" "It is e'en an aged man," said John, "infirm
and breathless, who is under the necessity, at this un-
seasonable hour, to seek relief in the open air. The
smoke of the fire, which, on account of the cold, he is
obliged to keep burning in the hearth, is like to stifle
him by reason of this cough." This statement seemed to
the dragoons to account naturally enough for the existence of the fire which they found blazing within, and
lulled their suspicions of its having been kept burning
for the accommodation of the party who had just fled
from the apartment. The soldiers, when they had
searched the dwelling and found nobody, entertained
themselves with what provisions they could find, and,
in the early morning, returned to Kilmarnock. Thus
the dream of the good old man, however it may be
accounted for, was the means employed by Providence
of saving a handful of helpless men, who, in the time of
their trial, sought refuge under his hospitable roof.

THE ERSKINES AS PREACHERS.

THE two brothers, Ebenezer and Ralph Erskine, were
both preachers, and remarkable men. Ebenezer was
born in 1680, and Ralph in 1685. Some one said of
Ebenezer that to hear him was "to listen to the
Gospel presented in its majesty;" and he excelled in
strength and leading power. But Ralph had more
of the orator, and of that subtlety of thought and fervour of emotion which met so remarkably in Samuel
Rutherford. In general literature, too, he was far in
advance of most of the ministers of his time, and
there was, according to tradition, a humanism in his

recreations that stumbled the more rigid, but attracted to him the mass of the people. The story of his practice on the "wee sinful fiddle," is so well known, that we do not repeat it; but there is another, showing the warmth of attachment to Ralph and his preaching. At West Linton, which was one of the early head-quarters of the Secession south of the Forth, there was a gathering of thousands to a sacrament, and the two brothers were present. The communion took place in the open air, on a beautiful green, beside the little river Lyne.

After the services, the ministers, in order to reach the manse, had to cross the stream on stepping-stones. A countryman from the far north had been so delighted and edified by Ralph's preaching that, to have a few words with him, he marched through the Lyne, step for step, beside him, with the water nearly up to his knees. Pulling out a large Highland snuff-horn, he put it in his hand, with the words, "O sir, take a pinch, it will do you meikle good." Ralph readily complied, and on his returning the horn, the worthy man, not knowing how to show his feeling, refused it, saying, "O sir, keep it, it will do me meikle good." On telling the story, and showing the gift at the manse dinner, his brother said, "Ralph, Ralph, ye hae blawn best, ye've brought away the horn," with a reference to the legend of the knight in the old tale of chivalry. It is a simple story, but it brings the two brothers near us, and lets us see how the time imprinted the little incidents on the memories of the people.

THE REV. DR. M'CRIE AND DUGALD STEWART.

WHEN the life of John Knox was first published by Dr. M'Crie, as nothing was expected, *à priori*, from the work of a Seceding clergyman, its great merit was not perceived for some time, especially by the *literati*. The way in which it first fell under the notice of the author's illustrious contemporary, Professor Dugald Stewart, was very remarkable. The professor, one Sunday, being confined at home with illness, and all the family at church, except his man-servant, he had occasion to ring his bell, to call up this faithful old attendant. To his surprise, John did not make his appearance. Again he rung the bell; but still without effect. After ringing a third time, he thought it necessary to step down stairs, to see what could possibly be the occasion of John's apparent negligence. On opening the door of the old man's apartment, he found him sitting at a little table, his eyes bent attentively upon a book, and his whole soul apparently engrossed by what he was reading. It was only on being shaken by the shoulder, that he rose from the trance of rapture in which he had been held by the book. Mr. Stewart was, of course, much surprised at the sudden turn which John's mind seemed to have taken in favour of literature; and he had the curiosity to ask what book it was which had captivated him so wonderfully. "Why sir," said John, "it's a book that *my minister* has written, and really it's a grand ane." The professor said he would take it up with him to his room, and try what he could make of it. He accordingly did so, and being once commenced, he found it fairly impossible to withdraw himself till he had completed the perusal of its whole contents. He next day waited upon Dr. M'Crie, to express the admiration he entertained for his performance, which he did in the highest possible terms. The author bowed to Professor Stewart's praises with the modesty of real genius, and replied by a compliment as exquisite as it was brief—'*Pulchrum est laudari a laudato*'—It is delightful to be praised by one who has himself gained the praise of mankind.

JAMES GUTHRIE'S COURAGE AND DEATH.

THIS Covenanter earned the hatred of the Earl of Middleton in a manner singularly characteristic both of the man and of the cause in which he was engaged. In a certain crisis Middleton proposed to aid the fallen fortunes of the King by raising a corps of Papists in the Highlands, and on account of this act of treason to Protestantism the General Assembly of the Church pronounced against him a sentence of excommunication; and it fell to the lot of Guthrie to administer from the pulpit this piece of wholesome discipline. Just prior to the time of service Guthrie received a letter—thought by some to have been written by the King—dissuading him from attempting to humiliate the nobleman in the open church. The warning only served to confirm the preacher in his purpose of obeying the Presbytery, and honouring God. That action cost the old man his life; for it was contrary to the nature of the Restoration statesmen to forgive an enemy. Guthrie was in due time arraigned on a paltry charge, which might have been equally brought against the best men of the country, and was sentenced to be hanged, and to have his head set up over the West Bow at Edinburgh. When his doom was pronounced, his heart was so wholly set upon Christ, that he came forth from the judgment-chamber with a heavenly countenance, which strangely contrasted with the profanity around him. He was an outcast from earth; but the gallows and market-cross at Edinburgh were to him the portals of heaven.

A belief in omens was common in his age, and Guthrie was not superior to the prevailing weakness. When, many years before, he had subscribed the Covenant, he was "stunned a little" by a circumstance which ruffled his composure—he met the hangman, in his uniform, passing along the street. This was an evil omen, according to the common belief, and Guthrie quite believed it to be so. What if the Covenant should entail death? The question was asked, the cost was counted, and from that hour there was no looking back. After his execution, Guthrie's remains were carried into a neighbouring church to be dressed by a number of ladies of quality; and a youth, more demonstrative than the rest, entered and anointed the body with an ointment which perfumed the whole building. Persons in sympathy with the Covenant also dipped napkins in the warm blood, declaring their intention of spreading them out before the Lord, who would avenge the innocent in his own time. Some time after Guthrie's death, a weird story gained currency in Edinburgh which, whether true or otherwise, shows the spirit of the times:—As the commissioner's carriage passed underneath where the head was spiked, some drops of blood fell upon the vehicle "which all their art could not wipe off." Men of science were consulted, and asked to account for the startling circumstance, first of the blood dripping at all, and then of the impossibility of wiping it out. Baffled and alarmed, the commissioner ordered a new covering for the carriage; but that did not mend the matter, nor remove the guilt. A crime had been committed, and his conscience could not rest.

A SOLDIER AT FORT-GEORGE.

The parish of Resolis is situated on the southern shore of the Frith of Cromarty, lying immediately to the east of the well-known Ferrintosh. In order to reach it from the coast of Nairn, one would require to cross the ferry of Fort-George, and strike athwart the peninsular district known by the name of the Black Isle. After a journey of some eight or nine miles over an immense wilderness of the most dreary moorland, lying along the entire back of the peninsula, you reach the church and manse of Resolis, situated in a spot which has lately been rendered a little more civilised looking than the desert around. At the period of our anecdote, Fort-George was garrisoned by an English regiment, which partook of the unusually profligate and debauched character of the British army at that time. As the neighbouring town of Campbeltown is at some distance from the Fort, wooden shambles had been erected close to the water's edge, immediately below the garrison, to serve as a flesh market for the convenience of the military. Having occasion one day to travel homewards by the route which, for more than one purpose, we have described, the Rev. Hector M'Phail was detained for some time below the Fort by the delay of the ferry-boat, which had to be summoned over from the opposite side. While he was standing at the water's edge, with his inseparable white pony, a soldier came into the shambles to purchase some meat, and asked the price of a quarter of mutton. The butcher named the sum. With a frightful oath, in which he pledged the everlasting salvation of his soul, the man refused to give the price, but ultimately, after a good deal of wrangling, agreed to the butcher's terms, and took up the meat to go away. All this while Mr. M'Phail, who was standing outside the shambles, overheard the conversation within, and, shocked at the awful jeopardy in which the soldier had placed his soul, was watching for an opportunity of addressing him upon the imminent danger of his condition. No sooner, therefore, had the man left the flesh market, than Mr. M'Phail contrived to throw himself in his way, and to engage him in conversation.

"A fine day, soldier." "A fine day, sir," replied the man, touching his cap. "Do you belong to the Fort?" "Yes, sir, and a dull enough place it is; nothing but drill and the blues." "You are an Englishman, I see; what is your name?" "Luke Heywood, your honour." "That seems a nice piece of mutton you have got." "So it is, sir, and cheap, too." "What did you give for it, may I ask?" The soldier named the price. "Oh! my friend," replied Mr. M'Phail, "you have given more than that." Luke Heywood looked astonished. "No, sir, I gave no more; there's the man I bought it from, and he can tell you what it cost." "Pardon me, friend; you have given your immortal soul for it. You prayed that God might damn your soul if you gave the very price you have just named; and now, what is to become of you?"

The ferry-boat was announced as ready, and Mr. M'Phail stepped on board; while Luke Heywood walked off with his purchase, and entered the Fort. Throwing off his cap, he sat down upon a form in the barrack, and in a short time his reflections turned upon his conversation with the stranger at the ferry. The gentleman's parting words were still fresh in his memory: "You have given your immortal soul for it; and now, what is to become of you?" "Really," thought he, "the stranger was quite right. I have a soul, though I had almost forgotten it; and I have pawned it for a bit of mutton, too. Well, I didn't mean that: but I have done it though; and now, what is to become of me?" The thought, even to a profligate, was anything but an agreeable one, so he tried to banish the occurrence from his memory. But it would not do; conscience was at its work, and refused to still its voice. The words of the stranger were pealing in his ears like the death-knell of his soul: "You have given your immortal soul for it; and now, what is to become of you?" In a perfect agony of terror he started from his seat, rushed bareheaded from the Fort, and arrived, all flushed and breathless, at the ferry in quest of Mr. M'Phail.

"Where is the gentleman?" cried Luke to the butcher. "What gentleman?" inquired the other. "The gentleman dressed in black clothes, and with a white pony, who told me that my soul was lost." "Oh! you mean Mr. M'Phail; he's the minister of Resolis, and you will have to go far enough till you catch him, for he has crossed more than half an-hour ago."

The ferry-boat being about to make a second passage across the water, Luke Heywood entered it, with the design of following the stranger with whose words he had been so painfully impressed. Inquiring at the ferrymen the route he must follow, Luke leaped from the boat as it touched the point of Fortrose, and started afresh upon his intensely exciting pursuit. We know not the feelings of the agitated traveller as he rushed bareheaded through the little town of Rosemarkie, or toiled all flushed and heated across the weary solitudes of Maol-bhui; we have not been informed regarding the astonishment of the shepherd or the cottar as an excited soldier hastily inquired whether he had seen anything of a clergyman upon a white pony—which was all the description he could give. He arrived, however, towards evening, at the manse of Resolis, and on demanding eagerly to see Mr. M'Phail, was immediately admitted. From the manse he came a new man, and went back to the garrison of Fort-George, singing—

> "He took me from a fearful pit,
> And from the miry clay,
> And on a rock He set my feet,
> Establishing my way."

Like the woman of Samaria, Luke Heywood now began to feel a love for the souls of others, and, with David, to say to his comrades, "Come, and I will tell you what God hath done for my soul." The word was "as fire within his bones," and he "could not but speak the things which he had seen and heard." He accordingly began to hold small prayer meetings in the barracks, and to expound the Scriptures to his fellow-soldiers. By degrees, however, the piety and zeal of the former profligate became known throughout the district; the people of God were amazed when they heard that, like Paul, he that had scoffed at them "in times past, now preached the faith which once he destroyed; and they glorified God in him." His prayer-meetings attracted others than the military, and the people began to flock from the neighbouring parishes to hear the expositions of this wonderful man. An old relation of the writer used to come down among the crowd from the parish of Ardclach, a distance of about *sixteen miles* from Fort-George; and his informant was personally acquainted with a godly old schoolmaster who had been a fellow-soldier of Luke's (and a very wild and thoughtless young man he was), but who, along with many others, owed his conversion to these prayer-meetings among the garrison.

THE LAST POPISH VICTIM IN SCOTLAND.

WALTER MILL, an old decrepit priest, who had been condemned as a heretic in the time of Cardinal Beaton, but had escaped, was at last discovered by the spies of his successor, Archbishop Hamilton, and brought to St. Andrews for trial. He appeared before the court so worn out with age and hardships, that it was not expected he would be able to answer the questions put to him; but, to the surprise of all, he managed his defence with great spirit. He was condemned to the flames; but such was the horror now felt at this punishment, and such the general conviction of the innocence of the victim, that the clergy could not prevail on a secular judge to ratify the sentence, nor an individual in the town so much as to give or sell a rope to bind the martyr to the stake, so that the Archbishop had to furnish them with a cord from his own pavilion. When commanded by Oliphant, the bishop's menial, to go to the stake, the old man, with becoming spirit, refused. "No," said he, "I will not go, except thou put me up with thy hand; for I am forbidden by the law of God to put hand on myself." The wretch having pushed him forward, he went up with a cheerful countenance, saying, "I will go unto the altar of God." "As for me," he added, when tied to the stake, his voice trembling with age, "I am fourscore years old, and cannot live long by course of nature; but a hundred better shall arise out of the ashes of my bones. I trust in God I shall be the last that shall suffer death in Scotland for this cause." So saying, he expired amidst the flames, on the 28th August, 1558. He was indeed the last who suffered in that cause, and his death was the death of Popery in the realm.

A BOY THEOLOGIAN.

DR. BALMER was a professor in the Secession Church Hall, and a man of more than ordinary parts. The first day he went with his mother to attend public worship at Jedburgh, having formerly gone with his father, during his life-time, to Morebattle, was one on which the sacrament of the Lord's Supper was dispensed. The action sermon, as it is called, was preached from a tent erected in a green adjoining the church. Robert sat before his mother on the grass. She, having never seen his demeanour in the public assembly before, was surprised and somewhat grieved by his apparent restlessness, but took no notice. However, when the services were concluded, and the little band which came from Eckfordmoss were returning, and talking by the way of what they had heard, and endeavouring to recall the particulars of the sermons delivered, he was found able to supply much of what the older people had forgotten. He had several times thus assisted them to the recollection, both of the heads of the discourses and of remarks made in illustration, when an elder who was among them, looking to his mother, said, "Margaret, do you know wha's laddie that is?" She might, no doubt, feel something of maternal pride, as she replied—"The boy is mine."

When about ten years of age, an old man, a neighbour, came frequently at leisure hours to converse with his parents. This person was harassed with doubts and fears about his interest in the Saviour. One day Robert listened while his mother argued with the poor man, and endeavoured to persuade him to dismiss his fears, and to commit himself trustingly to Christ. It was in vain. He still reiterated, "Christ will have nothing to do with me." Robert perceiving, it would seem, that the man was speaking under the influence of morbid feeling, and wilfully putting away consolation, at last put in his word. "Then what is the use of your aye talk talking about Him to my mother? If He'll have nothing to do with you, can't you let Him alone?" "Let Him alone, hinney!" the man replied, "I would not let Him alone for a thousand worlds." "O then," said the boy, "I'm thinking you'll do well enough."

ROBERT FLOCKHART AND THE BIBLE.

ROBERT FLOCKHART was a street preacher in Edinburgh, and had an aptness in quoting the Bible, and applying its truth to the souls of those he addressed. The Rev. James Robertson, who knew him well, tells us that he had a sort of instinctive dexterity with which he made the most simple incident subservient to the enforcement of Bible truths. For instance, speaking of the time when he first saw the sin-bearing Saviour, he said,— "Well, you know, after that, how I wondered that all the world did not see him too. I fell to telling all my comrades what a Saviour I had found; and there was one of them, a young lad—Edward Brown—that I took great pains to instruct in the ways of peace; but he was little the better of my concern about his soul, for he soon ran again into excess of riot. He was taken up on charge of having to do with a highway robbery, and, along with two other soldiers, was condemned to be hanged. The night before the execution, he sent for me, and said, 'You've been very kind to me, Flockhart; I want you to be my heir—to leave you all my effects.' So the morning came, when we were all ordered out to attend the execution. There were the three with the halters round their necks. I had heard o' 'mercy at the foot o' the ladder,' but I never saw it till then. For almost at the last moment a message came that there was a pardon for Edward Brown. 'Well, lad,' says I to myself, 'you've got your life, but I've lost my legacy; for a testament is of no force while the testator liveth.' But," turning to Mr. Robertson, with a beaming face, he added, "Isn't it precious that we're so sure that Jesus died; it is attested by so many 'infallible proofs.' 'He died for our sins according to the Scriptures.' We need not fear about losing our legacy because there's any doubt about the reality of his death. But we may fear something else. My wife had once a legacy left her by a lady. The lady was dead, beyond a doubt, but the lawyers got the legacy into their hands, and it was not easy, I assure you, gettin't out again. In fact, they wasted it among them, and my wife never never saw a sixpence o't. Had the kind lady been living, she would have had the business better managed. And isn't it doubly precious to 'know that our Redeemer liveth'? 'He liveth by the power of God.' He has made himself responsible to be the executor of his own will. When we put our case into his hands, he'll let none wrong us o' our legacy."

At another time, speaking of the risen Redeemer meeting his disciples on the shore of the sea of Tiberias, he observed,—"I suppose the kind salutation to them, 'Children, have ye any meat'? had a higher aim than the supply of their bodily wants. Ay, something was to be set right wi' Peter that day, and the plan Jesus took was wonderful like himself. He knew that the seafaring trade is a hungry trade, so, in order to keep Peter's temper sweet, he had a refreshment ready for him. And it was only after the meal was ended ('when they had dined') that he turned to him, and asked,—

'Simon, son of Jonas, lovest thou me?' He did not cut him short, and say, 'You denied me the other day, sir.' No, he took a more telling way of his own. The three askings would put Peter in mind of how often he had misbehaved in the high priest's hall before the cock crowed outside, and maybe the very 'fire of coals' on the shore might be just a picture of the fire at which he had warmed himself that cold night when the breath of a woman threw him down."

A MERRY GENTLEMAN'S ADVICE.

AFTER the burning of Patrick Hamilton in 1528, there was a great excitement in Scotland on religious matters. The friar Campbell who insulted him at the stake went distracted, and died in the utmost horror of mind, with the last appeal of the martyr ringing in his ears. This produced a deep impression on the popular mind, and even on those who were not apt to be affected with a mere passing prejudice. Many even in the University of St. Andrews began to call in doubt what they before held for a certain verity, and to espy the vanity of the received superstition. "Shortly after this," says Knox, "a new consultation was taken that some should be burnt. A merry gentleman, named John Lindesay, familiar servant to Bishop James Beatoun, standing by when consultation was had, said,—' My lord, gif ye burn any man, except ye follow my counsell, ye will utterly destroy yourselves. Gif ye will burn them, let them be burned in *how* [deep] *cellars*, for the reek of Mr. Patrick Hamilton has infected as many as it did blow upon.'" What immediate effect this advice had on those to whom it was tendered history saith not.

BREAD UPON THE WATERS.

A SCOTCH lady of social distinction, whose name for obvious reasons need not be mentioned, and whose husband had left her a competence, had two profligate sons, who wasted her substance with riotous living. When she saw that her property was being squandered, she determined to make an offering to the Lord. She took twenty pounds and gave it to the London Missionary Society. Her sons were very angry at this, and told her that she might just as well cast her money into the sea. "I will cast it into the sea," she replied, "and it will be my bread upon the waters." The sons, having spent all they could get, enlisted in a regiment, and were sent to India. Their positions were far apart, but God so ordered, in his providence, that both were stationed near good missionaries. The elder one was led to repent of his sins and embrace Christ. He shortly afterward died. Meanwhile the widowed mother was praying for her boys. One evening, as she was taking down her family bible to read, the door was softly opened, and the younger son appeared to greet the aged mother. He told her he had turned to God, and Christ had blotted out all his sins. Then he narrated his past history in connection with the influence the missionaries of the Cross had on his own mind, while his mother, with tears of overflowing gratitude, exclaimed,—"Oh, my twenty pounds! my twenty pounds! I have cast my bread upon the waters, and now I have found it after many days."

THE ASTRONOMICAL DISCOURSES.

IN the early part of this century, it was the custom that the clergymen in Glasgow should preach in rotation on Thursday in the Tron Church. On Thursday, the 23rd of November, 1815, this week-day service devolved on Dr. Chalmers. The entire novelty of the discourse delivered upon this occasion, and the promise held out by the preacher that a series of similar discourses was to follow, excited the liveliest interest, not in his own congregation alone, but throughout the whole community. He had presented to his hearers a sketch of the recent discoveries of astronomy—distinct in outline, and drawn with all the ease of one who was himself a master in the science, yet gorgeously magnificent in many of its details, displaying, amid "the brilliant glow of a blazing cloquence," the sublime poetry of the heavens. In his subsequent discourses, Dr. Chalmers proposed to discuss the argument, or rather prejudice, against the Christian Revelation, which grounds itself on the vastness and variety of those unnumbered worlds which lie scattered over the immeasurable fields of space. This discussion occupied all the Thursday services allotted to him during the year 1816. The spectacle which presented itself in the Trongate upon the day of the delivery of each new astronomical discourse, was a most singular one.

Long ere the bell began to toll, a stream of people might be seen pouring through the passage which led into the Tron Church. Across the street, and immediately opposite to this passage, was the old reading room, where all the Glasgow merchants met. So soon, however, as the gathering and quickening stream upon the opposite side of the street gave the accustomed warning, out flowed the occupants of the coffee-room; the pages of the *Herald* or the *Courier* were for a while forsaken, and during two of the best business hours of the day, the old reading-room wore a strange aspect of desolation. The busiest merchants of the city were wont, indeed, upon those memorable days, to leave their desks, and kind masters allowed their clerks and apprentices to follow their example. Out of the very heart of the great tumult, an hour or two stood redeemed, for the highest exercise of the spirit, and the low traffic of earth forgotten; heaven, and its high economy and its human sympathies and eternal interests, engrossed, for a while, the mind and the fancy of congregated thousands.

This series of discourses was published on the 28th January, 1817. In ten weeks 6,000 copies had been disposed of, the demand showing no symptoms of decline. Nine editions were called for within a year, and nearly 20,000 copies were in circulation. Never previously, nor since, has any volume of sermons met with such immediate and general acceptance. The "Tales of my Landlord" had a month's start in the date of publication, and even with such a competitor it ran an almost equal race. Not a few curious observers were struck with the novel competition, and watched with lively curiosity how the great Scottish preacher, and the great Scottish novelist, kept for a whole year so nearly abreast of one another. It was, besides, the first volume of sermons which fairly broke the lines which had separated too long the literary from the religious public. Its secondary merits won audience for it in quarters where evangelical Christianity was non-seated and despised. It disarmed even the keen hostility of Hazlitt, and kept him for a whole forenoon spell-bound beneath its power. "These sermons," he says, "ran like wild-fire through the country, were the darlings of watering-places, were laid in the windows of inns, and were to be met with in all places of public resort." They were received by all classes with acclaim, and their author was looked upon as one, who had done much to present the truths of Christianity in new forms, and to invest them with all the attractions of a fascinating eloquence; nor could any single volume be named which has done more than the "Astronomical Discourses," to soften and subdue those prejudices which the infidelity of natural science engenders.

SIR DAVID BREWSTER DISGUSTED.

DURING a severe illness in 1858, Sir David Brewster entertained a firm faith that death was at hand, and requested his pastor to pray for him as a dying man. It was then that his Christian faith was strengthened, and that he enjoyed a time of finding, after the long search of his life. During his convalescence, for he recovered, his daughter, Mrs. Gordon, read aloud to him. Among the books she read was a small one, entitled, "Perfect Peace," the memoir of a clever and scientific medical man, who accepted Christ after a severe struggle. He listened with his peculiar habit of vivid interest, combined, at first, with unqualified approbation. In the course of reading, they came to several of the biographer's laudatory remarks, such as the following,—"Notwithstanding his high talents, and great proficiency in professional and scientific knowledge, he talks with me in the most child-like manner on the things which concern his peace; indeed, he evinces as humble and teachable a spirit as ever I met with,"—"his humble and teachable spirit, notwithstanding his great literary and scientific attainments,"—"the pride of intellect was lost at the Cross of Christ."

These passages produced evident dissent, and when the last quoted was read, it caused an unpremeditated burst of disapprobation on the part of Sir David—more satisfactory than any set expressions could have been, and though vehement, were not bitter. "That disgusts me!" was his sudden and lively exclamation. "A merit for a man to bow his intellect to the Cross! Why, what can the highest intellect on earth do, but bow to God's word and God's mind thankfully?" and he added, with touching simplicity, "That's not *my* difficulty—what distresses me so much is, that I don't love the Bible enough."

DR. M'CRIE'S SINCERITY.

SIR GEORGE SINCLAIR, while attending the classes of the University, happened to get into conversation with a medical student, a man of learning and talents, but thoroughly sceptical in his religious opinions. The infidel stoutly maintained that no clergyman, possessed of any mental powers or liberal acquirements, *really* believed in the truth of what he preached. Sir George mentioned several clergymen to whom, in his opinion, such a suspicion could never be attached. "Can you suppose," he asked, "that Dr.," naming a reverend gentleman, "is not a sincere believer in the tenets which he preaches?" "Oh, he is a man of the world; he cannot believe in them." "What say you to Dr." so and so, naming him? "He is too much of a scientific man to be a believer," said the other, with a look of disdain. "Well, then," said Sir George, "can you say that Dr. M'Crie does not believe in the truths which he delivers?" The countenance of the sceptic fell, and, after a pause, he replied, "You have the advantage of me now; I must grant you that Dr. M'Crie would *not* preach such doctrines if he did not believe them." The sincerity of this devoted preacher closed the mouth of the gainsayer.

THE QUEEN'S TABLE AT BALMORAL.

THE REV. J. H. WILSON, who founded the "Ragged Kirk," Aberdeen, was invited by Her Majesty to Balmoral, and had the honour of dining with the Queen. During dinner wine was used, and as it went round the table Mr. Wilson passed it on, but did not touch it. On seeing this one present whispered to his neighbour, loud enough to be heard by others, that there was a gentleman at the table who did not take wine. The Queen, on hearing the remark, said, with great considerateness,— "Whoever dines at my table, it is my pleasure he may partake or refuse any beverage he pleases." During the course of the banquet, Her Majesty sent, by a special servant, one of the most magnificent bunches of grapes to Mr. Wilson, that she might thus acknowledge him as her most honoured guest.

MARY CAMPBELL AND THE GIFT OF TONGUES

THE intensely devoted and pious Mary Campbell of Gareloch fame, lived at Fernicarry, near Row, and was the subject, about the year 1830, of peculiar experiences, regarding which there was very great interest excited at the time in the West of Scotland. She, with many others, believed that the gift of tongues and other special gifts were to be vouchsafed to the Church, and that the advent of the Lord was at hand.

On a Sunday evening in the month of March, Mary, in the presence of a few friends, began to utter sounds to them incomprehensible, and believed by her to be a tongue such as of old might have been spoken on the day of Pentecost, or among the Christians of Corinth. This was the first manifestation of the restored "gift," for such it was imagined to be. She was anxious to ascertain what the tongue was, in order that she might, if strengthened to do so, repair to the country where it was intelligible, and there begin her long-contemplated labours. By and bye, she announced that she believed it to be the language of a group of islands in the southern Pacific Ocean; but as nobody knew the speech of the said islanders, it was impossible either to refute or corroborate her assertion; and, for the time, at least, she was unable to proceed in person in quest of the remote savages, whose mother tongue, she held, had been revealed to her.

MARY CAMPBELL'S BELIEF IN MIRACULOUS HEALING POWER.

AMONG many other strange incidents regarding this singular but intensely religious woman, the following may be given. It is Mary's own account of her recovery from a very serious illness, which had caused herself much suffering, and her friends much anxiety. The reader will bear in mind what is said in the previous anecdote with regard to belief in the restoration of the special gifts to the Church.

"On the Saturday previous to my restoration to health, I was very ill, suffering from pain in my chest and breathlessness. On the Sabbath I was very ill, and lay for several hours in a state of insensibility. Next day I was worse than I had been for several weeks previous, the agony of Saturday excepted. On Tuesday I was no better. On Wednesday I did not feel quite so languid, but was suffering some pain, from breathing and palpitation of my heart. Two individuals who saw me about four hours before my recovery, said that I would never be strong—that I was not to expect a miracle to be wrought upon me. It was not long after until I received dear brother James M'Donald's letter, giving an account of his sister being miraculously raised up, as in New Testament times; and in which he similarly commanded me to rise and walk also. I had scarcely read the first page when I became quite overpowered, and laid it aside for a few minutes; but I had no rest in my mind until

I took it up again, and began to read. As I read, every word came home with power, and when I came to the command to arise, it came home with a power which no words can describe; it was felt to be, indeed, the voice of Christ; it was such a voice as could not be resisted. A mighty power was instantaneously exerted upon me. I felt as if I had been lifted from off the earth, and all my diseases taken from off me at the voice of Christ. I was verily made in a moment to stand upon my feet, leap and walk, sing and rejoice."

Mary Campbell, who before this time had been confined to bed; from this moment, without any interval, returned to active life, became, as was natural, the centre of double curiosity and interest; spoke, expounded, gave forth the utterances of her power in crowded assemblies, and entered into the full career of a prophetess and gifted person. The M'Donalds, less demonstrative, and more homely, went on upon their modest way, attracting crowds of observers, without being thereby withdrawn from the composed and sober course of their existence; and thus a new miraculous dispensation was, to the belief of many, inaugurated in all the power of apostolic times, by these waters of the West.

ST. ANDREW AND SCOTLAND.

AFTER the ascension of our Lord, the name of St. Andrew is not mentioned in the New Testament, but he is believed to have travelled as a missionary through Asiatic and European Scythia; to have afterwards passed through Thrace, Macedonia, and Epirus, into Achaia; and at a city of Patra, in the last-named region, to have suffered martyrdom about 70 A.D. It is said that a Christian lady of rank, named Maximela, caused the body of St. Andrew to be embalmed and honourably interred, and that in the earlier part of the fourth century, it was removed by the Emperor Constantine to Byzantium, or Constantinople, where it was deposited in a church erected in honour of the twelve apostles. The history of the relic does not end here, for we are informed that about thirty years after the death of Constantine in 368 A.D., a pious Greek monk, named Regulus, conveyed the remains of St. Andrew to Scotland, and there deposited them on the eastern coast of Fife, where he built a church, and where afterwards arose the renowned city and cathedral of St. Andrews. Whatever credit may be given to this legend, it is certain that St. Andrew has been regarded from time immemorial as the patron saint of Scotland; and his day, November 30, is a favourite occasion of social and national reunion amid Scotchmen residing in England and other places where Scotchmen dwell.

BROWNLOW NORTH'S SUDDEN AWAKENING.

Mr. Brownlow North was the subject of a remarkable spiritual awakening, which he narrated to the students of the Edinburgh University in 1862. "It pleased God," he said, "in the month of November, 1854, one night when I was sitting playing at cards, to make me concerned about my soul. The instrument used was a sensation of sudden illness, which led me to think I was going to die. I said to my son, 'I am a dead man, take me up stairs.' As soon as this was done, I threw myself down on the bed. My first thought then was, now what will my forty-four years of following the devices of my own heart profit me? In a few minutes I shall be in hell, and what good will all these things do me for which I have sold my soul? At that moment I felt constrained to pray, but it was merely the prayer of the coward, a cry for mercy. I was not sorry for what I had done, but I was afraid of the punishment of my sin. And yet there was something trying to prevent me putting myself on my knees to call for mercy, and that was the presence of the maidservant in the room, lighting my fire.

"Though I did not believe at that time that I had ten minutes to live, and knew that there was no possible hope for me but in the mercy of God, and that if I did not seek that mercy I could not expect to have it, yet such was the nature of my heart and of my spirit within me, that it was a balance with me, a thing to turn this way or that, I could not tell how, whether I should wait till that woman left the room, or whether I should fall on my knees and cry for mercy in her presence. By the grace of God I did put myself on my knees before that girl, and I believe it was the turning-point with me. I believe that if I had at that time resisted the Holy Ghost—of course, I cannot say, for who shall limit the Holy Ghost?—but my belief is that it would have been once too often. By God's grace I was not prevented. I did pray, and though I am not what I should be, yet I am this day what I am, which, at least, is not what I was. I mention this because I believe that every man has in his life his turning-point. I believe that the sin against the Holy Ghost is grieving the Spirit once too often."

THE REV. DR. MACLEOD AND A WAIF.

THE REV. DR. NORMAN MACLEOD when in Dalkeith, in a letter to his mother, depicts a waif thus :—" On coming home one evening, I saw a number of boys following and speaking to, and apparently teasing, a little boy, who, with his hands in his pockets and all in rags, was creeping along close by the wall. He seemed like a tame caged bird which had got loose, and was pecked at and tormented by wild birds. I asked the boys who he was. 'Eh! he's a wee boy gaun' aboot beggin', without faither or mither!' He did seem very wee, poor child—a pretty boy, only nine years old. I found him near my gate, and took him in. I asked him to tell me the truth. He said his father was alive—a John Swan—in Kirkcaldy; that his 'ain mither' was dead; that he had a stepmother; that 'a month and a-week ago' he left them, for they used to send him to beg, to drink the money he got, and to thrash him if he brought none in, and that they sent him out one evening, and he left them. He got threepence from a gentleman, and crossed in the steamboat to Leith. He had heard that he was born in Kirkhill, near this, 'and that his mither lived there wi' him when he was a bairn.'

He got shelter in a stable, and there he has been ever since, begging round the district. Poor infant! Jessie, my servant, once a servant in some charitable institution, was most minute in her questionings about Kirkcaldy, but his answers were all correct and very innocent.

"Well, a few minutes after, Jessie came in. 'What,' said I, 'are you doing with the boy?' 'O, I gied him his supper, puir thing, and am making a shake down for him; and, ye see, I saw he was vera dirty, and I put him in a tub o' water, and he's staunin' in't 'e noo till I gang ben. That's the way we used to do in the Institution. Eh, if ye saw the boys frae the Hielans that used to come there! Keep me! I couldna eat for a week after cleanin' them, and wee Swan is jist as bad. I wadna tell ye hoo dirty he is, puir bairn! I couldna thole tae pit him tae his bit bed yon way. I cast a' his duds outside the door, and sent Mary Ann straight up tae the factor's for a sack for him; for ye see, whan we washed them in the Institution ——.' 'Be off,' said I, 'and don't keep the poor fellow in the tub longer.' I went in a few minutes after, and there I found him, or rather saw something like a ghost amongst mist, Jessie scrubbing at him, and seeming to enjoy the work with all her heart. 'How do you like it?' 'Fine, fine!' But just as I wrote the above word the door was opened, and in marches my poor boy, paraded in by Jessie—a beautiful boy, clean as a bead, but with nothing on but a large beautiful clean shirt, his hair combed and divided, and Jessie gazing on him with admiration, Mary Ann in the background. The poor boy hardly opened his lips; he looked round him in bewilderment. 'There he is,' said Jessie; 'I am sure ye're in anither warld the nicht, my lad. Whan were ye clean afore?' 'Three months syne.' 'War ye ever as clean afore?' 'No.' 'What will ye dae noo?' 'I dinna ken.' 'Will ye gang awa' and beg the nicht.' 'If ye like.' 'No,' said I, 'be off to your bed and sleep.' Poor child, if his mother is in heaven she will be pleased. If charity covers a multitude of sins, Jessie Wishart will get her reward."

THE REV. DR. LAWSON AND THE CAPTIOUS CHURCH MEMBER.

When Dr. Lawson received a call to Selkirk, there was one member of the church who opposed his settlement. This member took every opportunity to annoy the young minister, and put him out. One day, when on a diet of pastoral visitation, he came to this person's house, and being desirous of conciliating him, he entered into conversation with him in a very frank and friendly style. His mildness, however, had no mollifying effect; this person watched every opportunity to contradict and find fault with him. At length captiousness had the effrontery to assert, that the young minister had actually told a lie since entering the house, when he meekly said—"I am not aware of having committed so grave a misdemeanour as that with which you charge me." "Yes," rejoined the man, "you have; for, when I asked you to stay and take tea with us, you replied that you would not, and yet you have done both; is not this something like telling a lie?"

"You must have read the story," answered Mr. Lawson, "of the angels in Sodom who, when Lot pressed them to enter his house and lodge with him during the night, refused, and said, 'Nay; but we will abide in the street all night;' and instead of doing so, when Lot pressed them much, 'they turned in unto him, and entered into his house: and he made them a feast, and did bake unleavened bread, and they did eat.' Now, do you suppose that these angels told a lie? No, they only changed their mind; and so I too have just changed my mind, and have remained to partake of your fare." This proved a silencer to the individual who had, in his conceit, opined that he had caught the good man in a snare. The youthful Samson showed that the withes wherewith he was bound, were as tow when it toucheth the fire. This is the sort of treatment all such captious persons should receive, and if they were so dealt with in a good spirit, they would be made quieter, if not better, members of the Christian community

EBENEZER ERSKINE AND THE MURDERER.

The Rev. Ebenezer Erskine, after travelling, at one time, towards the end of the week, from Portmoak to the banks of the Forth, on his way to Edinburgh was, with several others, prevented by a storm from crossing that frith. Thus obliged to remain in Fife during the Sabbath, he was employed to preach, it is believed, in Kinghorn. Conformably to his usual practice, he prayed earnestly in the morning for the Divine countenance and aid in the work of the day; but suddenly missing his note-book, he knew not what to do. His thoughts, however, were directed to the command, "Thou shalt not kill;" and having studied the subject with as much care as the time would permit, he delivered a short sermon on it in the forenoon. Having returned to his lodging, he gave strict injunctions to the servant that no one should be allowed to see him during the interval of worship. A stranger, however, who was also one of the persons detained by the state of the weather, expressed an earnest desire to see the minister; and having with difficulty obtained admittance, appeared much agitated, and asked him, with great eagerness, whether he knew him, or had ever seen or heard of him.

On receiving assurance that he was totally unacquainted with his face, character, and history, the gentleman proceeded to state that his sermon on the sixth commandment had reached his conscience; that he was a murderer; that being the second son of a Highland laird, he had, some time before, from base and selfish motives, cruelly suffocated his elder brother, who slept in the same bed with him; and that now he had no peace of mind, and wished to surrender himself to justice, to suffer the punishment due to his horrid and unnatural crime. Mr. Erskine asked him if any other person knew anything of his guilt. His answer was, that so far as he was aware, not a single individual had the least suspicion of it, on which the good man exhorted him to be deeply affected with a sense of his atrocious sin, to make an immediate application to the blood of sprinkling, and to bring forth fruits meet for repentance; but at the same time, since, in providence, his crime had hitherto remained a secret, not to disclose it, or give himself up to public justice. The unhappy gentleman embraced this well-intended counsel in all its parts, became truly pious, and maintained a friendly correspondence with Mr. Erskine in after life.

THE REV. DR. JAMIESON AND THE SUGGESTED TEXT.

A REMARKABLE case occurred in the ministry of the Rev. Dr. Jamieson, author of the "Scottish Etymological Dictionary," which evinces the sympathy and long-suffering patience which the compassionate Saviour, who, on the morning of his resurrection, showed himself first to the weeping and desolate Mary Magdalene, bears to the humblest and the most solitary of his people. One week the Doctor, after returning from the meeting of Presbytery, prepared his lecture for the Sabbath forenoon; but after doing so, he found that he could not succeed in committing it to memory. No portion of it would adhere to his recollection. Various efforts were made, but all without avail. He felt that he could not deliver the lecture, and at last resolved to abandon the idea of attempting to give it at that time. But what was he to do? He had nothing else to put in its place. The Sabbath morning came, and he did not know the subject on which he was to speak. He went to the pulpit, sang and prayed, and still he had no text. During the singing of the second psalm, he resolved that, in the peculiar circumstances, he would throw himself upon his Divine Master, open the Bible, and take the first passage that would meet his eye. The only limitation made was that it should be in the Book of Psalms. The words on which his eye rested were, "Blessed is he whose transgression is forgiven, whose sin is covered; blessed is the man unto whom he Lord imputeth not iniquity" (Ps. xxxii. 1, 2); from which he preached with great ease and comfort.

In a few weeks the matter was explained. A poor woman, a member of the congregation, who lived in a house by herself, called on him and made the following disclosure:—Being in very poor and destitute circumstances, and seeing many of the wicked around her in the enjoyment of wealth, ease, and luxury, she began to think that God was unjust, and that He did not regard those who feared and served Him. These thoughts so affected her, that, after many painful struggles, she concluded that religion was a delusion, the Bible a fable, and that there was no God. Having done so, she resolved to lead the life of an Atheist. One Saturday night, she went to her bed without prayer—a thing which she had not done from her infancy. It was a night of agony. She could neither rest nor sleep; and towards morning the thought struck her that she would take farewell of God upon her knees. "And sir," said she, trembling and weeping, "I had the awful presumption to dictate to God, and to make this bargain with Him: I said, that if the Bible was true, and that if you were His servant, as you said you were, He would make you that forenoon preach from these words that I mentioned, 'Blessed is the man unto whom the Lord imputeth not iniquity.' If you did this, I engaged to serve God; and, if you did not do this, I was to abandon Him altogether. I came to the church in a state of mind that cannot be described. You opened the Bible, read these words, and preached from them. My bands were loosed, and I went home rejoicing. Oh! is not the Lord our God merciful and gracious, long-suffering, and slow to anger! And may we not say of Him, that He will not break the bruised reed, nor quench the smoking flax, and that He does not deal with us as our sins deserve; for as the heavens are high above the earth, so great is His mercy towards them that fear him?"

SEEKING FOR GOD IN THE SCOTTISH HIGHLANDS.

MANY years ago, and long before any awakening had taken place in Skye, a young girl, of little more than childish years, residing in a glen, which during the revival of 1812 was distinguished by much of divine power, became deeply impressed with the idea that God was not in her native isle. At the same time, she was overcome by the feeling that she must go in pursuit of Him where He was to be found. She stole away from her home, and travelled across the country to the usual ferry to the mainland. She made no secret of her errand, and as her relations had taken up the opinion that she had become insane, little attempt was made to recall her. So soon as she was out of Skye, she began to ask every passenger where she might find God, for that He was not in her country. Her question excited surprise, but as her manner expressed sincerity and deep earnestness, every one answered her soothingly, and was unwilling to interfere with the hallucination under which they conceived she laboured. At length she reached Inverness. The first person she met in the street was a lady, to whom she addressed her usual question. The lady was struck by her earnest manner, and engaged in conversation with her until assured of her sanity. "Come with me," at last the lady said, "perhaps I can bring you to where God is." She took her home, and next day being Sunday, took her to the house of God. For the first time the gospel was proclaimed in her hearing, and it came with power and blessing to her soul. She soon became a happy convert, and one of the brightest Christians of her day.

THE REV. ROBERT BRUCE OF EDINBURGH.

This minister of the gospel was a man of great power, and so impressed King James, that he said Mr. Bruce was worthy of half of his kingdom. He was a man that had much inward exercise, and had been often assaulted anent that great foundation truth if there was a God; which cost him many days and nights wrestling. When he had come to the pulpit, after being sometime silent, which was his usual way, he would say, "I think it is a great matter to believe there is a God," telling the people it is a greater thing to believe *that*, than they judged.

Great success attended his ministrations in Inverness, Edinburgh, and wherever he preached. A rather remarkable conversion under his ministry occurred on this wise. Mr. Henderson, who at his first entry to the ministry at Leuchars, was very prelatic, and by the Bishop of St. Andrews brought in against the parish's consent, so that, on the day of his admission, the church doors being shut by the people, they were forced to break in by a window to get him entrance. But a little after this, upon the report of a communion where Mr. Bruce was to help, he would needs, from a longing he had to hear and see such a man, go secretly there, and placed himself in a dark part of the church where he might not be known.

When Mr. Bruce was come to the pulpit, he did for a considerable time keep silence, as his manner was, which did some way astonish Mr. Henderson; but much more when he heard the first words wherewith he began, which were these,—"He that cometh not in by the door, but climbeth up another way, the same is a thief and a robber;" which did, by the Lord's blessing, at the very present take him by the heart, and had so great an impression on him, that it was the first mean of his conversion. When aged, and through infirmity of body confined to his chamber, where he was frequently visited by his friends, being asked by one of them how matters now stood betwixt God and his soul, he made this return,—"When I was a young man," said he, "I was diligent, and lived by faith on the Son of God; but now I am old, and not able to do much, yet He condescendeth to feed me with lumps of sense."

And that morning before the Lord removed him, he came to breakfast at his table, and having, as he used, eaten one single egg, he said to his daughter, "I think I am yet hungry, ye may bring me another egg;" but instantly thereafter falling into a deep meditation, and after having mused a while, he said, "Hold, daughter, hold; my Master calls me!"

With these words his sight failed him, whereupon he called for a Bible, but finding his sight gone, he said,—

"Cast up to me the 8th chapter to the Romans, and set my finger on these words, 'I am persuaded, that neither death, nor life, nor angels, nor principalities, nor powers, nor things present, nor things to come, nor height, nor depth, nor any other creature, shall be able to separate us from the love of God, which is in Christ Jesus our Lord.' Now," said he, "is my finger upon them?" When they told him it was, without any more, he said, "Now God be with you, my children; I have breakfasted with you, and shall sup with my Lord Jesus Christ this night," and so gave up the ghost, death shutting his eyes, that he might see God. Thus that valiant champion for the truth, who, in his appearing to plead for the crown and interest of Jesus Christ, knew not what it was to be daunted by the face and frowns of the highest and most incensed adversaries, was, by his Master, taken off the field, as more than a conqueror, and as the reward of much faithful diligence about the souls of others, and much pains and seriousness about making his own calling and election sure, had an entrance ministered unto him abundantly into the everlasting kingdom of his Lord and Saviour Jesus Christ.

SAINT COLUMBA RECEIVING A LESSON IN CHARITY.

SAINT COLUMBA spent much of his time in giving charity and procuring relief for the needy. He did this by every method in his power, beside praying for the blessing of God to increase their store. Still, he required a lesson in charity, and he received it thus. We are told, that after he had erected the monastery of Dunough, he ordered a hundred poor persons to be served with victuals every day at a certain hour, and appointed an almoner for that purpose. One day a mendicant came to apply for a share of this charity, but was told by the almoner that he could have nothing, as the appointed number had been already served. He came the second day, and was told in like manner that he was come too late, and that for the future he must come earlier, if he expected his share of the charity. The third day, however, he came as late as before, and when the almoner gave him the same reply as formerly, he bade him go and tell the abbot from him that he ought not to limit his charity by any precise rules which God had not prescribed, but always to give while he had, in whatever number, time, or manner, the poor should apply to him. Columba, upon receiving this message, ran hastily after the mendicant, who had then assumed a heavenly form, which gave him to understand to whom he was indebted for the counsel. From that day forward Columba laid aside his rules, and gave to all objects, at all times, provided he had any to bestow. If at any time he had not, his tears would flow, till God enabled him to relieve their wants. For this reason, the Saint was esteemed, what he really was, the common father and patron of the poor and needy.

THE GENERAL ASSEMBLY AND FOREIGN MISSIONS IN 1796.

THE subject of sending missionaries to the heathen was introduced for discussion to the General Assembly of the Kirk of Scotland in 1796. It soon appeared that there were considerable difference of opinion on the subject. The moderate party pronounced the idea to be "preposterous." One of their leaders argued that it "reversed the order of nature;" that "men must be polished and refined in their manners before they can be properly enlightened in religious truths;" that "the proposed method by missions was like teaching a child the *Principia* of Newton ere he is made at all acquainted with the letters of the alphabet;" that "the heathen did not need the gospel, as the savage had his own simple virtues after his own rude type, and that to send the gospel to him, and perhaps 'some of the vices of civilised society' along with it, might not tend to 'refine his morals or insure his happiness,' which reminds one of Prince Kung's request to Sir Rutherford Alcock— 'Now that you are going home, I wish you would take away with you *your opium* and *your missionaries.*'"

These sentiments roused the venerable Dr. Erskine. Starting to his feet, and stretching his arms towards the Moderator, he exclaimed, "Rax (reach) me that Bible!" and from it he quoted and enforced, with telling power, those texts in which an apostle declared himself a debtor to the barbarian as much as to the Greek, and pronounced the gospel to be the power of God unto salvation to every one that believeth. The Moderates, however, were not to be moved. One of them smelt in the young missionary societies and their "common fund," secret clubs that might be "turned against the constitution," and therefore he would oppose them. Since those days this same Church has done much to send the gospel to heathen lands, and at present is most zealous in the great missionary enterprise.

CHRISTIAN CHARITY OVERCOMING UNBELIEF.

JOSEPH BARKER, who was once an infidel, and lecturer against the Bible and Christianity, gives the following in his work, "Teachings of Experience." He says—A gentleman whose conduct left a very favourable impression upon my mind was Colonel Shaw, of Ayr, Scotland. He was a retired officer, but being a real Christian, and a good speaker, he employed a considerable portion of his time in preaching the Gospel. How it came to pass I do not exactly remember, but it was arranged that he and I should have a public discussion on the divine authority of the Bible. The discussion took place in the City Hall, Glasgow. The Colonel was so very kind and gentlemanly, that I found my task exceedingly difficult. It was very unpleasant to speak lightly of the faith of so good and true a man; or to say anything calculated to hurt the feelings of one so guileless and so affectionate. And many a time I wished myself employed about some other business, or engaged in contest with some other man. At the end of the second night's debate we were to rest two days, and the Colonel was so kind as to invite me, and even to press me, to spend those days with him

at his residence near Ayr. The Colonel had given his
good lady so favourable an account of my behaviour in
the debate, that she wrote to me enforcing her good
husband's invitation.

I went. I could do no other. The Colonel and his
venerable father met me at the station with a carriage,
and I was soon in the midst of the Colonel's truly
Christian and happy family. Neither the Colonel nor
any of his household attempted to draw me into controversy. Not a word was spoken that was calculated
to make me feel uneasy. There seemed no effort on the
part of any one, yet every thing was said and done in
such a way as to make me feel myself perfectly at home.
Love, true Christian love, under the guidance of the
highest culture, was the moving spirit in the Colonel's
family circle. A visit to the birth-place of Burns, and
to the banks of Bonnie Doon was proposed, and a most
delightful stroll we had, made all the more pleasant by
the Colonel's remarks on the various objects of interest
that came in view, and his apt and ready quotations of
passages from the works of the poet, referring to the
scenery amidst which we were moving.

On our return home I was made to feel at ease again
with regard to everything but myself. I felt sorry that
I should be at variance with my kind and accomplished
host, on a subject of so much interest and importance as
religion and the Bible. The thought that on the evening of the coming day I should have to appear on the
platform again as his opponent, was really annoying.
To talk with such a man privately, in a free and friendly
way, seemed proper enough, but to appear in public as
his antagonist, seemed too bad.

When we started from Ayr to Glasgow in the same
train, and in the same carriage, I felt as if I would much
rather have travelled in some other direction, or on a different errand. But an agreement had been made, and it
must be kept; so two more nights were spent in discussion.
But it *was* discussion—fair and friendly discussion—and
not quarrelling. Neither he nor I gave utterance to an
unkind or reproachful word. When the discussion was

over, the Colonel shook me by the hand in a most hearty manner in the presence of an excited audience, and presented me with a book as an expression of his respect and good feeling. I made the best return I could, unwilling to be too much outdone by my gallant and Christian friend. The audience, divided as they were on matters of religion, after gazing some time on the spectacle presented on the platform, as if at a loss what to do, or which of the disputants they should applaud, dropped their differences, and all united in applauding both, and the disputants and the audience separated with the heartiest demonstrations of satisfaction and mutual good will. The events of those days, and the impression I received of my opponent's exalted character, never faded from my memory. And though they had not all the effect they ought to have had, their influence on my mind was truly salutary. I have never thought of Colonel Shaw and his good, kind, Christian family, without affection, gratitude, and delight. He wrote to me repeatedly after my return to America, and his letters, which reached us when we were living among the wilds of Nebraska, were among our pleasantest visitants, and must be reckoned among the means of my recovery from the horrors of unbelief.

IRVING AND THE SCOFFER.

WHEN Edward Irving was in Glasgow, he attended a social party at the house of one of the members of his church. A young man was present who had permitted himself to talk profanely, in a manner now unknown, and which would not be tolerated in any party now-a-days. After expending all his little wit upon priestcraft and its inventions, this youth, getting bold by degrees, at last attacked Irving — who had hitherto taken no notice of him—directly, as one of the world-deluding order. Irving heard him out in silence, and then turned to the other listeners. "My friends," he said, "I will make no reply to this unhappy youth, who hath attacked the Lord in the person of his servant; but let us pray that this his sin may not be laid to his charge," and with a solemn motion of his hand, which the awe-struck diners-out instinctively obeyed, Irving rose up to his full majestic height, and solemnly commended the offender to the forgiveness of God.

AN ANTIQUE SCOTTISH MATRON.

As a certain minister was waiting for converse with his young communicants, an old woman, neatly dressed in kirtle and snood, like any well-to-do cottar's wife of the last century, was introduced. On asking her errand, she answers with a bright twinkle in her eye,—"Are na ye waiting for the young folk?" It is rejoined that she is "surely rather an old disciple." Her reply is,—"Only seventy-eight past; but to make a lang story short, I have just come from the country, have been studying baith sides of present controversies, and think your folks as near the truth as ony o' them, and having tried your gifts for my edification, I am anxious to become a member of your church, if you are willing to tak' me." On being reminded that it less concerned the minister what church one belonged to, than to be assured that we belonged to Christ, she replied, "Yes, but disna Christ demand a reasonable service? I have been upwards of sixty years a member of the kirk, but I have brought no certificate, for if I canna gie, to every man that asketh me, a reason of the hope that is in me, I am unfit to be a member ony gaet." She proved to be an expert Bible Christian, and by her ready wit and caustic humour, a dangerous antagonist in any religious controversy. An over zealous missionary once intruded into her house, and began to ask the character of some of her neighbours. Her answer was,—"I allow no one to meddle with me, and my Bible does not allow me to be a tale-bearer." On the same occasion, it being insinuated that she had far to go to her church, instantly she answered, "A willing heart maks licht heels."

DR. JOHN BROWN'S EARLY EXPERIENCES.

On the morning of the 28th May, 1816, writes Dr. John Brown, my eldest sister Janet, and I, were sleeping in the kitchen-bed, with Tibbie Meek, our only servant. We were all three awakened by a cry of pain—sharp, insufferable, as if one were stung. Years after, we two confided to each other, sitting by the burnside, that we thought that "great cry" which rose at midnight in Egypt must have been like it. We all knew whose voice it was, and, in our night clothes, we ran into the passage, and into the little parlour to the left hand, in which was a bed-closet. We found our father standing before us, erect, his hands clenched in his black hair, his eyes full of misery and amazement, his face white as that of the dead. He frightened us. He saw this, or else his intense will had mastered his agony, for taking his hands from his head, he said, slowly and gently, "Let us give thanks," and turned to a little sofa in the room; there lay our mother, dead. She had long been ailing. I remember her sitting in a shawl—an Indian one, with little dark-green spots on a light ground—and watching her growing pale with what I afterwards knew must have been strong pain. She had, being feverish, slipped out of bed, and grandmother, her mother, seeing her "change come," had called my father, and they, two, saw her open her blue, kind, and true eyes, "comfortable" to us all "as the day"—I remember them better than those of any one I saw yesterday—and, with one faint look of recognition to him, close them till the time of the restitution of all things.

"She had another morn than ours."

My mother was buried in a quiet little churchyard in Symington, lying in the shadow of Tinto, a place where she herself had wished to be laid. The funeral was chiefly on horseback. We, the family, were in coaches. I had been since the death in a sort of stupid musing and wonder, not making out what it all meant. I knew my mother was said to be dead. I saw she was still,

and laid out, and then shut up, and didn't move; but I
did not know that when she was carried out in that
long black box, and we all went with her, she alone was
never to return. When we got to the village all the
people were at their doors. One woman, the blacksmith
Thomas Spence's wife, had a nursing baby in her arms,
and he leapt up and crowed with joy at the strange
sight, the crowding horsemen, the coaches, and the nod-
ding plumes of the hearse. This was my brother William,
then nine months old, and Margaret Spence was his
foster-mother. Those with me were overcome at this
sight, he of all the world whose, in some way, was the
greatest loss, the least conscious, turning it to his own
childish glee.

We got to the churchyard, and stood round the open
grave. My dear old grandfather was asked by my
father to pray—he did. I don't remember his words; I
believe he, through his tears and sobs, repeated the
divine words,—"All flesh is grass, and all the good-
liness thereof is as the flower of the field; the grass
withereth, the flower fadeth, but the word of the Lord
endureth for ever;" adding in his homely and pathetic
way, that the flower would again bloom, never again to
fade; that what was now sown in dishonour and weakness, would be raised in glory and power, like unto His
own glorious body. Then to my surprise and alarm, the
coffin, resting on its bearers, was placed over that dark
hole, and I watched with curious eye the unrolling of
those neat black bunches of cords, which I have often
enough seen since. My father took the one at the head,
and also another smaller springing from the same point
as his, which he had caused to be put there, and unrolling
it, put it into my hand. I twisted it firmly round my
fingers, and awaited the result; the burial men, with
their real ropes, lowered the coffin, and when it rested
at the bottom, it was too far down for me to see it—the
grave was made very deep, as he used afterwards to tell
us, that it might hold us all—my father first and abruptly
let his cord drop, followed by the rest. This was too
much. I now saw what was meant, and held on, and

fixed my fist and feet, and I believe my father had some
difficulty in forcing open my small fingers; he let the
little black cord drop, and I remember, in my misery
and anger, seeing its open end disappearing in the gloom.

A FRUITFUL SERMON OF THE REV. DR. CHALMERS.

AFTER Dr. Chalmers passed through the spiritual crisis
which changed the whole spirit and style of his pulpit
ministrations, he achieved wonders; many under his
word were born again. One instance is given. It was
in the spring of 1812, and the preacher's text was John
iii. 16—" God so loved the world, that he gave his only
begotten Son, that whosoever believeth on him should
not perish, but have everlasting life." Two young men
heard this sermon, the one, the son of a farmer in the
parish; the other, the son of one of the villagers. They
met as the congregation dispersed. "Did you feel
anything particular in church, to-day?" Alexander
Paterson said to his acquaintance, Robert Edie, as they
found themselves alone upon the road. "I never," he continued, " felt myself to be a lost sinner till to-day, when
I was listening to that sermon." "It is very strange,"
said his companion, "it was just the same with me."
They were near a plantation, into which they wandered,
as the conversation proceeded. Hidden at last from all
human sight, it was proposed that they should join in
prayer. Screened by the opening foliage, they knelt on
the fresh green sod, and poured out in turn their earnest
petitions to the hearer and answerer of prayer. Both
dated their conversion from that day. Alexander
Paterson went shortly afterwards to reside in the neighbouring parish of Dairsie, but attended regularly on the
Sabbath at Kilmany Church. His friend, Robert Edie,
generally convoyed him part of the way home.

About one hundred yards from the road along which
they travelled, in the thickly-screened seclusion of a
close plantation, and under the shade of a branching
fir-tree, the two friends found a quiet retreat, where,

each returning Sabbath evening, the eye that seeth in secret looked down upon these two youthful disciples of the Saviour on their knees, and, for an hour, their ardent prayers alternately ascended to the throne of grace. The practice was continued for years, till a private footpath of their own had been opened to the trysting-tree; and when, some years ago, after long absence on the part of both, they met at Kilmany, at Mr. Edie's suggestion, they revisited the spot, and, renewing the sacred exercise, offered up their joint thanksgivings to that God who had kept them by His grace, and, in their separate spheres, had honoured each of them with usefulness in the Church. Mr. Paterson laboured for twenty-two years as a missionary in the Canongate of Edinburgh, not without many pleasing evidences that his labours have been blessed. And there is reason to believe that by his efforts in behalf of Bible and Missionary Societies, through means of Sabbath Schools and prayer meetings, and by the light of a guiding and consistent example, Mr. Edie's life, while one of active industry, has also been one of devoted Christian usefulness.

LIFE THROUGH DEATH.

MISS ELIZA FLETCHER was summoned from Paris to Scotland to the bedside of her friend, Marjory Smith, a minister's daughter at Kilwinning. This girl she had loved idolatrously, but not her religion; for her own strong religious impressions alternated with fits of wilful scepticism. Marjory knew this, and had laboured with all her gentle force to bring her to the humble acceptance of Jesus. And now on her death-bed she made one last solemn effort. She sent for her friend to her bedside, and a solemn scene ensued. Miss Fletcher tells the story herself:—

"Early next morning I was awoke from sleep by a voice at my bedside: 'Rise immediately, Miss Eliza; make haste, Miss Marjory is *very* ill, and wants to see you at once.' I sprang up; I think I was beside her in ten minutes. It was half-past four. When I entered the room, 'Eliza,' she said, 'I am glad you are there; I want to see you alone.' She made all go out. 'Now, Eliza,' she said, 'sit close beside me. I am dying, there's no use in concealing that or not speaking of it. I feel I am dying, and I wish to speak to you. Oh! Eliza, you have often talked lightly of Satan, heaven, hell. I know you have not yet given your heart to the Lord, and now I wish to tell you something. Last night Satan came to my bedside—it was no heated imagination—he was there,' she said, pointing to the other side. 'I *felt* his presence. He drew near, and held up to my terrified eyes all my past sins—sins, Eliza, long forgotten—and it was a terrible sight. I tried to drive him away by telling him I had come to Jesus. *You*, he said, such a sinner as *you*,—look; and I gazed at my sins. Again I told him of the blood which cleanseth from all sin. But are *you* washed? he argued; look again at your sins; there they are, you cannot deny *them*. Oh! Eliza, the conflict was so awful that the perspiration broke all over my body. At length I said, Well, Satan, I give it up. I *am* a sinner. I have committed all these sins, and far more; but I am not worse than Mary Magdalene, and she is in glory. The Saviour that took *her* there can, and will, take *me*. Then he pointed to the cold grave. Look at that dismal damp grave, how will you like to be there? Ah! Satan, I said, my dear Saviour has lain there before me, and the bed upon which he lay will be a sweet one for me. Then he fled. Now, dear Eliza, I tell you as a dying one—you will believe my *dying* words, won't you? There *is* a hell, there *is* a devil; and blessed be God, there is a heaven, and there is a Saviour. I speak to you solemnly; let my death be life to you.' She was exhausted. 'Marjory,' I said, throwing myself on the bed beside her, 'I *cannot* live without you.' Putting her hand tenderly on my shoulder, she replied, 'Oh, dear Eliza, get Jesus and *His* love, and you will do without me!'"

This appeal was not in vain, for Eliza became a noted Christian worker, and died a Christian death.

THE THREE REMARKABLE PARISHIONERS AT ARBIRLOT.

Arbirlot was Dr. Guthrie's first parish, and among those who belonged to it he refers to three of them thus:— In this population of a thousand parishioners, there were three units that stood out in a marked way from the rest. There was one dissenter, a very worthy man, a tailor, who travelled every Sunday, fair weather or foul, ten or twelve miles in order that he might worship with his own small sect of Old Light Seceders in Arbroath; there was one man who could not read, but he was an interloper, and not a native; and there was one man who did not attend church on the Lord's Day, and he was crazy. The first was much respected; the second was regarded as a curiosity, people pointing him out as the man who could not read; and the third nobody heeded, far less followed his example.

On the other hand, we had two or three as bad, immoral fellows as were to be found in the whole country, yet they were never out of church. I remember with no small satisfaction how I took the wind out of the sails of one of these in an attempt he made to mortify me, at the very time I was showing him kind and Christian attentions. He had been very ill, and was prepared to express his gratitude for my attentions on a day when I went to visit him, and when he expected me to do so. At that time the Voluntary Controversy was raging throughout the country, and a fierce and scurrilous attack had been made on me by a low pamphleteer in Arbroath. With this, which I had not seen but had heard of, this "fellow of the baser sort" had furnished himself, that he might annoy and mortify his minister by getting me to take it home and read it. So, no sooner had I finished praying with him, and was on my feet to go, than he said,—"Oh, Mr. Guthrie, here is a pamphlet about you!" I saw malignity gleaming in his eyes, and, suspecting the truth, turned round to ask, "Is it for or against me?" "Oh," he replied, "against you;" and never did a man look more mortified, more chopfallen than he, on my saying, with a merry laugh, "Ah, well, you may keep it; had it been for me, I would have read it. I never read anything that is against me!" This answer is one, which, if given in similar circumstances, would put an end to much mischief.

THE FRIENDS, OR QUAKERS, IN SCOTLAND.

WHEN the Friends began in Scotland they were harshly treated. They were excommunicated from the National Church, and otherwise looked upon as not sound in faith, nor what they should be in practice. This led them to explain many incidents as if they were judgments of God on their enemies. Thus Barclay remarks:—"Sir John Keith, who, in those days and afterward, was very violent against Friends, having in the year 1667 brought away under a guard several of his people from Inverury, where they had been previously imprisoned, the magistrates of Aberdeen, to whom they were delivered, after keeping them in confinement some time, caused them to be conducted through the streets, with great contempt and reproach, to the Bow Bridge, where a guard was provided to conduct them southward to Edinburgh, from shire to shire, as the worst of malefactors. When they had proceeded a little way out of the town, one of the prisoners, William Gellie, a man of very weakly and infirm habit, sat down; and the rest of the Friends followed his example, refusing to go further, unless horses were provided. Alexander, who attended, in order to see them set out, was much enraged, commanded William Gellie to rise and go forward on foot; and, because of his refusal, he struck him piteously.

"The Friends, however, continued to sit still; upon which the magistrate, with all his train, not being able to prevail in their purpose, returned to Aberdeen, and the Friends to their respective dwelling-places. But, what was remarkable, the first object that presented itself to this persecutor on reaching his own house was his son, who had, by a fall, broken his arm, and in the very same time that the father had been using his arm to strike the harmless servant of the Lord; which circumstance, thus coinciding, so awakened the conscience of this person, that he said (and afterwards told it to some Friends), *he would never strike a Quaker again.*

LORD BROUGHAM'S DECISION OF CHARACTER IN EARLY LIFE.

LORD BROUGHAM was born in Edinburgh, and attended the High School. When there, and as a boy, he displayed the wonderful powers of mind which were so conspicuous as a man. Lord Cockburn, who was at the same school, relates the following anecdote, which is characteristic:—" Brougham," he says, " was not in the same class with me. Before getting to the Rector's class, he had been under Luke Frazer, who, in his two immediately preceding courses of four years each, had the good fortune to have Francis Jeffrey and Sir Walter Scott as his pupils. Brougham made his first explosion while at Frazer's class. He dared to differ from Frazer, a hot, but good-natured old fellow, on some bit of Latinity. The master, like other men in power, maintained his own infallibility, punished the rebel, and flattered himself that the affair was over. But Brougham reappeared next day, loaded with books, returned to the charge before the whole class, and compelled honest Luke to acknowledge he had been wrong. This made Brougham famous throughout the school. I remember as well as if it had been yesterday, having had him pointed out to me as 'the fellow who had beat the master.' It was then that I first saw him." He who could set his master right when at school was likely to turn out a man of energy and success. This Brougham was, and in his case, the boy was the father of the man, and shows his unqualified devotion to truth as truth. It likewise illustrates the importance of being thoroughly confirmed in one's own mind in matters of more importance than that of Latinity, and thereafter holding fast to that which is true.

THE HUMANITY OF BURNS.

BURNS was tender in heart, and was benevolent in disposition. This tenderness comes out in his many poems, especially in his "Address to a Mountain Daisy" and "To a Mouse." And his benevolence finds expression in "Man is made to Mourn," and others of his productions. But he did not confine his love for man to words, but many were the deeds of kindness he did. An eyewitness has said, that returning home to his house in the Wee Vennel, Dumfries, one stormy wet night after dark, he discovered a poor, half-witted, street-strolling beggar woman, well known about the town, half-naked, drenched, and shivering, huddled together, almost insensible, on his own door-step. In those days there was no shelter of a police-office to which such a helpless vagrant could be removed, nor was there any house open at the moment to which she could be carried but his own. Mrs. Burns might, perhaps, be excused for hesitating to receive such an inmate, even for the night; but remonstrance was in vain. The insensible outcast, motionless, presumably unconscious, was carefully lifted in, and housed and sheltered under the Poet's hospitable roof till morning, when, not without breakfast, we may be sure, she was enabled to pursue her way. "Then shall the King say unto them on his right hand, Come, ye blessed of my Father, inherit the kingdom prepared for you from the foundation of the world: For I was an hungered, and ye gave me meat; I was thirsty, and ye gave me drink: I was a stranger, and ye took me in: Naked, and ye clothed me: I was sick, and ye visited me: I was in prison, and ye came unto me."

DRINK AND DEATH AT BLAIRGOWRIE.

THE REV. DR. GUTHRIE sent a letter to his eldest son from Blairgowrie in the month of May, 1859, in which he describes the terrible results of intemperance. In the letter he says:—"A wretched, ill-doing, drunken baker, had come on Thursday morning by the train from Dundee. He had been working there, and for some days past drinking hard. He had two children here, boarded with a woman, for whom, spending his money on drink, he had not been paying regularly. The woman, by letter, had dunned him for their board. The two bairns were crossing the bridge on their way to school in the morning, when they encountered their father. He bade them go up with him and see their grandmother, who lived some mile or so up the banks of the Ericht.

"It was a roaring flood, he was mad and moody after his days of debauchery. He took his lassie in the one hand, his boy in the other. About 1,000 feet above the bridge and the town, the banks approach, the bed grows rocky, and the whole body of the water shoots among horrid rocks, forming great, black, deep, swirling pools, through a very contracted channel. They reach the place. He takes off the laddie's cap, and, throwing it on the ground, says he will buy a better for him; does the same with his lassie's bonnet, then, standing on a rock about eight feet above the boiling flood, he seizes his boy and throws him in—he is shot off like an arrow. Some twelve feet farther down, there rises up from the black depths a rock which lifts its head about a foot above the surface, the stream roaring on each side. By a most merciful Providence, the boy was whirled within reach of it; he caught it, hung on, and got upon the rock.

"This must have been the work of a moment; he was safely there before the wretched drunkard had had time, I fancy, to complete his work, for the boy saw him next seize his little sister, and leap with her into the jaws of death. The poor laddie called to her to make for the rock. She cried, as she floated by along with her father, that he 'wadna let her;' and at that moment the boy saw the drowning monster actually raise his hand and press her poor head below the water, and then, in a moment, both vanished from his sight, while he stood screaming. A woman heard his cries; the alarm was given, a ladder was thrown from the bank, it reached the rock—a man passed over and rescued him. I went to see the place, and saw a commotion among the people that were scattered in groups all along the banks. A few steps brought me in sight of what I never shall forget. A deep hole lies behind a dam-dyke. A man had thrust a long pole into it, and, when I got to the spot, he was up to the middle in water, making his way to the shore, bearing in his arms the poor dead body of a bonny lassie. Her arms were extended, her head was lying on his shoulders, her face was ruddy. I thought it was a girl who had fallen in, and was not dead. But the outburst of grief, the cries and tears of women and children soon undeceived me. The body of the poor bairn, her yellow hair parted back from a sweet forehead, with a comely face, looking calm as if asleep, the face full of colour, but the little hands and arms deadly white, was laid on the bank. The sight was overwhelming enough to drive one mad with sorrow, rage, pity, horror, indignation. I spoke out to the multitude against drinking, and when one spoke of the body of the man lying, perhaps, in the same place, I said, if it were found, it should be hung up in chains; to which, to the credit of humanity, there was from some a loud and hearty assent.

"The only thing that calmed me was to look on that poor corpse, and think that, poor thing, this lassie was better dead than living,—with God, and in His arms, than to live and have a drunkard for her father. I expect God will bring much good out of this most horrid and unnatural tragedy. Strange that ministers will meet in General Assemblies and discuss this thing and that thing, nor address themselves aright and with self-denial to this spring and well-head of miseries and murders, the damnation of souls, and the ruin of our land."

A CAMERONIAN ELDER ON READING SERMONS.

THE REV. DR. WM. ANDERSON used to tell the following incident with much interest:—I had just, he said, been licensed to preach, and was despatched to Kirkintilloch, to officiate on the coming Sabbath. The mode of conveyance was by the night canal boat leaving Glasgow at 9 o'clock; the cabin of these vessels was so narrow that the knees of passengers sitting opposite touched. In the centre was a long narrow table, at the stern end of which sat a fiddler, whose duty it was to fill up the gaps between the political and theological discussions, which often made pleasant those otherwise weary night voyages. Opposite me sat an old grey-headed man, the whole make-up of whom indicated a Cameronian Elder of the "straitest sect," and on my right sat a young man, going to the same place, the twinkle of whose eye seemed to say, let us have some fun; and hardly had the boat left the wharf till he looked over to his old friend, and said, "Ay, David, man, say ye ha'e been in Glaskie, hae ye? What i' the world ha'e ye been there for, man? It's nae a journey that everybody taks; and abune a', wha wid hae expected tae see ye there?" "Weel, ye see," replied David, " ma dochter gat married tae a lad there, an' they wad ha'e me to gang thro' an' see them." " Weel, David, an' what think ye o' Glaskie?" "Oh, man, it's an awfu' place; it's abune a' ma thochts. I had nae idea o't, an' I'm jist gled to get awa' hame again." " Weel, David, an' wha did ye hear preachin'?" "Oh, ye ken, I gaed tae oor ain place, o' course; we ha'e a kirk in Glaskie, ye see." "But ye dinna mean to tell me, David, that ye didna gang to hear Tammas Chalmers, do ye?" "Aweel, aweel (scratching his head as if in a dilemma), I's no say that I didna, but then, do ye see, it was on Thursday nicht, an' I didna think there wad be meikle sin, when it wisna the Sabbath day; but, man, he's an awfu' man that: I never heard a man like him, for I was sittin', whan, an' afore I kent whaur I was, I was up on my verra feet, stretchin' o'er the beukboard, wi' my e'en wide starin', an' my mooth wide open, feared I wad lose a word. But ca' ye yon preachin'? Na, na, it was rank black prelacy; man, he read ilka word o't; na, na, nane o' that abomination for me—na, na."

I thought I might have a little banter with the old man also, and so I said, "David, you need not be so hard against prelacy, or read sermons, for ye know it is a fact, which you cannot deny, that ye read prayers yourself every morning." With a smile of contempt, mixed with pity, the old man fixed his eyes on me, and in a solemn tone said, "Laddie, ye'll no ken wha I am, or ye wudna speak that way; for onybody that kens me that has been an elder o' the Cameronian Kirk o' Kirkintilloch for abune thirty years, wudna set sic a sin to my door; na, na." "But, David, I have good ground for what I have said, and I know that you do read prayers every morning." At this reiterated charge, the old man's wrath began to wax warm, and rising to his feet, he exclaimed in a passion, "It's a lee, it's a lee; wha ever tald ye that I carena, but it's a black lee." Feeling that I had, perhaps, led him far enough, I said, "Be calm, David, and answer me a question; do ye not read the Psalms of David every morning?" "To be sure I do; but what has that to dae wi' the lee?" "Well, David, are not David's Psalms the best prayers ever written?" The face of the old Cameronian relaxed into a smile, as he sat down and exclaimed, "Ay, laddie, but ye ha'e caught me noo, ye ha'e caught me noo." "But, David," I continued, "I am afraid, that from the way you have been talking, you do not know what a sermon means." "I sud think," he rejoined, "I sud think that a man wha has been an elder o' the Cameronian Kirk abune thirty years, sud ken what a sermon means, if onybody kens." "Well, David, let me tell you that a sermon is a proclamation; now you know that when the king makes a proclamation, it is written on paper, and read at the Cross, and that it is not a proclamation unless it is read; now, you know that the gospel is the proclamation of the King of kings; therefore, as all proclamations must be read, so a sermon, being a proclamation, must be read, or it is not a sermon."

David looked dumfoundered; the boat had reached our destination, and the old Cameronian in stepping out, exclaimed, "Tuts, tuts, laddie, ye hae ower muckle Latin for me."

THE FATHER OF THE REV. DR. WARDLAW.

"Old Bailie Wardlaw" as he was called, the father of the Rev. Dr. Ralph Wardlaw, spent his life in a cheerful and charitable religiousness, and his end was in keeping with such a life, peaceful, serene, and happy. Being visited by some Christian friends during his confinement, he discoursed with them in his usual cheerful and pleasant way, and spoke, with humble but unfaltering confidence, of his hopes for eternity, founded on the Saviour's merits. One of the party, whose views of divine truth were of a kind which led him not only to indulge in gloomy feelings and anxious forebodings, but even to attach to these a certain religious worth, was somewhat scandalised by the brightness which seemed diffused over the soul of the dying saint, and he could not refrain from endeavouring to recall him to what he considered a more befitting state of mind. "Oh, Mr. Wardlaw," he said, "does it beseem us to pass through the dark valley without a struggle? Remember how it fared with our Master: was not his soul troubled within him, and was not he sorrowful even unto death?" "Aye," exclaimed the dying saint, rising on his couch, "it was even so; and oh! man, it is that very trouble and that very sorrow that make me go so lightly through the valley this day; surely *He hath borne our griefs, and carried our sorrows.*" Within a few hours of his departure, he repeated the words, "He which testifieth these things saith, Surely I come quickly: Amen. Even so, come, Lord Jesus." "That is," he added, "come quickly. But this is not to be understood as the language of impatience—come *instantly*—come now because it is my time. No, I would say, 'Come, Lord Jesus, come in Thine own good time, in Thine own way, and by Thine own appointed means; for those are always best. *Even so*, come, Lord Jesus.'" There is something in this akin to the faith of the Apostle when he exclaimed, "I know whom I have believed, and am persuaded that he is able to keep that which I have committed unto him against that day." This calm, serene reliance in the prospect of death rises to the sublime of piety.

JOY IN TEARS.

"MANY years ago, in a time of spiritual inquiry," says Dr. Moody Stuart, "a stranger, having an air of superior intelligence, called on me in distress of mind. In speaking to her, I was brought to a stand by her thorough knowledge of the letter and doctrine of the Scriptures; and finding I could add no instruction, I asked no further questions, but briefly opened and pressed the words, 'Christ Jesus came into the world to save sinners,' and ended with prayer. While I was speaking, a stream of silent tears began to flow, and she looked relieved, but was silent. A week after she returned, with her face bright with joy, to tell me that she had found that peace with God, which she had before been vainly seeking. I asked her, 'Why did you weep when you left last day?' 'I wept for joy.' 'And what gave you the joy?' 'I saw, as you were speaking, that Jesus came into the world to save sinners.' 'But you knew that before?' 'No.' 'Then what did you think?' 'I always thought that Jesus came into the world to save saints; and I wept for joy when I saw He came to save sinners.'"

THE SABBATH MARKET.

IN the year 1834 the Rev. Alex. Stewart, of Cromarty, visited the Duchess of Gordon at Gordon Castle, and when there, told an anecdote the Duchess often repeated with great animation. Hector Munro was a half-witted man, but like so many of the weak ones in this world, he was strong in the grace that is in Christ Jesus. He had a fair knowledge of sacred things and of the Bible, and was most careful in his religious duties. He was, though weak in intellect, much respected, and taken notice of by those who belonged to the better class of society. Mr. Stewart having invited him to pay him a visit at Cromarty Manse, he came most inopportunely on the Saturday afternoon, with the design of remaining all night, when the minister was busily engaged with his work for the Sabbath. Mr. Stewart was a man of genius as well as grace; his sermons were often the product of a high effort of intellect; and he was not constitutionally free from the senstiveness which might be ruffled at and resent such an interruption. But he overcame his discomposure, received and kindly entertained his guest, and found his reward in an intercourse more precious to him, and more memorable than the interrupted sermon.

Hector having come in his best clothes, the minister addressed him,—" Weel, Hector, ye've made yoursel' braw the day." "Hout ay, folk mak's themsel's braw tae gang tae thae vain markets, but I'se warrant the Sabbath's the best market, for it's there we get withoot money and withoot price. An', Maister Stewart, I'm thinkin' the Seterday's jist like the Christian's deathbed; he's dune his wark, an' he's wash't, an' he's clean, an' he lies doon, an' he waukens,—an' it's the Sabbath! An' HE was braw Himsel' that day," meaning thereby that Jesus was arrayed in a bright robe when He rose on the first day of the week.

DAVID HUME AND PRINCIPAL ROBERTSON;

Or, The Light of Nature and of Revelation.

DAVID HUME wrote an essay on the sufficiency of the light of nature, and Dr. Robertson wrote on the necessity of revelation and the insufficiency of the light of nature. Hume came one evening to visit Robertson, and the time was spent in conversation on this subject. The friends of both were present, and it is said that Robertson reasoned with unusual clearness and power. Whether Hume was convinced by his reasoning or not we cannot tell; but, at any rate, he did not acknowledge his conviction. Hume was very much of a gentleman in his manners, and, as he rose to depart, bowed politely to those in the room, while, as he retired through the door, Robertson took the light to show him the way. Hume was still facing the door. "Oh, sir," said he, "I find the light of nature always sufficient;" and continued, "pray, don't trouble yourself, sir," and so he walked on.

The door was opened, and presently, as he went along the hall, he stumbled over something concealed, and pitched down the steps into the street. Robertson ran after him with the light, and as he held it over him, whispered softly, "You had better have a light from above, Mr. Hume;" and raising him up, he bade him good night, and returned to his friends.

LORD HADDO'S SPIRITUAL CHANGE.

LORD HADDO thus records in his diary the history of his spiritual change. He says:—"About this time last year, 29th January 1849, or perhaps a few days earlier, I first began to change my habits of life. It was about seven o'clock in the evening that I received such a deep impression of eternity, that the effect has continued to the present day, and, by the blessing of God, will remain to my dying day. I had just dressed for dinner, when the sight of the clothes which I had thrown off, suddenly impressed me with the thought of dying; of undressing for the last time; of being unclothed of this body. I felt the terrors of dying unprepared, in a degree approaching to reality. In the bed I saw not a place of nightly repose, but a place intended to receive the dying struggle. In short, the prospect of death was impressed on my imagination with overwhelming force; and not of death only, but of eternity; of the day of judgment, an offended God, and the sentence to eternal torment. I felt the imperative necessity of preparing for death at any cost and any sacrifice. The prospect of heaven added little or nothing to my resolution. Safety was all I aimed at. This I felt was within my reach, and I grasped at it with the feelings of a drowning man.

"When I went to dinner, my poor wife saw from my expression that something had occurred; and when I began to speak, she fairly thought that I had lost my senses, till, after a few days, she herself embraced the same sentiments. Some musicians came, as usual at this hour, before the house. Their tune seemed to me utter discord, and they were sent away in disgust. What madness, I thought, to be fiddling, when heaven and hell are immediately before us.

"That evening and the next I read over Baxter's 'Saint's Rest,' and Wilberforce's 'Practical View,'—books which I had read before, but every word of which had now irresistible force. I felt the conclusion irresistible, that salvation must be sought and attained, though the path to it lay through fire and water, and that no hardships were worth a moment's consideration in comparison of so great a prize. In the same manner, the pursuits of my life hitherto appeared utterly frivolous—such as painting, etc. They could not advance me one step on the road to heaven. Till my title to salvation was assured, these occupations seemed an intolerable waste of time. After such an assurance, they could possess no interest for one whose thoughts and affections were in heaven. I mentally abandoned, without hesitation, everything, and resolved to make an entire change in my life, and to spend the whole day in the service of God, and to devote myself entirely to the *promotion of His glory.*" This change manifested itself in good works. During his life he walked in the footsteps of his Saviour, and died having the victory in the Lord.

THE OLD FERRYMAN ON THE FRITH OF FORTH.

ON the Frith of Forth lived an old ferryman, a man of much thought and observation, but of few words, a constant student of the Bible, and a firm believer in its truths. Among his patrons were two loquacious companions, whose business led them across the river on the same day once a-week. One of them, as he supposed, thought he could do without works if he had faith, and the other thought he could do without faith if he had works. Their conversation always turned upon some doctrinal point. The ferryman was frequently annoyed by the repetition of *faith* on one side and *works* on the other, because they were used in a sense so different from their real import, and so destructive of their Scriptural harmony. At length the patience of the old man failed him; he felt that he must interfere. He said nothing, but fell upon the following expedient. Upon one of his oars he painted "Faith," and upon the other, "Works." It was not long before the zealous but friendly disputants applied for a passage over the Forth. Upon entering the deepest part of the river, where the swollen water rushed down with some violence, the ferryman took in "Faith," and pulled away upon "Works" with all his might. The boat went round and round, much to the annoyance and terror of the two passengers. "Put out the other oar," said one of them in a loud and angry tone. "Very well," was the calm reply of the old man, at the same time taking in "Works" and putting out "Faith" alone, upon which he pulled.

The experiment with this oar produced the same result, and drove the witnesses of it to the conclusion that the ferryman was "out of his head." The old man, however, continued his "practical demonstrations" on the water until he thought the friends were prepared to see two things in connection. He then called their attention to the names painted on his oars. "I have tried your way," said he, "and yours; and you have seen the result. Now, observe my way." And giving a steady pull to each oar, the little boat soon acknowledged the power of their harmonious strokes by the straight and rapid flight which she took for the landing. "Thus it is," he added, "faith works by love."

A THIEF OUTDONE.

THERE lived in Ross-shire one of the "Men" called Alister Og, the godly weaver of Edderton, who was famous as a man of prayer and earnestness. On one occasion there came a pious man to consult him about the meaning of the counsel, "Pray without ceasing." On his arrival, he found Alister busy digging his croft. "You are well employed, Alister," he said, on coming up to him. "If delving and praying, praying and delving, be good employment, I am," was his answer, which met the inquirer's difficulty before he had stated it. Once, late at night, a stranger applied at Alister's door for a night's lodgings. His wife was unwilling to admit him, but Alister, "not forgetful to entertain strangers," at once invited him to come in, and gave him the best his house could afford. On rising next morning, the wife found that the stranger had gone, and had carried off a web which her husband had just finished to order. "Didn't I tell you," she said, after hurrying to Alister with the tidings of the theft, "not to admit that man; you yourself will now be suspected of doing away with the web, and what will become of us?" "I admitted the stranger," was her husband's reply, "because the Lord commanded me; and if there is no other way of defending His cause, He will send the man who stole the web back with it again." That day was very misty, and the thief spent it, wearily wandering, with the web on his back, over the hill of Edderton. After nightfall, as Alister and his wife were sitting by the ingle, they heard a knock at the door, on opening which, whom should they see on the threshold but their guest of the night before. He had wandered, not knowing whither, till his eye was arrested, and his course directed, by the light that twinkled in Alister's window; and now, much to his surprise and confusion, he finds himself throwing the web off his back in the house from which he had stolen it. He was thus outdone, and the words he received from Alister would, it is to be hoped, lead him to see that the way of transgressors is hard, and that a just and all-seeing God reigneth.

SIR JAMES YOUNG SIMPSON'S SUPERSTITIOUS FOREFATHERS.

SIR JAMES Y. SIMPSON, the "Beloved Physician," was descended from those who entertained notions of a superstitious kind, which were, less than a century ago, prevalent in Scotland. Several of his near relatives were men of mark in their native district, and noted for strong individuality of character. His grandfather, Alexander Simpson, was long remembered in Linlithgowshire as a man of great shrewdness, and highly skilled in the diagnosis and treatment of cattle-disease. His uncles were prudent and energetic men of business—all of them, like their father, adepts in farriery. To these qualities was added a dash of deep superstition. Cattle diseases that baffled their skill were at once ascribed to witchcraft, and characteristic expedients were resorted to for the removal of the spell. On an occasion when murrain threatened to empty the well-filled byre at Slackend, the old man took counsel with his sons, and pointed out that the plague could only be stayed by their giving up a cow to be buried alive. Accordingly, a grave was prepared in a field behind the byre, and the beast was led to its edge with great solemnity. "How shall we get her in?" asked one son. "Father will take the head, you will take the tail, and we will push at the side," was the ready answer. "I remember," says the narrator, "seeing the earth heaving as the soil was pushed in."

"Certainly," wrote Dr. Simpson in 1861, "some strange superstitions do remain, or, at least, lately did remain, among us. The sacrifice, for example, of the cock and other animals for recovery from epilepsy and convulsions, is by no means extinct in some Highland districts. In old Pagan and Mithraic times we know that the sacrifice of the ox was common. I have myself often listened to the account given by one near and dear to me, who was, in early life, personally engaged in the offering up and burying of a poor live cow as a sacrifice to the spirit of the murrain. This occurred within twenty miles of the metropolis of Scotland." The uncle, who became proprietor of Gormyre, was truly his father's son. "In the same district," Dr. Simpson continues, "a relative of mine bought a farm not very many years ago. Among his first acts, after taking possession, was the enclosing a small triangular corner of one of the fields within a stone wall. The corner cut off, and which still remains cut off, was the 'Gudeman's Croft,'—an offering to the spirit of evil, in order that he might abstain from ever blighting or damaging the rest of the farm. The clergyman of the Free Church, who told me the circumstances, added that my kinsman had been, he feared, far from acting honestly with Lucifer after all, as the corner which he had cut off for the 'Gudeman's' share was, perhaps, the most worthless and sterile spot on the whole property.

"Some may look on such superstitions and superstitious practices as matters utterly vulgar and valueless in themselves, but in the eyes of the archæologist they become interesting and important, when we remember that the popular superstitions of Scotland, as of other countries, are, for the most part, true antiquarian vestiges of the Pagan creeds and customs of our earlier ancestors; our present folk-lore being merely, in general, a degenerated and debased form of the highest mythological and medical lore of very distant times." The laird of Gormyre was known to have interrupted sowing for a day when two magpies flew across the field, in the belief that all the seed sown between the time of their appearance and sunset will be blighted. Another uncle was wont, when driving his cart along the road to Edinburgh, to return home at once, even though nearing town, if a hare crossed in front of him. Yet these men were intelligent above the average. They were industrious, persevering, and self-reliant; men who knew how to make money, how to keep it, and make it minister to their influence among their fellows.

IN A CLEFT OF THE GARRICK FELLS.

A LITTLE party assembled in a shepherd's house in Nithsdale to hear Peden—the prophet, as he was termed—expound the Word of God. While thus engaged, the bleating of a sheep was heard. The noise disturbed the little congregation, and the shepherd was obliged to go out and drive the sheep away. While so engaged, he lifted up his eyes and saw, at a distance, horse-soldiers coming towards his cottage. He hastened back to give the alarm. All instantly dispersed and hid themselves. Mr. Peden betook himself to the cleft of the rock, the

Cave of Garrick Fells, and soon the clatter of horses' hoofs and the ring of armour told him that his foes were at hand. But safe in the cleft he sat unmoved, and through an opening saw them gallop past, without any suspicion that he whose life they sought was so near. Thus a providential escape was secured through the simple bleating of a sheep.

THE WIGTON MARTYRS.

In the reign of Charles II., on the 11th of May, 1682, Margaret Wilson, a girl of eighteen years of age, and Margaret Lauchlison, an aged widow, were adjudged to die, because they refused to acknowledge the supremacy of any other than Christ in the Church. The sentence pronounced upon them was, that they should be fastened to stakes driven into the oozy sand that covers the beach of Wigton Bay, and left to perish in the rising tide. They were brought out to suffer for their faith in the presence of Grierson and Major Winram, and an immense concourse of spectators. "They did put the old woman first into the water," says the chronicler (no doubt with the expectation that the sight of her death-struggles would terrify the younger sufferer into submission), "and when the water was overflowing her, they asked Margaret Wilson what she thought of her in that case? She answered, 'What do I see but Christ wrestling there? Think ye that we are sufferers? No! it is Christ in us, for he sends none a warfare on their own charges.' Margaret then read the eighth chapter of the Romans, and sang Psalm xxv., from the seventh verse:—

'My sins and faults of youth
  Do Thou, O Lord, forgive;
After Thy mercy think on me,
  And for Thy goodness great,' etc.—

and did pray, and then the water covered her. But before her breath was quite gone, they pulled her up and held her till she could speak, and then asked her if she would pray for the king. She answered that she wished the salvation of all men, and the damnation of

none. Some of her relations being on the place cried
out, 'She is willing to conform,' being desirous to save
her life at anyrate. 'Dear Margaret, say God save the
King,' entreated another of the spectators. 'God save
him, if he will,' replied the poor girl, 'for it is his
salvation that I desire.' On hearing these words, the
bystanders cried out eagerly to Major Winram: 'Sir,
she has said it! she has said it!' upon which the Major
offered the oath of abjuration to her, either to swear it
or to return to the waters. She refused it, saying, 'I
will not; I am one of Christ's children, let me go.' And
then they returned her into the water, where she finished
her warfare."

KING ROBERT BRUCE AND THE SPIDER.
A Lesson in Perseverance.

IN the winter of 1306, King Robert Bruce had to leave
his Queen and seek shelter in an island called Rachrin,
on the coast of Ireland. After receiving the news of
the captivity of his wife and the execution of his brother
in the miserable dwelling he inhabited, he was reduced
to the point of despair. Bruce was lying one morning
on his wretched bed, and deliberating with himself
whether he had not better resign all thoughts of again
attempting to make good his right to the Scottish crown,
and, dismissing his followers, transport himself and his
brother to the Holy Land, and spend the rest of his days
in fighting against the Saracens, by which he thought,
perhaps, he might deserve the forgiveness of Heaven
for the great sin of stabbing Comyn in the church at
Dumfries.

When thus reflecting, and doubtful what he should
do, Bruce was looking upward to the roof of the cabin
in which he lay, and his eye was attracted by a spider,
which, hanging at the end of a long thread of its own
spinning, was endeavouring, as is the fashion of that
creature, to swing itself from one beam in the roof to
another, for the purpose of fixing the line on which it
meant to stretch its web.

The insect made the attempt again and again without success; and at length Bruce counted that it had tried to carry its point six times, and been as often unable to do so. It came into his head that he had himself fought just six battles against the English and their allies, and that the poor persevering spider was exactly in the same situation with himself, having made as many trials, and been as often disappointed in what it aimed at. "Now," thought Bruce, "as I have no means of knowing what is best to be done, I will be guided by the luck which shall attend this spider. If the insect will make another effort to fix its thread, and shall be successful, I will venture a seventh time to try my fortune in Scotland; but if the spider shall fail, I will go to the wars in Palestine, and never return to my native country more." While Bruce was forming this resolution, the spider made another exertion with all the force it could muster, and fairly succeeded in fastening its thread to the beam which it had so often in vain attempted to reach. Bruce seeing the success of the spider, resolved to try his own fortune, and as he had never before gained a victory, so he never afterwards sustained any considerable or decisive check or defeat. The spider taught the king a lesson in perseverance.

AN OLD STYLE OF PREACHING.

Justification by Works, and Justification by Faith.

THE REV. JOHN SIMPLE, a very zealous Scotch preacher of the seventeenth century, used to personate and act sermons in the old monkish style. At a certain time he preached upon that debate, Whether a man be justified by faith or by works? and acted it after this manner,— "Sirs, this is a very great debate; but who is that looking in at the door with his red cap? It is very ill manners to be looking in; but what's your name? Robert Bellarmine. Bellarmine, saith he, whether is a man justified by faith or by works? He is justified by works. Stand thou there, man. But what is he, that honest-like man standing in the floor with a long beard and Geneva cowl? A very honest-like man! draw near. What's your name, sir? My name is John Calvin. Calvin, honest Calvin, whether is a man justified by faith or by works? He is justified by faith. Very well, John, thy leg to my leg, and we shall hough [trip] down Bellarmine even now."

Another time preaching on the day of judgment, he told them,—"Sirs, this will be a terrible day; we'll a' be there, and in the throng. I, John Simple, will be, and all of you will stand at my back. Christ will look to me, and He will say, Who is that standing there? I'll say again, Yea, even as ye ken'd not, Lord. He'll say, I know thou's honest John Simple; draw near, John. Now, John, what good service have ye done to me on earth? I have brought hither a company of blue bonnets for you, Lord. Blue bonnets, John! What is become of the braw hats, the silks, and the satins, John? I'll tell, I know not, Lord; they went a gait of their own. Well, honest John, thou and thy blue bonnets are welcome to me; come to my right hand, and let the devil take the hats, the silks, and the satins."

A MUSCULAR CHRISTIAN.
The Parish of Lochcarron in the last Century.

THE REV. ÆNEAS SAGE, in the last century, was minister of the parish of Lochcarron, Ross-shire. He was a man of undaunted spirit, who did not know what the fear of man was. He had, however, the fear of God, and great zeal for the good cause in its highest perfection. He was the determined enemy of vice, and a true friend of the gospel. At the time of his induction, the state of the parish was very much the same as it was found by the presbytery to be in 1649, when, after visiting it, they reported that "there were no elders in it, by reason of malignancy — swearing, drunkenness, cursing, Sabbath profanation, and uncleanness prevailed." As to the church, there was found in it "ane formal stool of repentance, but no pulpit nor desks." The stool, if the only, was truly the suitable, seat for all the people of

Lochcarron in those days; but the more it was required, the less power there was to make it aught else than "ane formal" thing, as the solitary occupant of the church. Matters continued in this state till the induction of Mr. Sage, nearly eighty years after.

He was just the man for the work of breaking up the fallow ground of a field so wild, and a rich blessing rested on his labours. On the night of his arrival at Lochcarron, an attempt was made to burn the house in which he lodged, and, for some time after his induction, his life was in constant danger. But the esteem he could not win as a minister, he soon acquired for his physical strength. The first man in Lochcarron, in those days, was the champion at the athletic games. Conscious of his strength, and knowing that he would make himself respected by all if he could only lay big Rory on his back, who was acknowledged to be the strongest man in the district, the minister joined the people, on the earliest opportunity, at their games. Challenging the whole field, he competed for the prize in putting the stone, tossing the caber, and wrestling, and won an easy victory. His fame was established at once. The minister was now the champion of the district, and none was more ready to defer to him than he whom he had deprived of the laurel. Taking Rory aside to a confidential crack, he said to him,—"Now, Rory, I am the minister, and you must be my elder, and we both must see to it that all the people attend church, observe the Sabbath, and conduct themselves properly." Rory fell in with the proposal at once. On Sabbath, when the people would gather to their games in the forenoon, the minister and his elder would join them, and each taking a couple by the hand, they would drag them to the church, lock them in, and then return to catch some more. This was repeated till none was left on the field. Then, stationing the elder with his cudgel at the door, the minister would mount the pulpit and conduct the service. One of his earliest sermons was blessed to the conversion of his assistant, and a truly valuable coadjutor he found in big Rory thereafter. Many who were like Rory were reformed, and became strongly attached to religion. So that, on the death of Mr. Sage, his successor found an improved field for his labours, and was enabled to do much good.

BROWNLOW NORTH AND THE COLONEL.

WHEN Brownlow North was staying in London, he got a letter at breakfast, from a lady at Torquay, with whom he was only slightly acquainted, telling him that she had a son in London, a Colonel in the Guards, and asking him to call on him and speak to him about his soul, giving him his name and address. Mr. North did not at first like this. He did not care to intrude on a Colonel in the Guards whom he had never seen, and he knew the writer so slightly, that he hardly felt called on to do it. Still he kept the letter in his pocket, and it was like to burn a hole there. At last he resolved that he would call on him, but he secretly wished that he might not find him at home. On reaching his door he rung the bell, and asked if the Colonel was at home. "Yes, sir, he is," was the answer, and he walked in and found a tall, handsome man, with a long beard, very fashionably dressed. He was just about to go out to the Park. His hat was on, and he was pulling on one of his lavender kid gloves.

Mr. North began the conversation by saying, "Colonel, I have come to you on what you will think a strange errand. I am Mr. North. I had a letter from your mother yesterday morning, asking me to call on you and speak to you about your soul." "Oh, you are Mr. North," said the Colonel, taking off his hat; "pray sit down on the sofa. I had a letter from my mother, leading me to expect this visit." They conversed for a while together, when Mr. North showed him the danger of being of the world, living with it and perishing with it; and also the only possible way of escape through Jesus Christ, as the Saviour provided by God, and he urged him to leave the world and cleave to Christ. "But," said he, "you must do this out and out, and don't

be ashamed of it. Go to your club or to your mess, and
tell them that you have changed masters." The Colonel
indicated that he was not prepared for this. "I daresay," said Mr. North, "you shrink from it. You would
rather lead a forlorn hope, or brave any military danger.
The confession, however, would not be so difficult as it
seems at a distance. The lion is a chained one. I am
myself a proof of this now. Yesterday morning I got a
letter from a lady whom I scarcely knew, asking me to
go to a Colonel of the Guards whom I had never seen,
and speak to him about his soul. If you had got such
a message, you would not have liked it." "No," he said,
"I should not." "Neither did I. If any one had come
to me on such an errand a few years ago, I should have
turned him to the door, and I expected that you would
do so to me. But instead of that you have treated me
like a gentleman, given me a seat on your sofa, and
entered frankly into conversation with me, and I am
ashamed of my timidity." Difficulties in the way of
duty always become less as they are approached.

RICHARD CAMERON'S SUFFERING AND DEATH.

RICHARD CAMERON was a brave Christian man. He was
originally of the Episcopal persuasion, but having been
led to hear the Gospel preached in the fields, he forsook
the curates, and took license from the outed ministers.
He entered on his labours with all the ardour of a new
convert, who, tracing his first serious impressions to field-
preachings, could not bring himself to think with
patience of those who availed themselves of the Indulgence. Finding that he could not help preaching against
it, though he had come under a promise to refrain from
it, he retired for a time to Holland, but returned after
the stipulated period, in 1680, burning with a desire to
disburden his conscience. His sermons were filled with
predictions of the fall of the Stuarts, and the sufferings
of Scotland which would precede it. But his course was
brief; for in July of that same year, Bruce of Earlshall,

a violent persecutor, came upon him and his followers with a troop of dragoons, at a meeting held in a desert place called Airsmoss.

On seeing the enemy approach, and no way of escape, the people gathered close around their minister, when he offered up a short prayer, repeating thrice the memorable words, "Lord, spare the green, and take the ripe!" He then turned to his brother Michael, saying, "Come, let us fight it to the last; for this is the day that I have longed for, and the death that I have prayed for—to die fighting against the Lord's avowed enemies; and this is the day we will get the crown." And there, accordingly, he died, fighting manfully back to back with his brother. The enemy, foiled in their object, which was to bring him to an ignominious end, wreaked their vengeance on the inanimate body of the hero. They cut off his head and hands, and carried them to his father, who was then confined in the Tolbooth of Edinburgh, tauntingly inquiring if he knew to whom they belonged. "I know them, I know them," said the poor old man; "they are my son's, my dear son's. Good is the will of the Lord, who cannot wrong me nor mine." They were then fixed upon one of the ports of the city, the hands close to the head, with the fingers upwards, as if in the posture of prayer. "There," said Sir Robert Murray, "there's the head and hands of a man who lived praying and preaching, and died praying and fighting."

DONALD CARGILL KEPT FROM SUICIDE.

Mr. Donald Cargill was given to very much lawyer's work before his entry into the ministry, and while a student, and that with grievous temptations and fiery darts mixed in with it; and his too great reservedness, and not communicating his case to such as might have given him counsel and support under it, drove him to terrible excesses; in short, he came to the very height of despair; and through indulging melancholy, and hearkening to temptations, he at length came to take up a resolution to put an end to his miserable life. He was living then with his father, or some relation in the parish of Bothwell; and under the horrible hurry of those fiery darts, he went out once or twice to the river Clyde, with a dreadful resolution to drown himself. He was always, however, diverted by somebody or other coming by him, which prevented his design at the time. But the temptation continuing, and his horror by yielding to it increasing, he fell upon a method which he thought he would not be prevented in.

On a summer morning, very early, he went from the house where he stayed to a more unfrequented place, where there were some old coal pits, and coming up to one of them, was fully determined to step in; but when very near it, a thought struck him, that his coat he had upon him and vest being new, might be of some use to others, though he was unworthy to live, and so he stepped back and threw them off, and then came up to the very brink of the pit, and when just going to jump in, that word struck him,—"Son, be of good cheer, thy sins are forgiven thee." He said it came in with that power and life upon his spirit, which was impossible for him to express; and he did not know whether it was by an immediate impression of it on his mind, or a direct voice from heaven—which last he inclined to think; but it had such an evidence and energy accompanying it, as at once put an end to all his fears and doubts, and which he could no more resist than he could do the light of a sunbeam darted upon his eye.

The Rev. James Wodrow in the year 1681 went in and saw Mr. Cargill in Edinburgh Prison, a day or two before his death; and, after some conversation, asked him how he found matters with him? Mr. Cargill answered him, "As to the main point, my interest in Christ, and the pardon of my sins, I have no doubts there; neither have I been ever shaken since the Lord's condescension to me in my extremity, about twenty-five years ago—which I communicated to you a little after; and no thanks to me, for the evidence was so clear that I could never since once doubt; but then as to many other things, I have sad fears and damps. I see a dark and heavy cloud coming on the Church of Scotland—and our trial is not yet at its height."

M'CHEYNE AS A PREACHER.

The Rev. Robert M'Cheyne went about his public work with awful reverence. So evident was this that I remember, says his biographer, a countryman in my parish observed to me,—"Before he opened his lips, as he came along the passage, there was something about him that sorely affected me." In the vestry there never was any idle conversation; all was preparation of the heart in approaching God, and a short prayer preceded his entering the pulpit. After announcing the subject of his discourse, he used, generally, to show the position it occupied in the context, and then proceeded to bring out the doctrines of the text after the manner of our old divines. This done, he divided his subject, and herein he was eminently skilful. "The heads of his sermons," said a friend, "were not the milestones that tell how near you are to your journey's end, but they were nails which fixed and fastened all he said. Divisions are often dry, but not so his divisions,—they were so textual and so feeling, and they brought out the spirit of a passage so surprisingly." A simple incident was overruled to promote the ease and fluency of his pulpit ministrations.

From the very beginning of his ministry he reprobated the custom of reading sermons, believing that to do so does exceedingly weaken the freedom and natural fervour of the messenger in delivering his message. Neither did he recite what he had written. But his custom was to impress on his memory the substance of what he had beforehand carefully written, and then to speak as he found liberty. One morning, as he rode rapidly along to Dunipace, his written sermons were dropped on the wayside. This incident prevented him having the opportunity of preparing in his usual manner; but he was enabled to preach with more than usual freedom. For the first time in his life he discovered that he possessed the gift of extemporaneous composition, and learned, to his own surprise, that he had more composedness of mind and command of language than he had believed. This discovery, however, did not in the least degree diminish his diligent preparation. Indeed, the only use that he made of the incident at the time it occurred, was to draw a lesson of dependence on God's own immediate blessing rather than on the satisfactory preparation made. 'One thing always fills the cup of my consolation, that God may work by the meanest and poorest words, as well as by the most polished and ornate,—yea, perhaps, more readily, that the glory may be all His own.'"

TRIAL OF THE DUKE OF ARGYLL.

On the 16th of April, 1661, the Marquis of Argyll, who had been a prisoner in Edinburgh Castle since December, was brought to the bar of the Scottish Parliament to answer an indictment for high treason, and was wrongfully condemned to death. After transacting all his worldly business, he was accosted by George Hutcheson, an old, venerable minister of Edinburgh, who affectionately inquired,—"What cheer, my Lord?" "Good cheer, sir," he answered, "the Lord hath said to me from heaven, 'Son, be of good cheer, thy sins are forgiven thee.'" A sudden thrilling emotion overcame him; his eyes filled with tears of joy and rapture; he stepped aside to the window to compose himself. Then taking Hutcheson by the hand, he said,—"God is good to me, that He lets not out too much of His communications here, for He knows I could not bear it." "Before he went to death," Kirkton informs us, "he dined with his friends cheerfully, and, after dinner, went to secret prayer." When the procession of death was formed, surrounded by a faithful mourning band of noblemen and others who accompanied him, he thus addressed them,—"I could die like a Roman, but choose rather to die as a Christian. Come away, gentlemen, he that goes first goes cleanest."

In descending the stairs of his prison, he called for James Guthrie, also a prisoner, awaiting the same sentence of death. They embraced each other tenderly, bidding a mutual short farewell, expecting within a few short days to meet in the blessed realm where there is no sorrow or suffering, fraud or injustice. "My lord," exclaimed Guthrie, with a last grasp of the hand, his eye suffused with a tear which his own doom could not extort, "God hath been with you, He is with you, He will be with you; and such is my respect for your lordship, that if I were not under sentence of death myself, I would cheerfully die for you." Burnet, who was present on the occasion, records that "he came to the scaffold in a very solemn but undaunted manner." He spoke briefly to the people—rather uttering the religious thoughts which then occupied his mind, than indulging in any reflections on the political events in which he had borne so distinguished a part. He thus concluded,—"I desire not that the Lord should judge any man, nor do I judge any but myself. I wish that, as the Lord hath pardoned me, so may He pardon them for this and other things; and what they have done to me may never meet them in their accounts."

The moment before he laid down his head on the block, his physician, Cunningham, touched his pulse; it was beating at the usual rate—calm, regular, and strong. After taking leave of his friends "in a very gentle manner," says Kirkton, "distributing his tokens," and then engaging for some time in secret prayer, he gave the signal to the executioner. The axe fell, and on the boards of the scaffold rolled the head of the once mighty Argyll, mightiest in his death—the proto-martyr of his country's religion and liberty.

DR. NORMAN MACLEOD'S FIRST SERMON BEFORE THE QUEEN.

In a retrospect in his Journal, Rev. Dr. Macleod describes his first sermon before the Queen. He says,—"I had received an invitation to preach at Crathie when I was at Kirkcaldy. I refused to go. I had announced the opening of my church—after it had been closed for two months to be repaired—and it seemed to me that my duty to open it was greater than to accept of Mr. Anderson's invitation to preach before the Queen. The going there, therefore, was not sought for by me. I returned home at eight, Thursday night, and found a letter from Mr. A., stating that he asked me at the Queen's own request. My duty being clear, I accepted it. The weather was superb, and I was much struck with the style of the scenery.

"The Sunday at Balmoral was perfect in its peace and beauty. I confess that I was much puzzled what to preach. I had with me some of my best sermons (as people would call them); but the struggle, which had begun on Friday morning, was renewed—as to what was best in the truest, most spiritual sense for such an occasion; until, by prayer, I resolved to preach, without any notes, a sermon I never wrote fully out, but had preached very often, perhaps fifteen times, solely because I found that it had found human spirits, and had done good. It was from Matt. xi. 28-30; Mark x. 17-31. I tried to show what true life is—life in the Spirit—a finding rest through the yoke of God's service, instead of the service of self, and by the cross of self-denial instead of self-gratification, illustrated by the young man who, with all that way so promising, would not peril his happiness by seeking it with Christ in God. I preached with intense comfort, and, by God's help, felt how sublime a thing it was to be His ambassador. I felt very acutely how, for our sakes, the Queen and the Prince were placed in so trying a position, and was profoundly grateful for the way in which they had governed us; and so it was that I was able to look back from the future, and to speak as I shall wish I had done. It would be most ungrateful in me not to record this singular mercy of God to me; for I do know, and rejoice to record for the strengthening of my faith in prayer, that He did it. Thus I enjoyed great peace.

"In the evening, after daundering in a green field with a path through it which led to the high road, and while sitting on a block of granite, full of quiet thoughts, mentally reposing in the midst of the beautiful scenery,

I was roused from my reverie by some one asking me if I was the clergyman who had preached that day. I was soon in the presence of the Queen and Prince; when her Majesty came forward, and said with a sweet, kind, and smiling face, 'We wish to thank you for your sermon.' She then asked me how my father was—what was the name of my parish, etc.; and so, after bowing and smiling, they both continued their quiet walk alone. And thus God blessed me, and I thanked His name. I posted home by Glenshee—not well—and was in bed all the week. So ends my story. I read its commencement and ending to remind me how God is always faithful. 'O ye of little faith, wherefore did ye doubt?'"

MARTYRS AT PERTH.

On the 25th January, 1544, Helen Stark, her husband, and four others, were tried in Perth for holding meetings for conversing upon and explaining the sacred Scriptures, and were condemned. The men were sentenced to be hanged at the common place of execution, and Helen was to be drowned in a pool in the neighbourhood. Helen and her husband had lived together in the tenderest union, and, in the ardour of her affection, she implored, as a last request, that she might be permitted to die with him; but she had been sentenced to undergo a different kind of death, and the affecting request was denied. Being allowed to accompany him to the place of execution, she ministered to him consolation by the way, exhorting him to patience and constancy in the cause of Christ, and parting from him with a kiss, she expressed her feelings in these singularly touching words, the sincere effusion of the heart, for the occasion was too serious for mere theatrical display of sentiment: "Husband, be glad; we have lived together many joyful days, but this day, on which we must die, ought to be the most joyful of all to us both, because, now we shall have joy for ever. Therefore, I will not bid you good night, for we shall suddenly meet with joy in the kingdom of heaven."

Immediately after his execution, and the execution of his fellow-martyrs, she was led forth to a pool of water in the neighbourhood, to undergo the death to which she had been condemned. Upon reaching the pool, she prepared for her fate. Having several children—one of whom was an infant hanging upon her breast, a scene of the most affecting nature was exhibited, which strongly moved the spectators, many of whom could not refrain from shedding tears. Her affections being now strongly excited towards her orphan children, the thought of separation from them seemed for a moment to disturb the serenity of her mind, and she commended them to the compassion of her neighbours. But the most powerfully exciting cause of agitation and agony, was her parting with her sucking child. This beloved object, at whose couch she had often sung, in the joyousness of her heart, her favourite airs, she took from her bosom, and after fixing upon it a last look, full of the tender yearnings of a mother's heart, gave it to the friend who had undertaken to become its nurse. This struggle with parental affection made the sacrifice of her life the more trying, but it made it also the more magnanimous, the more sacred, the more acceptable to God. Recovering from the shock, she yielded herself to death with unwavering faith, calm tranquillity, and heroic fortitude. Without any change of countenance, she sees her hands and her feet bound by the executioner. Thus secured, and being tied in a sack, she was plunged into the water. After a momentary struggle, her redeemed spirit, emancipated from all its sorrows, was rejoicing before the throne of God; and may we not affirm that, next to the Saviour, among the first to welcome her into that happier state of being, were her own husband and his fellow-sufferers, who had reached it, perhaps, hardly an hour before?

A METHODIST MINISTER IN ORKNEY.

THE REV. THOMAS COLLINS was sent to Orkney, and laboured there with great zeal from 1835 to 1838. He was not very heartily received by some people, and was bitterly opposed by not a few. The country folk did not understand what Methodism was, and they were afraid of his theological views. After an open-air service, a poor, much conscience-smitten woman followed Mr. Collins to the house of a friend, where he gave her kindly advice. Before leaving the place, he sought out the humble home where she dwelt, in order to leave with her some instruction. Seeing that she had seven children, he prayed for them, and besought her to "bring them up in the nurture and admonition of the Lord," for, said he, "all their immortal souls are precious in the sight of the Saviour." This *all* was fatal to his influence. It broke the spell thrown over her. She exclaimed,— "*All* precious to God! Not one, out of so many, reprobated? Impossible. What heresy!" The woman's faith in her spiritual instructor had been shaken. To whom had she been listening? What terrible falsehood had well nigh beguiled her! From that day she held Mr. Collins to be a deceiver, and would never see or hear him more. On another occasion, a strong controversialist asked him,—" Do you believe in the perseverance of the saints?" "Certainly," was the unexpected reply. "Indeed! I thought you were a Wesleyan. I thought you did not." "O, sir, you have been misinformed; it is the perseverance of *sinners* that we doubt." This smart reply stopped the outflow of words, and the discussion ceased.

"A BEAUTIFUL FIELD IN EDINBURGH."

AFTER the Rev. Dr. Guthrie settled in Edinburgh, he set to work right earnestly to understand the wants of his parish, and the state of the population in the Cowgate. The valley where he laboured is spanned at one place by George IV. Bridge. Looking through the open railings, the stranger sees with surprise, not flowing water, but a living stream of humanity in motion beneath his feet. "It was there," writes Dr. Guthrie, "where one looks down on the street below, and on the foul, crowded closes that stretch, like ribs, down into the Cowgate, I stood on a gloomy day in the fall of the year '37. The streets were a puddle; the heavy air, loaded with smoke, was thick and murky; right below lay the narrow street of dingy tenements, whose toppling chimneys and patched and battered roofs were fit emblems of the fortunes of most of their tenants. Of these, some were lying over the sills of windows innocent of glass, or stuffed with old hats or rags; others, coarse-looking women, with squalid children in their arms or at their feet, stood in groups at the close-mouths—here, with empty laughter, chaffing any passing acquaintance, there screaming each other down in a drunken brawl, or standing sullen and silent, with hunger and ill-usage in their saddened looks. A brewer's cart, threatening to crush beneath its ponderous wheels the ragged urchins who had no other playground, rumbled over the causeway, drowning the quivering voice of one whose drooping head and scanty dress were ill in harmony with song, but not drowning the shrill pipe of an Irish girl, who thumped the back of an unlucky donkey, and cried her herrings at 'three-a-penny.' So looked the parish I had come to cultivate; and while contrasting the scene below with pleasant recollections of the parish I had just left—its singing larks, daisied pastures, decent peasants, and the grand blue sea rolling its lines of snowy breakers on the shore, my rather sad and sombre ruminations were suddenly checked. A hand was laid on my shoulder. I turned round to find Dr. Chalmers at my elbow.

"This great and good man knew that I had accepted an Edinburgh charge mainly for the purpose of trying what the parochial or territorial system, fairly wrought, could do toward christianizing the heathen down beneath our feet, and restoring the denizens of the Cowgate and its closes to sober, decent, and church going habits. Contemplating the scene for a little in silence, all at once, with his broad Luther-like face glowing with enthusiasm, he waved his arm to exclaim,—'A beautiful field, sir; a very fine field of operation.'" This field was brought in, and a rich harvest was produced, by the earnest husbandman, which is scattered over the world in the persons of honest, industrious, and Christian men and women.

THE IMPORTANCE OF DECISION.

"I ONCE attended an old man on his death-bed," said the Rev. Dr. Macleod. "He was very lonely, and very poor, and more than fourscore years of age. He was naturally very shy and timid, and suffering from many unbelieving doubts and fears. It was sad to see an old man so far from peace with his Father; yet he had been a church-member, and had led what is termed 'a quiet inoffensive life.' I found him, however, very earnest, inquiring, and thoughtful; but very weak in his faith as to the good-will of God towards *him*, and in the freeness of the gospel offers of pardon and grace to *him*. I felt much interested in him. One afternoon I was passing his door. I had seen him the day before. His illness seemed to be the lingering weakness of old age. It was within a few minutes of my dinner hour, and I had been labour-ing since morning. A strong impulse seized me to enter the sick man's house. But the flesh argued for delay, and pleaded fatigue and want of time, and to-morrow, etc. Yet the words, 'What thy hand findeth to do, do it,' rung in my mind.

"I entered, and found the old man very weak. 'O, sir,' he exclaimed, alluding to a previous conversation, 'is the Lord indeed willing to receive a poor sinner like me?' I again pressed a few truths upon his mind; and, when parting, I strongly urged the importance of be-lieving in the love of God to him through Jesus Christ. In bidding him farewell, I said, 'As freely as I offer you my hand, and with infinitely more love, does Jesus offer as *your* Saviour every possible good, and Himself as the greatest good of all. Believe, and *thou* shalt be saved!' He seized my hand eagerly, saying, 'I believe it!' and promised, according to my request, to resign himself, and all his concerns, in earnest prayer into Christ's hands the moment I left his poor and lonely room. 'You will pray for me, sir?' he asked, as I was departing. 'Yes,' I replied. 'To-day, sir?'—'This hour,' was my promise; 'but,' I added, 'no delay—no, not a minute!—remember you are to pray immediately to Jesus, and to tell Him all your cares, sins, and sorrows, and to commit your soul to His keeping now and for ever. Farewell!' I sent for a person to sit by the old man, as he seemed weaker than usual. In about half an hour after parting from him, the woman whom I had requested to attend him came running to my door with the intelligence, that *she had found him dead.*"

RETURNING GOOD FOR EVIL;

Or, Conquered by Kindness.

JAMES HARKNESS, who was one of the leaders of the Covenanters of Scotland, in the reign of Charles the Second, was once riding from his persecutors with a party of his friends among the wild mountains and solitary glens of Nithsdale, when they were surprised by a party of dragoons, who hastily surrounded them and took them prisoners. It was in vain to resist; they were in the firm grasp of the powerful foe, from which they could not extricate themselves. The commander of the party who apprehended them was a man of a cruel disposition, and he used them with great harshness. It appears that prisoners were frequently treated in a very barbarous manner by the soldiers who conveyed them to their place of destination. When they arrived in Edinburgh, to which place they were conveyed to be tried, they were put into a place of confinement, from which, before they were brought to trial, they succeeded in making their escape. They then proceeded homewards with all the secrecy and despatch they could, and passing Biggar, where the leader of the party who conducted them to Edinburgh happened at the time to be resident, they resolved to visit him. Their design in waiting on him was to put in execution a project which they had devised, for the purpose not of injuring, but of frightening one who had caused them so much trouble and inconvenience.

As they approached his house he observed them, and at once knew them to be the prisoners who were recently under his charge. He could not understand how they had possibly got free, and dreading mischief from them, he hid himself. At the door they asked civilly for the captain, and said they wished to see him on particular business. His wife, who had been apprised of the character of her visitors, said he was not at home. Harkness began to fear lest their intention should be defeated, when a little boy standing near said, "I will show where my father is," and forthwith conducted them to the place of his concealment. They instantly dragged him out, as the soldiers used to do the Covenanters from their hiding-places, and appeared as if they were going to take his life. They imitated in all respects the manner in which the dragoons shot the wanderers in the field. Having furnished themselves with a musket, probably from his own armoury, they caused him to kneel down while they tied a napkin over his eyes, and ordered him to prepare for immediate death. The poor man, in the utmost trepidation, was obliged to submit. He bent on his knees, and, being blindfolded, he expected every moment that the fatal shot would be fired into his body. Harkness, after an ominous silence of a few seconds—a brief space, doubtless of intense anxiety and agony to the helpless captain—fired, but fired aloft into the air. The shot went whizzing over the head of the horror-stricken man, who, though stunned with the loud and startling report, sustained no injury. Having thus, by way of chastisement, succeeded in making him feel something of what the poor Covenanters felt when their ruthless foes shot them without trial or ceremony in the fields, they took the bandage from his eyes, and raised him almost powerless with terror to his feet.

The circumstance made a deep impression on his mind; he saw he was fully in the power of the men who had thus captured him, and that, notwithstanding, they had done him no harm. Surprise and gladness took the place of the fear of death and of the anguish of despair in the grateful man's bosom. He confessed that the sparing of his life was owing to their Christian clemency, and to the merciful character of their religious principles. He was deeply affected by a sense of the favour shown him, at a time when he had nothing before him but a prospect of immediate death, and determined to change his life. He became a new man.

THE ANNIVERSARY OF A DELIVERANCE AT HADDINGTON.

JOHN CROUMBIE of Haddington was an amiable, bountiful, singularly pious, and every way memorable Christian man; as well as a rather ungainly, grim-visaged, over-scrupulous, nervous, and eccentric old bachelor. He was a travelling dealer or chapman, and was, indeed, about the best of this class. The most conspicuous feature in his secular character was an unbending and even chivalrous integrity; and the richest, or at least the rarest quality of his Christian nature was his zeal and almost prodigal liberality in the cause of his Lord. So fine a soul could almost afford to be peculiar, to live in a rough-spun bodily presence, and to do without some congenial graces of manner and appearance. Then the world never knows aught of those inward experiences which sometimes modify the whole exterior of such a deep, still spirit, as this inflexible, sternly and tenderly pious, and, to Christ's cause, open-handed country merchant. To John Brown, the Commentator, and to some few more that knew him by heart, he was both lovely and beloved in no common degree. His experiences, too, were varied, and he had, at least, one of the most extraordinary kind to carry to the grave with him, enough to make most men nervous and strange for life. He sold gunpowder. The store where he kept it was in a cellar right below the shop.

One summer evening, as he sat at the shop-window over his ledger, an apprentice went below stairs, candle in hand. A spark from the candle did its work;

the barrel exploded; the lad was killed; the flooring and window were blown to pieces, and John Croumbie was lifted into the air, and thrown up the street the length of the old Tron, where, in the strangest manner possible, he was set down safe and sound—except from the slight effects of his fall. This Tron, the public weighing machine, was just half-way between his window and the Cross—a flight of some one-and-thirty yards. The shop doors being supposed shut for the night, the good man was doubtless projected by, and likewise carried safely within, the range of the explosion, the terrible fragments going with him, instead of dashing about him; if not dashing him to bits, as they might have done but for his guardian angel, the Providence of God. It was, in any case, a most solemn and memorable event. Its influence on his sombre and susceptible mind was deep and permanent. As long as he lived he religiously observed the anniversary of this deliverance from death. Regularly as the day came round, he shut himself within his bed-chamber the whole day long. The hours were spent in thanksgivings for the mercy of not having been hurried, all too suddenly, into the nearer and everlastingly fixed presence of Him who is the reintrying and heart-searching Jehovah. He remembered the mercies of the Lord, and dedicated himself anew to his service. This was a means of grace which tended to keep the heart of honest John Croumbie right, and enabled him to value at their worth the things of earth and time. Deliverances remembered in this spirit will always have a sanctifying effect.

DR. CHALMERS' INTEGRITY.

In Dr. Chalmers' journal we meet with the following:— "Left Kilmany on horseback for Kirkcaldy. Was annoyed with the peculiarities of my horse, and gave way to an old habit of vehemence on the subject. This must be carefully guarded against." We are informed, by Dr. Hanna, that the annoying peculiarity of the horse was the habit of suddenly depositing his master upon the

earth with no great respect to gentleness in the act. At
first, the Doctor was much interested, by noticing the
relative length of the intervals between each fall. One
fall, however, was so severe, that he ordered his servant
to sell the horse forthwith. "You must conceal none of
his faults," said Dr. Chalmers, "and be sure and tell that
he has thrown his master ten times." "And who will
buy him," said the servant, "if I tell all that beforehand?" "I cannot help that," was the reply; "I will
have no deception practised." The horse was finally ex-
changed for one of Baxter's works. The quiet and
faithful manner in which he served his new master for
many years, led to the suspicion that the annoying
peculiarity formerly exhibited, was owing to "the singularly restless and energetic horsemanship of the rider."
Nor does it fail to show forth the Doctor's love for "the
truth, the whole truth, and nothing but the truth."

CHALMERS AND THOLUCK.

WHEN Professor Tholuck of Halle was in Edinburgh in
1846, Dr. Chalmers took an early opportunity of spending an evening with him at the house of the friend with
whom he resided. "Dr. Chalmers," says this friend,
"seated himself on a low chair close to the learned
German, and listened with an air of genuine docility to
all he said, throwing in a stray characteristic observation
now and then, always, however, in the way of encouragement, never in the way of contradiction. Dr. Tholuck
had published some verses of a religious character, which
had given umbrage to some sect or other. He showed
the lines to Dr. Chalmers, who, admiring them, observed
that he had often been taken to task himself for a
similar latitudinarianism; 'for, my dear sir,' he added,
'some people have a fine nose for heresy.' While Dr.
Chalmers was sitting in this posture, drinking in all that
was said to him, Tholuck turned to his host, and said,
in German, that he had never seen so beautiful an old
man.

"The words coming out so suddenly in an unknown

tongue, instantly changed the whole expression of Dr. Chalmers' face from that of happy acquiescence, to one of puzzled amazement, which was, in the highest degree, comic, and this effect was not lessened by his eager putting of the question,—'What is it, sir, that he says?' —a question impossible to answer, and yet not easy to evade. The result of this interview was an amount of mutual confidence and esteem, as deep and sincere as it was sudden. Dr. Tholuck took an early opportunity of returning the visit, and spent some hours with Dr. Chalmers, urging upon him, in the most direct and homely way, the necessity of directing his mind to the study of the German theology, for, as it was from that quarter the bane had come which was poisoning the simple faith, so it was there alone that the antidote could be found. The day before Tholuck's departure, Dr. Chalmers called upon him and found him at his midday repast. He sat with him only for a few minutes, and said little, but looked at him constantly with an expression of earnest interest and affection. He rose to take leave, and, instead of taking him by the hand, he threw his arms round his neck and kissed him, while 'God bless you, my dear friend,' broke with apparent difficulty from his overcharged heart. After he was gone, it was noticed that a tear had gathered in the eye of him who had received the apostolic benediction and seal of brotherhood from one he loved and venerated so much. His only observation was a half-muttered, half-spoken, *eben ein kuss*—even a kiss!"

BROWNLOW NORTH TURNING A LETTER TO ACCOUNT.

AFTER Mr. Brownlow North became an evangelist, he was taunted by those who knew his past career, and this sometimes with more than a tinge of spite. One evening Mr. North was about to enter the vestry of a church in one of our northern towns, in which he was going to preach, when a stranger came up to him in a hurried manner, and said,—"Here is a letter for you of great importance, and you are requested to read it before you preach to-night." Thinking it might be a request for prayer from some awakened soul, he immediately opened it, and found that it contained a detail of some of his former irregularities of conduct, concluding with words to this effect: "How dare you, being conscious of the truth of all the above, pray and speak to the people this evening, when you are such a vile sinner!"

The preacher put the letter into his pocket, entered the pulpit, and, after prayer and praise, commenced his address to a very crowded congregation; but before speaking on his text he produced the letter, and informed the people of its contents, and then added,—"All that is here said is true, and it is a correct picture of the degraded sinner that I once was; and oh! how wonderful must the grace be that could quicken and raise me up from such a death in trespasses and sins, and make me what I appear before you to-night, a vessel of mercy, one who knows that all his past sins have been cleansed away through the atoning blood of the Lamb of God. It is of His redeeming love that I have now to tell you, and to entreat any here who are not yet reconciled to God to come this night in faith to Jesus, that He may take their sins away, and heal them." His hearers were deeply impressed by the words he spoke, and that which was intended to close his lips was overruled to open the hearts of the congregation to receive his message.

KNOX'S PRAYER FOR SCOTLAND.

DURING the troublous times of Scotland, when the Popish courts and aristocracy were arming themselves to suppress the Reformation in the land, the cause of Protestant Christianity was in imminent peril. Late on a certain night John Knox was seen to leave his study, and to pass from the house down into an inclosure to the rear of it. He was followed by a friend; when after a few moments of silence, his voice was heard as if in prayer. In another moment the accents deepened into intelligible words, and the earnest petition went up from his struggling soul to heaven,—" O Lord, give me Scotland, or I die!" Then a pause of hushed stillness, then again the petition broke forth,—" O Lord, give me Scotland, or I die!" Once more all was voiceless, noiseless, when, with a yet intense pathos, the thrice-repeated intercession struggled forth,—" O Lord, give me Scotland, or I die!" And God gave him Scotland in spite of Mary and her Popish missionaries. For Knox's influence has been the greatest of any man in Scotland, and has done much to determine her ecclesiastical, social, educational, and political institutions—Knox's prayer was heard and largely answered.

FLOCKHART'S IMPORTANT SCHOOL-LESSON.

ROBERT FLOCKHART tells us in his life that, soon after his conversion, he commenced a school in which he taught children to commit to memory portions of Scripture. He had done this himself when a boy, and he found it had been blessed to him. He says:—" One passage which I learned at that school was Isaiah i. 18, 'Come now and let us reason together, saith the Lord; though your sins be as scarlet, they shall be white as snow; though they be red like crimson, they shall be as wool.' This text the Lord hid in my heart for fully twenty years. During all that time, I had clean forgotten it. At length the Lord was pleased to afflict me, and bring me into the wilderness that he might draw me to himself, as it is written, 'I have loved thee with an everlasting love; therefore with loving-kindness have I drawn thee.' The Spirit of God strove with me through the once crucified, but now glorified Saviour, to lead me to pray. I said, 'I do not know how to pray, or what to say.' Then it came into my mind that I could offer the Lord's Prayer only. Then, methought I felt not satisfied with praying the Lord's Prayer only; and now that the task I learned so long ago at Mr. Robertson's school came into my mind, 'Come now, and let us reason together, saith the Lord,' etc., etc., I repeated that blessed portion of God's Word, and the Lord came to me, and I came to him, and pleaded the fulfilment of that sweet promise.

"I now understood why the Lord required me to confess my sins and transgressions; it was that his justice might be glorified, in my eternal punishment for breaking his law, and living a life of rebellion against him. When, therefore, I repeated the words, 'Though my sins be as scarlet, they shall be as white as snow; though they be red like crimson, they shall be as wool,' I had the full assurance of faith that God had heard and answered this my first prayer. Thus, judging from my own case, I thought that portion of God's Word instilled into the children's young hearts might afterwards be productive of great good, though I might not live to see it. It might, I thought, be twenty, or even thirty years before the seed sown would ripen into fruit. No matter, the attempt ought to be made, and the result left with God. The attempt, therefore, I did make, praying at the same time that, as in my own case, the fruits of my labours might appear (even though it should be many years hence) in the lives of at least some of my pupils."

LIVINGSTONE'S MODESTY.

WHEN David Livingstone returned to his native country for the second time, the great explorer and heroic missionary was received everywhere with honour and applause. He was, as he himself says, cheered and welcomed as a man and a brother. But amid all the exciting scenes through which he passed, he was ever the same retiring and modest Scotchman. He went with his daughter Agnes to see the launching of a Turkish frigate from Mr. Napier's yard, when he saw eight thousand tons weight plunged into the Clyde, which sent a wave of its water to the other side. The Turkish Ambassador, Musurus Pasha, was one of the party at Shandon, and he and Livingstone travelled in the same carriage. At one of the stations, they were greatly cheered by the Volunteers. "The cheers are for you," Livingstone said to the Ambassador, with a smile. "No," said the

Turk, "I am only what my master made me; you are what you made yourself." When the party reached the Queen's Hotel, a working man rushed across the road, seized Livingstone's hand, saying, "I must shake your hand," clapping him on the back, and rushed back again. "You'll not deny, now," said the Ambassador, "that that's for you."

AN OLD-FASHIONED SAINT OF THE PENTLAND HILLS.

JUST at the foot of the Pentland Hills lay, years ago, an old farm-house, of the plainest kind, built of rough stone, and roofed with thatch, but shaded by venerable trees, and cheered by a "bonnie burn, wimpling" over its pebbly bed. That was the home of Sandy Morrison, an old-fashioned Presbyterian elder. In exterior, Sandy was rough, tall, and ungainly. The only thing about him really attractive was his large clear hazel eye, which lay beneath his shaggy brows.

Sandy had a perfect trust in the Providence of God. "The Lord reigneth," he would say, "everything is wisely ordered, and will come out right in the end." If you said, "Not surely the sins and follies of men," he would reply as follows:—

"Sins and follies are ours, and we suffer for them; but God overrules them for His glory. You see the eddies in the stream yonder; they twist and turn a' sorts o' ways, but they go wi' the current at last. In the storm, sticks, stanes, and dirt come tumbling doun frae the hills; but in the valley yonder, they lie a' quiet enough, and, in the simmer time, will be covered wi' grass and daisies. In the same way, it seems to me, God works a' things according to the counsel o' his ain will." This accounts for Sandy's peace and joy. "You see," said he, explaining the matter in his peculiar fashion, "years gane by, I believed jist as ithers dae, wha ha'e a form o' godliness, but deny the power thereof. I didna understand, an', abune all, I didna love God. I was worryin' aboot this, that, and the other. Things were nae richt; wife an' I were puir, ye ken, and had to work hard; but we didna mind that sae lang as we had health an' strength. We lived in a bonnie place; the sun shone cheerily on oor bit housie, amang the roses an' honeysuckles that my auld mither had planted wi' her ain hand—an' mair than that, the Lord sent us a bonnie bairn. Hech! the wee thing seemed an angel in disguise, wi' its yellow hair, dimplin' cheeks, and blue een! It was the licht an' glory o' oor hame; but the Lord took her to himsel'. O how we grat when we laid her in the yird! and Mary (that's my wife's name) began to fail. She couldna tell what was the matter wi' her. The doctor said she had a weakness in the chest. But it made oor hame unco dowie-like. Everything seemed to gae wrang, and I murmured sair against the Lord. The world looked waefu', and I would have liked to dee. But I began to think—I seemed to come to mysel'; yet my mind was unco dark. Then I read the Bible and prayed. Oor neebor, auld Mr. Wallace, a guid man, tauld us to look to the Rock o' Ages, and see if the Lord wadna open for us the fountain o' consolation. Then I saw, but not very clearly at first, that there was anither warld— anither kingdom-like, speeritual an' eternal—as auld Mr. Rutherfurd wud say. This warld is only a husk or shell —the substance, the speerit, is anither. An' a' is fu' o' God. Then I saw wee Mary, whose body we had laid in the grave, walkin' in that warld o' licht an' peace. I heard her singin' there wi' the angels o' God; I heard the voice o' Jesus there, saying—Peace, peace! It cam' like the sweetest music to my puir heart! Then I understood hoo blind, unbelievin', an' wicked I had been, an' I said to mysel', 'What's the use o' murmurin'? The Redeemer liveth, an' blessed be His name; I will jist put mysel' an a' I ha'e under the shadow o' His wings.'

"Says I to my wife, 'Mary, we maun believe in God —He's a', an' in a'. He gave us oor bonnie bairn, an' He's ta'en her again; for she was His mair than oors; an' noo she's an angel; she winna come to us, but we'll gang to her. An' noo ye maun be comforted.' An' then we kneeled doon thegither, and prayed to the God o' oor faithers, the God o' oor bairn, an' were comforted. Then the world appeared to me in a new licht. It was filled wi' the holy presence o' God. I saw that a' was His— licht an' darkness, simmer an' winter, sorrow and joy, death an' life; an' that He was governin' a' things according to the counsel o' His ain will."

REV. WILLIAM WILSON AND THE SOLDIER.

ONE evening, as the Rev. William Wilson, of Perth, was passing along the streets of that town, three soldiers, then quartered in it, happened to walk behind him, who were indulging in the utterance of the most profane and blasphemous language. One of them, on some frivolous account, declared it to be his wish, that God Almighty might damn his soul in hell to all eternity. Mr. Wilson immediately turned round, and, with a look of dignity and compassion, said, "Poor man, and what if God should say Amen, and answer that prayer?" Mr. Wilson passed on. The man seemed to stand petrified, and, on going home to his quarters, was in such distraction of mind, that he knew not whither to turn for relief. He was soon afterwards seized with fever, under which he continued to suffer the most awful forebodings of eternal misery. His case was so singular, that many Christians went to visit him, to whom he invariably said he was sure of being beyond the reach of mercy, and that God had sent his angel to tell him so.

One of them asked him to describe the appearance of the person who had pronounced this doom on him. He did so, and the visitant at once perceiving that it must have been Mr. Wilson, inquired if he would wish again to see him. "Oh," said he, "I would wish above everything to see him, but he would not come near a wretch like me." Mr. Wilson was soon brought; and he told him of the way of salvation through Christ crucified, and encouraged him to flee for refuge to lay hold upon the hope set before him. His words being accompanied by Divine power, the poor soldier was enabled to believe in Christ, and thus found peace and comfort to his troubled soul. He soon afterwards recovered, and became a very exemplary Christian; and as he felt the army unfavourable to a religious life, Mr. Wilson, at his request, used his influence, and procured his discharge. He settled in Perth, became a member of the church, attached himself steadily to Mr. Wilson, and was, through life, a comfort to him, and an ornament to the Christian profession. He became a soldier of the Cross, and fought nobly the battle of an earnest Christian life. From being a blasphemer, he became known as one who, in childlike humility of soul, bent the knee, and looked to heaven with the words on his lips, "Abba, Father."

"IF YE KENNED HOW I LOVE HIM."

A POOR idiot, who was supported by his parish in the Highlands of Scotland, passed his time in wandering from house to house. He was silent and peaceable, and won the pity of all kind hearts. He had little power to converse with his fellow-men, but seemed often in loving communion with Him who, while He is the High and Holy One, condescends to men of low estate. Yeddie, as he was called, was in the habit of whispering to himself as he trudged along the highway or performed the simple tasks which any neighbour felt at liberty to demand of him. Once, when a merry boy heard him pleading earnestly in prayer, he asked, "What ghost or goblin are you begging favours of now, Yeddie?" "Neither the one nor the tither, laddie," he replied; "I was just having a few words with Him that neither yoursel' nor I can see, and yet with Him that sees the baith of us!"

One day Yeddie presented himself in his coarse dress and hob-nailed shoes before the minister, and, making a bow, much like that of a wooden toy when pulled by a string, he said, "Please, minister, let poor Yeddie eat supper on the coming day with the Lord Jesus." The minister was preparing for the observance of the Lord's

Supper, which came quarterly in that thinly settled region, and was celebrated by several churches together, so that the concourse of people made it necessary to hold the services in the open air. He was too busy to be disturbed by the simple youth, and so strove to put him off as gently as possible. But Yeddie pleaded, "Oh, minister, *if ye but kenned how I love Him*, ye wud let me go where He's to sit at table." This so touched his heart that permission was given for Yeddie to take his seat with the rest. As the service proceeded, tears flowed freely from the eyes of the poor "innocent," and at the name of Jesus he would shake his head mournfully, and whisper, "But I dinna see Him." At length, however, after partaking of the bread and wine, he raised his head, wiped away the traces of his tears, and, looking in the minister's face, nodded and smiled. Then he covered his face with his hands, and buried it between his knees, and remained in that posture till the parting blessing was given and the people began to scatter. He then rose, and, with a face lighted with joy and yet marked with solemnity, he followed the rest. One and another from his own parish spoke to him, but he made no reply until pressed by some of the boys. Then he said, "Ah, lads, dinna bid Yeddie talk to-day! He's seen the face of the Lord Jesus among His ain ones. He got a smile frae His eye and a word frae his tongue; and he's afeared to speak lest he lose memory o't, for it's but a bad memory he has at the best. Ah! lads, lads! I ha' seen Him this day that I never seed before. I ha' seen wi' these dull eyes *yon lovely Man*. Dinna ye speak, but just leave poor Yeddie to His company."

When Yeddie reached the poor cot he called "home," he dared not speak to the "granny" who sheltered him, lest he might, as he said, "lose the bonny face." He left his "parritch and treacle" untasted; and, after smiling on and patting the faded cheek of the old woman, to show her that he was not out of humour, he climbed the ladder to the poor loft where his pallet of straw was, to get another look and another word "frae yon lovely Man." And his voice was heard below, in low tones:

"Ay, Lord, it's just poor me that has been sae long seeking Ye; and now we'll bide thegither and never part more! Oh, ay! but this is a bonny loft, all goold and precious stones! The hall o' the castle is a poor place to my loft this bonny night!" And then his voice grew softer and softer till it died away. Granny sat over the smouldering peat below, with her elbows on her knees, relating in loud whispers to a neighbouring crone the stories of the boys who had preceded Yeddie from the service, and also his own strange words and appearance. "And, beside a' this," she said in a whisper, "he refused to taste his supper—a thing he had never done before, such a fearfu' appetite he had! But to-night, when he cam' in, faint wi' the long road he had come, he cried, "Nae meat for me, granny; 1 ha' had a feast which I will feel within me while I live; I supped with the Lord Jesus, and noo I must e'en gang up the loft and sleep wi' Him!"

When the morrow's sun arose, "granny," unwilling to disturb the weary Yeddie, left her poor pillow to perform his usual tasks. She brought peat from the stack and water from the spring. She spread her humble table, and made the "parritch"; and then, remembering that he went supperless to bed, she called him from the foot of the ladder. There was no reply. She called again and again, but there was no sound above, except the wind whistling through the openings in the thatch. She had not ascended the rickety ladder for years, but anxiety gave strength to her limbs, and she soon stood in the poor garret which had long sheltered the half-idiot boy. Before a rude stool, half-sitting, half-kneeling, with his head resting on his folded arms, she found Yeddie. She laid her hand upon his head, but instantly recoiled in terror. The heavy iron crown had been lifted from his brow, and, while she was sleeping, had been replaced with the crown of the ransomed, which fadeth not away.

Yeddie had caught a glimpse of Jesus, and could not live apart from Him. As he had supped, so had he slept —with Him!

GOOD SEED STRANGELY SOWN ON THE BANKS OF THE TWEED.

SOME years ago, a lady, while strolling along the banks of the Tweed, near her own mansion, either mislaid or accidentally dropped a new copy of Reid's "Blood of Jesus," bearing her name and address. There, among the grass, the flowers, and the drifting leaves of autumn, it lay until a rainy season flooded the river. The uprising waters, surging over the grassy banks, swept it out into the current, and carried it downwards for many miles. At last it floated aside towards a mill-dam, where, along with much wreckage brought down by the flood, it became fast in the mill heck. Here it was discovered by a working man, who came from some distance to the saw-mill to procure a load of wood. He took it home and read it, and at once he became deeply earnest about his soul's salvation. After awhile he gave himself to Christ, and has since endeavoured to live as a poor blood-washed sinner should do. Several other unconverted persons have also been blessed by reading this precious little volume. In this marvellous manner the Lord was pleased to carry the glad tidings to several careless persons, making the waters an instrument in bearing the saving message.

A LAMB OF CHRIST'S FLOCK.

LET me tell you, says the Rev. Robert Murray M'Cheyne, a word of a gentle lamb whom Jesus gathered, and whom I saw on her way from grace to glory. She was early brought to Christ, and early taken to be with Him where He is. She told her companions that she sometimes fell asleep on these words—" Underneath are the everlasting arms." She said she did not know how it was, but somehow she felt that Christ was always near her. When seized with her last illness, and told that the doctors thought she would not live long, she looked quite composed, and said,—" I am very happy at that." She said that she could not love Jesus enough here, that she would like to be with Him, and then she would love Him as she ought. To her tender, watchful relative, she said,—"I wonder at your looking so grave. I am surprised at it, for I think I am the happiest person in the house. I have every temporal comfort, and then I am going to Jesus." After a companion had been with her, she said,—"Margaret quite entered into my happiness; she did not look grave, but smiled; that shows how much she loves me." When sitting one evening, her head resting on a pillow, she was asked, "Is there anything the matter, my darling?" "Oh," she said, "I am only weak. I am quite happy. Jesus has said, 'Thou art mine.'" Another day, when near her last, one said to her,—"Have you been praying much to-day?" "Yes," she replied, "and I have been trying to praise, too." "And what have you been praising for?" "I praise God," she said, "for all the comforts I have. I praise Him for many kind friends. You know He is the foundation of *all;* and I praise Him for taking a sinner to glory."

HIS WORD IS AT STAKE.

GRANDLY did the old Scottish believer, of whom Dr. Brown tells us in his "Horæ Subsecivæ," respond to the challenge of her pastor regarding the ground of her confidence. "Janet," said the minister, "what would you say, if after all He has done for you, God should let you drop into hell?" "E'en's (even as) He likes," answered Janet. "If He does, He'll lose mair than I'll do." At first sight Janet's reply looks irreverent, if not something worse. As we contemplate it, however, its sublimity grows upon us. Like the Psalmist, she could say, "I on thy word rely" (Ps. cxix. 114, metrical version). If His word were broken, if His faithfulness should fail, if that foundation could be destroyed, truly He would lose more than His trusting child. But that could never be. "For ever, O Lord, thy word is settled in heaven. Thy faithfulness is unto all generations." Well, then, might Janet encourage herself in the Lord her God, and say, "God hath spoken in his holiness; I will rejoice."

THOMAS CAMPBELL CLOSING HIS LIFE.

Thomas Campbell, the poet, was born July 27, 1777, and died July 15, 1844. His end was peace. On the 6th June, 1844, Campbell was able to converse freely with those around him, but his strength had become reduced, and on being assisted to change his posture, he fell back in the bed insensible. Conversation was carried on in the room in whispers; and Campbell uttered a few sentences so unconnected, that his friends were doubtful whether he was conscious or not of what was going on in his presence, and had recourse to an artifice to learn. One of them spoke of the poem of "Hohenlinden," and pretending to forget the author's name, said, he heard it was by a Mr. Robinson. Campbell saw the trick, was amused, and said playfully, in a calm but distinct tone, "No; it was one Tom Campbell." The poet had—as far as a poet can—become for years indifferent to posthumous fame. In 1838 he had been speaking to some friends in Edinburgh on the subject.

"When I think of existence," he said, "which shall commence when the stone is laid above my head, how can literary fame appear to me—to any one—but as nothing? I believe when I am gone, justice will be done me in this way—that I was a pure writer. It is an inexpressible comfort, at my time of life, to be able to look back and feel that I have not written one line against religion and virtue." Religious feeling was, as the closing scene approached, more distinctly expressed. A friend was thinking of the lines in "The Last Man," when he heard, with delight, the dying man express his belief in life and immortality brought to light by the Saviour. To his niece he said, "Come, let us sing praises to Christ." Then pointing to the bedside, he added, "Sit here." "Shall I pray for you?" she inquired. "Oh yes, he replied," let us pray for each other." After she had done so, the dying poet expressed himself "soothed and comforted." The next day, at a moment when he appeared to be sleeping heavily, his lips suddenly moved, and he said,—"We shall see —— to-morrow," naming a friend who was dearly beloved, and who had been long departed this life. On the morrow the Poet of Hope passed away, believing in Him

> "Who captive led captivity,
> Who robbed the grave of victory,
> And took the sting from death."

A CHARACTER AT WEST LINTON.

There was what is usually called "*a character*" in the Rev. James Mair's congregation, Linton, who not unfrequently tried a temper so very irritable. His name was Walter Jackson. He was a "Sir Oracle" of his kind, and to his opinions, especially of the minister's sermons, the people looked with considerable interest. He was, however, as such characters generally are, an unjustly severe critic, his task being rather to find fault than to commend. He manifested his mind of the preacher by his attitudes in the pew. When pleased, which was seldom, he sat erect, and looked the preacher in the face; when dissatisfied, he gradually turned round till his back was towards the pulpit.

Dr. Husband, of Dunfermline, was a popular preacher. His fame had reached West Linton; the people were on the tiptoe of expectation; and when he did come and preach, they were all delighted; but they "held their peace" till Walter's judgment was known. He listened attentively for awhile, but to the surprise of the congregation, he gradually turned his back upon him. The Doctor himself noticed it, and afterwards facetiously remarked, that the man's behaviour told that in his his estimation "the preaching was no great thing, and that after all there was in it a great deal more whistling than red land."

The prayers of even godly men at that time were very long and heavy, comprehending sometimes a system of divinity. Jackson was notorious for length. He was attending a funeral at Hallmyre. The company had assembled in the barn to get some refreshment, and, having partaken, he was asked to return thanks. He commenced in right good earnest with the fall of Adam, and was going down from one great Bible doctrine to another, till patience was exhausted, significant looks passed among the mourners, one by one they deserted the barn, and the funeral procession started for Newlands churchyard. When Walter came to a close, and opened his eyes, he found himself alone, and on inquiry discovered that the procession was fully a mile on its way. His conceited soul was chafed. From this others might learn a lesson as to how and to what length to pray, as well as the importance of treating others as they desire others to treat them.

THE DUKE OF BUCCLEUCH AND THE HERD-BOY.

On one occasion the old Duke of Buccleuch bought a cow in the neighbourhood of Dalkeith, where he lived, and left the creature to be driven home the next morning. Early the following day the Duke was taking a walk, very plainly dressed, and saw a boy trying in vain to drive the cow to his place. The animal was so unruly that the lad could do nothing with her, and, not knowing who the Duke was, he bawled out to him in broad Scotch: "Hie, man! come here, an' gie's a han' wi' this beast." The Duke walked slowly on, not seeming to notice the boy, who still kept calling on him to help. At last he cried out in distress, "Come here, man, an', as sure's onything, I'll gi'e ye half I get."

The Duke could hold out no longer, but went and did as he was desired. "And now," said he to the boy, as they trudged along together, "how much do you think you will get for the job?" "I dinna ken," was the reply; "but I'm sure of something, for the folks at the big hoose are guid to a' bodies." When they came to a lane near the house, the Duke slipped away from his companion, and entered by a different way. Calling his butler, he put a sovereign into his hand, saying, "Give that to the lad who has brought the cow." He then returned to the end of the lane where he had parted with the boy, so as to meet with him on his way back. "Well, how much did you get?" asked the Duke. "A shilling," said the boy, "and there's half o't to ye." "Surely, you must have more than a shilling," returned the Duke. "No," said the boy, "sure that's a' I got; an' d'ye no think it's plenty?" "I do not," said the Duke; "there must be some mistake; and as I am acquainted with the Duke, if you return, I think I'll get you more."

They went back accordingly, and the Duke rung the bell, ordered all the servants to be assembled. "Now," said the Duke to the boy, "point me out the person who gave you the shilling." "It was that chap there wi' the apron," he said, pointing to the butler. The dishonest man fell on his knees, confessed his fault, and begged to be forgiven; but the Duke indignantly ordered him to give the boy the sovereign, and quit his service immediately. "You have lost your money," said the Duke, "your situation, and your character by your deceitfulness: learn for the future that honesty is the best policy." The boy now found out who it was that had helped him to drive the cow; and the Duke was so pleased with his honesty and manliness, that he sent him to school, and helped him forward in life.

AN EXPLANATION.

On one occasion, the Rev. Mr. Kidston, Stow, had gone to a country farm house to preach, and baptise the farmer's son. The service, as was then customary, took place in the large barn, or threshing-floor. which was usually filled with the neighbours and friends, who received their invitation from the pulpit on the previous Sabbath, the misdemeanour of *private* baptism being thus avoided. When the services were concluded, the minister, and a few more intimate friends, remained to dinner with the family. When the time came for drinking to the health and happiness of the child, Mr. Kidston gave the following toast:—"Here's wishing the health and long life of the wean; and may he be a better man than his father." All heartily joined in the same, except the farmer himself whose countenance fell, and whose tongue became dumb during the remainder of the afternoon. Mr. Kidston mounted his pony to depart. The farmer stood beside him. "Good night," said the minister. "It's no good night yet, sir," replied the farmer, who took hold of the bridle, and led the pony forward. When they had cleared the homestead, and were a little on the way, Mr. Kidston asked the farmer the meaning of his conduct, and whether anything had been done to offend him. After a little pause, the farmer said, "I want to know, sir, whether you have heard anything ill of me?" "No, John," replied Mr. Kidston, "I have not. Is there any ill I should have heard?" "I know of none, sir," said John; "and yet at the baptism to-day, you affronted me before all my family and friends, by wishing my wean to be a better man than his father." "Oh," said the minister, quickly, "is that all?" "Yes," quoth the farmer, "that is all, and it is bad enough." "I am ashamed of you, John," said Mr. Kidston; "are you such a fool as not to wish every child you have to be better than yourself?" "Oh," said the farmer, as the light broke in upon him, "is that all?" "Yes," replied the minister, "that's all." "Good night, then," said John; and they parted. The explanation made all things clear, and sent the farmer home in a happier frame of mind, and the minister himself from the experience gained.

THE LAST MARTYR OF THE COVENANT.

RENWICK was brought to trial on the 8th February, 1688, charged with disowning the King's authority, teaching that it was unlawful to pay the cess-tax, and recommending his followers to come armed to the field-meetings. He admitted and defended these views. The tax, he contended, was unlawful, both because it was oppressive, and because it was imposed for the suppression of the gospel. "Would it have been thought lawful," he said, "for the Jews, in the days of Nebuchadnezzar, each to bring a coal to augment the flame of the furnace to devour the three children, if they had been so required by the tyrant? And how can it be lawful either to oppress people for not bowing down to the idols which the King sets up, or for their brethren to contribute what may help forward their oppression?" He was, of course, found guilty, and sentenced to be executed within three days. He was asked by the Justice-General if he would like longer time. He seemed, however, to be wearied of life, and was anxious to be gone. "It is all one to me," he said, "if protracted, it is welcome; if shortened, it is welcome. My Master's time is the best."

The execution of his sentence, however, was delayed for a few days, during which the most earnest efforts were made to induce him to retract his opinions. His ability and winning eloquence, his gentle demeanour, together with his youth and beauty, produced an unwonted effect on the hardened members of the Privy Council. Men who had sentenced Hackston to be hacked to pieces by a coarse and clumsy hangman, and had approved of the shocking barbarities perpetrated on the aged Donald Cargill, shrank from putting to death his disciple, so young and amiable, and yet so courageous and firm, and entreated him to save his life by acknowledging the Royal authority. The King's Advocate, Sir John Dalrymple, also used his influence with him, but in vain. The Bishop of Edinburgh, when his importunities had failed, said compassionately, "It was a pity he was of such principles, for he was a pretty lad." Even the Roman Catholic priests showed their anxiety that the interesting youth should ask for pardon, which they assured him would be immediately granted, but he continued firm in his refusal. It is probable that his incessant and wearing-out labours, his wanderings and watchings, his sickness and solitude, had somewhat affected his mind, and made him long for the rest of his grave. On the morning of his execution, he wrote to a friend, "Death to me is as a bed to the weary." His feelings might have been different, if he had known that deliverance for the Church and the country was close at hand.

On the 17th of February, he was brought to the scaffold in the presence of a multitude greater than had ever before thronged the Grassmarket. He first sang the 103rd Psalm, and read the 19th chapter of the Book of Revelations, which describes the advent and conquering career of Him who is called "Faithful and True," the Avenger of the blood of His saints upon the false prophet, and the wild beast, and the kings of the earth and their armies. He then prayed.

His address to the spectators was, as usual, drowned by the beating of drums. But once when there was a momentary pause, looking up to the clouds gathering on a lowering February sky, he was heard to say, "I shall soon be above these clouds; then shall I enjoy Thee and glorify Thee, O my Father! without interruption, and without intermission for ever." Renwick was only twenty-six years of age when he was put to death. He was the last who suffered martyrdom in Scotland for Christ's "Crown and Covenant." A few months later, the principles for which he had laid down his life were recognised as the foundation of the revolution settlement. What was capitally punished in February as treason, was adopted by the Legislature of both countries in November as the palladium of their liberties.

DR. HENRY AND THE WEARISOME MINISTER.

ABOUT 1790 the Rev. Dr. Henry, author of the "History of England," was living at a place of his own in his native county of Stirling. He was about seventy-two, and had been for some time very feeble. He wrote to Sir Harry Moncrieff that he was dying, and thus invited him for the last time,—"Come out here directly. I have got something to do this week; I have got to die." Sir Harry went, and found his friend plainly sinking, but resigned and cheerful. He had no children, and there was nobody with him except his wife. She and Sir Harry remained alone with him for about three days— being his last three—during a part of which the reverend historian sat in his easy chair, and conversed, and listened to reading, and dozed. While engaged in this way, the hoofs of a horse were heard clattering in the court below. Mrs. Henry looked out, and exclaimed that it was "that wearisome body," meaning a neighbouring minister, who was famous for never leaving a house after he had once got into it.

"Keep him out," cried the Doctor, "don't let the cratur in here." But before they could secure his exclusion, the cratur's steps were heard on the stair, and he was at the door. The Doctor instantly winked significantly, and signed to them to sit down and be quiet, and he would pretend to be sleeping. The hint was taken; and when the intruder entered, he found the patient asleep in his cushioned chair. Sir Harry and Mrs. Henry put their fingers to their lips, and, pointing to the supposed slumberer as one not to be disturbed, shook their heads. The man sat down near the door, like one inclined to wait till the nap should be over. Once or twice he tried to speak, but was instantly repressed by another finger on the lip, and another shake of the head. So he sat on, all in perfect silence, for about a quarter of an hour, during which Sir Harry occasionally detected the dying man peeping cautiously through the fringes of his eyelids, to see how his visitor was coming on. At last Sir Harry tired, and he and Mrs. Henry, pointing to the poor Doctor, fairly waved the visitor out of the room; on which the Doctor opened his eyes wide, and had a tolerably hearty laugh, which was renewed when the sound of the horse's feet made them certain that their friend was actually off the premises. A lesson is here taught to ministers who frequent the chambers of weak and dying men.

MAJOR-GENERAL BURN'S DREAM.

MAJOR-GENERAL ANDREW BURN, who became a decided Christian after the death of his brother, had a very striking and significant dream, which was more than a dream. He thus gives it:—

"I thought I was sitting, a little before daylight in the morning, with my deceased brother, on the wall of a churchyard, situated in a neighbourhood where we had

lived many years together. He remained silent for some
time, and then asked me if I would not go with him into
the church. I readily consented, and immediately rising
up, walked with him towards the porch, or outer gate,
which I thought was very large and spacious; but, when
we had passed through it, and came to the inner door
that led directly into the body of the church, some way
or other, but how I could not well conceive, my brother
slipped in before me; and when I attempted to follow—
which I was all eagerness to do—the door, which slid
from the top to the bottom, like those of some fortified
towns on the Continent, was instantly let down more
than half-way, so that I found it requisite to bend myself almost double before I could possibly enter. But as
I stooped to try, the door continued falling lower and
lower, and, consequently, the passage became so narrow
that I found it altogether impracticable in that posture.
Grieved to be left behind, and determined to get in, if
possible, I fell down on my hands, and tried to squeeze
my head and shoulders through; but finding myself still
too high, I then kneeled down, crept, wrestled, and pushed
more eagerly, but all to no purpose. Vexed to the last
degree, I, yet unwilling to be left outside, came to the
resolution of throwing off all my clothes, and crawling
like a worm; but being very desirous to preserve a fine
silk-embroidered waistcoat, which I had brought from
France, I kept that on, in hopes of being able to carry it
with me. Then, laying myself flat on my face, I toiled,
and pushed, and strove; soiled my embroidered waistcoat, but could not get in after all. At last, driven
almost to despair, I stripped myself entirely, and forced
my body between the door and the ground, till the rough
stones and gravel tore all the skin and flesh upon my
breast, and, as I thought, covered me with blood. Indifferent, however, about this, and perceiving I advanced
a little, I continued to strive with more violence than
ever, till at last I safely got through. As soon as I stood
upon my feet on the inside, an invisible hand clothed
me in a long white robe; and as I turned round to view
the place, I saw a goodly company of saints—among

whom was my brother—all dressed in the same manner, partaking of the Lord's Supper. I sat down in the midst of them, and, the bread and wine being administered to me, I felt such seraphic joy, such celestial ecstasy, as no mortal can express."

A MISTAKE OF THE INTELLECT.

IN the early ministry of Dr. Chalmers, he had been given to scientific studies, and published a pamphlet, in which he reflected severely upon such ministers as did not do the same. Years after, this pamphlet was cast up to him in the General Assembly, to show his inconsistency in then urging what he now discarded. Having acknowledged himself the author of the pamphlet, he added,—"Alas, sirs! so I thought in my ignorance and pride. I have now no reserve in declaring that the sentiment was wrong; and, in giving utterance to it, I penned what was outrageously wrong. Strangely blinded that I was! What, sir, is the object of mathematical science? magnitude, and the proportions of magnitude. But then, sir, I had *forgotten two magnitudes. I thought not of the littleness of time; I recklessly thought not of the greatness of eternity.*"

DR. WILLIAM ANDERSON ON MINISTERS' STIPENDS.

"WILLIE ANDERSON," as the Rev. Dr. Anderson, of Glasgow, was familiarly called, was a great favourite on the platform, and by his pawkie straightforwardness, carried all before him. He was once addressing a crowded meeting in the City Hall on some Church finance business or other, when he had occasion to speak of ministers' stipends — at that time a more delicate subject for a minister to speak about than now. And he dashed into the shabby treatment they received in something like the following style. "If a doctor comes to see you when you are dying, he will drug you, and drug you, and in gratitude to him you will add a codicil to your will to the effect that he receives a considerable sum over and above his bill of fees. If a lawyer come to see you and make out your will, you will instruct your immediate attendants to give him a beautiful statuette or a gold ring in recognition of his services, for which services he will take care to be well paid besides. But for the minister, who, perhaps, alone of all the three does you any real service—who visits you daily, and pours out his sympathy and instruction into your soul, you not only have no acknowledgment of service to make, but you often do not even bequeathe to him the poor reward of thanks."

One would think that courage could hardly venture further than this. But this was not all. The audience by this time were on fire with the justice of this droll exposure of unequal treatment for ministers. And Anderson burst out in one of his good-natured furies into this further appeal. "And why should we be singled out for this unthankful treatment? I will ask this assembly of Glasgow merchants and professional men,—Are we less gifted as a class? Have we less intellect or scholarship? I appeal to yourselves. We beat you in the classes of your boyhood. We took the best prizes out of your hands at college. And we could have distanced you in your own line of things if we had become merchants, or doctors, or lawyers." When he had got to this point he was able to do anything with the audience; and he struck in forcibly with the business in hand, and carried his resolution *nem. con.*

DR. NORMAN MACLEOD'S LAST HOURS.

ON the morning of Sunday, the 16th of June, 1872, Dr. Macleod was so much better that his brother left him in comparative comfort, and when Professor Andrew Buchanan saw him some hours afterwards, he was surprised at the great improvement which had taken place. He felt so refreshed after taking some food, about seven in the morning, that he asked his wife to sit beside him while he told her the deeper thoughts that were possessing his soul. "I believe I will get better," he said, "but I wish you to record for my good, and for our good afterwards, that in this hurricane I have had deep thoughts of God. I feel as if He said,—'We know one another, I love you, I forgive you; I put my hands round you,' just as I would with my son Norman," and here he laid his hand tenderly on his wife's head. "I have had few religious exercises for the last ten days. If my son were ill I would not be angry with him for not sending me a letter. But I have had constant joy, and the happy thought continually whispered, 'Thou art with me!' Not many would understand me. They would put down much that I have felt to the delirium of weakness, but I have had deep spiritual insight."

When he was speaking of God's dealings, the expression of his face and his accents were as if he was addressing One actually present. Still more intimately, it seemed, than ever, his fellowship was with the Father and the Son. He again repeated that he believed he would get better, and that his latter days would be more useful than any former ones. "I have neglected many things. I have not felt as I ought how awfully good God is; how generous and long-suffering; how He has 'put up' with all my rubbish. It is enough to crush me when I think of all His mercies" (as he said this he was melted in tears); "mercy, mercy, from beginning to end. You and I have passed through many lifestorms, but we can say with peace, it has been all right." He added something she could not follow as to what he would wish to do in his latter days, and as to how he "would teach his darling children to know and realise God's presence." Some hours afterwards two of his daughters came to kiss him before going to church. "He took my hands in both of his," one of them writes, "and told me I must come to see him oftener. 'If I had strength,' he said, 'I could tell you things would do you good through all your life. I am an old man, and have passed through many experiences, but now all is perfect peace and perfect calm. I have glimpses of heaven that no tongue, or pen, or words, can describe.' I kissed him on his dear forehead and went away, crying only because he was so ill. When I next saw him he was, indeed, 'in perfect peace and perfect calm.'"

The church bells had for some time ceased to ring, and the quiet of the Lord's-day rested on the city. His wife and one of his sons were with him in the drawing-room, where he remained chiefly sitting on the sofa. About twelve o'clock Mrs. Macleod went to the door to give some directions about food. The sudden cry, "Mother, mother!" startled her, and when she hurried in she saw his head had fallen back. There was a soft sigh, and, gently as one sinking into sleep, his spirit entered into rest.

THE SIMPLICITY OF FAITH.

Dr. WILLIAM ANDERSON was journeying to Kilsyth to help in the revival which was then going on. He met with a boy who told him of the death of his little brother. The lad seemed sure that his brother had gone to heaven. Dr. Anderson asked him for the ground of his confidence. He replied, "Because he had faith." "But," said the Doctor, "how do you know?" "Weel, sir, when he was dying, he seemed afraid. I told him to trust in Jesus. He asked me what that meant—what he was to do. I said, 'Pray to Him.' He replied, 'I'm too weak: I'm not able to pray.' Then I said, 'Just hold up your hand—Jesus will see you, and know what it means.' And he did it. Now, was not that faith?" Dr. Anderson was a great theologian, yet he often pointed to that dying lad with the uplifted hand as a beautiful illustration of the simplicity of faith.

RESIGNATION TO THE DIVINE WILL.

An Incident in the Scottish Highlands.

THE following remarkable anecdote is currently related in the Highlands:—A farmer, whose wealth, wisdom, and beneficence gave him great sway in his elevated hamlet, was fortunate in all respects but one. He had three very fine children, who all in succession died after having been weaned, though before they gave every promise of health and firmness. Both parents were much afflicted; but the father's grief was clamorous and unmanly. They resolved that the next should be suckled for two years, hoping by this to avoid the repetition of such a misfortune. They did so, and the child by living longer only took a firmer hold of their affections, and furnished more material for sorrowful recollection. At the close of the second year he followed his brothers, and there were no bounds to the affliction of the parents. There are, however, in the economy of Highland life, certain duties and courtesies which are indispensable, and for the omission of which nothing can apologise. One of these is to call in all their friends and feast them at the time of the greatest family distress.

The death of the child happened late in the spring, when sheep were abroad in the more inhabited straths, but from the blasts in that high and stormy region, were still confined to the cot. In a dismal snowy evening, the man, unable to stifle his anguish, went out lamenting aloud for a lamb to treat his friends with at the "late-wake." At the door of the cot, however, he found a stranger, standing before the entrance. He was astonished on such a night to meet a person so far from any frequented place. The stranger was plainly attired, but had a countenance expressive of singular mildness and benevolence; and addressing him in a sweet impressive voice, asked him what he did there amidst the tempest.

He was filled with awe which he could not account for, and said that he came for a lamb. "What kind of a lamb do you mean to take?" said the stranger. "The very best I can find," he replied, "as it is to entertain my friends, and I hope you will share of it." "Do your sheep make any resistance when you take away the lamb, or any disturbance afterwards?" "Never," was the answer. "How differently am I treated," said the stranger. "When I come to visit my sheepfold, I take, as I am well entitled to do, the best lamb to myself;

and my ears are filled with the clamour of discontent by those ungrateful sheep, whom I have fed, watched, and protected."

He looked up in amazement, but the vision was fled. He went, however, for the lamb, and brought it home with alacrity. He did more; it was the custom of these times—a custom, indeed, which was not extinct till after 1745—for people to dance at late-wakes. It was a mournful kind of movement, but still it was dancing. This man, on other occasions, had been quite unequal to the performance of this duty; but at this time he immediately on coming in, ordered music to begin, and danced the solitary measure appropriate to such occasions. The reader must have very little sagacity or knowledge of the purport and consequences of visions, who requires to be told that many children were born, lived, and prospered afterwards in this reformed family.

HUGH M'KAIL—HIS LAST HOURS.

HUGH M'KAIL was a young man about twenty-six years of age. Because he joined the insurgents in Galloway, in 1665, he was captured, and, after being tortured, he was condemned to die.

On the Friday night, the night immediately preceding his execution, he went to bed a little after eleven, and his cousin, Dr. Matthew M'Kail, lay with him, and relates how soundly he slept, "which the said Mr. Matthew knew, having slept very little that night because of a pain in his head, wherewith he was frequently troubled." About five in the morning, M'Kail arose and woke his comrade, John Wodrow, saying pleasantly, "Up, John! you are too long in bed; you and I look not like men going this day to be hanged, seeing we lie abed so long;" but soon passing to serious thoughts suggested by their situation, "Now Lord," he prayed, "we come to Thy throne, a place we have not been acquainted with. Earthly kings' thrones have advocates against poor men; but Thy Throne hath Jesus an advocate for us. Our supplication this day is not to be free of death, nor of pain in death, but that we may witness before many witnesses a good confession."

When he came to the place of execution, "he appeared," says the old memoir, "to the conviction of all who formerly knew him, with a fairer, better, and more staid countenance than ever they had before observed. When Hugh M'Kail suffered, there was scarce ever seen so much sorrow in onlookers. Scarce was there a dry cheek in the whole street or windows at the Cross of Edinburgh."

When upon the scaffold, he said, "Although I be judged and condemned as a rebel amongst men, yet I hope, even in order to this action, to be accepted as loyal before God. Nay, there can be no greater act of loyalty to the king, as the times now go, than for every man to do his utmost for the extirpation of that abominable plant of Prelacy, which is the bane of the throne and of the country. I heartily submit myself to death, as that which God hath appointed to all men because of sin. I praise God for his fatherly chastisement, whereby He hath made me in part, and will make me perfectly, partaker of His holiness."

Standing on the ladder, with the fatal napkin over his face, he lifted it for a moment, and, in the highest ecstasies of assurance and devotion, exclaimed, "As there is a great solemnity here, of a confluence of people, a scaffold, and people looking out of windows; so there is a greater and and more solemn preparation in heaven of angels to carry my soul to Christ's bosom." His closing words were the famous anthem of triumph—the "Farewell and Welcome"—which the after-martyrs so commonly repeated. "Now I leave off to speak any more to creatures, and turn my speech to Thee, O Lord! Now I begin my intercourse with God, which shall never be broken off. Farewell, father and mother, friends and relations; farewell, sun, moon, and stars! Welcome, God and Father! Welcome, sweet Lord Jesus, the Mediator of the New Covenant! Welcome, blessed Spirit of Grace, God of all consolation! Welcome, glory! Welcome, eternal life! WELCOME, DEATH!"

THE REV. DR. MACLEOD AND THE POOR WOMAN.

ONE evening, said the Rev. Dr. Macleod, after a laborious day, I was passing, in the street of a small provincial town, a house which had been an hospital in "the cholera year," and which since then, had been occasionally used for any cases of fever, or dangerous disease, occurring among the resident or vagrant poor. Again, by one of those strange suggestions that come—we hardly know how or whence at the time—I was induced to ask if there was any one in the hospital; but again the flesh pleaded for delay. Yet I could not somehow pass the door without inquiry, although I almost smiled at my impulse to do so as being superstitious. I was told that a poor woman was there who seemed to be dying of consumption. She had been found a few days before as a beggar on the highway. I entered the room where she lay. I found her confined to bed, an emaciated creature, with skeleton hands and sunken eyes, a severe cough, and apparently about fifty years of age. She did not know me; and all I knew of her was, that she was very poor and very lonely in the world, and a stranger.

After a few ordinary observations about her weak state of body, when she expressed her sense of hopelessness as to recovery, I said, "I suppose when you die, no one in the world, poor woman, will miss you." "No one cares for me," she replied, in a tone of sadness. "No one?" I asked. "No, sir, not one that I know of." "Do you not think that God cares for you?" I said kindly to her. "I don't know," she replied, in a half whisper, turning her eyes away. "He knows you, at all events," I said. "No doubt of that, sir." "And is it not something," I continued, " to be known personally—even you with all your cares, and pains, and anxieties—to the great God who made heaven and earth, and who is able, at all events, to supply every want of your body and soul?" "Ay, sir, I did not think of that. It is something, indeed!" "But what," I asked, "if this God has an interest in you—cares for you—loves you?" "O sir! I have been a great sinner—a great sinner." "God knows that better than you do," I replied, "and He hates your sins with an infinite hatred; but what if that same God, nevertheless, commands you, saying, 'Believe in the Lord Jesus Christ, and thou shalt be saved,' and beseeches you to be reconciled to Himself? and says to you, 'Come now, and let us reason together, though your sins be as scarlet, I shall make them white as snow'?" and then I spoke to her for a long time of the love of God to lost sinners.

I have been privileged to address the same words of truth and life to many a sinner, in health and sickness. I have seen in many cases the power of the truth, through God's grace, to enlighten the mind and change the heart; but never did I behold so visible an effect produced upon a human spirit, in the same time as upon that poor and unknown woman! Even as the mercury is seen slowly rising in the tube when heat is brought near it, so did her heart and soul seem to rise more and more to God, in faith, love, hope, and penitence, as the grand theme of the love of Jesus was presented to her. At first she looked thoughtfully; then she raised herself up in bed; then clasped her hands, and lifted her eyes to heaven, and often exclaimed, "Oh! thank God! thank God! that I have heard such words as these!"

After remaining more than an hour, and praying with her, she besought me to come back next day. I promised to do so, but earnestly urged her immediately to pray to Jesus Christ, and to tell Him her whole heart—to confess her sins to Himself, and to ask, nothing doubting, the blessings which I had taught her to expect from Him. She gladly promised to do so, but said, "Don't forget to-morrow, sir." "Never fear," I replied, "if I am alive and able to come; but, remember, there is no to-morrow given us! Don't you forget to-day; 'for now is the accepted time, now is the day of salvation.'" "God bless you, sir!—oh, thank God! thank God!" were the last words I heard.

I called, according to promise, next day at the door of the small hospital, and found *she had died the night before, and was already buried!* What her name was or history I never could learn; but I have good hope that the name of that poor woman will be found in the Lamb's book of life!

THE REV. DR. RITCHIE AND THE SWEARER.

Dr. Ritchie, of the University of Edinburgh, was one day preaching in Tarbolton Church against profane swearing in common conversation, while one of his principal heritors, who was addicted to that sin, was present. This gentleman thought the sermon was designedly addressed to him, and that the eyes of the whole congregation were fixed upon him. Though he felt indignant, he kept his place till the service was concluded, and then waited on the preacher and asked him to dine with him, as he was quite alone. The invitation being accepted, the gentleman after dinner thus addressed the minister:—

"Sir, you have insulted me to-day in the church. I have been three times in church lately, and on every one of them you have been holding me up to the derision of the audience; so I tell you plainly, sir, I shall never enter the church of Tarbolton again, unless you give me your promise that you will abstain from such topics in future, as I am resolved I shall no more furnish you with the theme of your discourse."

Dr. Ritchie heard this speech with calmness, and then looking him steadfastly in the face, thus replied: "Very well, sir; if you took to yourself what I said to-day against swearing, does not your conscience bear witness to its truth? You say you will not enter the church till I cease to reprove your sins; if such is your determination, it is impossible you can enter it again; for which of the Commandments have you not broken?" On observing his firmness, and feeling that he was wrong, the gentleman held out his hand to Dr. Ritchie, a mutual explanation took place; and while the minister would abate none of his faithfulness, the heritor endeavoured to overcome his evil habits.

BURNS IN PAISLEY.

Paisley has been distinguished for the literary tastes of some of its sons, now occupying a high place in the temple of fame. Here, too, was the scene of some of Burns's saddest, and, we hope, of some of his happiest moments. Let us relate one anecdote, as told by a gentleman, long a medical practitioner there. One afternoon, seated in his own house, his wife came running to him, exclaiming,—" Oh, Doctor, there's a man away into the Bailie's house opposite, whom I am sure is Burns the poet. I knew him, by his picture, the moment I saw him." The Doctor was at first dubious of, and strongly inclined to laugh at, his wife's supposition; but upon her earnest entreaty, he put on his hat and went across to the Bailie's, to ascertain if there was any truth in her notion. The Bailie hearing the sound of the Doctor's voice on the stair, conversing with his servant, called him up. "Is Burns with you?" inquired the latter. "He is, Doctor. Come in," said the Bailie, and, taking him up stairs, introduced the two.

After sitting a short time, the Doctor prevailed on them to come over and drink tea with him. "Burns," he said, relating the meeting many years after, "was a man once seen you could never forget. There was a something noble in his look and conversation that rivetted the impression he created indelibly in your memory." At first he was very dull and dispirited, but the hearty hospitality and warmth of his new friend at last opened his heart, and he told him that that day he had been delivering the first edition of his own poems, published by subscription. At almost every house he called, the moment his name was mentioned the door was unceremoniously shut in his face; he was treated like one whose very name carried the plague with it. Poor Burns, how much reason has the world to take blame to itself for thy follies! How cold, thankless, and cruel was its treatment of thee! and what although the trodden worm turned upon its oppressor!

A few years after this, one winter night, there

was a marriage party. All were merry and joyous. The mirth and pleasure was at its height, when one of the guests observed to a good-looking woman,— "Where's your husband? I have not seen him this half-hour." "Oh, I don't know, he's often out of sight when wanted," replied she, smiling. "Come away and let us seek him out—we're missing him sadly." The two ranged through the house, but the absent man was not there. Going into the garden, they saw, stretched upon the grass, looking up at the clear moon and into the starry dome above him, the master spirit of all Scotland, his thoughts dwelling in contemplation even beyond the region of the stars, and far beyond the frivolities of time. The sound of their voices aroused him, and he accompanied them into the house. That night, or next day, was penned the first outline of the "Address to Mary in Heaven," long after written fully out. Poor Burns! yet noble-hearted Burns!

THE DUKE OF GORDON AND THE FARMER;

Or, Go Directly to the Lord.

IN the north of Scotland a Protestant tenant who rented a small farm under Alexander, second Duke of Gordon, having fallen behind in his payments, a vigilant steward, in his Grace's absence, seized the farmer's stock, and advertised it to be sold by auction on a fixed day. The Duke happily returned home in the interval, and the tenant went to him to supplicate for indulgence. "What is the matter, Donald?" said the Duke, as he saw him enter with sad downcast looks. Donald told him his sorrowful tale in a concise natural manner; it touched the Duke's heart, and produced a formal acquittance of the debt. Donald, as he cheerfully withdrew, was staring at the pictures and images which he saw in the ducal hall, and expressed to the Duke, in a homely way, a wish to know what they were. "These," said the Duke, who was a Roman Catholic, "are the saints who intercede with God for me." "My lord Duke," said

Donald, "would it not be better to apply yourself directly to God? I went to muckle Sawney Gordon, and to little Sawney Gordon; but if I had not come to your good Grace's self, I could not have got my discharge, and both I and my bairns had been turned out from house and home."

THE REV. DR. LAWSON GIVING A WISE ANSWER.

WHEN Dr. Lawson, of Selkirk, travelled to London, he had in the coach with him two men who evidently suspected that they had got a minister and a simpleton with them. They acted accordingly, but he seemed not to heed it. At last one of them put to him, rather abruptly, the startling question,—"How is it, sir, that a man such as I take you to be can refuse to believe that Socrates and Plato, Epictetus and Seneca, and other such wise and virtuous men among the heathen, have a place among the blessed of heaven?" "God," replied the wise and good man, "has told us in His Word, that 'Where no provision is, the people perish,' and that 'there is no other name given under heaven among men whereby they must be saved, but the name of Jesus;' but whether it please Him in any other way to make known this name to such celebrated heathens as those you have mentioned, I do not find that He has anywhere expressly informed me. I feel that I ought not to attempt 'to be wise above what is written,' and that it is not for me to 'limit the Holy One of Israel.' If it please God in His mercy, and through faith in His Son, to take you and me to heaven, and that we shall find there Socrates and Plato, I am sure we will be glad, indeed, to meet them; and if we shall not find them in heaven, I am also sure the Judge of all the earth will be able to assign a reason for their absence, and that none in heaven will be either able or willing to dispute either the justice or the wisdom of His sovereign arrangements."

During this conversation, Dr. Lawson had clasped his hands together, and had continued to twirl the one thumb round the other. Piqued at the "clincher" he had received to his question, his fellow-traveller asked him,—"Pray, sir, do you always do that?" imitating, at the same time, the Doctor's motion with his thumbs. "No," was the philosophic reply, "I sometimes do *this*," and he twirled his thumbs in the reverse way. The two wiseacres thought it best to let him alone, and so the Doctor had peace and quietness during the remainder of the journey. A fool is none the worse sometimes of being answered according to his own folly.

EBENEZER ERSKINE AND THE BLASPHEMERS.

WHEN crossing the Forth from Leith to Kinghorn, Ebenezer Erskine had the unhappiness to find himself in the midst of ungodly passengers, who took the most unhallowed liberties with their Creator's name. For a time he was silent, but at last, unable to suppress his concern, and solicitous to curb their blasphemous tongues, he rose from his seat, and taking hold of the mast, uncovered his head, waved his hat, and cried aloud,—"O yes! O yes! O yes!" Having thus secured the attention of the astonished passengers and crew, he repeated in a solemn and impressive manner that commandment of the moral law which they were flagrantly violating,—"Thou shalt not take the name of the Lord thy God in vain, for the Lord will not hold him guiltless that taketh His name in vain." Without adding a single word, he quitted the mast, covered his head, and resumed his seat. The giddy company, however, resolved to harden themselves against the striking reproof. They began first to elbow each other, then to titter, and at last to be avenged on their kind reprover, they burst into a fit of loud laughter. Their conversation soon became as profane and offensive as before. Among the rest, a lady, laying aside the delicacy of the sex, and regardless alike of the authority of God and the maxims of politeness, seemed to find a malicious pleasure in giving emphasis to almost every sentence, by intermixing the sacred name, accompanied with smiles of derision and contempt, obviously intended to mortify the venerable man. It pleased God, however, to second the despised warning of His servant, by an alarming admonition of His providence.

When they had got to the north of Inchkeith, a tempest suddenly arose; the heavens became black with clouds, the sea raged, the danger was imminent; the pilot, unable to keep hold of the helm, assured them that their fate was inevitable. This unexpected alteration of circumstances produced, at least, a temporary change on their spirit and appearance. Their sportive gaiety gave place to consternation and despair. The same lady, who had acted so insolent a part towards the faithful clergyman, overwhelmed with dismay, now sprang across the boat, and clasped her arms around his neck, exclaiming, "O, sir, if I die here, I will die with you." Through the Divine patience and forbearance, however, they weathered the storm, and reached the harbour in safety. It is hoped that the future life, at least of the ungodly woman, without any knowledge of the fact, furnished some evidence that to her the arm of the Lord had been revealed.

ST. COLUMBA AND THE ROBBER.

Though Saint Columba loved peace, he at the same time ever sought to maintain the strictest order and discipline. He admonished and reproved with freedom, and, when the case required it, with sharpness. If that did not serve, without any regard to persons, he proceeded to higher censures. Thus, at the hazard of his life, he excommunicated some of the nobility, among whom were the sons of Connel, after having first admonished and reproved them to no purpose. John, one of the excommunicated, continued to persecute and harass the good, and to live by rapine and plunder. Thrice had he robbed the house, and carried off the effects of a worthy hospitable man who used to lodge the Saint whenever he came his way. On the third time, Columba met him as he was carrying off his booty, and earnestly entreated him to leave it. He followed

him all the way to his boat, which lay at Camus, in
Ardnamurchan, and even waded after him into the sea
with his fruitless petitions. The plunderer and his
company scorned and laughed at him. The Saint at
length, lifting both hands to heaven, prayed to God to
glorify Himself by avenging and protecting His people.
He then sat down on an eminence, and thus addressed a
few who were along with him,—"God will not always
bear to have those who love and serve Him to be thus
treated. That dark cloud already forming in the north,
is fraught with this poor man's destruction. The cloud
spread, the storm arose, and, between Mull and Colonsay,
overtook the boat, which, no doubt, the greed of the
plunderer had too deeply loaded. "His fate, though
just," says the historian, "was much to be lamented."

STUDY AND STUDY.

Though Brownlow North was a well educated man, he
was not trained for the ministry, and did not adopt the
usual method of preparing his addresses. In one of the
towns in the North of Scotland, soon after he commenced
his public labours, there was a minister who had the
welfare of his flock much at heart, and who, seeing how
Mr. North's labours were blessed, gave him the use of
his church, and often listened to him with pleasure
himself, but constantly remarked,—"Oh, Mr. North, if
you would only study more, you would do still more
good." "What sort of study do you mean?" was the
reply, "for I devote three hours every morning before
leaving my room to reading the Bible, and to meditation
and prayer, and during the day I think of Divine truths
as much as possible." "Oh," said the minister, "that is
all well; but if you would arrange your addresses with
more method, they would be more instructive." "Well,
as you advise it so strongly, I will try what I can do
before next Sunday." And accordingly he did meditate
much upon the arrangement of his next address, so as
to put it into a more "connected form."

Sunday arrived, and a great crowd of hearers assembled, so that every space for standing as well as sitting room was occupied, and, after prayer and praise, he commenced his address. For the first five minutes the ideas that he had arranged came out in nice order, when, suddenly, his chain of thoughts was broken, and all he had intended to say passed entirely from him, and a dead silence ensued. It was a trying moment, and most men would have found it overpowering. Not so Mr. North. He knew that his mission was not of man, and did not depend on the method in which his discourses were arranged, but on the power of the Holy Spirit. He therefore frankly told the congregation of the advice he had received, of his endeavour to follow it, and his complete failure, as the whole train of thought had passed away from his mind. "But," he added, "there is one subject that has not passed away, and that is, that many of you are sinners, ready to perish, and I know the way of life, because it is God's way." He then delivered a most powerful address as the Spirit gave him utterance, which was much blessed to several of those who heard him.

INVITATION TO PUBLIC WORSHIP.

A SABBATH School Teacher in Edinburgh was visiting in a close, and in one of the top flats of a stair, found a poor family living in a small but clean room. It was at once seen that intemperance and its dreadful evils had not entered the dwelling. From conversation with the father and mother, it was soon discovered that it was one of those cases where, from the long illness of the father, the family had fallen from comparative comfort to poverty. He was now, however, better, and had been able for some time to work a little, so as to keep his family from destitution, but by no means to enable them to live in comfort. Having learned so much of their worldly concerns, their visitor next began to speak of the concerns of their higher nature.

They were asked if they ever went to church. "No," said the father; "we used to go long ago, before I took ill, but we went no more after that." "But," said the visitor, "you have been better for a good while." "Oh!" said the father, "nobody ever asked me to come; no one seemed to care about us." "Well, I'll ask you now," was the response. "Come with me, and you and your family will be welcome." He was directed to a church where he would hear the gospel from the lips of a faithful minister. Next Sabbath, several of the children were at the Sabbath-school, and the father and mother, and some of the family, were at church. They continued to be regular attenders at the sanctuary, and adorned the doctrine of God their Saviour by a consistent walk and conversation in the world. A word of encouragement is never lost. It not unfrequently finds its way into hearts ready to receive it, and brings forth a rich harvest.

MODERATISM: ITS FASCINATION AND EVIL INFLUENCE.

This form of religion obtained to a considerable extent in Scotland, and especially Edinburgh, at the end of last century. It is indeed a pregnant proof of the still dominant and triumphant position of the latitudinarian and Laodicean spirit of the age of Principal Robertson, that it continued to draw to itself so large a proportion of the very flower and promise of the rising race. It was still the strong and gaining cause, and, like every other strong and gaining cause, rallied around it the whole crowd of the weak and the wavering; while the intellectual and literary lustre, which a few celebrated names had thrown around it, imparted to it a peculiar fascination for the young and the aspiring. It thus numbered in its ranks the great body of the brighter and more genial spirits of the time, as well as many others who were neither bright nor genial, but had a keen ambition, at least, to be esteemed such. It was, in fact, the religion of the court party, of the literary coteries, and of fashionable society. It was the religion of Principal Robertson, of Lord Melville, and of all the world, save only a few pious women, and old-fashioned, however worthy, and well-meaning ministers, of whom fame knew nothing. So said Edinburgh Society at least.

It was, in short, the strong and central stream of the world, and even of the religious world; and, therefore, by the simple force of its current, drew to itself, and carried along with it, all the straws. It is not surprising that the great majority of young and unformed hearts, however originally well disposed, gave way beneath this influence. Nothing, indeed, could stand before it but the most serious views, and the deepest convictions of the truth. To resist was to pass at once beneath the shadow of the cross; was to go forth to Christ without the camp bearing his reproach. Some had cause to remember long afterwards the keen "ordeal of scorn" which the modest profession of evangelical sentiments cost in some of the new town circles, and how even the mere fact of attending "such places" as Lady Glenorchy's or the Tolbooth Church provoked the wondering and contemptuous smile. In academic circles the prevailing tendency took a more theoretic direction. What in general society was Laodicean indifference and ungodliness, was here heterodoxy. A certain freedom and laxity of faith was the fashionable mode. The profession of a strict orthodoxy was deemed the mark of a mean and narrow spirit; a certain boldness of heterodox speculation and free thinking, the proof of a large and enlightened mind. So easy a road to intellectual eminence was sure to be well trodden. It is always easier to mount a badge than to fight a battle, to join a set than achieve for one's self anything good or great in any field of thought or action. So, while a few strong spirits were boldly broaching and defending error, the feeble crowd aped it.

A good story illustrative of this is told by the Rev. Dr. Burns, Kilsyth, as having come under his own knowledge. A young country minister, of large vanity and small mind, eager to tread this ready road to fame, was in the habit of dropping hints among his friends that his orthodoxy on certain deep speculative points was not altogether to be trusted, and dabbled a good deal in the buying of, or, at least, looking at, books which he never read. In this way he came under the notice of a shrewd Edinburgh bookseller, whose shop he frequented during the Assembly sittings, and who seems at once to have taken his measure. He invited him to take tea at his house, giving him to understand that he would find there a literary reunion suited to his taste and his studies. On going there he was at once introduced to a grave and reverend senior whom he had never seen, but whom he at once concluded to be one of the chief lights of the theological world. Accordingly, he fastened himself to this man for the evening, and was soon embarked on the wide sea of theological discussion and speculation. He modestly hinted his heretical doubts and misgivings, and was gratified beyond measure by the kindly interest with which his companion mourned his youthful aberrations, and hoped that he might yet live to embrace other and sounder views. After an evening spent much to his own satisfaction, he rose to leave, and in quitting the room, asked his host in a whisper, " Who is that reverend gentleman with whom I have been speaking most of the evening?" "Oh, do you not know who that is? It is the head beadle of the Tolbooth Church!"

GEORGE BUCHANAN'S TRUTHFULNESS AND HUMILITY.

IN the month of September, 1579, the learned George Buchanan was visited by some of his learned friends, among whom were Andrew Melvin, James Melvin, and his own cousin, Thomas Buchanan, provost of the collegiate church of Kirkhaugh. Having heard that his "History of Scotland" was in the press, and the author indisposed, they hastened to Edinburgh to pay him a final visit. Upon entering his apartment, they found Buchanan, the most learned man and greatest genius of the age, employed in the humble though benevolent task of teaching the horn-book to a young man in his service. After the usual salutations,—"I perceive, sir," said

Andrew Melvin, "you are not idle." "Better this," replied Buchanan, "than stealing sheep, or sitting idle, which is as bad." He then showed them his dedication of his "Historie" to the king, and Melvin having perused it, remarked that it seemed in some passages obscure, and required some emendations. "I can do no more," said Buchanan, "for thinking of another matter." "What is that?" rejoined Melvin. "To die. But I leave that and many other things to your care." The visitors then proceeded to the printer's office to inspect the work which had excited such high expectations. They found it had proceeded as far as the passage which related to the interment of David Rizzio, and being alarmed at the coldness with which the historian had expressed himself, they requested the printer to desist. Having returned to Buchanan's house they found him in bed. In answer to their friendly inquiries, he informed them that he was "even going the way of welfare."

His kinsman then proceeded to state their apprehensions respecting the consequences of publishing so unpalatable a story, and to suggest the probability of its inducing the king to prohibit the entire work. "Tell me, man," said Buchanan, "if I have told the truth." "Yes, sir," replied his cousin, "I think so." "Then," rejoined the dying historian, "I will abide his feud and all his kin's. Pray God for me, and let Him direct all." "And so," adds the historian, "by the printing of his chronicle, that most learned, wise, and godly man, ended this mortal life."

PROFESSOR WODROW MEASURING HIS GRAVE.

THE REV. JAMES WODROW, that was called to take the Professorship of Theology in the University of Glasgow in 1692, was an eminently pious man. He lived for many years in the daily view of death and eternity, and waited and wished for it. Some considerable time before he died, he was sitting one morning in his fore-room, that was upon the street, when Mrs. Wodrow came in to him. The bell, commonly called the dead-bell, rang before the windows. After he had listened to the cryer, and heard who was to be buried that day, he said to his wife,—"My dear, how sweet and pleasant would it be to me, were it possible, to hear that bell going through the streets for my death; but that is a foolish wish— the Lord's time is best, and I wait for it." Principal Stirling's lady came in one day to see him, the summer, or that save one, before he died. He happened to speak of death, as pretty frequently he did, and he said to her,—"Mrs. Stirling, do you know the place in the new kirk-yard that is to be my grave; for in that burial-place the masters of the college have particular allotments made, and there is one for the professor of divinity?" She answered she did. "Then," says he, "the day is good, and I'll go through the Principal's garden into it, and take a look of it." Accordingly they went, and when they came to the place, as near as she could guess, she pointed it out to him—next to Principal Dunlop and her own son, and only child. Mr. Wodrow looked at it, and lay down upon the grass, and stretched himself most cheerfully on the place, and said, with the greatest composure,—"O, how satisfying would it be to me to lay down this body of mine in this place, and be delivered from my prison; but it will come in the Lord's time."

PATRONAGE AND POPULAR PREACHERS.

On the 10th April, 1810, James Hogg, the "Ettrick Shepherd," and his father, went to the funeral of George Monncie, who had been removed by sudden death from the head of a large family. As the company arrived, each received a glass of whisky, and then they sat conversing, sometimes about common topics, but for the most part about the parish ministers, what subjects they had of late been handling, and how they had succeeded.

One man said in the course of conversation, "I do not deny it, David, your minister is a very good man, and a very clever one too; he has no fault but one." "What is that?" said David. "It is patronage," said the other. "Patronage!" said David, "that cannot be a fault." "Not a fault, sir? But I say it is a fault; and one that

you and every one who encourages it, by giving it your
countenance, will have to answer for. Your minister
can never be a good shepherd, for he was not chosen by
the flock." "It is a bad simile," said David; "the flock
never chooses its own shepherd, but the owner of the
flock." The greatest number of the inhabitants of that
district being dissenters from the Established Church,
many severe reflections were thrown out against the
dangerous system of patronage, while no one ventured
to defend it save David, who said, that if one learned
man was not capable of making choice for a parish, the
populace was much less so, and proved, from Scripture,
that man's nature was so corrupted, that he was unable
to make a wise choice for himself, and maintained that
the inhabitants of this country ought to be thankful
that the Legislature had taken the task out of their
hands.

As a farther proof of the justice of his argument, he
asked, whether Jesus of Nazareth or Mahomet was the
best preacher? The other answered that none but a
reprobate would ask the question. "Very well," said
David, "Mahomet was one of your popular preachers;
was followed and adored by the multitude wherever he
went, while He who spoke as never man spake, was
despised and rejected. Mahomet gained more converts
to his religion in his lifetime than has been gained to
the true religion in eighteen hundred years. Away with
your popular preachers, friend! they are bruised reeds."
His antagonist was non-plus'd; he only could answer,—
"Ah, David, David, ye're on the braid way!"

PREACHING SEVENTY YEARS AGO.

In those days, it was not unusual to preach from the
same text for successive weeks and months—a whole
system of doctrine and of practice being opened up and
reiterated from Sabbath to Sabbath. For example, the
text being "Repent and believe the gospel," several
sermons were occupied in telling what the gospel was—
its doctrines and its duties; then on "Believe"—the

evidences of the gospel, its truth and certainty; and next repentance was treated of, and its connection with faith, all under the same text. One does not wonder that under a system like this, the giving out of a new text was quite an era; every eye and ear were stretched out and fixed; every Bible ready to be opened, as if it had been a "latter will." The next text comes, it is Jude 20, 21, "Building up yourselves on your most holy faith," etc.; again the truth to be believed was treated of, the nature of faith in connection with these truths, its holy character and influence, with the practical lessons thence resulting, etc., etc., in a long series of discourses stretching on from week to week. On this plan, no doubt, much sound doctrine was brought out, and the hearers, if not too impatient, got very good matter on which to meditate, but certainly the mode was not attractive, and superinduced tedium, while it did not do justice to the fulness and variety of the Divine Word. Let it be observed, however, that the expositions of large portions of the Bible, by way of lecture, formed always the first part of the forenoon's worship, although the reading of a whole chapter was not at that time practised in any of the Presbyterian churches as a regular part of the service.

At Borrowstounness, a younger minister, however, who at this time acted as assistant to the aged minister of the parish, introduced a new text at least every second Sabbath. He went upon the maxim, "*Bonus textuarius est bonus theologus,*" and, accordingly, the first quarter or more of the hour, or of the hour and a half, consisted of parallel texts made to bear on the illustration of the passage in hand, after which he lightened, and even thundered. This copious divine, on his removal to a church in England, found that it behoved him to abbreviate much to suit the English taste. The first half hour, at least, he had to cut off, and became, in respect of length, an ordinary preacher. The system thus described was still in full force during the first quarter of the present century in the church of Borrowstounness. Preaching from the text, "Behold I stand at the door and knock," the then minister of the parish, the Rev. Dr. Rennie, discussed, seriatim, from Sabbath to Sabbath, in separate discourses, the "bars" of the door at which he knocked, and then, finally, the "uses" and corollaries derivable from the whole disquisition. In this way, and with the lengthened recapitulation by which each successive discourse was introduced, often so protracted as to render a very small portion of new matter needful, it will not be surprising that, as happened in the present instance, the Sabbaths of a whole quarter of the year were often consumed in the discussion of one single theme.

THE REV. DR. M'GAVIN AND THE DESERTED CLIMBING BOY.

On dismissing, on one occasion, the senior Bible-class, writes Dr. M'Gavin, Dundee, a stranger lad introduced himself, and asked permission to join it. He was a youth of about sixteen years of age, plain in features, and of unpretending address, somewhat diminutive in size, and very neat and tidy in his attire. He was, of course, told that he would be welcome, and was encouraged to be punctual. This intimation, however, did not seem to be sufficient, as he still lingered and looked abashed. At length with tearful confusion he whispered, "I am afraid sir, you will think me bold, for I cannot read as yet; but I have now put myself to school, and hope to read very soon; only I was very anxious to join the class, and hope you will not refuse me." The statement and the spirit of the lad excited interest, and I asked him his name. The question seemed to awaken intense emotion, and he replied—

"Sir, I am ignorant of my real name, but my former master called me John Shaw." "What!" said I, "have you no parents, or friends, or home?" "Alas!" was his reply, "I have known very little of any of them in my lifetime. All that I know of myself and parentage is, that when I was about seven years of age, my mother, for a half-mutchkin of whisky sold me to John Denny, the chimney-sweep, and I have never seen her since."

The progress of this young volunteer in spiritual knowledge was rapid and steady. Without bright parts or great capacity, he discovered a quiet perseverance and intense thirst for truth, which overcame all obstacles, and stored up treasures of Bible knowledge. In many conversations with John, I found that his soul continually yearned in secret after his heartless mother. One evening John came to me with a beaming countenance, and said, "Sir, I have found my mother." It turned out that she was a vagrant beggar, and notorious drunkard; and that she had on that day sought her boy and demanded money.

"And what do you mean to do with her?" said I. "I have come," he replied, "to ask your advice; but I think of taking a house for her and me, that we may have a home together." To prove the lad, I sought fully to apprise him of the difference of his mother's habits from his own—of the unlikelihood of his subduing her restless and vagrant disposition—of the impossibility of his supplying her insatiable craving for intoxicating drink, and of the utter discomfort that he might expect in such a home.

He seemed to listen for a while with conscious pain, not unmingled with impatience, until, as if no longer able to restrain himself, he started to his feet, and said, "I know, sir, that what you say is all too true, but yet in the sight of God she is my own mother still. I have been so long in this world without any one to love me, that you cannot know how my heart warms to her. With her habits, she must be a burden and trouble to somebody; and who has a better right to bear them than her 'ain bairn'? Sir, I'll take her home; we'll read the Bible, and pray together every night, and who can tell but the Lord may yet give her a new heart. Maybe she has never had a chance of well-doing before; at all events, it is worth more than one effort, and with God's help I'll try it." And he would have done it. The noble soul which formed the resolution had decision to execute it. His vow was registered in heaven, where holy purposes, like infants called at birth, are stored.

But God, who accepted the intention, arrested its accomplishment.

A few days after the last recorded interview, the shocking tidings were announced that an apprentice of Deacon Craigie had fallen from a roof of four storeys in height, and was killed on the spot. Alas! it was no other than my hopeful scholar. The young outcast, who had sought a first home for himself and mother, never found it on earth; but God had suddenly prepared for him a happier and better one, where he should "weep, and wander, and be weary" no more. Hard even to the last had been his pillow, and there were none to smooth it; but he needed it not. His life, like his death-stroke, was sharp and soon over; but it was significant, and its lesson is not lost. His remains were borne to their final resting-place, as a last token of their respect, on the shoulders of his fellow-workmen; and although no kindred were there, many a moistened eye in men unused to weep told that the foundling chimney-sweep was missed, and mourned when he left us. As I stood musing beside that grave, while the gravediggers were fulfilling the last sad offices, I was roused by a hand being suddenly laid on my arm, when I became conscious of the presence of a bronzed and haggard woman, in the tattered garments of a beggar, in whose hoarse voice and staggering gait could at once be recognised the whine of the mendicant, and the maudlin whimper of drunkenness, as she groaned out, "Oh, sir, that was my laddie! and what is to become of me?" As I tore myself away from the shocking spectacle, I went home musing, as I leave my readers to do, of the mystery of the Providence which gave such a parent to such a son, and of the triumph of that grace which could rear such a son from such a mother.

THE OUTER AND INNER MAN.

THE late Rev. Dr. Wardlaw, when a young man, was fair to look upon; and like the early fathers of the Congregational denomination, he now and again went on a tour through the country to preach the gospel. In the summer of 1811, the young preacher, Mr. Wardlaw, visited Banff on a tour through the North of Scotland, and was by no means strictly clerical in his costume, but wore topped boots and other articles of dress corresponding to the necessities of a journey on horseback. This circumstance, added to the remarkably elegant appearance of the preacher, rather stumbled the faith of a lady, one of the old school. She looked wonders, as she saw the young minister ascend the pulpit stairs; but as he entered on his subject, she was seen to become most grave and attentive. When he had finished his discourse, she looked round to another lady—a person of an exceedingly different cast of mind—and exclaimed, "O woman! was na' that a great sermon for sic a young man? But, O he's o'er braw and o'er bonny!" "O'er braw!" replied the lady, "Fat signifies a man's claes, if there be plenty o' furniture in's mind? And to find fau't with the dear young man, because he's bonny, is something like a reflection on the Creator himself"—a rebuke both reverent and sensible.

EDWARD IRVING'S DYING HOURS.

In December, 1834, Edward Irving entered Glasgow with uplifted hands and words of thanksgiving and blessing in his heart and on his lips. He thought he had a great work to accomplish in that centre of life and wickedness and sorrow; and so he had; but it was no longer to labour or battle that God had called his servant. He had come not to work, not to fight, but to die. Never death-bed appealed with more moving power to the heart. His mother and sister had come to see him, and his life-long Kirkcaldy friends watched him in the last struggle.

With fluctuations of despairing hope, Dr. Martin, his father-in-law, and his son, wrote to the anxious sisters. Sometimes there were better symptoms—gleams of appetite, alleviation of pain; but throughout all, a burning fever, which nothing could subdue, consumed away the fainting life. "Your mother and I are at Mr. Taylor's," writes Dr. Martin, on the 4th December; "he is a most devout believer in the reality of the gifts, of Mr. Irving's Divine commission, etc., and has hardly ever faltered in his faith that Edward is still to recover strength; till this morning Isabella has never had a doubt of it." This was on Thursday. As the week waned, the frame, which enclosed that spirit, now almost wholly abstracted with its God, died hourly. He grew delirious in those solemn evenings, and "wandered" in his mind. Such wanderings! "So long as his articulation continued so distinct that we could make anything of his words, it was of spiritual things he spoke, praying for himself, his church, and his relations." Sometimes he imagined himself back among his congregation in London, and in the hush of his death-chamber, amid its awe-stricken attendants, the faltering voice rose in broken breathings of exhortation and prayer. "Sometimes he gave counsel to individuals; and Isabella, who knew something of the cases, could understand" what he meant. Human language has no words, but those which are common to all mental weakness, for such a divine abstraction of the soul, thus hovering at the gates of heaven. Once in this wonderful monologue, he was heard murmuring to himself sonorous syllables of some unknown tongue.

Listening to those mysterious sounds, Dr. Martin found them to be the Hebrew measures of the 23rd Psalm—"The Lord is my Shepherd," into the latter verses of which the dying voice swelled as the watcher took up and echoed the wonderful strain—"Though I walk through the valley of the shadow of death, I will fear no evil." As the current of life grew feebler and feebler, a last debate seemed to rise in that soul which was now hidden with God. They heard him murmuring to himself in inarticulate argument, confusedly struggling in his weakness to account for this visible death which, at last, his human faculties could no longer refuse to believe in, perhaps touched with ineffable trouble, that his Master had seemed to fail of His word and promise.

At last that self-argument came to a sublime conclusion in a trust more strong than life or death. As the gloomy December Sunday sank into the night shadows, his last audible words on earth fell from his pale lips. The last thing like a sentence we could make out was, "If I die, I die unto the Lord. Amen." And so, at the wintry midnight hour, which ended that last Sabbath on earth, the last bonds of mortal trouble dropped asunder, and the saint and martyr entered into the rest of his Lord. Amen! He who had lived to God for so many hard and bitter years, enduring all the pangs of mortal trouble, in his Lord at last, with a sigh of unspeakable disappointment and consolation, contented himself to die. Nothing more need be added to that last utterance, which rounds into a perfection beyond the reach of art, this sorrowful and splendid life. So far as sight or sound could be had of him, to use his own touching words, he had "a good voyage," though in the night and in the dark. And again let us say, Amen!

TWO KINGS AND TWO KINGDOMS IN SCOTLAND.

In 1596, when the design of recalling the Popish lords was ascertained, the celebrated Andrew Melville accompanied a deputation of the clergy to Falkland, where James VI. then resided. They were admitted to a private audience, when he thus addressed the King:—" Sir, we will always humbly reverence your Majesty in public, but since we have this occasion to be with your Majesty in private, and since you are brought into extreme danger, both of your life and crown, and, along with you, the country and the Church of God are like to go to wreck, for not telling you the truth and giving you faithful counsel, we must discharge our duty, or else be traitors both to Christ and you. Therefore, Sir, as divers times before I have told you, so now again I must tell you, there are two kings and two kingdoms in Scotland; there is King James, the head of the commonwealth, and there is Christ Jesus, the King of the Church, whose subject James VI. is, and of whose kingdom he is not a king, nor a lord, nor a head, but a member. We will yield to you your place, and give you all due obedience; but again, I say, you are not the head of the Church; you cannot give us that eternal life which we seek for even in this world, and you cannot deprive us of it. Permit us then freely to meet in the name of Christ, and to attend to the interests of that Church of which you are a chief member.

THE DISRUPTION.

THE Disruption of the Church of Scotland took place on Thursday the 18th May, 1843. The opening sermon was preached by Dr. Welsh from the text,—" Be fully persuaded in your own mind." On its conclusion the General Assembly adjourned from the High Church to St. Andrew's Church, George Street, Edinburgh. At half-past two o'clock Dr. Welsh arrived—took the chair, and opened the proceedings with prayer. He then entered his protest, and read the grounds on which it rested. Having handed it to the clerk, he vacated the chair, and left the Assembly, followed by a large body of adhering ministers and elders. On that day there met two men well known in Edinburgh society, and to the country generally. The one, Lord Rutherfurd, and the other, Lord Jeffrey. Lord Rutherfurd was one of those who had little or no faith in the honesty and sincerity of the non-intrusionists, and joined in the sneer of those who admitted that, *perhaps*, nine or ten of the men who had most deeply committed themselves might sacrifice their living and churches and come out. Lord Rutherfurd, along with Lord Jeffrey, had gone that day to a place which would overlook the line of the expected procession, in the hope rather that sinister predictions might be verified, than that honour, and courage, and fidelity, might be vindicated and exemplified.

At last the long-looked for moment arrived—the door of St. Andrew's Church was opened, and there issued forth Chalmers, Welsh, and Macfarlane, followed by a long continuous line of hundreds of their less known but not less determined brethren, and the Church of Scotland was on the streets, and Free. They were received with the greatest enthusiasm as they went along to the large hall at Tanfield, Canonmills, which was already filled to overflowing by a solemn and excited throng. The procession was one to be long remembered. The eye could not number the blackening train—the prediction was not fulfilled, and the result was the exclamation,—"The fools! thus to leave their fat livings for a whim!" Lord Jeffrey took a different view of the matter, and a truer and a nobler one. With deep emotion, his eye—that sharp piercing eye—filled with tears, he uttered the words,—"Thank God for my country! there is not another country in the world where such a deed could have been done." Dr. Chalmers was chosen moderator, and, on taking the chair, said, "I propose that we shall begin the business of this Assembly by an act of worship—with praise and prayer to God, on the duties and prospects which lie before us." He then gave out the 43rd Psalm, from the third verse, when all stood and sung the solemnizing lines :—

> "O send thy light forth and thy truth;
> Let them be guides to me,
> And bring me to thine holy hill,
> Ev'n where thy dwellings be."

In this way the Free Church of Scotland began.

JOHN WELSH AND HIS WIFE.

JOHN WELSH, of Ayr, was sent as an exile into France, where he and his wife resided for sixteen years. St. Jean d'Angely was the last sphere of usefulness occupied by Welsh in France; his ministry here was famous, and became as remarkable as it had been in his own country. His life for some few years was happy apparently, until, upon the rise of the hostility of Government towards the Reformed religion, the city was besieged; and in this extremity Welsh showed that he was not unequal to some of the duties of warfare. In particular, he displayed one piece of heroism, so remarkable that it averted the calamities hanging over the city and led to the terms of capitulation; the King himself was at the siege, and he remained at St. Jean d'Angely for a number of days after it had capitulated, to refresh his army.

During this interval, Welsh was earnestly entreated by his friends not to appear in public on the Sabbath, because the celebration of Protestant worship so near the Court was unknown in France; it would give offence; it might even expose his life to danger. He would not, however, be dissuaded. He determined to officiate as usual, which he did to a congregation more than ordinarily numerous, a vast auditory having been drawn together, partly by the novelty of Huguenot preaching almost within hearing of royalty. Whilst he was proceeding with the service, the King sent the Duke of Espernon with some military to apprehend him. Beholding their approach, and knowing the Duke's rank from his apparel, Welsh, in a tone of authority, demanded of the people that they should make way for the marischal, and provide seats for him and his attendants, that they might listen to the Word of God. Either conscience-stricken, or perceiving the impolicy of so harsh an action as that of making prisoner a man enjoying so large a measure of popular favour, the Duke, instead of interrupting the preacher, sat down and heard him to the close of the service. After this he conducted him to the King to answer for his temerity.

The King, who was incensed, demanded how it came to pass that he dared to preach heresy so near his person. "Sire," said Welsh, "if you did right, you yourself would come and hear me preach, and you would make all France hear me likewise; for I preach not as those men whom you are accustomed to hear. My preaching differs from theirs in these two points: First, I preach that you must be saved by the death and merits of Jesus Christ, and not your own; and I am sure your own conscience tells you, that your good works will never merit heaven for you. Next, I preach that, as you are

King of France, you are under the authority and command of no man on earth. Those men whom you usually hear, subject you to the Pope of Rome, which I will never do."

Welsh, when he said this, no doubt referred to the doctrine commonly taught by Romanist preachers, and more especially to that inculcated by Cardinal Bellarmine, in his "Treatise of the Pope's Power in Temporal Causes," published in 1610, and which had excited no small interest at that time, engaging the grave deliberations of the Parliament of Paris, which decided the question against the Cardinal, and ordered his book to be suppressed. Indeed, the greatest writers of the Gallican Church maintained that the King of France had no superior on earth in temporal matters.

Louis felt flattered by the coincidence of Welsh's doctrine respecting the independent power of kings with his own ideas, and with the decision of the Parliament of Paris; and with the utmost good humour he said—"*Hé bien, vous seriez mon ministre*" ("Well, well, you shall be my minister), at the same time calling him "Father"—a title of reverence.

The King, however, was a deceiver; his treatment of the town was base and perfidious, and despotism and Romanism soon asserted their sway within its walls. Very remarkable, however, the King did not forget John Welsh; he commanded the captain in guard of the town to show all manner of kindness to "his minister," place sentinels before his dwelling-house, and provide waggons to convey him and his family to Rochelle. Rochelle was the Jerusalem of France, but it was surrounded with armies; to go to Geneva would be a long, expensive, and dangerous journey.

His physician advised him to seek permission to return to his native country, to breathe his native air, but this the King, James I., peremptorily denied; only if he chose he might come to London to be dealt with. Mrs. Welsh had an interview with the King. The King asked, who was her father. "John Knox," was the reply. "Knox and Welsh!" exclaimed the King;

"the devil never made sic a match as that." "It's right like, sir," said she, "for we never speird [asked] his advice." His Majesty next inquired, how many children her father had left, and if they were lads or lasses? "Three," she said, "and they were all lasses." "God be thanked," cried James, lifting up both his hands; "for if they had been three lads, I had never buiked [enjoyed] my three kingdoms in peace." She urged that the King would give her husband his native air. "Give him his native air!" the King exclaimed; "give him the devil!" "Give that to your hungry courtiers!" she indignantly rejoined. The King at last told her that, if she would persuade her husband to submit to the bishops, he would grant her request. Lifting up her apron, and holding it towards his Majesty, she heroically said, "Please, your Majesty, I'd rather kep [receive] his head there!" The memorialist to whom we are indebted for this anecdote adds, after recording it, that King "James stood in great awe of Mr. Welsh, who often reproved him for his habit of profane swearing. If he had at any time been swearing in a public place, he would have turned round and asked if Welsh was near."

THE REV. ROBERT MORISON AND THE ARTIST.

Mr. John Kelso Hunter in "The Retrospect of an Artist's Life," says:—In 1841 I was sent to Bathgate, and my mission there was to paint the picture of the Rev. Robert Morison. He was a jolly man in every sense of the word. I was for four days an inmate of his house, and in that time I painted his likeness. We had much agreeable conversation during the process, much of which was free, off-hand joking, touching the truth as we passed it, without cramming each other's truths down each other's throats, and we had in after years better fruit than comes out of the most of party discussions.

One example will show this better than a long description. One day I was speaking of being in a public house getting a dram; it was the first day that I went into Bathgate, and I was relating the same to Mr.

Morison. He put on such a serious face, and looked in mine, and enquired with such a seriousness, as was almost laughable. "Does a sensible man like you drink whisky?" I said, "Yes," "Dear me, I thought that the like o' you would be daft enough without it." This was said with so much good humour, that it left a mark, and the conversation went on to other subjects. We did not dwell long on anything at a time. "Laying joking aside," said his reverence, "you never have been much given to drink, and it's well for you that it is so." "How do you know that I have never been given to drink?" His answer was, "You would not have had the same buoyancy in your person, nor such elasticity in your step if you had, nor the same steadiness of hand. You have such a flow of animal spirits, that you don't need the aid of artificial stimulants, and I have no doubt but were you using spirits, it would make you sad, instead of exciting you to joyous thoughts; and I should think that insanity would follow readily in your case, were you to depend on stimulants. You cannot expect always to possess the same flow of spirits which you do now; yet you will long desire to do so. It is then when nature fails, that art would step in; and you would fancy that you were benefited when you were only hurrying faster down the hill."

I looked his portrait of me in the face. I saw that part of it was like, and it was now in my power to stop the other portion from being like. I had never at any time taken too much drink, but I found my mind upset, and a stupor bordering on insanity present. Whisky depressed me. The critic was right in the preface; and that night when I went to bed, in imitation of King David, I lay there, talked with myself, and was silent. On Friday night the portrait was finished, and I was to start for Glasgow at eight o'clock next morning, but was to be sure and visit Mr. Morison in his bedroom before starting. I entered, he rose on his elbow on the bed, gave me good morning, and with a smile enquired, "Well, what is to be the wind-up?" I said I had prepared to make a speech like a Socialist. "It's a fine thing to be social," he said; "now for the speech." I took the furthest back part of the room where he lay, and said: "Mr. Morison—Sir, you have been a circumstance acting on my organisation with such force, when you least expected it, that I have resolved from this time henceforth, till I find myself the worse from wanting it, should drink of any kind be offered me through kindness or otherwise—I hope to see your apparition, tall, not ghastly, stand between the mug and me—and I'll not taste it."

He sat up, held out his arms, and said, "Come, till I embrace you." I took a hap, step, and loup into his arms, and wintled ower beyond him in the bed, kissed him, and bade him an affectionate farewell in the meantime. I called him father ever after, and he called me son. I kept the pledge for twenty-six years; and when sunk with disease, only then used a little stimulant as medicine. Few days in that long period but some time of the day my father Morison has been remembered by his son. I never see a man the worse of drink, but up he comes. Had it not been for him, the same fate might have been mine. My life since, as to my avoiding strong drink, has been a monument to the memory of the Rev. Robert Morison of Bathgate.

HUME'S SCEPTICISM AND GRIEF.

DAVID HUME, the author of the "History of England" and other works, was known by Dr. Carlyle of Inveresk, who describes him as a man of social and benevolent temper, and one of the best-natured men in the world. He was branded with the title of an Atheist, on account of the many attacks on revealed religion which are to be found in his philosophical works and in many places of his history. Dr. Carlyle never believed, however, that Hume's sceptical principles had laid fast hold on his mind, but that his books proceeded rather from affectation of superiority and pride of understanding, and love of vain glory. He was confirmed in this opinion after Hume's death by the following incident related to him by the Hon. Patrick Boyle. When Hume and he were both in London, at the period when Hume's mother died, Mr. Boyle, hearing of it, soon after went into his apartment—for they lodged in the same house—when he found him in the deepest affliction, and in a flood of tears.

After the usual topics of condolence, Mr. Boyle said to him,—"My friend, you owe this uncommon grief to your having thrown off the principles of religion, for if you had not, you would have been consoled by the firm belief that the good lady, who was not only the best of mothers, but the most pious of Christians, was now completely happy in the realms of the just." To which David replied,—"Though I threw out my speculations to entertain and employ the learned and metaphysical world, yet, in other things, I do not think so differently from the rest of mankind as you may imagine." To this testimony Mrs. Carlyle was a witness, and the whole incident is another proof that when the human soul is stirred to its depths, it can be satisfied with nothing but what religion supplies.

THE REV. DR. FERGUSON'S HYMN—
"He loved Me and Gave Himself for Me."

ABOUT four miles from the large and thriving town of Dundee, in the East of Scotland, stands Panmure House, the property of the Earl of Dalhousie. The late Earl, finding that he had really no use for it—since he rarely removed from Brechin Castle—let it out on a lease of several years' duration to a wealthy Dundee mill owner. This gentleman thought it proper to repair the great house considerably when he took possession of it—and it may well be called "great," for there are said to be as many windows in it as there are days in the year. When the repairs were all finished he gave an entertainment to the masons, joiners, and upholsterers who had been at work on the repairs. Mr. Miller, for that was the gentleman's name, took the chair himself, and his lady and daughter graced the meeting with their presence. The rule of the entertainment, when the eatables had been disposed of, was that every one present should either sing a song or tell an anecdote.

When it came to the turn of one young man in the company, he modestly declined, and insisted that he neither could sing a song nor tell a story. But all the company pressed him to perform his part, and refused to let him off. Thus solicited, the young man stood up, and with a meek and subdued aspect of countenance, yet with a clear and melodious voice, sang the hymn by the Rev. Dr. Ferguson, "He loved me and gave Himself for me," which, some way or other, he had met with and had committed to memory. As he rendered in a tender manner the words,

"O when I stand 'mid yonder shining throng,
   And on fair Canaan's coast my Saviour see,
I'll add this chorus to my swelling song,
   'He lovéd me and gave Himself for me,'"

the spiritual effect produced was as deep as it was unexpected. Mr. Miller, who was himself a good man, and member, if not elder, in the Free Church, struck in at once, and said that "they were all certainly very much obliged to their young friend for singing so beautiful a hymn, and for his own part he was so anxious to catch all the words that he would be still more obliged to him if he would sing it again."

Thus encouraged, if the vocalist had performed his part well the first time, the second performance was yet more overpowering. Observing that a deep impression rested upon the whole company, Mr. Miller very properly proposed to turn the assembly into a prayer-meeting—to which all present heartily agreed. Thus the programme, which concluded with music and dancing, was changed into Bible-reading, praise, and prayer; and all through the power of Christian faithfulness and sacred song. Next day the young man wrote out several copies of the hymn, both for the dining-room and the kitchen, and for weeks the servants might be heard singing at their work in all the rooms and corridors of Panmure House, "He loved me and gave Himself for me."

CARLYLE AND EMERSON.

THESE two men were together in Dumfries-shire in the month of August in 1833. Many were their walks, and talks on themes of vastest moment. Emerson gives us in a letter an account of a most suggestive incident and utterance. He says:—"We went to walk over long hills, and looked to Criffel, then without his cap, and down into Wordsworth's country. There we sat down and talked of the immortality of the soul. It was not Carlyle's fault that we talked on that topic, for he has the natural disinclination of every nimble spirit to bruise itself against walls, and did not like to place himself where no step could be taken. But he was honest and true, and cognisant of the subtle links that bind ages together, and saw how every event affects all the future. "Christ died on the tree; *that* built Dunscore Kirk yonder: *that* brought you and me together. Time has only a relative existence."

REV. JOHN PATISON PREACHING THE WORD.

THE late Rev. John Patison, of Edinburgh, having occasion to preach one Sabbath day in Dundee, had, previously to his leaving his home, laid aside and ordered to be packed up with some other necessary articles, a certain note-book, which contained a sermon on which the good man had bestowed considerable pains, and which he hoped might not be unacceptable to the congregation of Christians who then enjoyed the stated labours of the late excellent Mr. M'Ewen. On his arrival in Dundee, however, which was not till Saturday evening, and, examining the contents of his saddle-bags, he found the note-book missing, nor had any other been substituted in its place. He was, therefore, late as it was, obliged to make choice of a new subject, and to cast his thoughts together upon it in the best manner he could, and, after all his pains and all his prayers, was not a little apprehensive that such defective preparation would not only affect the respectability of his appearance in the pulpit, but in some measure mar the success of his work. "Not by might," however, "nor by power, but by my Spirit, saith the Lord."

It happened, in His adorable providence, on the afternoon of that Sabbath, that a poor fish-woman, notorious for clamour and profanity, stumbled into the meeting, and felt the sermon, particularly in the application, come home with such life and peculiar energy to her soul, as instantly to produce the most happy effect on the dispositions of her heart and tenor of her conduct. On Monday she attended with her fish-basket as usual, but O, how changed! Instead of her former noise and profanity, she was quiet and calm as a lamb; instead of asking from her customers double or triple the value of her fish, she spoke to them with discretion, and told them the lowest price at once. Surprised at this new behaviour of the woman, some who were present, judging she might be indisposed, began to inquire after her health: one of them, in particular, said to her,—"Dear! Margaret, what is the matter with you? you are not at all as you used to be." "No," replied Margaret, "and I hope never shall. It pleased God to lead me yesterday to Mr. M'Ewen's Meeting-house, where I heard words I shall never forget, and found something come over me the like of which I never knew before." This woman lived to give the most satisfactory evidence of the soundness of her conversion, by a walk and conversation becoming the gospel.

THE BOY WHO BECAME A CAPTAIN.

THERE lived in a Scotch village a boy, Jamie by name, who set his heart on being a sailor. His mother loved him very dearly, and the thought of giving him up grieved her exceedingly, but he showed such an anxiety to go and see the distant countries which he had read about, that she finally consented. As the boy left home, the good woman said to him,—"Wherever you are, Jamie, whether on sea or land, never forget to acknowledge your God. Promise me that you will kneel down, every night and morning, and say your prayers, no matter whether the sailors laugh at you or not." "Mother, I promise you I will," said Jamie, and soon he was on shipboard bound for India. They had a good captain, and as several of the sailors were religious men, no one laughed at the boy when he kneeled down to pray. On the return voyage, things were not quite so pleasant. Some of the sailors having run away, their places were supplied by others, and one of these proved to be a very bad fellow.

When he saw Jamie kneeling down to say his prayers, this wicked sailor went up to him, and giving him a sound box on the ear, said in a very decided tone, "None of that here, sir." Another seaman who saw this, although he swore sometimes, was indignant that the young sailor should be so cruelly treated, and told the bully to come up on deck, and he would give him a thrashing. The challenge was accepted, and the well-deserved beating was duly bestowed. Both then returned to the cabin, and the swearing man said, "Now, Jamie, say your prayers, and if he dares to touch you, I will give him another dressing." The next night the devil tempted Jamie to do a very foolish thing. Satan does not like to have anyone say his prayers, or do right in any way, and so he put it into the young sailor's mind that it was quite unnecessary for him to be creating such a disturbance in the ship, when it could easily be avoided, if he would only say his prayers very quietly in his hammock, so that nobody would observe it. Now, see how little he gained by his cowardly proceeding. The moment that the friendly sailor saw Jamie get into his hammock without first kneeling down to pray, he hurried to the spot, and, dragging him out by the neck, he said,— "Kneel down at once, sir! do you think I am going to fight for you and you not say your prayers, you young rascal!"

During the whole voyage back to London, this reckless, profane sailor, watched over the boy as if he had been his father, and every night saw that he kneeled down and said his prayers. Jamie soon began to be industrious, and, during his spare time, studied his books. He learned all about ropes and rigging, and, when he became old enough, about taking latitude and longitude. Several years ago, the largest steamer ever built, called the Great Eastern, was launched on the ocean, and carried the famous cable across the Atlantic. A very reliable, experienced captain was chosen for this important undertaking, and who should it be but little Jamie, the sailor boy. When the Great Eastern returned to England, after this successful voyage, Queen Victoria bestowed on him the honour of knighthood, and the world now knows him as Sir James Anderson.

A SPECIAL PROVIDENCE AT ARBIRLOT.

Dr. Guthrie, in his autobiography, writes as follows:—
"A merciful interposition of God's hand occurred during my ministry at Arbirlot. I had gone to the rocks on the east side of Arbroath that culminate in the noble promontory of the 'Red Head,' on a day when the waves were, so to speak, 'running mountains high.' Though the tide was making, a considerable breadth of the rocks that shelved at a sharp angle into the sea lay bare; I leaped down on one, and had no sooner lighted on the slippery weeds that covered it, than my feet went out from below me, and, laid flat on my back, with my face to the sky and my feet to the sea, I was off, like a ship at her launch! Instantly taking in all the danger, I gave myself up for lost. I could swim, but in such a sea I would have been dashed in pieces against the rocks. By God's providence the very extremity of the danger had the effect, not of confusing, but of calming my mind.

I remembered that the rocks there, formed of what is called 'plum-pudding stone,' had often nodules that, consisting of harder matter, had resisted the action of the waves, and rose above their polished surface. I remembered also how, but the very day before, I had got the heels of my boots armed with iron, and it came on me like a flash of lightning that, if I pressed firmly against the rock in my descent, I might peradventure catch a projecting nodule and be saved—brought to a standstill by that. This flashed on my mind like an inspiration; and, through the divine blessing, by this device I was plucked from the jaws of death—saved, when nothing else short of a miracle could have saved me. There are few who have not experienced, some time or other, providential deliverances equally remarkable." Such facts are worth many arguments on behalf of the doctrine that God exercises a providential care over man. He watches over the swallows which fall to the ground, and over man still more.

BENEVOLENCE AND FIDELITY REWARDED AT OCHILTREE.

LADY GLENCAIRN was a singular child both of providence and grace. Her birthplace was the village of Ochiltree. In that village, side by side, there lived a weaver, who had three daughters, and a widow, who had an only son. The son left his widowed mother to enlist in the army, and go abroad as a common soldier. Time passed on; the infirmities of years came on the lone widow, amid which her humble neighbour showed her much kindness. Her boy being far away, and never heard of, the weaver was as a son to her, and when at length she died, he laid her head in the grave. Years passed on, and when the grass had grown green on the widow's grave, and her son had been long forgotten, the news rang through Ochiltree that the widow's son had come back again: "he that was lost was found." From round to round, from step to step, the soldier boy had risen, till he returned to his fatherland governor of the Leeward Islands, and the possessor of an immense fortune.

On inquiring into the circumstances of his mother's latter years and death, his ear was filled and his heart was melted with the story of her humble neighbour's kindness. The weaver had proved a son to the soldier's mother, the soldier would be a father to the weaver's daughters; and so, settling on them his whole fortune, he educated and reared them in a style becoming their future rank. Two of them were afterwards married in England. The third wore the honours of the house of Glencairn, and when lady of the lands on which, when a little bare-footed, sun-browned, gleesome child, she used to feed her father's cow, she was wont to say that the herd lassie was as happy singing on the lea as now when she was lady of all these lands. This child of providence was also a daughter of grace, and used all the influence which her noble rank and high character gave, in favour of evangelical truth.

LADY GLENCAIRN APPOINTING A MINISTER.

THE death of a pious and worthy minister had left the pulpit of Ochiltree vacant. The farmers, affected by the Socinianism of the neighbouring parishes, had resolved to have no more fanatics in Ochiltree; and, in compact with the ungodly ministers around, they fixed on their man, a cold lifeless preacher. This settled, and counting all secure, three of them agreed to ride next day to Edinburgh, where Lady Glencairn resided, from whom they, as the representatives of the people, expected to get a promise in favour of their nominee. Some bird of the air carried the news of this well-laid plot to Miller Sampson. Like a wise man, he kept the secret to himself. It was the summer time. Sampson was up at the peep of day, and the sun rose on our friend breasting the hills between Ochiltree and Edinburgh.

The well-mounted farmers, little dreaming who was a-head of them, took it easily. By the time Sampson had come in sight of Edinburgh, he heard the tramp of horsemen behind him. It went to Sampson's heart; for he saw that, though he had the strength of his namesake, they would outstrip him in the race. However, the sun by this time was well-nigh down; and it instantly occurred to him that the farmers, having themselves and their horses to bait, would postpone till to-morrow their visit to Lady Glencairn, unless the sight of him should awaken their alarm; and so, if he could conceal himself, he might steal a march on them in the morning, and be the first, after all, to get her ladyship's ear. Sampson, in a moment, cleared the ditch, and lay safe in the bosom of a broom-bush. The farmers jog merrily on, little thinking who listens and lies beneath the broom.

So soon as Sampson, cautiously peeping out, found that the foe are out of sight, he issued forth; and in the hope the farmers would be content to enjoy the comforts of the Harrow Inn, he pressed on to Edinburgh, where he immured himself in some obscure lodging. He was up next morning with the dawn, and away to Coates' House, where her ladyship lived. So soon as Sampson counted that the servants were awake as well as he, his strong arm was thundering at the door. On demanding at that untimely hour to see her ladyship, he was rebuffed by her lackey, and very summarily told to go about his business, for nobody could, or should, see her ladyship at such an hour. Sampson, however, stood to his point; told the servant "he maun see Lady Glencairn," and bade him go and tell her ladyship that "Miller Sampson from Ochiltree maun see her ladyship on business that winna wait." He made good his entrée, unraveled the plot to her ladyship, and left her with the assurance that the nominee of the farmers would not be presented, and, what was then sufficient security to the pious people of Scotland, that she would be guided by Dr. Erskine in filling up the charge. Sampson, making his best bow, walked forth with a buoyant step.

As Sampson was going out, the farmers were coming in. The sight of the strong man of old never filled the Philistines with more dismay. The truth flashed upon the farmers; and as he walked forth with an air, and cast on them a look which very plainly said, "You are a day behind the fair," one of the farmers was heard to say, "There goes Miller Sampson; our meal's a' daigh!" (dough). The farmers found the matter settled; and thus, through the piety, energy, and generalship of a humble man, the parish of Ochiltree was speedily blessed with an efficient and evangelical minister.

MONTAGU STANLEY, THE ACTOR.

Mr. Montagu Stanley was an actor, and attained eminence in his profession. He went to Edinburgh to fulfil an engagement, and when there came under the influence of religious truth. The following reflections, written by him in 1837, show the state of his mind. He said :—"I was passing along one of those crowded by-streets, which serve as a link of connection between two others of magnitude, and in which is situated one of those tokens of the refinement, and too often the depravity, of populous capitals—a small theatre—when my attention was arrested by an object that forcibly struck me, from the singular contrast it presented to another, and a very different one.

"At an angle of the building, which abruptly recedes from the direct line of the street, and at some height from the ground, a large door was formed in a wall of the theatre, apparently for the purpose of receiving and hoisting into the building objects of considerable magnitude. It was closed, while beneath it, on the pavement, lay one of those mimicries of nature used in the gorgeous pageants of a drama—the scenic representation of a sun, surrounded by rays of tarnished gold; the paint in many places had detached itself from the canvas, and was hanging in loose patches; the brilliancy of the original colours, sadly faded, were still further impaired by the thick coating of dust and smoke that obscured their lustre; while here and there were large rents crossing the image, and betraying the coarse texture of the material beneath, and meagre nature of the imitation. A man, of the lower class of servants that hang around the walls of a theatre, was watching, and seated on the pavement, apparently waiting for the opening of the door above. While dozing listlessly in the heat of noon, two or three ragged, dirty children were collected round the sides of the tattered scene in gazing wonder. It was intensely hot; the sky was without a cloud, and the atmosphere surcharged with light, refracted the sun's rays in all directions, glancing from windows, pavement, and every object upon which they fell, till the eyes ached with the excess; while a full unbroken flood of splendour seemed poured upon the battered and worn scene from the meridian sun, as if in mockery of his wretched type that lay beneath.

"It was a sad comparison thus forced upon the mind, and not confined to the trifling forms that for a moment fixed my attention. It was a striking and beautiful image of Truth before which the artificial resemblances of life sink into something worse than mere insignificance. It seemed a species of blasphemy on the bright and glorious sun, that man should dare degrade its image by an imitation at once so feeble and contemptible as that coarse daub of paint and canvas showed; and yet how often had its tinselled splendour been used to add enchantment to the circean scenes of temptation for which it was framed!—how often it had aided in the intoxicating draughts of pleasure which those walls had witnessed, where the intellect is often squandered upon objects the least useful that can engage the mind of man, and the feelings are vitiated by the false sensibilities engendered in the fascinating circle of the drama! Then it had attracted the gaze of hundreds, and, in the absence of reality, applause had been lavished on its gaudy resemblance; now, brought into the light of noon, how despicable it appeared!

"How would those who then admired have turned in disgust away, wondering what infatuation could for a moment have led them to look upon it with any other feeling? Even such is sin—even so we hurry on, regardless of the real nature of what we are admiring and lavishing our time upon—and even so we shrink with disgust, and turn from it when exposed before us in the bright rays of the Sun of Truth. Oh! the littleness of life and its objects, which so engrossingly call on our hours and energies; what atoms we pursue—what trifles chain our admiration!

"The attendant, too, as we watched the mockery before him—indifferent to the contrast presented to his eyes, careless of the force in the comparison, intent only on his painted charge, and ignorant of the great lesson placed so palpably in view, was an apt type of myriads who pass through life, regarding only the creations of their own hands, and unmindful of the light which their Creator's Sun of Righteousness poured full before them. I turned in silence from the place, and pondered deeply as I passed homewards; but the impression was soon worn away, in the hurry and turmoil of other work; and, when recalled, I looked back with regret upon the lessons I had suffered to fade from my mind. Alas! alas! they are the links of that invisible chain of love and thought with which our Creator would draw us towards Himself; but, carelessly, we let them glide through our hands, till, looking back, we learn to count 'their value by their loss.'"

Shortly after this Mr. Stanley resolved to leave the stage and betake himself to a new course in life. The 28th April, 1838, was the last night of his dramatic career, and that night he thanked God who had called him from darkness to light, and emancipated him from what was called by him a "most ungodly profession." His life afterwards was not long, but it was eminently Christian, and he found out the difference experimentally between the theatrical and the real.

DICKSON'S HYMN, "JERUSALEM, MY HAPPY HOME."

A PRESBYTERIAN minister of the United States—an American by birth, but of Scottish parentage—happening to be in the city of New Orleans, was requested to visit an old Scottish soldier who had wandered thither, and, having been attacked by the yellow fever, was conveyed to the hospital in a dying state. On announcing his errand, the sick soldier told him, in a surly tone, that he desired none of his visits—that he knew how to die without a priest. The minister replied that he was no priest, but a Presbyterian clergyman, come to read to him the Word of God, and to speak of that eternity to which he seemed drawing near. The Scot doggedly refused all conversation, and, after lingering a few minutes, the minister was reluctantly compelled to take his leave.

Next day, however, he called again, thinking the reflections of the man on his own rudeness might secure a better reception on a second visit; but the soldier's tone and manner were equally rude and repulsive. He turned himself in bed with his face to the wall, as if determined to hear nothing and relent nothing. As a last effort to gain attention, the minister bethought himself of the hymn, well known in Scotland, the composition, as it is supposed, of David Dickson, of Drone, one of the worthies of Scotland:—

> " Jerusalem, my happy home,
>   Name ever dear to me;
> When shall my labours have an end,
>   In joy and peace and thee?"

This hymn his Scottish mother had taught him to sing when a child, to the tune of "Dundee." He began to hum his mother's hymn to his mother's tune. The soldier listened for a few minutes in silence, but gradually turning himself round, his countenance relaxed, and, with the tear in his eye, he inquired, "Who learnt you that?"

"My mother," said the minister.

"And so did mine," replied the now softened and relenting soldier, whose heart was melted by the recollections of infancy, and who was now prepared to give a willing ear to the man that had found the key to his Scottish heart.

REV. JOHN MILNE'S EARNESTNESS.

THE REV. JOHN MILNE, of Perth, was in some respects a remarkable man, and was much beloved by all who knew him. He was earnest and simple-minded, and ever had a word to utter for the Master. He never refused invitations to preach for his neighbours. He went out on missionary tours, holding "revival" meetings, preaching in barns, or in the open air, or to the workpeople in factories. He never missed an opportunity of trying to do good. If travelling in a railway carriage, he would engage the passengers in religious conversation. If he hired a cab, he would speak to the cabman about being "saved." If he saw a poor woman carrying a basket, he would offer to help her, saying, "that we ought to bear one another's burdens." If a man begged from him, he would give a coin, and tell him to "beg for his soul." To fishermen mending their nets, he would say, that he too was a fisherman, and he wished to catch men. To stone-breakers he would say that he was a stone-breaker, trying to break stony hearts. He would often accompany the policemen in their night-rounds, and with the help of the lanterns read to them verses out of the New Testament. He has been known to travel amid the smoke and soot of a railway engine, that he might "convert" the stoker.

He would tell boys selling newspapers that he had a newspaper that never grew old, meaning his Bible. When he saw any one in mourning, he would go up to them, speak of their bereavement, say that he sympathised with them, and so did Christ. When the Queen came to Perth to uncover a statue of Prince Albert, Mr. Milne was anxious that she should receive some spiritual benefit at his hands. He wished to present her with a copy of a favourite hymn. He found no opportunity of doing it personally, but Lord Mansfield introduced him to General Grey, who assured Mr. Milne that the hymn would be presented to the Queen. When Mr. Milne went to India, he began his work as soon as he was on board ship. He conversed with the passengers, held meetings with them, and preached to them. He watched for opportunities of speaking to the seamen. He gave the boys sixpences to learn verses of the Scriptures, and he even succeeded in getting the captain to join with him in private prayer.

In Calcutta, he visited through the lanes and gulleys of the old town—a place unknown to most of the European population. He made his way into several families, in spite of what he called "worldly etiquette," when he knew they were in trouble, or on the occasion of sickness or death. Many a time, now more than twenty years ago, did Mr. Milne stop the writer of this on Perth Bridge, on the North Inch, or by the river side, look at his bundle of books, and ask how he was getting on with "Ovid," or "Virgil," or "Homer." Then would follow an invitation to his Bible-class. His manner was so simple, his character so transparent, that as soon as he spoke it was evident that he had but one object in view, and that was to lead the soul to the living Lord, that it there might enjoy rest, pardon, and peace.

AN OLD HEARER AT THE CROMARTY FRITH.

THE REV. JOHN CAMPBELL, when preaching in the North of Scotland and Orkney Islands, went down the Frith of Cromarty to Drummond, where an old man who enjoyed his sermon, told him of a Scotch bishop who used to preach in that quarter. This bishop asked one of his old hearers why he had forsaken him? "Because I got no good," said Donald Munro. "But should you not wait at the pool, Donald?" "No, I expect no good at your pool." "Oh, but did not the man at Bethesda get a cure at last?" "Yes, but he had some encouragement. He saw others cured now and then, but I never knew one who was cured at your pool."

SEED EARLY SOWN IN THE HIGHLANDS.

A GOOD many years ago, there was a society formed in Scotland, for the purpose of establishing, circulating or ambulatory schools, among the mountains, and in the valleys and glens of the Highlands, where it was impossible that the population, so widely scattered, could have access to the means of education provided by the parochial schools, and which were frequently placed at a distance of ten, or twenty, or even thirty miles from many of the hamlets or dwellings of the people. Great success attended this Christian and benevolent enterprise, and multitudes flocked to the schools, both old and young, to acquire the power of reading the Word of God in their native language. A considerable effort had therefore to be made by the society to obtain the necessary funds to enable them to support and multiply their schools; and on one occasion they sent a deputation to London to endeavour to interest in their object those wealthy individuals, of whom there are not a few in that great city, who were natives of Scotland, or in some way connected, or interested in, that part of the kingdom.

A learned and respected clergyman of Edinburgh was one of such a deputation; and, among many others, called upon a late opulent and esteemed baronet, who was by birth a Scotchman, and who had returned some time before from India, where he had spent a long period of his useful and honourable life. To him the Rev. Doctor stated his case, and preferred a claim for some assistance in behalf of the Gaelic schools. The worthy baronet listened with the greatest patience, and seemed to feel the deepest interest in the object; and, after a considerable pause, he said :—" Well, Doctor, I cannot be indifferent to such a cause as you have now set before me. I was born in the Highlands of Scotland, and at a very early age was deprived of both my parents. I was committed to the care of a very pious and worthy woman, who brought me up in a retired cottage, in a wild part of Inverness-shire. To that good woman I owed much; she kept me and cared for me as if I had been her own child, and she was particularly anxious to bring me up in the fear of God, and in the knowledge of His Word. I have before me, at this moment, her appearance and figure as she taught me to read the Bible, and especially when (as she regularly did every night), after putting me to bed, she either repeated to me, or made me repeat to her, some text of the Scriptures. One of these texts I well remember. It was this, 'Except a man be born again, he cannot see the kingdom of God.' These words, as she wrapped the bed-clothes around my neck, and kept patting me on the shoulder, she pronounced again and again, until they were so imprinted on my memory, that I have never forgotten them to this day. And during the long years I have spent in India, and amidst all my many wanderings and occupations, the image of

that worthy woman has often been before me; and these
words of the Bible, and many others that she taught me,
have been present to my mind, and have, perhaps, kept
me from much evil. I honour the work in which you
are engaged, in giving to the Highlanders the means of
reading the Word of God. Here is my donation to you,
which I give with the greatest cheerfulness; and if you
will step up stairs with me to the drawing-room, my wife
and daughters have each of them a purse, in which there
will be something for so good a purpose." It is almost
unnecessary to add, that the Doctor left the baronet's
house with a handsome donation from every member of
the family, for the funds of the Gaelic School Society.
The seed sown in the young mind had taken root, and in
after days had produced fruit to the Saviour's praise.

REV. DR. MUIR ILLUSTRATING THE INFLUENCE OF A FLOATING CHAPEL.

THE following interesting statement was made by the
late Rev. Dr. Muir, of St. Stephen's Parish, Edinburgh,
in a sermon preached in behalf of the Edinburgh and
Leith Seaman's Friend Society. "In the course of ministerial duty, I was called to visit, on his death-bed, a fine
youth, who, after several voyages and perilous escapes,
was laid down in consumption. It was a considerable
time before, that he had been seized with this disorder,
and there was, also, little doubt that harsh treatment,
during one of his voyages, had aggravated the malady
and confirmed it. On his way home he had been carried
to an English sea-port, where the opportunity was given
him of attending the floating chapel; and, situated as
he was, he could not have been able to attend divine
worship, had not such a provision been made for seamen.
And I state these particulars that you may the better
learn the frame of his mind, as I inform you, that, amidst
all his sufferings (which were particularly trying), his
gratitude for having had that opportunity of hearing
the gospel was unbounded.

"He frequently recurred to it. He spoke of it with satisfaction. He often mentioned it with tears of delight. He said that he saw the hand of God in bringing him, by chastenings, to a place where he was told of the love of God to lost sinners. He said that the Bethel-ship had been the house of the Lord to him—as a refuge—as an ark to him. And well I remember the emphasis with which he said,—'O! the sound of those psalms and hymns, and the words of those prayers, and the texts of the Bible. They came on my heart, after the long voyage in which there was no Sabbath, and no God to me—they did come on my heart as voices and messengers from heaven. I was then made thoroughly to know the gospel-salvation. And I found the very Saviour whom my sinful and weary soul needed.' And, let me add, that he blessed the Saviour to the last; that he died committing his soul in peace to the Saviour; that even when near his latter end, he still connected his eternal hopes with the privileges he had received at the seamen's chapel; and that his afflicted mother, while she could not but weep at the loss of her sailor boy, was enabled to rejoice in tribulation for the glorious rest on which his soul had entered, and blessed God for the Bethel-ship where her son had first experienced the preciousness of the Saviour."

TORTURE AND CONSCIENCE AT EDINBURGH.

WILLIAM CARSTARES, after being arrested, was, after examination, subjected to torture. One of the bailies of Edinburgh, and the executioner, had been ordered to be present to conduct the operation, and the King's smith was also in attendance, with a new pair of thumbkins of an improved construction, by which much greater force could be applied to the screw. Carstares' thumbs were put in, and screwed down till the sweat of his agony poured over his brow and down his cheeks. The Duke of Hamilton, who was entirely opposed to the torturing system, rose and left the council-room, followed by the Duke of Queensberry, who exclaimed to the Chancellor, "I see he will rather die than confess." All the reply Perth made was to order the executioner to give another turn, which was given with such violence, that Carstares broke silence, and cried out,—"The bones are squeezed to pieces!" "If you continue obstinate," roared the Chancellor, "I hope to see every bone of your body squeezed to pieces!" Again and again he was asked, would he answer the queries of the Council; and assured, that if he did not, he should be tortured day by day while he had life. General Dalzell at last, in a rage, left his seat at the table, and, coming close to the prisoner, vowed that he would take him and roast him alive the next day if he would not comply.

Carstares did not waver for a moment from his resolute refusal. A sterner test must be applied, and the order was given for the boot. While his thumbs were still held fast in the thumbkins, the boot was brought forward, and an attempt made to fit it on. The hangman, however, had only been in office since the 15th of August (when his predecessor had been consigned to the "Thieves' Hole" for nearly beating a beggar to death), and was so inexpert, that he could not adjust the boot and the wedge. He had to take it off after a good deal of bungling, and applying himself anew to the thumbkins, the screw was turned again and again, until Carstares appeared to be on the verge of a swoon. The torture had lasted "an hour" according to the minute of Council, "near an hour-and-a-half" according to the victim's own report, when "the Lords thought fit to ease him of the torture for that time." The executioner was ordered to remove the thumbkins, but when he attempted to loosen them, he found it beyond his strength to undo what he had done, and the King's smith had to be called to fetch his tools to revert the screw before the broken and mangled thumbs could be released. Carstares was then sent back to the Tolbooth, with due notice, that if he remained "obstinate," he would be tortured with the boot by a skilled operator next morning at nine o'clock.

THE RELIGIOUS INFLUENCE OF MOUNTAINS.

The Rev. George Gilfillan, in writing of the successor of his father, the Rev. Mr. Brechin, says:—I had some interesting little talk with Mr. Brechin, and enjoyed much his strong sense, good taste, and subtle reflection. He accompanied me on my return as a student to Edinburgh, as far as where moors described were separated from the hill-side, sloping down to the level of Strath-Rennie, by a little bridge. We sat down to rest ourselves on the ledge. It was the afternoon of an August day, and the sullen face of the moorlands was all smiling with purple heather, and humming with bees and winged insects of every kind. I never had found him so communicative. He said he had come to Strath-Rennie a disappointed man, and perplexed, moreover, with terrible doubts; but added,—"Blessings on these dark rugged hills (they were towering up to the north-west, like a saw of ebon-coloured iron, distinctly defined against a glowing sky), I would not exchange what I have learned of God—Jesus—man—myself, amid their silent circuit, for ten thousand worlds!" As he wrung my hand in parting, he said, "My dear lad, you may—you must, with your temperament—doubt, but, for God's sake, never disbelieve, never despair, and you will come at last to that resolution of your doubts which only patience, prayer, and peace of conscience can bestow." He turned rapidly down the valley, and I pursued southwards my lingering and lonely way. I never saw him again.

SCOTCH ITINERATING PREACHERS.

At the end of the last century, Greville Ewing, John Campbell, Robert and James Haldane, with other congenial spirits, were preachers who moved from place to place as preachers to the poor, and all those who would hear their message. The distribution of tracts, the founding of Sabbath-schools, and the familiar and fervent preaching of the gospel in neglected villages, were their earliest enterprises, and owe to them, in Scotland, at least, their first origination and impulse. In the year 1797, Mr. Ewing and his friend, Mr. Gairie, of Perth, a very holy man and useful preacher, set out on an itinerary tour for preaching and giving tracts. They had hired a gig, and set out from Edinburgh on a fine summer morning, having a large store of religious tracts to give away or scatter on the road during their progress. They came to Livingstone to breakfast.

When standing on the landing step of the inn, Mr. Gairie, looking about, saw a venerable, hoary-headed man making way to them from the other side of the square, who said to them,—" Good-morrow, gentlemen; from Edinburgh, I presume?" "Yes, sir." "Any news? we usually expect news from travellers from Edinburgh." "Oh," said Mr. Gairie, "old friend, here is the best news we have got,"—taking a tract, "'Good news of the way of salvation,' written, I think, by Simeon of Cambridge. Will you take one?" The old gentleman was, no doubt, taken by surprise,—for the admirable essaying to do good in this way was just commenced,—thanked Mr. Gairie, and went away with it. Mr. Ewing then asked his friend—" Do you know to whom you have given the tract?" "No, how could I know him? I never was here in my life before. Do you know him?" "Yes, it is no other than the old minister of the parish. His name is Wishart, one of the Wisharts of Kinneal old church, afterwards joined to Bo'ness." He was long a recluse, having gone through many domestic afflictions, and was, by this time, left alone. He used to say he was like a violin with all its strings broken. May we not hope the "Good News" enlivened him in his solitude and in his declining days? He died in 1801.

CARLYLE IN SORROW.

MRS. CARLYLE died on Saturday, April 21st, 1866. For forty years she was the true and loving helpmate of her husband"—we quote his own words—"and by act and word unweariedly forwarded him, as none else could, in all of mostly that he did or attempted. She was snatched away from him, and the light of his life as if gone out." She was buried in the centre of the ruined roofless choir of the old Abbey Church of her native town. After her death, no summer passed, as long as health allowed, in which Carlyle did not go to Haddington to visit the grave, and also the house in which his wife had spent her early years, and under whose roof they had first met. It was with a feeling of sympathetic awe that the inhabitants of the ancient town, who were familiar with his aspect, would see the venerable pilgrim revisiting these shrines of his heart. The sexton said to one who had made a pilgrimage to the grave of Mrs. Carlyle, "Mr. Carlyle comes here from London now and then, to see the grave. He is a gaunt, shaggy, weird kind of old man, looking very old the last time he was here. He is to be brought here to be buried with his wife. He comes here lonesome and alone. When he visits the wife's grave, his niece keeps him company to the gate; but he leaves her there, and she stays there for him. The last time he was here, I got sight of him, and he was bowed down under his white hairs, and took his way up by that ruined wall of the old cathedral, and around there and in here by the gateway, and he tottered up here to this spot."

Softly spoke the gravedigger and paused. Softer still, in the dialect of the Lothians, he proceeded: "And he stood here awhile in the grass, and then kneeled down and stayed on his knees at the grave; then he bent over, and I saw him kiss the ground; aye, he kissed it again and again; and he kept kneeling, and it was a long time before he rose and tottered out of the cathedral, and wandered through the graveyard to the gate where his niece stood waiting for him." It is to this period of his life that we owe one of the most solemn and pathetic, and also one of the most comforting, of all his letters that we have yet been privileged to see. Writing on the 12th February, 1869, to Erskine, he says: "I was most agreeably surprised by the sight of your handwriting again, so kind, so welcome! The letters are as firm and honestly distinct as ever; the mind, too, in spite of its frail *environments*, as clear plumb-up, calmly expectant, as in the best days: right so; so be it with us all, till we quit this dim sojourn, now grown so lonely to us, and our change come! 'Our Father which art in heaven, hallowed be Thy name, Thy will be done;' what else can we say? The other night in my sleepless tossings about, which were growing more and more miserable, these words, that brief and grand prayer, came strangely into my mind, with an altogether new emphasis, as if *written*, and shining for me in wild pure splendour, on the black bosom of the Night there; when I, as it were, *read* them word by word, with a sudden check to my imperfect wanderings, with a sudden softness of composure which was much unexpected. Not for, perhaps, thirty or forty years had I once formally repeated that prayer; nay, I never felt before how intensely the voice of Man's soul it is; the inmost aspiration of all that is high and pious in poor human nature; right worthy to be recommended with an 'after this manner pray ye.'"

AN EDINBURGH BOARDING SCHOOL ANECDOTE.

WHEN a young girl at school in Edinburgh, says a lady, I often spent my Saturdays at Morningside, with some school companions. The parents of the girls whom I visited were members of the Free Church, and intimate friends of Dr. Chalmers, who also resided at Morningside. It was toward the close of a beautiful autumnal Saturday, just at that hour when all nature looks so calm and lonely, that some of my friends and I were returning to the house after a walk. The sun was beginning to set in gorgeous beauty, casting its golden beams all around us, when suddenly, at a turn of the road, we met Dr. Chalmers, who was also returning home after taking his usual walk. He being well acquainted with the young people who were with me, I was introduced, and O how happy I was! I think I see him now, as I saw him then, although many years have passed, and many changes have been mine.

That calm and lovely face, with heaven stamped on it; that soft, white, silvery hair, and the red cotton handkerchief tied loosely round his neck! His voice, with the Scotch accent, to me so sweet, still at times thrills in my ears like sweetest music. Dr. Chalmers asked me about my studies, which were my favourites; and then, when shaking hands and bidding me good-bye, he said:—"But oh! my dear young friend, seek above all knowledge to know Christ." Though constitutionally a timid girl, I replied, "I will try; and wish to be so good, and hope to meet you in heaven." "Cling to Christ, then," he said, "and we will meet again—if not here, up there," pointing upward as he spoke. I never met him again; he died in the May following. His words did not die with him. They live still, for they will remain with me for ever.

FIRMNESS AND LOVE IN RAGGED-SCHOOL WORK.

THE REV. DR. GUTHRIE tells a touching anecdote of his Ragged School, to show the power of Christian firmness and love when brought to bear on the obdurate and the depraved. During one season, Mr. Gibb, the teacher, was not a little cast down by finding that, as the skies grew warmer, the school grew thinner, and the roll shortened with the length of the day. It was necessary to pass a law, which was done with the approbation of the school, that no boy shall go away from school until he is prepared to remain away altogether, or to submit on his return to a certain measure of punishment. The law was passed with acclamation, and our teacher thought all was right. Next day, however, a dozen had absconded. On being brought back, they said they wished to remain at school; but the four ringleaders refused obedience, declining the punishment. Mr. Gibb was resolved to make an example; but though he told them that as he had threatened so he must perform, and that they must either submit to be punished or go away, they were obstinate, and refused to yield, which to him was a great grief, as they were biggish boys, and stood most of all in need of such a school.

He could not break them—he resolved to try to bend by an appeal to their better feelings, and said, "Boys, we will not compel you to accept of the food and instruction of which hundreds like you would be glad who have it not. If you like to remain, submit to the rules, and you are welcome. Will you do it?" "No, sir," "Would you have me tell a lie by not acting up to my word?" "No, sir." "Would you like to remain, and be allowed to do as you please?" "No, because we would go wrong, sir." "Why, then, not submit to the rule you agreed to?" "We'll stop if you'll no lick us, sir—if you'll no give us palmies." "Boys, were you ever punished before, and why?" "Because we deserved it." "And don't you deserve it now? Take it, and be done with it."

After trying them in this manner for some time without any success, Mr. Gibb addressed them in a farewell speech, suited to the taste and calibre and character of those he spoke to, saying—"Well, then, boys, I think I have done; I can do nothing for you; I dare not let you pass. You are going away, and it may be that I shall never see you more. Perhaps I shall see you rich and respectable men. Perhaps I shall see you masters of a fine shop, standing behind the counter, with your hair nicely curled, and dressed like gentlemen. Or, may be, when I am an old man, and walk leaning on a staff, I shall see you rolling by in a fine carriage, drawn by two grey horses, attended by grand servants; and when you see me, you will say, 'Look, there's the ragged-school master that used to lick us when we were laddies. Here, Mr. Gibb, there's something to put in your pocket.' Now, these things may be; but ah! my boys, I much fear that if ever I see you riding, it will be in one of those dark, gloomy carriages, with the locked door and iron gratings, conveying you—you know where to?" "Yes, sir," "And is it not likely, if you go away from the school, that you will be obliged to sink to begging again? And then your next step down will be to stealing; and down and down you go. But whether I may see you again in this world or not, I do not know. One thing, however, is certain, we shall meet again—and where?"

Their heads, before erect, now began to hang down; and as one or two answered, "At the last day, sir," they and the greater number of the children, as if by a sudden shock of electricity, burst into tears. The superintendent of work, who had worn the red coat for upwards of thirty years, turned on his heel, and the tear glistened in the old soldier's eye, while nothing was to be heard but sobs and sighing. Now was Mr. Gibb's time to drive home the wedge; and so, though nearly overcome himself, he said, "All that I ask of you now, my boys, is a shake of your hand, and we part good friends." This being done by him, the assistant teacher, and old veteran, nothing now remained for the poor fellows but to go. Moving slowly to the door, and all the while crying bitterly, they shook hands with their companions and—went? No; all remained! They melted on the threshold, yielding to the master's last appeal, fairly conquered, and proving the almost omnipotent power of Christian wisdom, combined with Christian affection.

A LILY AMONG THORNS IN DUNDEE.

Dr. M'Gavin in his "Scottish Pastorate," sets before his readers a lily among thorns in the following touching sketch:—In a humble home of single apartment and scanty furniture in Dundee, which tells of extreme poverty, yet scrupulously clean, to prove that propriety and principle can shed attraction o'er the lowliest lot, lies a lovely young female, alone, and in hopeless consumption. The features are of the finest Grecian mould, and might have been a model for the statue of an ancient goddess, while the complexion, as yet only beautiful by its affliction, pales all comparison with the purest alabaster. This child of nature's nobility has been born to hard fortune. Her father, fallen by profligacy from commercial competency, has long abandoned his family to destitution. One by one the children have faded into the grave before the struggles of stern poverty and feeble constitution, until now this last victim is awaiting her precocious removal, and the broken-hearted mother is toiling hopelessly to prevent the quenching at her hearth of this "only coal that is left." The girl herself, now sixteen years of age, has, until lately, been entirely giddy and godless, misspending her Sabbaths in bed, or in reading the worthless stories of the worst London journals, and refusing to attend any religious instruction. But failing health had compelled to serious conviction, and by a seasonable discourse on the solemn words, "It is a fearful thing to fall into the hands of the living God," she has been led through great concern to seek salvation in the finished work of the Lord Jesus Christ.

Now, she is conscious that her days are numbered, and she is waiting the end. A smile always greets you on entrance. Ask how she is, the answer is, "Wonderfully well." "Have you had a good night?" "Oh yes." "Did you sleep well?" "Well, the cough is too constant to let me sleep much, but I do not need much sleep, being always in bed, and getting snatches by day as well as by night." "Are you not lonely?" "Oh no! by day, if I weary, I can get a promise from my Bible to comfort me, and by night, I have a good God and Saviour, who is present with me." "Is your pain easier?" "The stitch has been rather distressing from the severity of the cough, but oh! dear sir, what is that? one moment of heaven will be more than an ample recompence for it all." "Are you not afraid to die, and vexed to leave your mother alone?" "Sometimes I am deeply grieved for my mother, for she has had many sorrows, and she will have none to cheer her when I am gone. But the blessed Jesus, who has taken away the sting of death from my soul, will comfort her in my departure, and I leave her fearlessly, where I trust my own soul, on His care."

"Is there anything you want for, Lily" (and this was spoken in an apartment that almost rebuked the inquiry, because it seemed to want everything, even to the necessaries of life)? The ready answer was,—"No, I thank you; it is but little that I need, and everybody is so kind to me, that I have more than I can take." Thus from this humble couch were daily preached, to the end, lessons of sweet content in poverty, of sunny cheerfulness in lonely pain and sorrow, and of fearless hope and confidence in death, which, in one so young and so uneducated, could only be produced by the grace of the Holy Ghost in that simple heart, and that failed not to proclaim truths to many which still survive, in the conversion of some, and the spiritual improvement of others.

MOFFAT'S FIRST SERMON TO THE HEATHEN.

Dr. Moffat used to tell the story of his first missionary sermon. "It happened, one evening, soon after I began my journey up the country, that I found my way to the homestead of a Dutch Boer, of whom I begged a night's lodgings. It was nightfall, and the family must soon go to rest. But first, would the stranger address some words of Christian counsel to them; might they hear what he has to say? Gladly I assented, and the big barn was resorted to. Looking round on my congregation, I saw my host and hostess, with their family of three boys and two girls. There were crowds of black forms hovering near at hand, for this surly Boer had some hundred Hottentots in his service, but never a one was there in the barn.

"I waited, hoping they might be coming. But no; no one came; still I waited, as expecting something. 'What ails you,' said the farmer; 'why don't you begin?' May not your servants come too?' I replied. 'Servants!' shouted the master; 'do you mean the Hottentots, man? Are you mad, to think of preaching to Hottentots? Go to the mountains and preach to the baboons; or, if you like, I'll fetch my dogs, and you may preach to them!' This was too much for my feelings, and tears began to trickle down my cheeks, for my heart was too full to hold. After a pause I opened my New Testament, and read out for my text the words,—'Truth, Lord; yet the dogs eat of the crumbs that fall from their master's table. A second time the words were read, and then my host, vanquished by the arrow from God's quiver, cried, 'Stop!

you must have your own way. I'll get you all the Hottentots, and they shall hear you.' He was as good as his word. The barn soon filled with rows of dark forms, whose eager looks gazed at the stranger. I then preached my first sermon to the heathen. I shall never forget that night."

THE HIGHLAND WIDOW AND HER SON.

A HIGHLAND widow, bearing her only son in her arms, went away to seek assistance from a relative to pay her rent. She was suddenly overtaken, in a wild glen among the mountains, by what was long recalled by her fellow-villagers as "the first May storm," that after attempting in vain for some time, with her infant in her arms, to buffet whirling eddies, she laid the child down among the heather and ferns in the deep cleft of a rock, with the brave resolve, if possible, to make her own way home, through the drifting sleet, and obtain succour for her little one. So was found, by the anxious neighbours, next morning, stretched cold and stiff on a snowy shroud. But the cries of the babe directed them to the rock crevice where it lay, all unconscious of its danger, and from which it was rescued in safety. Many long years afterwards, that child returned from distant lands a disabled soldier, covered with honourable wounds. The first Sabbath of his home-coming, he entered the Gaelic Church, Glasgow, to get shelter from a heavy fall of snow.

It was on a Communion Sabbath. The subject of the discourse was the Love of Christ. In illustrating the self-sacrificing nature of that "love which seeketh not her own," the preacher narrated the above story of the Highland widow, whom he had himself known in his boyhood. And he asked,—"If that child is now alive, what would you think of his heart, if he did not cherish an affection for his mother's memory, and if the sight of the poor tattered cloak which she had wrapt round him, in order to save his life at the cost of her own, did not fill him with gratitude and love too deep for words? Yet, what hearts have you, my hearers, if, over those memorials of your Saviour's sacrifice of Himself, you do not feel them glow with deeper love, and with adoring gratitude?" A few days after this, a message was sent by a dying man, requesting to see the clergyman. The request was speedily complied with.

The sick man seized the minister by the hand, and, gazing intently on his face, said,—"You do not, you cannot recognize me. But I know you, and knew your father before you. I have been a wanderer in many lands. I have visited every quarter of the globe, and fought and bled for my king and country. I came to the town a few weeks ago in ill-health. Last Sabbath I entered your church—the church of my countrymen—where I could once more hear, in the language of my youth and heart, the gospel preached. I heard you tell the story of the widow and her son"—here the voice of the old soldier faltered, his emotion almost choked his utterance; but recovering himself for a moment, he cried, "I am that son!" and burst into a flood of tears—"Yes," he continued, I am that son! Never, never, did I forget my mother's love. Well might you ask what a heart should mine have been, if she had been forgotten by me! Though I never saw her, dear to me is her memory, and my only desire now, is to lay my bones beside hers in the old churchyard among the hills. But, sir, what breaks my heart and covers me with shame, is this—until now, I never saw, with the eyes of the soul, the love of my Saviour in giving Himself for me—a poor, lost, hell deserving sinner. I confess it, I confess it!" he cried, looking up to heaven, his eyes streaming with tears; and pressing the minister's hand close to his breast, he added, "It was God that made you tell that story. Praise be to His holy name, that my mother has not died in vain, and that the prayers which, I was told, she used to offer for me, have been at last answered; for the love of my mother has been blessed by the Holy Spirit for making me see, as I never saw before, the love of the Saviour. I see it; I believe it. I have found deliverance in old age where I found it in my childhood—in the cleft of the rock—but it is the Rock

21

of Ages!" and, clasping his hands, he repeated with intense fervour,—"Can a mother forsake her sucking child, that she should not have compassion on the son of her womb? yea, they may forget, yet will I not forget thee."

"GIVE ME A BAIRN'S HYMN."

I HAVE just been reading, says a well-known writer, through eyes brimming with tears, the narrative of Dr. Guthrie's last hours. They were all in perfect keeping with his noble and beautiful life. For threescore years and ten, Guthrie had been patterning after Jesus, who "went about doing good." To the last, he was the same simple-hearted, genial, child-like creature; in genius, a full-grown man; in simplicity, a child. His love of children was a passion with him. He had eleven of his own, one of whom, Johnnie, had gone home to heaven in his infancy. For the poor outcast lads and lassies of the wretched Cowgate, in Edinburgh, Dr. Guthrie's heart went out in tenderest compassion. He visited them in their miserable whisky-cursed homes. He organised for them the first ragged-school ever established in Scotland. And, among all his printed productions, his "Plea for Ragged-Schools" is the most characteristically touching and eloquent. When the great pulpit orator came to die, he grew more and more like a child himself. He felt like a babe on the bosom of Jesus. The sight of a little grandchild, who came into his dying chamber, brought a smile over his pale face, and he whispered,—"Put her up." When lifted on the bed, she crept up to him and kissed him, and he nodded his head, and said, sweetly, "My bonnie lamb!"

During those last hours, he found great solace in the singing of dear old favourite psalms and spiritual songs. But of none was he so fond as of simple Sunday-school melodies. When they asked him on one of the last nights of his life, "What shall we sing for you?" he said quickly, "Give me a bairn's hymn." So they sang for the veteran pilgrim, "Jesus, Tender Shepherd hear me," and "There is a happy land, far, far away." Glorious old hero of the Cross! His theology was all narrowed down to one word—Christ. His faith was the faith of a little child. When asked, "Have you that Saviour now?" he promptly answered, "Yes, I have none else." Then he was heard to murmur to himself, "Over on the other side," and kept ejaculating, "Happy, happy, happy!" And so he fell asleep in Jesus, without a struggle or a sigh. The last of earth was the beginning of the everlasting weight of glory. To-day, Scotland weeps over the silence of her most gifted tongue. But the voice has passed into the harmonies of heaven, and Guthrie is singing a *bairn's hymn* before the throne."

BAD DRINK FOR A CHILD.

A WISE and far seeing doctor in delivering an address to a working class audience in Edinburgh, we mean the genial and large-hearted author of "Rab and his Friends," said,—"The stomach is almost the first thing that goes wrong in children, and generally as much from too much being put in, as from its food being of an injurious kind. A baby, for nine months after it is born, should have almost nothing but its mother's milk. This is God's food, and it is the cheapest and best, too. No child should get meat or hard things till it gets teeth to chew them, and no child should get a drop of whisky, or any strong drink, unless by the doctor's orders. Whisky to the soft, tender stomach of an infant, is like vitriol to ours; it is a burning poison to its dear little body, as it may be a burning poison and a curse to its never-dying soul. As you value your children's health of body, and the salvation of their souls, never give them a drop of whisky; and let mothers, above all others, beware of drinking when nursing. The whisky passes from their stomach into their milk, and poisons their own child!

"I was once, many years ago, walking in Lothian Street, Edinburgh, when I saw a woman staggering along very drunk. She was carrying a child; it was lying over her shoulder. I saw it slip, slippin' farther and farther back. I ran, and cried out, but, before I could get up, the poor little thing, smiling over its miserable mother's shoulder, fell down like a stone on its head on the pavement; it gave a gasp, and turned up its blue eyes, and had a convulsion, and its soul was away to God, and its little, soft, waefu' body lying dead, and its idiotic mother, grinning and staggering over it, half seeing the dreadful truth, then forgetting it, and cursing and swearing. That was a sight! so much misery, and wickedness, and ruin. It was the young woman's only child. When she came to herself she became mad, and is, to this day, a drivelling idiot, and goes about for ever seeking for her child, and cursing the woman who killed it. This is a true tale, too true, and should be a warning to all mothers."

A ST. MONANCE FISHERMAN'S TRIUMPH IN DEATH.

THERE lived a good Christian fisherman in the village of St. Monance, on the coast of Fife. His name was Andrew Davidson, and he was the owner and captain of a fishing boat called *The Rose in June*. The herring season came, and Andrew Davidson and his little crew prepared to go to sea. He had but lately been married, and, before leaving home, he knelt down with his young wife, and asked God to keep her safely while he was away; but she noticed, and her heart sunk within her at the thought, that he said not a word about his own safety.

On Monday, 15th December, 1872, the boats started to their grounds, and soon thereafter a strong easterly wind began to blow, which increased to a gale by midnight, at which time the sea was running very high. The gale was accompanied by torrents of rain, and lasted with extreme severity till Tuesday. The most of the St. Monance boats made for Elie harbour, which they reached with great difficulty and danger. An anxious crowd of women and children, made up of the families of the absent fishermen, gathered on the beach and along the shore. Every eye was strained across the waters to catch the first glimpse of the returning boats. One by one they struggled in, and shouts of joy and thankfulness arose from one and another as a husband, a brother, a father, or a son sprang ashore. But *The Rose in June* did not come. Driven by the storm, and dashed upon the rocks, she had become a total wreck. Turned bottom upwards, her crew of six men clung to her sides with desperate energy. No other boat was near to help or save them, and, all around, the wild waves were rolling and roaring, threatening every moment to tear each man from his hold and dash him to pieces on the sharp rocks. Andrew Davidson thought of Jesus in that hour of peril, and, in the face of certain death, that thought did for him what nothing else in the world could have done—it made him happy. It may have been that he remembered then how Paul and Silas glorified God in the prison of Philippi, for he shouted, loud and clear above the storm,—"Now, boys, let's sing a hymn of praise to God!" and at once he began and sang this verse,—

> "Jesus, lover of my soul,
>   Let me to Thy bosom fly,
> While the nearer waters roll,
>   While the tempest still is high:
> Hide me, O! my Saviour, hide,
>   Till the storm of life be past;
> Safe into the haven guide,
>   O! receive my soul at last."

The voices could be heard by those on the shore above the noise of the tempest and the tumult of the waters. Ere the hymn was closed, one of the fishermen became unconscious, and the boat was caught by an immense wave, and carried on the top of it to a considerable distance at a fearful rate. When it left her, she was struck on the broadside by a heavy sea, and thrown on her beam ends, after which, another sea made a breach right over her, and carried away Skipper Davidson, who left this world and entered heaven with a song of praise on his lips.

A sad silence fell upon the men who had been trying to join in that song of praise. For awhile no one spoke. At last, John Allan, the mate of the little vessel, who was also a believer in Jesus, exclaimed,—" Come, my lads, let us go on with the hymn that our skipper is now finishing in heaven." And then those brave men, rocking on their wrecked boat, with the waves dashing, and the wild winds wailing around them, sang on till they had finished the hymn.

Just as they were finishing these last words, another huge wave burst over the boat, and the young mate was carried away to join his friend and shipmate in that blessed world—

"Where, anchored safe, his weary soul
Shall find eternal rest,
And not a wave of trouble roll
Across his peaceful breast."

The rest of the crew of that wrecked boat escaped with their lives. But they never forgot the scene they had witnessed during that terrible storm. And no sermon ever preached about the preciousness of Jesus could make such an impression on their minds as was made by that memorable scene. They felt, deep down into their very souls, that the truth in Jesus is the best of all truth, because it satisfies us and makes us happy.

HEALING BY FAITH AND PRAYER.

THE REV. THOMAS HOG was ordained minister of Kiltearn in 1655, and was a most spiritually minded man. In prayer he was most solemn and fervent; the profoundest reverence, the lowest submission, and yet a marvellous boldness and intimacy with God, attended his engagements in this exercise. It might be truly said of him, as of Luther, when he prayed, it was *tanta reverentia, ut si Deo, et tanta fiducia, ut si amico,*— "with as much reverence as if he were speaking to God, and with as much boldness as if he had been speaking to a friend." The strength of his faith was proof against discouragement; none ever beheld him perplexed on account of difficulties. Having once committed his cause unto the Lord, he could wait with assurance of a happy event, and he obtained many remarkable and even extraordinary returns. On one occasion, a good woman having come to Mr. Hog with a sore lamentation that her daughter was distracted, Mr. Hog charged one or two devout persons, for he frequently employed them on extraordinary occasions to set apart a day and night for fasting and prayer, and then to join with him in prayer for the maid the next day. Accordingly, when the time of their appointment for a joint concurrence in the duty came, he wrestled for the distressed person till she recovered her senses, and became as quiet as ever she was before.

Another case is that of a daughter of the Laird of Parks, his brother-in-law, who, being lodged with him, and being seized with a high fever, and little hope of life left, Mr. Hog, who loved the child dearly, consulted with his wife whether there was any cause, either in him or her, of the Lord's contending with their friend while under their care; and acknowledging their offences jointly to the Lord in prayer, with the iniquity of the child, the fever instantly left her, and she was restored to health. In like manner, a child of the Rev. Mr. Thomas Urquhart, having been at the very point of death, those present pressed Mr. Hog to pray, for he was now become so revered, that none other would, in such cases, pray when he was present; upon which he solemnly charged them to join fervently with him, and having wrestled in prayer and supplication for some time, the child was restored to health. This was the manner of this godly man's life. He offered up an effectual fervent prayer, and it prevailed. The cases given above, and others as wonderful, are testified to by witnesses whose words are worthy of all acceptation, and if they be looked upon as extraordinary, it must be remembered Hog was an extraordinary man, and he lived in an extraordinary time.

REV. DONALD CAMPBELL AND SATAN.

The Rev. Donald Campbell, minister of Kilmichael, Glassery, Argyleshire, lived in the seventeenth century, and laboured in an extensive parish, where the labours of Knox had made little impression on the minds of the priests or the people. He had, therefore, many varied experiences of more than an ordinary character. The following curious anecdote is told of him by the more credulous of the people. In any case, the anecdote contains a good deal of moral and spiritual teaching. One evening, as the minister of Glassery, exhausted with fasting and fatigue, was returning from a distant part of his extensive parish, he was assailed by Satan, whether *in propria persona*, or through the agency of some human emissary, or by internal suggestion, informants were not certain, although it was evident the most of them were rather inclined to the first opinion. The enemy tempted him to abandon the ministry. Being foiled on this point, he represented to him the inexpediency of exhausting his strength with such multiplied and harassing labours. Here, also, failing of his object, he at last attempted to excite self-righteous thoughts in his bosom by representing the merits of his services. To all these darts, Donald Campbell opposed the shield of faith, the harness of humility, and the sword of the Spirit, which is the word of God, and was victorious. The Devil left him for a time, but met him again when not far from his own house, and threatened to do him some bodily injury. To this threatening the man of faith replied, that the Devil had not power over a child of God, except by permission, and he reposed perfect confidence in the protection of Him who was the God and Creator of them both.

Finding that he could not succeed by any of the means hitherto employed, Satan affected to sympathise with him in the fatigue he must feel after the day's labour, and counselled him, instead of going round by the bridge across the river, which separated him from his house, to take the nearer road by a ford. This advice, although to all appearance kind and harmless, was rejected, on the principle that none of the suggestions of Satan, however expedient in appearance, are ever on any account, or any occasion, to be followed. Donald Campbell, therefore, proceeded by the way he originally intended. But just as his horse (for he was riding) was entering upon the bridge, Satan caused him to stumble against the parapet, and dislocate his rider's little toe. Satan exultingly exclaimed, " Hadst thou but taken *my* advice, thou hadst escaped that affliction; and is this the reward thou receivest for thy services? This the protection thou enjoyest from thy Master?" "'I had rather,'" meekly replied the man of God, "'be a doorkeeper in the house of my God, than to dwell in the tents of wickedness. For the Lord God is a sun and shield: the Lord will give grace and glory: no good think will He withhold from them that walk uprightly. O Lord of hosts, blessed is the man that trusteth in thee.'"

PRIESTLY CURSING; ITS EFFECTS.

An example of the way priests preached and cursed is given in a defence made by a friar, William White, in answer to the charge made against him of having calumniated the clergy.. His defence was delivered in the parish church, St. Andrews, in the presence not only of the doctors and masters of the University, but of several dignitaries of the Church. His theme was, "Verity is the strongest of all things." His discourse on cursing was, that if it were rightly used, it was the most fearful thing upon the face of the earth, for it was the very separation of man from God, but that it should not be used rashly and for every light cause. "But now," said he, "the avarice of the priests and their ignorance of their office have caused it to be evil spoken of; for the priest, whose office it is to pray for the people, stands up on the Sunday, and cries, 'One has tint (lost) a spurtle; there is a frail broken beyond the burn; the gudewife of the other side of the gate has tint a horn spoon; God's displeasure and mine I give to them that know of the gear, and restore it not.'" To show how the people mocked their cursing, he told, that, after a sermon he had at Dunfermline, he came to a house where gossips were drinking their Sunday's penny, and he, being dry, asked for a drink. "Yes, father," said one of the gossips, "ye shall have drink, but ye maun (must) first resolve a doubt which has risen among us, *to wit*, what servant will serve his master best on least expenses?" "The good angel," said I, "who is man's keeper, who makes great service without expense." "Tush," said the gossip, "we mean no such high matters; we mean, what honest man will do the greatest service for the least expense?" "And while I was musing," said the friar, "what that should mean, he said, 'I see, father, that the greatest clerks are not the wisest men. Know ye not how the bishops and their officials serve us husbandmen? Will they not give us a letter of cursing for a plack, to last for a year, to curse all that look over our dyke, and that keeps our corn better than the sleeping boy that will have three shillings of a fee, a sark, and a pair of shoon in the year; and, therefore, if their cursing dow (can) effect anything, we hold the bishops the best cheap servants that are within the realm."'

THE PREVAILING ARGUMENT.

Professor Henry Drummond, the author of "Natural Law in the Spiritual World," in addressing a meeting of students belonging to the Edinburgh University, told them of an incident which produced a marked impression upon them. It was to this effect,—"Some years ago, in the University, there was a fine, manly fellow, a medical student, a very Hercules in strength, but as gentle and lovable as he was strong. He was immensely popular, the captain of the football club, and not a cricket match was considered complete without him. He was a man of good intellectual gifts as well. He caught typhoid fever while attending the Royal Infirmary, and soon he lay dying in a private ward. One of the house physicians, an earnest Christian and

successful soul-winner, spoke to him about God and
eternity. The dear fellow listened, became anxious, and
eagerly heard the story of redeeming love. 'Will you
give yourself to Jesus?' asked the doctor. He did not
answer for a space, and then earnestly regarding the
man of God, he said,—' But don't you think it would be
awful mean just to make it up now, at my last gasp,
with One I have rejected all my life?' 'Yes, it would
be mean; but, dear fellow, *it would be far meaner not
to do it.* He wants you to do it now, for He has made
you willing, and it would be *doubly* mean to reject a
love that is pursuing you even to death.' The dying
man saw the point, and apprehending the greatness of
that exceeding love, he cast himself upon the Eternal
Heart of Mercy, and passed away in sweet peace and
blessedness."

MICHAEL BRUCE AND THE PARAPHRASES.

MICHAEL BRUCE, who was born in Kinnesswood on 27th
March, 1746, was the author of some parts of the paraphrases which have been so long used in public worship
in Scotland. The circumstance which first led Bruce to
write them has been rendered memorable in the district
by its contributing, at the same time, to form a taste for
sacred music among its inhabitants, for which they are
still somewhat celebrated. About the period to which
this refers, a farmer, of the name of Gibson, settled in
the village with his family, and one of them, afterwards
a preacher in connection with the Established Church,
took delight in teaching this art to such villagers as
would receive his instructions. Among the youths who
benefited by his lessons, was one John Buchan, who,
after residing in several towns with a view to improve
himself in his profession as a mason, returned to his
native village, where he taught church music, and introduced a number of new tunes which he had learned in
the places he had visited. Till then, "the old eight,"—
French, Dundee, York, Elgin, Newton, London, Martyrs,
Abbey—as they are now emphatically called, were con-

sidered the only tunes which it was lawful to sing in country congregations, and, consequently, were all that was deemed necessary or proper to learn; but in town churches a few others had begun to be added to the number.

In the summer of 1764, Michael Bruce joined Buchan's class. At the time of his doing so, mere doggerel rhymes were sung by the pupils of the practising school. Buchan knowing Bruce to be both a poet and a scholar, requested him to furnish the class with verses which might be substituted for the ones used, which were destitute of sentiment, and calculated to produce a ludicrous effect when sung to solemn airs. With this request Bruce complied, and wrote a number of hymns, which soon became popular, and parts of these are embodied in the paraphrases. Among these are,—

> "O happy is the man who hears
> Instruction's warning voice;
> And who celestial Wisdom makes
> His early, only choice."—*Para. xi.*

> "Few are thy days, and full of woe,
> O man, of woman born!
> Thy doom is written, 'Dust thou art,
> And shalt to dust return.'"—*Para. viii.*

> "The beam that shines from Sion hill
> Shall lighten ev'ry land;
> The King who reigns in Salem's tow'rs
> Shall all the world command."—*Para. xviii.*

In this humble way, these verses of praise were produced which have been the means by which thousands, all over the world, have wafted their praises to Him who receives the praises of Israel.

THE WIFE OF THE REV. JAMES FRASER, OF ALNESS.

THE REV. JAMES FRASER, of Alness, was a Christian minister of more than ordinary piety and unction. He was much esteemed, and exercised an influence for good far beyond his parish. He had, however, a thorn in the flesh in the person of his wife, who was a cold, unheeding, worldly woman. Never did her godly husband sit down to a comfortable meal in his own house, and often would he have fainted from sheer want of needful sustenance but for the considerate kindness of some of his parishioners. She was too insensate to try to hide her treatment of him, and well was it for him on one account, that she was. His friends thus knew of his ill-treatment, and were moved to do what they could for his comfort. A godly acquaintance arranged with him to leave a supply of food in a certain place, beside his usual walk, of which he might avail himself when starved at home. Even light and fire in his study were denied to him on the long, cold, and wintry nights; and as his study was his only place of refuge from the cruel scourge of his wife's tongue and temper, there, shivering, and in the dark, he used to spend his winter evenings at home. Compelled to walk in order to keep himself warm, and accustomed to do so when preparing for the pulpit, he always kept his hands before him as feelers in the dark, to warn him of his approaching the wall at either side of the room.

In this way, he actually wore a hole through the plaster at each end of his accustomed beat, on which some eyes have looked that glistened with light from other fire than that of love, at the remembrance of his cruel wife. But the godly husband had learned to thank the Lord for the discipline of this trial. Being at a Presbytery dinner alone, some one of the gentlemen proposed as a toast, the health of their wives, and, turning to Mr. Fraser, said,—"You, of course, will cordially join in drinking to this toast." "So I will, and so I ought," Mr. Fraser said, "for mine has been a better wife to me than any one of yours has been to you." "How so?" they all exclaimed. "She has sent me," was his reply, "seven times a-day to my knees in my closet, when I would not otherwise have gone, and this is more than any of you can say of yours." The company was silent.

MARTYRDOM IN GLASGOW.

About the year 1538, persecution raged in Scotland, and many faithful ones were consigned to the flames. So much was this the case, that emulation began to operate among those who sought to destroy the righteous. Cities vied with cities as to which was to have the most honour, as some thought, in burning heretics. Were Edinburgh and St. Andrews to have all the glory? the Archbishop of Glasgow seems to have inquired, and answering "No," to have sought victims to render his city illustrious. He found two — Jerome Russell, a cordelier friar, and Alexander Kennedy—who, it seems, though only 18 years of age had, by his poetical effusions, distinguished himself as a child of genius. They were brought to trial in Glasgow, before the bishop and his court, aided by some agents from Edinburgh, more skilful than themselves, perhaps, in ensnaring, or more insensible than they to pity. Kennedy (and his youth must be his excuse) was faint-hearted; he would, it is said, have recanted the opinions which he had avowed, but his death was determined on—and for him there was no place for repentance. When he found there was no escape, his vigour of mind returned—the Spirit of God again gave happiness, enabling him to exclaim: "O Eternal God, how wondrous is that love and mercy thou bearest to mankind, and unto me the most miserable above all others; for even now, when I would have denied thee and thy Son, thou hast pulled me from the very bottom of hell, and makest me to feel that heavenly comfort, which takes from me that ungodly fear wherewith before I was oppressed. Now, I defy death; do what you please; I praise God I am ready." Russell was superior to fear—he never quailed—but, in words which should have been powerful over the minds of his murderers, he said: "This is your hour and power of darkness; now sit ye as judges, and we stand wrongously accused, and more wrongously to be condemned; but the day shall come when our innocency shall appear, and that ye shall see your own blindness to your everlasting confusion. Go forward and fulfil the measure of your iniquity!"

When they were being led to the place of execution, Russell, moved by the fragile frame and former weakness of his fellow-sufferer, comforted him thus: "Brother, fear not; more potent is He that is in us, than he that is in the world; the pain that we shall suffer is short, and shall be light; but our joy and consolation shall never have an end; and therefore let us contend to enter in unto our Master and Saviour by the same strait-way which he has trod before us; death cannot destroy us, for it is already destroyed by Him for whose sake we suffer." The flames raged around them, but they fainted not. The voice of praise only burst from their lips. They died; but from their ashes arose others to avenge their wrongs and extend their doctrines.

A FILIAL PRAYER ANSWERED IN ABERDEEN.

The Rev. John Smith was the pastor of the Congregational Church, Blackhills, near Aberdeen. He was not only much given to prayer, but, like David of old, he earnestly looked up for an answer, so much so, indeed, that almost every providence was regarded by him as in some way or another an answer to prayer. The last time he visited his pious and respected father, he requested him, before parting, not to feel any pecuniary inconvenience without letting him know. His father promised to apply to him if he should at any time be in need of assistance. It was not long after this when the aged parent was seized with a complaint which terminated in his removal to that land where there is no sickness. While on the bed of affliction, he found it necessary to apply, through the medium of a friend, to his son for a little help. Mr. Smith, to his great grief, found himself destitute of money, and could not remit the smallest sum to his afflicted parent. This was no ordinary trial. He had, however, one resort under all his trials and under all his difficulties, namely, the throne of grace. The application from his aged parent reached him on a Saturday; he was engaged to preach in Aberdeen next day.

While on his way to town on the Lord's day morning, he prayed fervently that the Lord would enable him to fulfil his promise, and speedily relieve the wants of his kind father. He, however, saw no way in which he could expect to be able to send immediate relief. He arrived in town, and preached according to his appointments. In the evening, after closing the last service, as he was about to leave the chapel, a lady, whom he had never before spoken to, came up to him and said,—"Sir, you do not leave town to night?" Being answered that he was not intending to do so, "then," said she, "be kind enough to call on me to-morrow morning, as I wish particularly to see you before you leave town." He called accordingly, and, to his surprise, the lady presented him with a guinea, saying, you have but a limited income, and may be in need of this. With a heart overflowing with gratitude for this unexpected answer to prayer, he returned home, enclosed the gift in a letter, and sent it to his worthy father. His father received it, read the letter, blessed God that he had such a son, stretched himself in his bed, immediately breathed his last, and entered the joys of his Lord. These circumstances were communicated to Mr. Smith by return of post. It is well to mark the doings of the Lord.

THE DUKE OF ARGYLL AND MR. DARWIN.

THE DUKE OF ARGYLL, in a lecture he delivered under the auspices of the Glasgow Young Men's Institute, on "What is Science?" said that he never thought the theory of development due to Mr. Darwin in the least degree inconsistent with Divine purpose and design; but many scientific men in the world are more Darwinian than Darwin himself was:—"I have seen some letters published in scientific journals, from which it was quite obvious that the writers rejoiced in Darwin simply because they thought that Darwin had dispensed with God, and that he had discovered some process entirely independent of design, which eliminated altogether the idea of a personal Creator of the universe. Now it so happens that I have some means of knowing that this was not the attitude of Mr. Darwin's own mind. In the last year of his life Mr. Darwin did me the honour of calling upon me in my house in London, and I had a long and very interesting conversation with that distinguished observer of nature. Darwin was above all things an observer. He did not profess to be a theologian or a metaphysician; it was his work in the world to record facts, so far as he could see them, faithfully and honestly, and to connect them with theories and hypotheses, which were constructed, at all events, for a temporary convenience, as all hypotheses in science must be before being proved.

"But in the course of that conversation I said to Mr. Darwin, with reference to some of his own remarkable works on 'Fertilisation of Orchids,' and upon 'The Earthworms,' and various other observations he had made of the wonderful contrivances for certain purposes in nature—I said it was impossible to look at these without seeing that they were the effect and the expression of Mind. I shall never forget Mr. Darwin's answer. He looked at me very hard and said, 'Well, that often comes over me with overwhelming force; but at other times,' and he shook his head vaguely, adding, 'it seems to go away.' This is exactly the language which we have expressed in a remarkable passage in the book of Job, in which that truth is expressed which every Christian holds—that in nature we cannot see the Creator face to face, and that there are difficulties and veils between Him and the visible methods through which He works. *Behold, I go forward, but He is not there; backward, but I cannot perceive Him; on the left hand where He doth work, but I cannot behold Him; He hideth Himself on the right hand that I cannot see Him.*'"

22

ST. KENTIGERN AND KING MORKEN.

ST. KENTIGERN, otherwise called St. Mungo, was the local apostle of the kingdom of Strathclyde, and belonged to the latter part of the sixth century. He had a renowned controversy with King Morken, to whom he applied for what was necessary to support himself and the priestly followers that attended him. Morken replied in a manner that showed he had the power of sarcasm, whatever may be said for its seemliness. "Was it not," said the king, "a pet precept of the saint, 'Cast thy care upon the Lord, and He will care for thee?' Now," continued his majesty, "here am I who have no faith in such precepts, who do not seek the Kingdom of God and His righteousness; yet, for all that, are not riches and honours heaped upon me?" This was intended to prove that practice and the saint's doctrine were not in harmony, and that, consequently, the latter was not true. In vain the saint pleaded that it was part of the Divine policy and government to afflict good and holy people with the wants of the body, and to heap the world's wealth on the ungodly—it was to both a trial, giving an opportunity for acts of beneficence and self-sacrifice. The prince would by no means see the logic of this, and told St. Kentigern to have done with words and come to deeds. There were the royal granaries full of produce, and there were the Christian priests starving. There would be something to believe in if the God in whom they trusted would bodily transfer these good things into their hand and thereby supply their wants.

The saint, not being able to convince the heathen king, retired into his oratory and prayed. In the intensity of his sufferings he began to weep, and then, behold! as the tears filled and flowed from his eyes, so began the waters of the Clyde to swell into a mighty flood. The river overflowed the banks where the royal granaries were, and, carrying them down the stream, deposited the whole at the saint's very door, beside the Molindinar stream, which flows through Glasgow to join the Clyde. This, however, did not convince the king, who, on being visited by the saint, abused the man of God. For this act he was divinely visited with a heavy bodily affliction, which fell not only on the king, but also on his chief adviser, Cathen, who, though he worked in secret, was known by St. Kentigern to have taken a mischievous delight in prompting the unhappy king throughout the whole affair. In this way, says the legend, the Christian religion found its way to the heart of the people on the banks of the Clyde, and imparted to them a principle of life by which they have flourished ever since.

AN AWFUL PROVIDENCE AT KIRRIEMUIR.

Rev. Richard Penman was the pastor of one of the Independent churches of Aberdeen, and, before his settlement, was in the habit of going from place to place preaching the gospel. For a season, he remained in the town of Kirriemuir, and preached with great acceptance. During his stay there, a circumstance of a very awful and awakening nature took place. Mr. Penman was frequently in the habit of preaching in the fields to great numbers who were disposed to listen to the gospel. On one of these occasions, while Mr. Penman was preaching, a young man, about twenty years of age, was moving to and fro, and endeavouring in various ways to draw away the attention of the multitude from what was said. The preacher perceived and felt the disturbance, and found it necessary to speak to the young man regarding the sin and danger of such conduct. This, however, did not avail, and again it was found necessary to stop and address him in a still more pointed manner. Among other emphatic statements made to him, he was told that that opportunity might be the last he ever would enjoy of hearing of the only way of deliverance from sin and ruin. At length the services ended, or rather were brought somewhat abruptly to a close, when the people dispersed, and went to their respective homes. On the following morning, Monday, a messenger came somewhat hastily to the house where the preacher was lodged, and astounded him by the following affecting exclamation,—

"Oh, sir, the man whom you addressed last night was found dead upon his bed this morning!" This very awful dispensation of Providence produced an impression in the town of Kirriemuir, and in all the surrounding country, which for many years was not effaced.

PATRICK SIMSON AND KING JAMES.

THERE were brave men in the pulpits of Scotland three hundreds of years ago. Among these was the Rev. Patrick Simson, who, when uttering words for God, respected not the persons of men. He did not fail even to let the king know the mind of the Lord regarding his conduct, as the following incident will show. Upon Tuesday, the 8th of February, 1572, Edinburgh was thrown into a state of excitement and lamentation by the news that a cruel murder had been committed, on the preceding night, upon the Earl of Murray in his own place at Donnybristle, by the Earl of Huntly. He went out from King James VI. and set fire to Donnybristle House, so that the Earl of Murray was forced to come out to see it, and being discovered, he was killed, and, as history says, "cruellie demained"—beheaded—and the Sheriff of Moray was likewise killed. The king went forth to hunting that morning as if nothing had occurred, and, hunting about Inverleith and Wardie, he saw the fire, which had not died out, but was not moved at the sight.

Aware of being popularly suspected of having been privy to the horrid deed, he sent for four of five of the ministers, and desired that they would "cleare his part before the people." They said, if he were innocent, he should arrest Huntly, and try him for the deed. This, however, he would not do. A few days after the murder, Mr. Patrick Simson preached before James VI. at Stirling, and took for his text the words,—"The Lord said to Cain, where is Abel thy brother?" Gen. iv. 9. In the course of his sermon the minister said to the king,—"Sir, I assure you, in God's name, the Lord will ask you, 'Where is the Erle of Moray, thy brother?'"

This startled the king, and he replied, before all the congregation,—" Mr. Patrick, my chalmer door was never steiked upon you; ye might have told me anything ye thought in secret." He replied, "Sir, the scandal is public." After the service was over he was sent for, and went up to the Castle to meet His Majesty with the Bible under his "ockster," affirming that the "buik" would plead for him. The brave minister of Christ was privileged to preach before the same king six years after this, and he lost none of his influence, but gained it by being faithful even to those who were high in position, and to the one man in the realm who wore a crown and wielded a sceptre.

PROVOST DRUMMOND'S BENEVOLENCE.

UPWARDS of a hundred years ago Sir George Drummond was the Lord Provost of Edinburgh. He was chosen no less than six times to fill the civic chair, and was greatly esteemed and renowned for the benevolence of his disposition. One day as he was coming into the city by what was a suburb then, the West Port, he saw a funeral procession leaving the door of a humble dwelling and setting out for the churchyard. The only persons composing the funeral company were four poor-looking old men, seemingly common beggars, one at each end of a spoke, and none to relieve them; there was not a single attendant. The provost at once saw that it must be a beggar's funeral, and he therefore went forward to the old men, saying to them, "Since this poor creature now deceased has no friends to follow his remains to the grave, I will perform that melancholy office myself." He then took his place at the head of the coffin. They had not gone far till they met two gentlemen who were acquainted with the provost, and they asked him what he was doing there. He told them that he was going to the interment of a poor friendless mendicant, as he had none else to do it, so they turned and accompanied him. Others joined in the same manner, so that there was a respectable company at the grave. "Now," said the kind-hearted provost, "I will lay the old man's head in the grave," which he accordingly did, and afterwards saw the burial completed in a decent manner.

When the solemnity was accomplished, he asked if the deceased had left a wife or family, and learned that he had left a wife, an old woman, in a state of perfect destitution. "Well, then, gentlemen," said Provost Drummond, addressing those around him, "we meet in rather a singular manner, and we cannot part without doing something creditable for the benefit of the helpless widow; let us each give a trifle, and I will take it upon me to see it administered to the best advantage." All immediately contributed some money, which made up a respectable sum, and was afterwards given in a fitting way to the poor woman; the Provost also afterwards placed her in some way of doing, by which she was able to support herself without depending on public relief.

A SENSIBLE ADVICE TO A MINISTER.

INDEPENDENCY has never been either wealthy or strong in the rural parts of Scotland. On one occasion in a country place, the minister and deacons of an Independent Church were assembled at their monthly meeting in the house of one of the "brethren." After their consultation, the house-keeper's curiosity was somewhat awakened to know the "serious" that had to occupy their attention. It transpired that the funds were somewhat low, upon which Janet, with a smile, and a humorous twinkle in the eye, which tempered the force of the caustic remark, said—"Some of you seem to think ye've naething to dae but to sit on Sabbath mornin' glowerin' at the plate, as if ye were countin' the bawbees, and searching the pockets, and weighin' the hearts o' the folk as they gang in. Wae's me, I shouldna like to be you. My temper's gey short at the best, but it would gang clean aff a' thegither, like a knotless thread, if I had to sit and see every week what I've seen now and again. It gar'd me grue the last time I was gaun into the chapel to see our neibour in the next farm flinging in his big penny wi' as grand an air as if it had been, as it should hae been, a crown piece. Richt behin' him was widow Chalmers; and as we met at the door I could see her takin' her saxpence out from between her Bible and handkerchief and spearmint, an' slippin' it into the plate. She had wrocht hard for the saxpence, but she gied it as cheerfully as if she had been puttin' it into the hand o' the Lord, an' no into a pewter plate. I just thocht at the time that that saxpence was a pairt o' hersel', but my neibour penny was nae mair than a round bit o' common copper. The minister is to blame for no tellin' us from the pulpit mair than he does, what is the duty and privilege o' gi'en to the Lord. It's the Lord's treasury, an' no his." Turning round to her pastor, she said— "My man, ye're young yet, an' ye've muckle to learn, and though ye're my minister, let me say that ye shouldna be blate in declarin' the hale counsel o' God."

DR. ANDREW THOMSON PREACHING A SERMON WITHOUT UTTERING A WORD.

A MIDNIGHT revel, full of hollow vanity and dissipation, was going on one Saturday night in the city of Edinburgh. The people of the house in which the revel was being held, were a family of some note, which belonged to the St. George's Church congregation. Its minister, Dr. Andrew Thomson, had been out late that night to visit a sick member of his flock. On his return home, his eyes chanced to light on this house, whose windows were brilliant with the glare of festivity. The minister paused as he saw the shadows of the dancers on the window-blinds of the drawing-room; he could hear the sounds of music and the voices of the revelry. Taking his resolution, he stepped up to the doorway, and rang the bell. Without speaking a word to the servant who opened the door, he went upstairs, entered the room, and stood up in the midst of the dancers.

Had a spirit from the other world appeared, the party could not have been thrown into a state of greater embarrassment and confusion. The music ceased, the dancers stood still; a silence, as awful as death, followed; while the bold intruder surveyed the company with a stern glance. Not a word did he utter; not one tongue was moved to ask, "What doest thou?" As the penetrating glance of reproof fell in turn on each one of the confounded revellers, every countenance fell, and the bravest quailed. The piercing eye and solemn presence having accomplished the work of admonition, the minister retired amid the same unbroken silence. It was a bold stroke, but God blessed it, and it was the beginning of a work of the revival of genuine Christianity and reformation in many a family in the Scottish metropolis.

THE PIOUS HIGHLAND SOLDIER IN AMERICA;
Or, Drill and Review.

THERE are many ways of testing Christians, and some of these are not very accurate. The following incident brings out one which can never fail in the circumstances. It took place during the American Revolutionary War, when the strictest order required to be kept, and when care needed to be taken lest the enemy should get an advantage. One night near the British camp, not far from the river Hudson, a Highland soldier was caught creeping stealthily back to his quarters, out of the woods. He was taken before the commanding officer, and charged with holding communication with the enemy. The case of Major André was then very recent; and no Briton was disposed to be merciful toward a suspected friend of the Americans. The poor Highlander pleaded that he had only gone into the woods to pray by himself. That was his only defence.

The commanding officer was himself a Scotchman and a Presbyterian; but he felt no tenderness for the culprit. "Have you been in the habit, sir, of spending hours in private prayer?" he asked sternly. "Yes, sir." "Then down on your knees, and pray *now*," thundered the officer. "You never before had so much need of it." Expecting immediate death, the soldier knelt, and poured out his soul in a prayer that for aptness, and simple expressive eloquence, could have been inspired only by the piety of a Christian. "You may go," said the officer, when he had done. "I believe your story. If you had not been often at drill, you could'nt have got on so well at review." And the poor soldier saved his life by proving himself to have practised habitual communion with God.

JOHN MACK, SOLDIER AND MINISTER.

A REMARKABLE minister had at one time a church in Clipstone. His name was the Rev. John Mack, and he had been originally a weaver in Scotland, his native country. One day in Glasgow he met with a recruiting sergeant, who induced him to believe that if he joined the army he should have plenty of time to read, and thus led him to accept the fatal shilling. His enlistment caused intense grief to his God-fearing parents; but while on service, he became a decided Christian. His regiment happened to be stationed at Leicester; he took the liberty of calling upon Robert Hall. For a few moments the illustrious preacher looked at the soldier, but spoke not a word. Seeing Mr. Hall was smoking, Mack took out his pipe, lit it, and began to smoke too. When Mr. Hall did speak, he was all kindness. Having listened to his visitor's life-story, he pressed the soldier to dine with him, and to take his place the same evening in giving the address at prayer-meeting. The congregation, as well as their pastor, were amazingly interested. Mr. Hall, at the close of the service, introduced Mack to the leading members, and on the following Sunday requested him to occupy his pulpit.

The immediate consequence was, that the friends purchased Mack's discharge, though the Colonel, well aware of his value, threw every obstacle in the way. Mack entered the college at Bristol, and after a brief curriculum, was settled as the minister at the church at Clipstone. Sent by the missionary society as a deputation to Scotland, he sought out his only surviving parent at Glasgow.

The poor mother was living in a very humble abode, and failed to recognise her son, refusing to believe that this grave and fine-looking minister could possibly be her own child. But he remembered how once, when he was a boy, teasing his mother by eating up the potatoes as fast as she peeled them. She had given him a tap, and unintentionally wounded his wrist with the knife she was using. Whenever she afterwards saw the scar, she used to stroke his wrist, and in tender tones say to him: "Never mind, my bonnie bairn, your mother will ken ye by that when ye are a man." He turned back the sleeve of his coat, and looking earnestly in her face, and pointing to the mark, said: "Mither, mither! dinna ye ken *that?*" She looked at him for a moment, and exclaiming, "My bairn! my bairn!" rushed into his arms. Then together they lifted up their voices and wept. On the following Sunday he had to preach in the church in Glasgow, which his mother attended. She chose a seat where she could best see and hear her son. The beadle came to her and intimated that a more retired pew would be more suitable for her. "Dinna ye ken that I am the preacher's mither?" "Hoo was I to ken that? But if ye are the preacher's mither, the best seat in the kirk is nane too guid for ye."

So long as she lived, her son was able to add to her comforts, and to brighten her declining days. Mr. Trestrail declares that Mack was in humour and wit quite the match for Robert Hall, and he had also a marvellous power of pathos.

SIMPLE-MINDED ANSWERS.

THERE used to be in many parts of Scotland a class of persons who were looked upon with a kindly eye, and were objects of great interest to children. We refer to those who were called "naturals," half-witted, or daft. They were, when let alone, generally quiet and agreeable, but if aroused, they were sometimes violent. They frequently went to the church, and took an interest in what was said. Generally the minister of the parish paid them regard, and liked to keep their goodwill. Sometimes they gave utterance to sentiments and phrases which became common property. One of those wise fools, by his keen reply to a clergyman, gave rise to the proverb, "The mair fool are ye, as Jack Amos said to the minister." On a Sunday morning the minister, as he was on his way to the kirk, discovered daft Jack Amos whittling. "Jack," asked the clergyman, "can you repeat the fourth commandment? Which is the fourth commandment?" "I dare say, sir, it'll be the ane after the third," answered Jack, whittling on. "Can you repeat it?" "I'm no sure about it." The clergyman repeated it, but as Jack whittled on, he changed his tactics. "But, Jack, what is the reason you never come to church?" "Because you never preach on the text I want you to preach on." "What text would you have me preach on?" "On the nine-and-twenty knives that came back from Babylon." "I never heard of them before." "It is a sign you never read your Bible. Ha, ha, ha! sic fool, sic minister!" The clergyman gave up the daft Jack, and went away to search for his odd text. He found it in Ezra i. 9; and the story going abroad, gave rise to the proverb.

Another of these poor "naturals" was Jamie Fleeman, whose witty saws were long remembered in Aberdeen. While he was dying, one of the group about him said— "I wonder if he has any sense of another world?" "Oh no," answered someone; "he is a fool; what can he know of such things?" Jamie, overhearing the talk, opened his eyes, and looking the rude speaker full in the face, said—"I never heard that God seeks what he did not give; but I am a Christian, and dinna bury me like a beast." Then he died. On the small granite stone that marks his resting-place, his last prayer is chiselled— "Dinna bury me like a beast."

THE REV. DR. GUTHRIE AND THE IRISHMAN.

WHEN the Rev. Dr. Thomas Guthrie took up his abode in Edinburgh as a minister, he was determined to visit all the people in his parish, no matter whether they attended his church or not. This enabled him to understand the social condition of the city, and it frequently brought him into contact with rather strange characters. His courage, both moral and physical, was always equal to any emergency, and, by his wisdom, he made many enemies fast friends. While engaged in visiting the poor, he came one day to the door of an Irish Roman Catholic, who was determined that the Doctor should not enter his house. "You must not come in here," said he; "you are not called nor wanted." "My friend," said the Doctor, "I'm going round my parish to become acquainted with the people, and have called on you only as a parishioner." "It don't matter," said Paddy. "You shan't come in here;" and lifting the poker, he said, "If ye come in here, I'll knock ye down."

Most men would have retired or tried to reason, the Doctor did neither, but drawing himself up to his full height, and, looking the Irishman in the face, said— "Come, now, that's too bad. Would you strike a man unarmed? Hand me the tongs, and then we shall be on equal terms." The man looked at him in great amazement, and then said—"Och, sure, you're a quare man for a minister! Come inside." And feeling rather ashamed of his conduct, he laid down the poker. The Doctor entered, and talked in a way so entertaining and instructive, as to win the man. Pat, when the Doctor arose to go, shook his hand warmly, and said—"Be sure, sir, don't pass my door without giving me a call," which invitation Dr. Guthrie took advantage of to the good of both the man and his family."

THE REV. DR. BEGG AND THE RADICALS.

THE REV. DR. BEGG, parish minister of New Monkland, was a bold man, and would not say behind a man's back what he was not prepared to say to his face. At the time of what were called the Radicals, upwards of fifty years ago, he, although always an advocate for reasonable reform, yet, because some of them maintained theories of spoliation, to be promoted by force and civil war, and were supplying themselves with pikes and other instruments, denounced them from the pulpit, and declared that it was an attempt on the part of the "scum of the earth" to become rulers of the nation. It was alleged at that time that some of the leaders of the revolutionists in Airdrie were proposing to divide the different estates. Each was making his selection of considerable property in the neighbourhood. Some were for Airdrie House, others for Cavinhill, others for Rochsoles. One said,—"John, I think I would just be contented wi' your house and garden." *My* house!" exclaimed John, with the utmost astonishment and indignation, "Are you going to become a public robber?" This class became very violent, and threatened to shoot all who opposed them, and Dr. Begg among the rest. The worthy minister did not care for all their threatenings; at the same time, he sent his son James, then a child, covered with blankets, in a cart, with all the rest of the family, to the neighbouring manse of Slamannan, ten miles distant, and inland far from the scene of strife. But Dr. Begg himself would not move, lived in the manse, performed his duties, continued to denounce what he regarded as unsound views from his pulpit, and walked the streets of Airdrie as if nothing had happened. The agitation soon passed away, and the minister and his parishioners were on as good terms as ever. Honest words when judiciously spoken never produce lasting animosity.

THE REV. DR. MACDONALD AND THE PREACHING CURE.

THE REV. DR. JOHN MACDONALD, called most worthily "The Apostle of the North," itinerated a great deal, and preached the gospel wherever he went. He was greatly beloved and honoured by the common people, who heard him gladly, and to whom it was his delight to make known the gospel. He did so in season and out of season, and some times in peculiar circumstances. The following may be taken as an illustration of some of the incidents of his laborious life. During one of his many journeys, he caught a severe cold, and refusing to delay for rest and some necessary means of cure, he became at last seriously ill. The pores of his skin became so closed up, that the usual means of producing perspiration entirely failed, and to induce this was deemed essential to his recovery. His old friend, Hector Holm, heard of his illness, and went to see him. When Hector found out what was required for his cure, he went about among the houses round the manse, and asked the inmates to assemble to hear a lecture from the minister. The people immediately collected, and when the kitchen of the manse was full, Hector went to Dr. Macdonald's bed-room, and told the minister that the people were assembled, and were expecting a lecture.

Dr. Macdonald, who had known nothing of Hector's proceedings, said that he could not rise to speak to them. "But will it not be hard," replied Hector, "to send them away without a word?" "But how can I manage to speak to them in my present state?" Holm, seeing that the minister had begun to consider how his opportunity could be used, suggested that he should sit up in bed wrapped in blankets, while the people sat in the passage outside the bed-room, and that he should read and expound a passage of Scripture. To this Dr. Macdonald at once agreed, and so the people came, and the minister began to address them. Becoming interested in his subject, his usual fervour warmed him up, and before the lecture was concluded, he was wet with copious perspiration. He then lay down, slept quietly all night, and awoke quite well in the morning. Hector used to say that he was the best physician Dr. Macdonald ever had. "A dose of preaching was the only prescription he gave." This his patient had often found to be a delight to his heart, but on this occasion it was a cure to his body also.

ROBERT POLLOK'S FIRST PUBLIC SERMON.

ONE day when Robert Pollok, author of "The Course of Time," was taking a walk with Mr. David Marr, a fellow student, being in a curious thoughtful state of mind, and, talking a word now and again about preaching and making discourses for the pulpit, they agreed to give one another a text, and not leave the house again till each of them had written a sermon. Mr. Marr gave Pollok these words in 1 Kings xviii. 21,—"If the Lord be God, follow him: but if Baal, follow him." Pollok wrote a sermon from these words at two sittings, and never transcribed it. This was the sermon he preached on the 3rd of May, 1827, in Dr. John Brown's Church, Rose Street, Edinburgh. His fame, by the publication of his Poem, had attracted a large audience, and when he entered the pulpit, they looked at him with eagerness and deep interest. He was pale, thin, and study-worn, and, indeed, seemed something angelic in his look. After the introductory exercises, conducted by Dr. Brown, Pollok rose, engaged in a short prayer, read his text, and proceeded in the delivery of his discourse with a firm voice and a steady look, calm, and collected. The first head he delivered with ease and readiness; but immediately announcing the second head, he hesitated, paused momentarily, tried to go on, and stopped! For a moment he looked expressively to his brother, seated directly before him in the back seats, with a look never to be forgotten. He tried once more to go on, and again stopped. He then made a decided stand, in attitude of determined recollection, as if he had been thinking over the discourse entirely alone; and thus, after a short pause, during which he retained perfect self-possession, so that the audience never seemed to lose confidence in him, nor to be in the least distress, he recalled the sentence which had escaped him, and went on from that to the end, calmly and collectedly as before.

Considering all things, the weakness of the preacher in body, the first time of his preaching in public, the largeness and intelligence of his audience, and the excitement produced by the recent publication of his great poem, this was a remarkable instance of self-possession. This was the impression of many who were present, and the Rev. Dr. Belfrage, Slateford, on retiring from the church, said to his brother, "Was there ever such self-possession?" Thus began a ministry which ended on earth a few months after.

DUNCAN MATHIESON'S CONVERSION.

DUNCAN MATHIESON, Huntly, was a long time in great distress of mind when he was about twenty-two years of age. He left his native place and went to Edinburgh, thinking that there, by means of some eminent preachers, he might be spiritually delivered. At last, not finding rest, wearied and anxious, he left for home. Those who saw him at once discovered he was greatly changed. His fierce temper was checked. The lion had, to a certain extent, become a lamb. All the town heard of it, and pitied the poor lad who had, as they thought, gone mad. His state was sad, indeed, and yet he sighed for light and liberty. This came to him fully in the following way: "I was," he himself states, "standing on the 10th December, 1846, at the end of my father's house, and meditating on that precious word which has brought peace to countless weary ones; 'God so loved the world, that He gave His only begotten Son, that whosoever believeth in in Him should not perish, but have everlasting life' (John iii. 16). I saw that God loved me, for I was one of the world; I saw the proof of his love in the giving of his Son Jesus. I saw that 'whosoever' meant anybody and everybody, and therefore *me, even me*. I saw the result of believing—that I should not perish, but have everlasting life. I was enabled to take God at his word. I saw no one, but Jesus only, all in all in redemption. My burden fell from my back, and I was saved. Yes, saved!

"That hour angels rejoiced over one more sinner brought to the Saviour, and new songs rang through the courts of that city to which I had now got a title, and of which I had now become an heir. Bunyan describes his pilgrim as giving three leaps of joy as his burden rolled into the open sepulchre of Christ. I could not contain myself for joy; I sang the new song, 'Salvation through the Blood of the Lamb.' The very heavens appeared as if covered with glory. I felt the calm of a pardoned sinner; yet I had no thought about my safety. I saw only the person of Jesus. I wept for my sin that had nailed Him to the Cross, and they were tears of true repentance as a toll between me and the cross; now it came freely as the tear that faith wept. I felt I had passed from death unto life—that old things had passed away, and all things had become new."

A PRAYER WONDERFULLY ANSWERED.

HUGH MILLER gives an account of a wonderful answer to prayer in his "Memoirs of William Forsyth." He says, Saunders Macivor, the mate of the ship "Elizabeth," was a grave and somewhat hard-favoured man, powerful in bone and muscle, even after he had considerably turned his sixtieth year, and much respected for his inflexible integrity and depth of his religious feelings. Both the mate and his devout wife were especial favourites with Mr. Porteous of Kilmuir—a minister of the same class as the Pedens, Renwicks, and Cargils of a former age; and on one occasion when the sacrament was dispensed in Cromarty parish, and Saunders was absent on one of his continental voyages, Mrs. Macivor was an inmate of the manse. A tremendous storm burst out in the night-time, and the poor woman lay awake, listening in utter terror to the fearful roaring of the wind, as it howled in the chimneys, and shook the casements and doors.

At length, when she could lie still no longer, she arose, and crept along the passage to the door of the minister's chamber. "O, Mr. Porteous," she said, "Mr. Porteous, do ye no hear that? and poor Saunders on his way back frae Holland! O, rise, rise, and ask the strong help o' your Master!" The minister accordingly rose, and entered his closet. The "Elizabeth," at this critical moment, was driving onwards through spray and darkness, along the northern shores of the Moray Frith. The fearful skerries of Shandwick, where so many gallant vessels have perished, were close at hand; and the increasing roll of the sea showed the gradual shallowing of the water. Macivor and his old townsman, Robert Hossack, stood together at the binnacle. An immense wave came rolling behind, and they had but barely time to clutch to the nearest hold, when it broke over them half-mast high, sweeping spars, bulwarks, cordage, all before it in its course. It passed, but the vessel rose not. Her deck remained buried in a sheet of foam, and she seemed settling down by the head. There was a frightful pause. First, however, the bowsprit and the butts of the windlass began to emerge; next the forecastle. The vessel seemed as if shaking herself from the load; and then the whole deck appeared as she went tilting over the next wave. "There are still more mercies in store for us," said Macivor, addressing his companion; "she still floats." "O, Saunders, Saunders!" exclaimed Robert, "there was surely some God's soul at work for us, or she would never have *cowed* yon!"

THE REV. WILLIAM LINDSAY OF LETHAM, AND THE APPRENTICE;

Or, "After Many Days."

THE REV. WILLIAM LINDSAY, Independent minister, Letham, Forfarshire, was a useful servant of Christ in his day and generation, and had many encouraging proofs of the power of his ministry. One of these, of an interesting character, was made known to him in the summer of 1822. One Sabbath, at that period, a person presented himself to the minister of the quiet little village, as coming from Edinburgh. After public worship, they retired to the manse, when the following conversation took place: "Well, Mr. Lindsay," said the stranger, "this is a day I have long wished to see, and I have peculiar delight in worshipping with you to-day." Mr. Lindsay interposed, and said, "Why, sir, I do not well understand what you mean." The stranger replied by asking the minister if he remembered preaching in Townhead long ago. "Yes," said Mr. Lindsay, "and that is just fifteen years ago." "You are quite right, it is just about that time," said the stranger; "I was then an apprentice to a shoemaker who lived not far from Townhead. Feeling a desire to hear your sermon—not, indeed, from any superior motive, but from a strange feeling I had, I asked my master, the night before, whether he would permit me to go. He said if I would perform a piece of work which he instantly prescribed, he would allow me to go, but not otherwise.

"I considered the task equal to a prohibition, and I have no doubt it was so designed by my master. But anxiety to hear the sermon was the master feeling, and enabled me to overcome the difficulty. I arose early next morning, and toiled incessantly till I finished my task at the very hour your meeting was to take place. My work was inspected and approved of, and I was permitted to go to the sermon. You had commenced the service when I arrived, and when the prayer was conducted, I pushed forward to near the table at which you stood, and there listened to all that was said." Mr. Lindsay here interrupted the stranger by saying, " Oh, I remember quite well a shoemaker boy with his shirt-neck loose, his face as black as a sweep, furrowed with lines made by the running down of perspiration." "That boy," said he, " is the man that is now before you. You, sir, preached from the faithful saying (1 Tim. i. 15). It arrested my attention, and I have no doubt that I found the Saviour that night. I am now in Edinburgh, and in business, and it has given me no ordinary happiness to hear you preach once more, and grasp your hand." This unexpected testimony came like a Divine blessing on Mr. Lindsay's soul, who resolved to sow more liberally the seed of the kingdom beside all waters.

THOMAS LERMONT AND HIS PROPHECY.

THOMAS LERMONT, "The Rhymer," a name which Scotland formerly viewed with reverence almost equal to that which Orpheus obtained in Greece, was recognised in the combined character of prophet and poet. He lived during the 13th century, and during the year 1283, predicted the death of King Alexander III. On the night preceding the king's death, visiting the Castle of Dunbar, he was interrogated by the Earl of March in the jocular manner which he was wont to assume with this reputed prophet, if to-morrow should produce any remarkable event. The said Thomas Lermont, fetching a heavy sigh from the very bottom of his heart, is reported to have expressed himself to this effect. " Alas for to-morrow! a day of calamity and of misery! Before the twelfth hour, shall be heard a blast so vehement, that it shall exceed those of every former period; a blast which shall strike the nations with amazement, shall reduce those who hear it to a state of insensibility, shall humble what is proud, and what is fierce shall level to the ground!"

The solemnity of this denunciation made some impression on the Earl and his companions; but having next day continued on the watch till the ninth hour, without being able to remark any unusual appearance in the elements, they began to deride Thomas as a driveller, and afterwards hastened to enjoy their wonted repast. The Earl had scarcely placed himself at the table, and the hand of the dial pointed towards the hour of noon, when a messenger appeared before the gate, and with importunate strokes demanded instant admission. On entering the castle, and being questioned regarding the news, he exclaimed, "I do indeed bring news, but of a lamentable kind, to be deplored by the whole realm of Scotland! Alas! our renowned king has yesterday ended his life at Kinghorn." When the messenger paused, the Earl and his companions roused themselves as from a profound sleep; and beating their breasts in the agony of despair, acknowledged that the prediction of Thomas Lermont had been fatally verified. This is but one of many predictions uttered by this strange man, who is represented as having to a large degree the spirit of divination, a spirit said to be possessed by more than Lermont in that age.

SCOTCHMEN AN ARGUMENT FOR THE BIBLE.

There are such things as "living epistles," and these can be read and known of all men. When these confront an unbeliever, he is put to silence. This was the case in the experience of the celebrated Thomas Paine. One evening I found, said a correspondent to a New York paper, Paine haranguing a company of his disciples on the great mischief done to mankind by the introduction of the Bible and Christianity.

When he paused: "Mr. Paine," said I, "you have been in Scotland; you know there is not a more bigoted set in the world than they are in their attachment to the Bible; it is their school-book, and their churches are full of Bibles. When a young man leaves his father's house, his mother always, in packing his chest, puts a Bible on the top of his clothes." He said it was true. I continued, "You have been in Spain and Portugal, where they have no Bible, and there you can hire a man for a dollar to murder his neighbour, who never gave him any offence." He assented. "You have seen the manufacturing districts of England, where no one man in fifty can read (fifty years ago there was no Sunday Schools); and you have been in Ireland, where the majority never saw a Bible. Now," said I, "you know it is a historical fact, that in one county in England or Ireland there are more capital convictions in six months than there are in the whole population of Scotland in twelve. Besides, this day there is not one Scotsman in the alms-house, state prison, bridewell, nor penitentiary of New York. Now, then, if the Bible were as bad as you represent it, they who use it would be the worst members of society; but the contrary is the fact, for our prisons, alms-houses, penitentiaries, are filled with men and women whose ignorance or unbelief prevented them from reading the Bible." It was now near ten o'clock, p.m.; Mr. Paine answered not a word, but lifting a candle from the table, walked up stairs, leaving his friends and myself staring at one another. This argument of fact put to silence the gainsayer.

LORD HAILES AND AN INFIDEL.

Lord Hailes was a learned lawyer, an upright judge and accurate historian, and an able defender of divine truth. To a person of his Lordship's research and benevolence, there is always ready access, especially in such departments of literature as were known to be his favourite pursuits. The correspondence of John Pinkerton, published in 1830, brought to light an anecdote of Lord Hailes, which brings out in striking light some traits of his character. Pinkerton was a man of great talent, industry, and research, but his mind was unhinged as to religion, and there is no doubt of his infidelity. He wrote repeatedly to Lord Hailes on the subject of Scottish antiquities, and received prompt and polite answers. After he publicly avowed infidelity, this intercourse was checked by the learned judge.

On 29th December, 1785, Lord Hailes wrote Mr. Pinkerton,—"It surprised me not a little to see you, in your Essay, declare war against the Old Testament, but what you say will do little harm; for it is plain that you have not studied the subject sufficiently. What you say of the similarity of style throughout the Old Testament convinces me that you have never read *Lowth de Hebraica Poesi*, or his *Translation of Isaiah*. It is not incumbent on me to enter into a discussion of that subject, or of others of the like nature. But I would seriously recommend it to you to set down what you have said in the shape of queries, and then subjoin your answers; this will show you that you have been in too great a hurry. The queries to be thus: *Who* was Boyle? *Who* were the wisest Rabbis? *When* did they live? *How* should *their* authority be the best? This is for yourself, and not written with any view of obtaining an answer. I have only to beg, that in your publications, my name may not be mentioned as a correspondent of yours; at least, while you can perceive no difference between Jehovah and the demon of barbarous nations, or between the religion of the Jews and that of the Hottentots." This letter, though never designed to meet the public eye, conveys an idea of the firmness and purity of the character of the writer, and will gratify many who have received delight from the writings of this distinguished judge.

THE REV. JOHN MARTIN'S TRUST IN THE LORD.

The Rev. John Martin, near the beginning of this century, was well-known in and around the town of Forres. He was one of those who were commonly called "missioners," who established the Independent Churches in the north of Scotland. Like his Divine Master, he went about doing good to the bodies and souls of men, and met the calls of duty and benevolence, as they came, to the full extent of his power, and even sometimes beyond it. But the barrel of meal and the cruise of oil were never quite exhausted. One year, when the collectors of the Bible Society made their annual call for his subscription, his finances were very low. There were only ten shillings in the house, and no immediate prospect of more coming in. He gave it entire. One of the collectors said, "Really, Mr. Martin, this is too much for you." He replied, with a smile, "It is not too much for the Lord."

The first post brought him a letter enclosing a guinea from a friend, more than a hundred miles distant. Handing it over to Mrs. Martin, with a tear in his eye, he remarked, "Here, Eliza, there is the money again, after a short loan, with good interest." His habit of trusting the Lord is brought out in a conversation he had with a military gentleman, one of his stated hearers, who had long been in a weakly state, and whom Mr. Martin frequently visited in his affliction. This gentleman said to him on the occasion of one of his visits,—"Why, Mr. Martin, if I had the power over the pension list, I would actually have you put upon half-pay for your long and faithful services." The minister replied,—"Ah! my friend, your master may put you off in your old age with half-pay, but my master will not serve me so meanly. He will give me full pay all along. Through grace I expect a *full* reward." This humble servant of Christ lived as seeing the invisible, and trusted the Lord for all he required.

ROBERT ANNAN THE CHRISTIAN SWIMMER.

ROBERT ANNAN, Dundee, attained such ease and power in the water that he was named "The Water-dog," and this mastery he successfully turned to one of the noblest uses, that of saving life. In his latter days he was an earnest Christian worker, who delighted to rescue the perishing, both bodily and spiritually. In this good work he lost his life. On the morning of Wednesday, 31st July, 1867, he rose at four o'clock, and spent a long season in secret prayer. Some of the neighbours heard the sound of his wrestlings, and remarked to his wife that Robert had been "very busy with his God that morning." He returned to breakfast as usual, and after family worship spent half an hour in secret prayer. He then took a piece of chalk, and wrote upon the pavement "ETERNITY," and on the gate "DEATH," and went to his work at the docks. In two hours he met death, to him in Christ a vanquished foe, and entered eternity, to be for ever with the Lord. He was a powerful swimmer. "Swimming," he said, "was a gift bestowed on him by God, and he desired to use it for the glory of God." The first life he saved was that of his brother Ebenezer. When boys they were one day bathing; Ebenezer could not swim, and, going beyond his depth, began to sink. Robert, alarmed by his cry, swam to the spot, and dragged him to the shore. In the course of a few years, in the latter part of his life, he had saved at least six or seven lives. In one day he saved two. After having rescued the first of these he went home, and putting on a good suit of clothes, he said with a smile, "I should not like to jump in again and spoil my good clothes; and yet I don't think I could resist the temptation." On returning to the harbour he heard the cry raised that another boy was drowning, and instantly plunging in, good clothes and all, he plucked the youth from the jaws

of death. One boy whom he was saving he held up in
the water, and all the while spoke to him of Jesus, saying,
"Trust in Jesus, He will save you from eternal death."
When his wife expressed a fear that he would one day
lose his life in saving others, he replied, "Dear Jeanie,
could I look on a fellow-creature perishing, and not endeavour to save him?"

About twelve o'clock on the Wednesday referred to, a
boy, eleven years old, fell into the water, and Robert,
hearing the cry, plunged in to save him. Having
reached the spot where the boy was struggling for
life, he laid hold on him, and bidding him "hang on by
his neck," he made way for the shore. But the current
proved too strong for even the strong swimmer, and two
boats put off to his assistance. The child was saved, but
the man of God went down. He might have saved himself by letting the boy go. But he did not so. The
self-sacrificing and Christ-like man would save another
if he perished himself. Waving his hand, as if bidding
farewell—so says a spectator of the scene—and with a
smile on his face, he laid himself on his back and went
down. Down? No; not down, but up; for the man
himself, the nobler part, washed in the blood of Christ,
and clad in the beauty of holiness, went up to be forever
with his God.

THE REPENTANT PUBLICAN;

Or, no Terms with God.

THE REV. WILLIAM BURNS was preaching one evening,
in the open air, to a vast multitude. He had just
finished, when a man came timidly up to him and said,
"O, sir! will you come and see my dying wife?" Burns
consented, but the man immediately said, "Oh! I am
afraid when you know where she is you wont come."
"I will go wherever she is," he replied. The man then
tremblingly told him that he was the keeper of the
lowest public-house in one of the most wretched districts
of the town. "It does not matter," said the missionary,
"come away." As they went, the man, looking up in

the face of God's servant, said, earnestly, "O, sir! I am going to give it up at the term." Burns replied, "There are no terms with God." However much the poor trembling publican tried to get Burns to converse with him about the state of his soul and the way of salvation, he was unable to draw another word from him than these,—"There are no *terms* with God." The shop was at last reached. They passed through it in order to reach the chamber of death. After a little conversation with the dying woman, the servant of the Lord engaged in prayer, and while he was praying, the publican left the room, and soon a loud noise was heard, something like a rapid succession of determined knocks with a great hammer. Was this not a most unseemly noise to make on such a solemn occasion as this? Is the man mad? No. When Burns reached the street, he beheld the wreck of the publican's sign-board strewn in splinters upon the pavement. The business was given up for good and all. The man had in earnest turned his back on his low public-house, and returned to the Lord, who had mercy upon him, and unto our God, who abundantly pardoned all his sins. Nothing transpired in his after-life to discredit the reality of his conversion.

REV. THOMAS HOG'S MARVELLOUS RESTORATION TO HEALTH.

The Rev. Thomas Hog was minister of Kiltearn, Ross, and was a remarkable man. He had much of the prophetic spirit, and the interpositions of the providence of God on his behalf, were very remarkable. An instance of this kind, which is authenticated, occurred about the year 1676, when he was apprehended for attending private conventicles. When put to trial, he joyfully submitted to a prison, rather than bind himself from preaching, and was therefore sent to the Bass Rock. The air of the place, and the close confinement, however, soon affected his health, which brought him into peculiar and great danger. In this situation, a physician was called from Edinburgh, who gave it as his opinion that, unless he was liberated, there was no hope of his recovery, and advised him to supplicate the Council for liberation for a short space of time, that means might be used for the recovering of his health. Mr. Hog hesitated to address them, for reasons of his own. The doctor, however, of his own accord, and without owning Mr. Hog in it, drew up a petition for him to the Council, in the strongest terms he could devise; and the better to ensure a hearing, the clerk's dues were liberally paid.

The petition was read, and some of the lay lords interceded for Mr. Hog, and said, while he was at liberty, he lived more quietly, and traversed not the country so much as other Presbyterians did. Upon which, Archbishop Sharp, taking up the argument, said that the prisoner did, and was in a capacity to do, more hurt to their interests, sitting in his elbow chair, than twenty others could do by travelling from this land to the other; and if the justice of God was pursuing him, to take him off the stage, the clemency of the government should not interpose to hinder it; and therefore it was his opinion, that if there were any place in the prison worse than another, he should be put there. This motion having been seconded by another of the prelates and their supports, was accordingly put to the test, and it carried. The order was, therefore, issued,—"*The closest prison in the Bass for him,*" which was speedily put in execution. When the keeper intimated the order, Mr. Hog raised himself up, with some difficulty, in his bed, to read the sentence, "which," said he, "was as severe as if Satan himself had penned it." William Balloch, his servant, being with him when he was carried down to a low nasty dungeon in the Bass, fell a-weeping, and cried, "Now, master, your death is unavoidable." Upon this, the good man's eyes were directed to the Lord as his physician, and turning to his servant, with a countenance full of joy, he said, "Now that men have no mercy, the Lord will show himself merciful; from the moment of my entering this dungeon, I date my recovery." So it fell out, for the very next day he recovered, to admiration, and was in a short space as well as ever.

And yet, afterwards, when any would have been speaking of the archprelate Sharp in his hearing, he never showed any resentment, but sometimes would have said, somewhat merrily, "Commend him to me for a good physician!"

AN ARGYLESHIRE MINISTER'S DREAM.

In the parish of Glassery, Argyleshire, the Rev. Donald Campbell was minister shortly after the Reformation. The people were careless, ignorant, and utterly worldly. Though Mr. Campbell laboured hard, he did not see the fruit of his labour, although he earnestly desired to see the same. This weighed heavily on his mind. He wrote bitter things against himself, and began to question whether the Lord had sent him into the vineyard. It occurred to him that the Lord might have his secret ones, where the eye of man could discover none but the children of this world. While the mind of the faithful pastor was thus agonized, he one night dreamed, and a voice came unto him in his dream, saying, "Arise, if thou wouldst behold the death of a Christian." He awoke and listened, for his dream was so vivid, that he at first thought he must have been awake. He listened, but heard only the howling of the wintry wind, and the dashing of a mountain thunder shower. The war of elements without harmonised with the tumult in his own mind; and while meditating on his dream, and adoring God in the tempest, he again fell asleep. His dream returned, and a voice, articulate as from an angel's lips, rung in his ear, and repeated, "Arise, if thou wouldst behold the death of a Christian." He arose in haste, and went upon his way towards a ford upon the river which divided his parish. The river, subject to those sudden inundations which distinguish mountain streams, was just beginning to swell; but Donald Campbell, alive only to the object of his mission, heeded not the stream, nor felt the storm.

He passed over, and proceeded to a cottage at some distance towards the mountains. He entered, and found at the point of death an aged man, one of his parishioners,

whom he had noticed at church, but in whom he knew
nothing to mark him out from his neighbours. The
minister sat down upon the pallet of straw, and immediately recognised the language of Canaan from the
lips of a poor Highland disciple. To the refined ear, its
accent might sound uncouth, its idiom barbarous; but it
was the language of faith, confident, triumphant faith,
and, to the man of God, its sound was the sweetest he
ever heard, or hoped to hear, until the melody of the
full choir of paradise burst upon his enraptured sense.
His prayers were answered, his longing satisfied. Like
Elijah, he had fancied that the thousands around him
had bowed the knee to Baal, and that he only was left
of the servants of God. Jehovah did not descend to
inform him, "I have reserved unto myself seven thousand
in Israel, who have not bowed the knee to Baal, and
whose lips have not kissed him;" but a lowly disciple
reproved his unbelief, by showing that a child of God
may be found in the midst of Popery, like Obadiah of
old in the court of Ahab. Donald Campbell spent the
night with this heir of heaven, thus lowly lodged in a
cottage of clay; and when the spirit winged its flight to
take possession of the inheritance prepared from before
the laying the foundations of the world, he assisted the
widow in paying the last honours to a body lifeless now,
but destined one day to shine with all the lustre of an
angel! He could sympathise with her the better, for he
also had cause for grief. For years he had longed for a
companion, and he found him but the moment before he
was snatched from his arms. Still he learned two important lessons from the events of the night. There
may be fruit of a minister's labours where he is not
privileged to see it, and the proper and unfailing companionship of a Christian is that of his risen Lord, the
"Friend that sticketh closer than a brother."

SEEING AND BELIEVING.

Mr. Donald Brotchie, Chaplain to Seamen, Greenock,
says that one day he was visiting among the ships, con

versing with some of the seamen, and pressing upon them the necessity of personal religion. The men were smoking their pipes, just after dinner, when the mate of a vessel—a smart, cheerful looking person—came forward, and among other things, said—" How is it that you are always talking to seamen about the Lord Jesus?" "Just because I cannot speak to them of a better friend." "You tell them to believe in Him. Did you ever see Him?" "No, I never have." "And how in the world can you tell men to trust in, and expect salvation through, one you never saw?" "O, perfectly well." "I can't see any sense in that," he said. "Well, now, young man," said 'I "you will soon be going to sea with this vessel, and you may, before you clear the coast, encounter a gale of east wind, find yourself on a lee shore, with your ship strained, and your sails riven. In such a condition, the weather looking worse, and night coming on, you will naturally think of some place of refuge. And if, on consulting your chart, you find there is such a place within your reach, you will make up your mind, put up your helm, and, when your ship falls off, square away your yards, and make for the refuge. When you come to the place marked in your chart with an anchor, you will clew up your sails, bring your ship's head to the wind, and when she loses headway, you will sing out to the man on the prow, with the stopper in his hand, 'Let go the anchor!' Suppose the man were to cry back to you, 'No, sir, I don't see the ground,' would you not at once conclude that either the man was deranged, or was so green a hand that he ought never to have been on board a ship?" "Just so." "Well, tell me on what principle you trust your ship and your life to ground you never have seen and never can see?" "O," said he, "we go by our chart." "Just so, all right; and," holding up my Bible, I said, "we go by our chart, and it is an infallible one, but yours is not. It tells us of the only sure ground—the atoning work of Christ. He, having died for our offences, and risen again for our justification, is now at the Father's right hand, making intercession for us. Our faith, like your anchor, which penetrates the veil of water, and

takes hold of the unseen ground beneath, penetrates the
veil between us and the eternal world, and takes hold of
our once crucified, but now unseen Lord and Redeemer,
and so rides out the storm of life in peace and safety."

A SWEARER REPROVED IN HUNTLY.

Using oaths in ordinary conversation is common in many
parts of the north of Scotland. Those who use them
are sometimes unconscious of the sin they are committing, and the pain they cause to others. And, frequently, they have been cured of the bad custom in a
peculiar manner. The following instance is one out of
many. The present Duke of Gordon's grandfather was
one night at the town of Huntly, on a journey southward. While he enjoyed himself with his friends in a
room fronting the street, a company of a marching
regiment was drawn up under the windows to answer
to the muster roll, and to have their clothes examined
by their officer. The gentleman, who had probably been
raised from the ranks, more for his courage than his
breeding, had a strong inclination to find fault; and
whenever anything displeased him, imprecated damnation upon himself and the men.

The Duke, who had an utter abhorrence to common
swearing, was uneasy, and expressed his warm wishes
that the review might quickly be over. "If your Grace,"
said one of his retinue, "will excuse my farther attendance upon this journey, I will clear the coast of this
man of words without noise or bloodshed." "'Tis a
bargain," said his Grace. On this the gentleman stepped
down into the street, took his station behind the officer,
pulled off his hat, and as the first swore, the other, with
the grave solemnity of a parish clerk, pronounced aloud,
"Amen!" The officer, turning hastily about, asked the
gentleman what he meant? "I am joining with you in
prayer," said he. "I thank you, sir," said the officer,
"but I have no farther need of a clerk upon this occasion.
Soldiers! to the right about—March." The Duke and
his company who witnessed this droll scene from the

windows, were much diverted; and Mr. Innes (for that was the gentleman's name) had leave to return to his own house next morning.

A SECOND JENNY GEDDES AND THE CHARTIST.

DURING the agitation which took place before the great Disruption of 1843, strange incidents took place, which sometimes served to show how readily the thoughts of the people went back to the old Covenanting times. In January, 1840, a Non-Intrusion meeting was held in Dumfries, at which the Rev. Drs. Elder, Begg, and Guthrie, spoke in the midst of much interruption raised by a body of Chartists. At the close of their addresses, one of the leading Chartists of the town rose to reply to what had been advanced. He did so in a very offensive way, his speech bordering on profanity. Dr. Guthrie understood the situation at once, and whispered to Dr. Elder,—"We are in a scrape with this fellow, and must watch our opportunity to get out of it." After the man had gone on for a few minutes, he came out with strong expressions in reference to the Scriptures, and made allusions of an objectionable character. Dr. Guthrie, starting from his seat, and raising himself to his full height, lifted his long arm above his head, and exclaimed, in a voice of thunder, "Shocking! shocking! I call on all Christian men and women to leave this meeting," and, as he strode out of the church, he was followed by the chairman and the greater part of the audience. The Chartists then attempted to put their leader in the chair, but at that point there rose from a seat close to the pulpit, a woman belonging to the humbler ranks of life— Mrs. Ewart, the wife of a working mason—"a second edition" of Jenny Geddes, not flourishing her stool, but collaring the proposed chairman, calling out, in no gentle terms, "Come doon, come doon;" and, suiting the action to the word, she summarily effected her purpose. She was a powerful and vigorous matron, and how completely public opinion was in her favour, was seen from the applause with which she was greeted on the spot—the allusions made to Jenny Geddes, and from a testimonial afterwards presented "in approbation of her spirited and praiseworthy act." Such incidents serve to show how readily in the minds of the Scottish people the events of the present link themselves on to the memories of the past.

JOHN KNOX'S VOCATION.

THE castle of St. Andrews being held by the Reformers after Archbishop Beaton's death, Knox, for safety, repaired thither with his pupils from Langniddrie and Ormiston, and taught in a chapel, the ruins of which, is still called Knox's kirk. The stated preacher at the castle was one John Rough, who was a few years younger than Knox. This man, feeling himself overwhelmed by the responsibility which the leadership of the Protestant cause had upon him, urged Knox to share his work; but Knox declining at first, he preached a sermon on the right of a congregation to elect a minister, and the responsibility by one, if he refused the call; and, addressing Knox, said—"Brother, you shall not be offended, although I speak unto you that which I have in charge, even from all those who are here present, which is this: In the name of God, and of His Son, Jesus Christ, and in the name of all that presently call you by my mouth, I charge you that you refuse not the holy vocation; but, as you tender the glory of God, the increase of Christ's kingdom, the edification of your brethren, and the comfort of me, whom you understand well enough to be oppressed by the multitude of labours, that you take the public office and charge of preaching, even as you look to avoid God's heavy displeasure, and desire that He shall multiply His graces unto you." Then, addressing the congregation (one of whom was Sir David Lindsay, of the Mount), said—"Was not this your charge unto me? and do ye not approve this vocation?" They all answered, "It was, and we approve it." At these words, Knox suddenly burst into tears, and left the assembly. It is recorded that "his countenance and behaviour from that day till the day that he was compelled to present himself in the public place of preaching, did sufficiently declare the grief and trouble of his heart, for no man saw any sign of mirth from him ; neither had he pleasure to accompany any men for many days together." In this way the divine call came to the great Scotch Reformer, and the voice of God in that call he obeyed, with what results his noble life showed.

KNOX CLOSING HIS LIFE.

AFTER a life full of conflict and trial, John Knox lay down to die, in the year 1572. He was visited by many persons of distinction, and by the ministers, elders, and deacons of the Church. He delivered a message to each class, and, in some instances, he became prophetic. To the preachers he said,—"There is one thing that grieveth me exceedingly; you have sometimes seen the courage of the Laird of Grange in the cause of God, and now that unhappy man is casting himself away; I pray you go to him from me, and tell him, that unless he forsake that wicked course he is in, the rock wherein he confideth shall not defend him, nor the carnal wisdom of that young man, whom he counteth half a god (which was young Leshington), shall yield him help; but he shall be shamefully led out of that nest (meaning Edinburgh Castle), and his carcase hung before the sun ; for his soul is dear to me, and, if it were possible, I would fain have him saved." The Laird, though spoken to by the preachers, did not change his course, and, in a year after, the Castle was taken, and he was hanged before the sun.

The night before Knox's death, he slept some hours with great disquietude, whereupon, when he awaked, those about him asked how he did, and what it was made him moan so heavily ? To whom he answered,— "In my lifetime I have been assaulted with temptations from Satan, and he hath often cast my sins in my teeth, to drive me to despair; yet God gave me strength to overcome all his temptations : but now the subtle serpent takes another course, and seeks to persuade me that my labours in the ministry, and the fidelity that I have shewed in the service have merited heaven; but, blessed be God, it brought to my mind these Scriptures, 'What hast thou that thou hast not received?' and, 'Not I, but the grace of God in me,' with which he is gone away ashamed, and shall no more return. And now I am sure that my battle is at an end, and that without pain of body, or trouble of spirit, I shall change this mortal and miserable life for that happy and immortal life which shall never have an end." After which, one who had prayed by his bed asked him if he had heard the prayer. "Yes," said he, "and would to God that all present had heard it with such an ear and heart as I have done;" adding, "Lord Jesus, receive my spirit." With which words, without any motion of hands or feet, as one falling asleep, rather than dying, he ended his life. Men of all ranks were present at his burial. The Earl of Moray said, when the coffin was placed in the grave,— "There lies the body of one who, in his lifetime, never feared the face of man!"

"OUR BAIRN THAT'S DEEIN'."

THE gift of praying is not an uncommon one in Scotland, but that does not always mean the possessor of said gift could vary his words and phrases to suit the circumstances in which he may be placed. Too often it meant that a set of words were almost always employed, no matter what were the wants to be presented to the ear of the Heavenly Father. The late Dr. James Hamilton had a capital illustration of how general prayers and "oblique sermons" fail to satisfy the soul in the emergencies of life. A Scotchman, who had but one prayer, was asked by his wife to pray by the bedside of their dying child. The good man struck out on the old track, and soon came to the usual petition for the Jews. As he went on with the time-honoured quotation, "Lord, turn again the captivity of Zion," his wife broke in, saying: "Eh! man, ye're aye drawn out for the Jews; but it's *our bairn* that's deein'!" Then clasping her hands, she cried, "Lord, help us, or give us back our darling, if it be thy holy will; and if he is to be taken, oh, take him to thyself." That woman knew how to pray, which was more than her husband did. And in her prayer she honestly poured out her heart's needs before God.

An "oblique sermon" is not a prayer. An audible meditation or a doctrinal dissertation is not a prayer. Telling the Lord a hundred things He knows better than we do is not prayer. If persons who lead in prayer had as vivid a conception of what they want, and as earnest a desire to get it, as this poor woman, would there be as many complaints about long prayers as we hear?

DR. WILLIAM RITCHIE AND HIS VIOLIN.

THE REV. DR. WILLIAM RITCHIE, of St. Andrew's Church, Glasgow, was exceedingly fond of music, and had taught his church to admire both vocal and instrumental music combined. They determined, if possible, to secure an organ to assist in aiding the praise in public worship, but were not allowed to do so by the Presbytery, which were of the "opinion that the use of organs in the public worship of God, is contrary to the law of the land and constitution of our Established Church." This did not, however, prevent Dr. Ritchie cultivating his favourite art. He loved the violin especially, and had both a big and a small one, which he frequently used. Though popular with his own congregation, who were devoted to him, and admired his ministrations, he was not so well liked by his brethren, who thought he acted an unministerial part by playing on the violin. In the year 1807, he was waited upon by a deputation of ministers, to advise him to give up his performance on these instruments on a Saturday night, that he might be the better prepared in spirit for the sacred duties of the Sabbath day. When they arrived, Dr. Ritchie asked them to come in, and he would let them hear one of his favourite tunes, and then they could judge for themselves whether such music was calculated to produce evil or good results. They consented to remain, and he begged them not to interrupt him in the performance till he was done, which would be, at most, in a few minutes. Taking the largest instrument into his hands, he played with care and feeling his own most favourite tune, the "Old Hundred." The effect was marked. One of the chief divines was entranced, and could not refrain from saying, "Oh, 'tis a heavenly sound! please let us hear it again." Some of the others were also enraptured. Dr. Ritchie, marking the favourable impression made, played several sacred pieces to the admiration of the deputation, some of whom declared themselves converts to the beneficial effect upon the mind of sweet sounds.

TRUE TO CONSCIENCE.

AFTER the Disruption of 1843, there were many cases among the humble in life, where conscience and God were obeyed rather than man, though obedience to the "still small voice" entailed sacrifice. Among these, two instances may be given. At Latheron, where the majority of the people had gone out with the Free Church party, the leading heritor, a gentleman of high rank, resolved to make one more effort before yielding. His farm-grieve, who was also manager of his extensive estates, had been with him for a great many years, probably not less than twenty, and on his services he placed the highest possible value; and he having adhered to the Free Church, it might perhaps be supposed that his example had influenced the other servants and tenants also, so it was resolved to select him for the first assault. One day, therefore, his master called him, and having stated how much annoyed he was, that he and all the other servants and tenants had left the good old kirk, how long they had been together, and how well pleased and satisfied he always had been with him, he added, "I fear this foolish breach will be the means of separating us, unless you come back to the kirk, for it will never do for me and you to be at different kirks; so think of it, and come with me, and we will continue good friends, as we have always been." The poor grieve was, of course, taken by surprise; but, being a man of good sense and resolution, as well as firmness, he at length said that he was sorry that his honour—for he was an honourable—had thought of interfering in a matter of this kind; that they certainly had been long together; that he felt he had endeavoured to serve him faithfully to the best of his ability, and was willing to do so still; but that if this was to depend on his joining the Establishment in its now altered state, he was quite ready, rather than do so, to leave his honour's service at the first term. This decided and suitable reply settled the whole matter, and saved the other servants from being interfered with; for the grieve's services were too valuable to be dispensed with, and he was never again questioned on the subject.

Another gentleman, who held an extensive sheep-farm in one of the parishes of Sutherland, was very desirous that all in his employment should adhere to the Establishment. One day, in the summer of 1843, when his shepherds had occasion to meet at sheep-washing or sheep-shearing, he rode up to the place accompanied by his son, and, addressing "the manager," said that he had brought a paper for them all to sign. He was going to a distant part of his farm, and would call for it on his return, when he expected to find that all had signed it. The paper contained the following declaration—"We, the undersigned, adhere to the Established Church of Scotland." When this gentleman and his son had left, the manager (an excellent and very intelligent man) addressed the shepherds—"Well, men, I know what I'll do; but don't let me influence you. What do you say? Will you sign?" An emphatic and unanimous "No!" was the reply. "Well, but," continued the manager, "don't you think that it would be more respectful to sign *something*, rather than to return the paper blank?" and turning the other side of the paper, he wrote—"We, the undersigned, adhere to the Free Church of Scotland." This he himself signed first, and then all the shepherds adhibited their names. When the gentleman and his son rode back, he asked the manager—"Well, is that paper signed by you all?" "Yes, sir," replied the manager, "we have all signed it, but *on the other side.*" The gentleman turned the paper round, examined it silently, pocketed it, and rode off without uttering a word. He never afterwards gave the slightest annoyance to any of his shepherds because of their adherence to the Free Church.

BENEVOLENCE STIMULATED IN GLASGOW.

ON one particular occasion, Mr. Robert Carrick, banker, Glasgow, was waited upon by a deputation of two or three respectable citizens for his subscription to the Royal Infirmary, then in its infancy. They expected that he, being one of the wealthy men of the city at the time, and knowing the urgent circumstances of the case, would head the list of subscribers with a handsome donation. To their mortification and surprise, he would put his name down for only two guineas. When they respectfully besought him to give something more, he waxed wroth, and was for drawing back his miserable pittance; but recollecting himself for a moment, he stated that he really could not *afford* to give them any more; and he literally bowed them out of his miserly room, encased as it was, with millions of money, in the shape of bills and other documents. Their next call was on old Mr. John M'Ilquham, who was then a manufacturer, doing a good business. When the deputation, who had just left the banker, approached the merchant, he put on his spectacles, and glanced at the list of subscribers. He mused and commented on the trifling subscription of Mr. Carrick. "Bless me," he said, "has he only given you *twa guineas* for such a benevolent purpose?" "Not more," they replied, "and when pressed for more, he said he could not afford to give any more." "What is that you say?" asked Mr. M'Ilquham. They repeated the answer, which apparently roused his ire and astonishment.

He rose from his seat with animation, and called to his cash-keeper and confidant, "Jamie, bring me the Ship Bank book and a cheque, and the ink-bottle and a pen." With these materials before him, he filled up a cheque on the bank for £10,000. "Now, Jamie," said he, "run down as fast as you can to the bank, and take care and be sure and bring that money to me, and the gentleman of the deputation, here, will just kindly wait till you return." Of course they agreed to do so, not knowing at that moment anything about the impending circumstance. The cheque was presented at the bank table, and Mr. Carrick stared as he looked over it again and again. "Go back," he said, "young man, to Mr. M'Ilquham, with my compliments, and tell him he has committed some mistake." "What!" exclaimed the indignant manufacturer, when that message was communicated to him, " will Banker Carrick not give me my own money? I've greatly more than this in his hands, so go back instantly, and tell him from me there is no mistake on my part." On this fresh, but imperative message, Mr. Carrick got uneasy in his chair and alarmed. There had been an understanding between him and his excellent customer that when an unusual large supply of money was wanted, previous notice should be given. To see how matters stood, the banker felt it necessary to repair to the warehouse of Mr. M'Ilquham. As he entered, he said, "What's wrong wi' ye the day?" "Wrong with me! nothing in the least degree," was the reply; "wrong wi' me, praise be blest! but I am dumfoundered, and suspect that there's surely something very far wrong with yourself and the bank, for my friends—these douce decent gentlemen, sitting *ben* yonder—have assured me, that in your own premises, and out of your own mouth, you declared you could not afford to give them scrimp twa guineas for this praiseworthy purpose; and if that be the case, I think it high time that I should remove some of my deposits out of your hands."

This led to a most agreeable result. The banker took the pen in hand, and scribbled down his name to the subscription paper for fifty guineas, and Mr. M'Ilquham, on seeing this, cancelled his cheque for the ten thousand pounds, and the gentlemen of the deputation went away amazed, and perfectly delighted with this reception.

DR. ERSKINE MODERATING A CALL.

Among the venerable, estimable, and most efficient characters of a former age, the name of the Rev. Dr. John Erskine will always be conspicuous. An anecdote is told of him which brings out more than one of his characteristics.

The parish of Ratho, within the bounds of the Presbytery of Edinburgh, had become vacant, and a presentation had been issued by the noble Earl, in whom the patronage was vested, in favour of an individual who was obnoxious to the people, or, at least, who had not their consent to his becoming their pastor and spiritual instructor. In default of this, Dr. Erskine strongly opposed his induction in the Church courts. His opposition was, however, fruitless; the necessary forms were ordered to be gone through, and the admission to take place. And with a refinement of cruelty not unknown in those days, Dr. Erskine was appointed to preside at the moderation of the call. This he did in obedience to his ecclesiastical superiors. With his staff in his hand, he walked from Edinburgh to Ratho, a distance of eight miles, on the morning of the appointed day. Not being well acquainted with the place or the road, and immersed in deep thought, he went a considerable way beyond the church, and stopped only when he thought that he had made a mistake, and had gone farther than was necessary. Meeting a man coming towards him, and dressed, apparently, in his Sunday suit, he conjectured that he might be going to the church, and inquired the road thither. The man told the doctor that he had travelled a good bit too far, but that he would conduct him to the church, as he was going there himself.

In the door of the porch, and at the entrance to the churchyard, stood the patron peer and some others, who, observing Dr. Erskine to be fatigued, invited him to take some refreshment before entering upon the duties of the day. This offer he gently declined, and passed directly into the church, and to the pulpit. He went through the services with dignity and calmness, and fulfilled his mission. On returning from the church he was again accosted by the patron, who entreated him to rest a while and accept some refreshment. His calm, yet firm and solemn answer, was to the effect,—"I feel obliged by your politeness, my Lord, but 'If thou wilt give me half thine house, I will not go in with thee, neither will I eat bread nor drink water in this place: for so was it charged me by the word of the Lord.'" (1 Kings xiii. 8, 9.) And the good Doctor walked his way back to Edinburgh without a rest or even a halt. He did his duty severely, without doubt, but fully as unto the Lord.

THE GOSPELS OF ST. MARGARET.

St. Margaret, Queen of Scotland, lived in the first half of the thirteenth century, and was a remarkably pious Queen. Her care for the honour of the realm and the discipline of the Church was great, and her deeds of benevolence were many. Her biographer, Turgot, Bishop of St. Andrews, narrates one incident of her life which may go to prove, he says, what the holiness of her life was. She had a book of the Gospels beautifully adorned with gold and precious stones, and ornamented with the figures of the four Evangelists, painted and gilt. All the capital letters throughout the volume were radiant with gold. She had always felt a peculiar attachment for this book, more so than for any of the others which she usually read. It happened that as the person who carried it was once crossing a ford, he let the book, which had been carelessly folded in a wrapper, fall into the middle of the stream. Unconscious of what had occurred, the man quietly continued his journey; but when he wished to produce the book, suddenly it dawned upon him that he had lost it.

Long was it sought, but nowhere could it be found. At last it was discovered lying open at the bottom of the river. Its leaves had been kept in constant motion by the action of the water, and the little coverings of silk which protected the letters of gold from becoming injured by contact with the leaves, were swept away by the force of the current. Who could have imagined that the book was worth anything after such an accident as this? Who could have believed that so much as a single letter would have been visible? Yet, of a truth, it was taken up from the middle of the stream so perfect, so uninjured, so free from damage, that it looked as if it had not been touched by the water. The whiteness of the leaves, and the form of the letters throughout the volume continued exactly as they had been before it had fallen into the stream, except that on the margin of the leaves, towards the edge, the least possible mark of water might be detected. The book was conveyed to the Queen, and the miracle was reported to her at the same time, and she, having thanked Christ, valued it much more highly than she had done before. "Whatever others may think, I," adds Bishop Turgot, "believe that this wonder was worked by our Lord out of His love for this venerable Queen."

PEDEN'S PREVAILING PRAYER.

ALEXANDER PEDEN, the prophet, was powerful in prayer, and in all the extremities of his eventful life, he had recourse to the throne of grace. Many a time was he in danger, but he escaped, and often, like his Master, he passed through the midst of his enemies, and went his way. At one time, Peden and some others of the "hill men" were hotly pursued for a considerable way both by horse and foot soldiers. They took to the hills, which had so often proved to them a refuge. When weary, and all but worn out, they at last succeeded in getting some little height between them and their persecutors. When Peden saw they were so far safe, he stood still, and said,—"Let us pray here, for if the Lord hear not our prayer and save us, we are all dead men." This is what all the company felt. He then prayed, saying,— "O Lord, this is the hour and the power of thine enemies; they may not be idle. But hast thou no other work for them than to send them after us? Send them after them to whom thou wilt gie strength to flee, for our strength is gane. Twine them about the hill, O Lord, and cast the lap of thy cloak over puir auld Saunders, and thir puir things, and save us this ane time, and we will keep it in remembrance, and tell to the commendation of thy guidness, thy pity and compassion, that thou didst for us at sic a time." And in this he was heard, for a cloud of mist immediately intervened between them and their persecutors; and, in the meantime, orders came to go in quest of James Renwick, and a great company with him, and Peden and those who were with him escaped.

AN OLD TAR SWEEPING OUT DARKNESS.

CAPTAIN BROTCHIE, the devoted friend of seamen, found an old sailor one day leaning by the door of the Sailors' Reading Room, Greenock, whom he knew to be anxious about spiritual things. He was still in bondage, and afraid of the future. The Captain inquired kindly into the state of his mind. Robert had made many spasmodic efforts to soften his heart and make it better, but all to no purpose. In answer to inquiries, he said his heart was as hard as ever, and he feared it would never be better. He was invited into the Reading Room. As soon as they entered, Captain Brotchie locked the door, and began to close the shutters. Wondering at these movements, the sailor began to inquire what this all meant. It was answered "Be not alarmed, you are about to be taught a very important lesson." After a large brush used for sweeping the place had been put into his hand, the last shutter was closed. "Now, Robert," said the Captain, "put out the darkness." "I cannot," he replied. "Oh, take the brush, man," said the Captain, "and drive right and left, and see whether you cannot drive it out of the place." "Oh, no, that won't put out the darkness," he answered. He was then asked, "Well, can it not be put out?" "Oh yes," he replied, "but not that way." "And is it not strange," the Captain remarked, "that a simple act accomplishes what a thousand men could not by any amount of physical force! If I simply take my little finger and pull back the shutter, I will let in the light, and the darkness will be gone." "It is quite true," said Robert. "Come then, friend," urged the Captain, "let in the light! Let in the truth as it is in Jesus! Let in that glorious light about the love of God: God so loved you, that He gave His only-begotten Son to die that you might live. Jesus died for you, and put away your sin by the sacrifice of himself; let that truth into your soul. Now that Jesus has suffered in your room and stead, your sin is taken away, and the mercy of God is as free to you as the water you drink or the air you breathe. Let these truths into your soul as I have let the light into this room by putting back the shutter."

By this time the tears were coursing down the cheeks of the old tar in amazement and gratitude. He exclaimed, "I never saw the way to peace in that light before." The poor man was bathed in tears, and felt he was free from the load of condemnation. Before they separated the Captain said he had another lesson to teach Robert. "You often," he said, "went to meetings among the anxious, and sang, and prayed, and shouted; was much excited, and had happy feelings; but these were like the morning cloud and early dew, which soon pass away, and that because you knew not the truth. Now, observe, this room is full of light at present. We have enough to serve for a whole month, have we not? I may put on the shutters, may I not?" "Oh no," said the happy man, "if you put to the shutters, we shall be in darkness." "Why?" asked Captain Brotchie, "what has my putting to the shutter to do with putting out the light?" "I do not know," answered the sailor, "but so it is, that if you put to the shutter the light is kept out." "Is it not this, Robert," said the Captain, "that you cannot get the rays of the sun separate from the sun itself? If you want to retain the light, you must keep up the connection between you and the orb of day. So be careful to walk in the light. In a few verses, the

Saviour says seven or eight times, 'Abide in me.' Run the race that is set before you, looking to Jesus as your everlasting Saviour, and Prince of Peace." Robert went home in gladness, and soon thereafter died in peace. His last words were, "Christ is precious; I can trust in Him."

THE MOTHER OF THE ERSKINES;
Or, a Providential Deliverance from the Grave.

A MOST remarkable deliverance from the grave was experienced by the mother of the celebrated Ralph and Ebenezer Erskine. Strange though it may appear, it could be said she died and was buried before her renowned sons were born. She wore on her finger at the time of her death a rich gold ring, which, from some domestic cause or other, was much valued by the family. After the body was laid in the coffin an attempt was made to remove the ring, but the hand and the finger were so much swollen, that it was found impossible. It was proposed to cut off the finger, but as the husband's feelings revolted at the idea, she was buried with the ring on her finger.

The sexton, who was aware of the fact, formed a resolution to possess himself of the ring, and therefore, on the night of her burial, he opened the grave and coffin. Having no scruples about cutting off the finger of a dead woman, he provided himself with a sharp knife for the purpose. He lifted the stiff arm, and made an incision by the joint of the finger; instantly the blood flowed, and the woman arose and sat up in her coffin! The grave-digger fled with affright, while the lady made her way from her narrow tenement, and walked back to the door of her dwelling, where she stood without and knocked for admittance. Her husband, who was a minister, sat conversing with a friend. When the knock was repeated, he observed, "Were it not that my wife is in her grave, I should say that was her knock." He arose hastily and opened the door. There stood his dear companion, wrapped in her grave-clothes, and her uplifted finger drooping blood. "My Margaret!" he exclaimed. "The same," said she; "your dear wife, in her own proper person; do not be alarmed." The lady in question lived seven or eight years after this occurrence, and became the mother of several children, among whom was the persons to whom we have referred.

A PRETENDED MIRACLE EXPOSED.

THE late Sheriff Henry Glassford Bell, in one of his works, says there was a chapel in the neighbourhood of Musselburgh dedicated to the Lady of Loretto, which, from the character of superior sanctity it had acquired, had long been the favourite resort of religious devotees. In this chapel, a body of the Catholic priests undertook to put their religion to test, by performing a miracle. They fixed upon a young man who was well-known as a common beggar in the streets of Edinburgh, and engaged to restore to him, in the presence of the assembled people, the perfect use of his eyesight. A day was named, on which they calculated they might depend on this wonderful interposition of divine power in their behalf. From motives of curiosity, a great crowd was attracted at the appointed time to the chapel; and the blind man made his appearance on the scaffold erected for the occasion. The priests approached the altar, and after praying very devoutly, and performing other religious ceremonies, he, who had previously been stone blind, opened his eyes, and declared he saw all things plainly. Having humbly and gratefully thanked his benefactors—the priests—he was permitted to mingle among the astonished crowd, and receive their charity.

Unfortunately, however, for the success of this deception, a gentleman from Fife, of the name of Colville, determined to penetrate, if possible, a little into the mystery. He prevailed upon the subject of the recent experiment, to accompany him to his lodgings in Edinburgh. As soon as they were alone, he locked the chamber door, and either by bribes or threats, contrived to win from him the whole secret. It turned out, that in his boyhood, this tool, in the hands of the designing, had been employed as a herd by the nuns of the convent of Sciennes, then in the neighbourhood of Edinburgh. It was remarked by the sisterhood, that he had an extraordinary facility in " flipping up the lid of his eyes, and casting up the white." Some of the neighbouring priests, hearing accidentally of this talent, imagined that it might be applied to good account. They accordingly took him from Sciennes to the monastery, near Musselburgh, where they kept him till he had made himself an adept in this mode of counterfeiting blindness, and till his personal appearance was so much changed, that the few who had been acquainted with him before, would not be able to recognise him. They then sent him to Edinburgh to beg publicly, and make himself familiarly known to the inhabitants as a common blind mendicant. So far everything had gone smoothly, and the scene at the chapel of Loretto might have had effects on the minds of the vulgar, had Colville's activity not discovered the gross imposture. Colville, who belonged to the congregation, instantly took the most effectual means to make known the deceit. He insisted upon the blind man's appearing with him next day at the cross of Edinburgh, where the latter repeated all he had told Colville, and confessed the iniquity of his own conduct, as well as that of the priests. To shelter him from revenge, Colville immediately afterwards carried him off to Fife; and the story, with all its details, being speedily disseminated, exposed the Catholic clergy to more contempt than ever.

BURNS ON TRUE MANHOOD.

SINCE Carlyle wrote his " Sartor Resartus" the tendency to judge people by their dress is less marked than it used to be. Robert Burns failed not to express himself vigorously about it. Walking in Leith, Robert met an old acquaintance, and he stopped to have a crack with him, and a dandy friend who was with him, said afterwards that he was surprised he should stop to speak to such a shabby looking fellow as that. "What," said the manly poet, "do you suppose it was the man's clothes I was speaking to, his hat, his coat, his boots? No! it was the man within, and, let me tell you, that man has more sense and worth in him than nine out of ten of my city friends." That was the man who was worthy to write the poor man's noblest song:—

> "What though on hamely fare we dine,
>   Wear hodden grey and a' that,
>   Gie fools their silks and knaves their wine,
>   A man's a man for a' that.
> For a' that and a' that,
>   Their tinsel show, and a' that,
> The honest man, though o'er sae poor,
>   Is king o' men for a' that."

AN HONEST STREET ARAB IN EDINBURGH.

In Edinburgh two gentlemen were standing at the door of a hotel one very cold day, when a little boy, with a poor, thin, blue face, his feet bare, and red with the cold, and with nothing to cover him but a bundle of rags, came and said, "Please, sir, buy some matches?" "No! don't want any," the gentleman said. "But they are only a penny a box," the little fellow pleaded. "Yes; but you see we do not want a box," the gentleman said again. "Then I will gie ye twa boxes for a penny," the boy said at last. "And so, to get rid of him," the gentleman, who tells the story in an English paper, says, "I bought a box. But then I found I had no change; so I said, "I will buy a box to-morrow." "O, do buy them the nicht, if you please," the boy pleaded again. "I will rin and get ye the change, for I am verra hungry." So I gave him the shilling, and he darted away; and I waited for him, but no boy came. Then I thought I had lost my shilling; but still there was that in the boy's face I trusted, and I did not like to think bad of him. Well, late in the evening, a servant came and said a little boy wanted to see me. When he was brought in I found he was a smaller brother of the boy that got my shilling, but, if possible, still more ragged, and poor, and thin. He stood a moment diving into his rags, as if he was seeking something, and then said, "Are you the gentleman that bocht the matches frae Sandie?" "Yes." " Weel, then, here's fourpence oot o' yer shillin.' Sandie canna come; he's no weel. A cart run ower him and knocked him doon, and he lost his bannet, and his matches, and your sevenpence; and baith his legs are broken, and he's no weel at a', and the doctor says he'll dee. And that's a' he can gie ye the noo," putting fourpence down on the table, and then the poor child broke down into great sobs.

"So I fed the little man," the gentleman goes on to say, "and then I went with him to see Sandie. I found that the two little things lived with a wretched drunken stepmother; their own father and mother were both dead. I found poor Sandie lying on a bundle of shavings. He knew me as soon as I came in, and said, "I got the change, sir, and was comin' back, and then the horse knocked me doon, and baith my legs are broken. And O, Reuby, little Reuby! I'm shair I'm deein'! and wha will tak' care o' ye, Reuby, when I'm gane? What will ye dae, Reuby?" Then I took the poor little sufferer's hand, and told him I would always take care of Reuby. He understood me, and had just strength to look at me as if he would thank me; then the light went out of his blue eyes, and, in a moment,

"He lay within the light of God,
 Like a babe upon the breast,
Where the wicked cease from troubling,
 And the weary are at rest."

Reuby was looked after, educated, and cared for in every way.

GOD NEVER DIES—A WIDOW'S FAITH.

IN the *Christian Treasury* for 1845, it is recorded that there dwelt in the east of Scotland, a pious minister of the gospel who had laboured in connection with a small but respectable congregation for a number of years. In the midst of his active career of usefulness he was suddenly removed by death, leaving behind him a wife and a number of helpless children. The small stipend allowed him by his congregation had been barely sufficient to meet the current expenses of his family, and at death no visible means were left for their support. The death of her husband preyed deeply upon the heart of the poor afflicted widow, while the dark prospect which the future presented filled her mind with the most gloomy apprehensions. By her lonely fireside she sat—the morning after her sad bereavement—lamenting her forlorn and destitute condition, when her little son, a boy of five years of age, entered the room. Seeing the deep distress of his mother, he stole softly to her side, and placing his little hand in hers, looked wistfully into her face, and said,—"Mother, mother, is God dead?" Soft as the gentle whisper of an angel did the simple accent of the dear boy fall upon the ear of the disconsolate and almost heart-broken mother. A gleam of heavenly radiance lighted up for a moment her pale features. Then snatching up her little boy, and pressing him fondly to her bosom, she exclaimed, "No, no, my son, God is not dead; He lives, and has promised to be a father to the fatherless, and a husband to the widow. His promises are sure and stedfast, and upon them I will firmly and implicitly rely." Her tears were dried, and her murmurings for ever hushed. The event proved that her confidence was not misplaced. The congregation over whom her husband had worthily presided, generously settled upon her a handsome annuity, by which she was enabled to support her family, not only comfortably, but genteelly. The talents of her sons, as they advanced in years, soon brought them into notice, and finally procured them high and honourable stations in society.

HUGH MILLER PUBLICLY CATECHISED.

It was the custom some years ago, in some parishes in the north of Scotland, for the pastor at stated intervals to publicly examine the members of the congregation in the Westminster Assembly's Catechism.

Working men and their children were put through this ordeal before the whole people, but the rich were frequently treated with more consideration. On the 30th day of February, 1826, Hugh Miller, when nearly 24 years of age, was catechised by the Rev. James Stewart, of Cromarty. As he was called upon to stand up before two or three hundred people, he felt it was far from being a pleasant position. He stood before the minister as conspicuous as Saul among the people — his face changing from crimson to pale, and pale to crimson, and endeavoured, with faltering speech, to answer the recondite questions in theology which were put to him. The minister, in the most solemn manner, asked and received, among others, the following questions and answers:— "Who is the Holy Spirit?" "The third person of the Holy Trinity." "Is he a person?" "He is termed so in the Scriptures." "Do you recollect any particular passages of Scripture which show him to be a distinct person?" Here Hugh Miller was silent, and felt confused.

The good minister helped him out of his difficulty by remarking,—"I thought from your readiness in answering me my first two questions that you would answer me this one too. In what form did the Spirit appear at the baptism of our Saviour?" "In the form of a dove." "Yes. The Spirit, then, is a person, not a mere influence proceeding from the Father and the Son as some believe. In what manner were we baptised?" "With water, in the name of the Father, Son, and Spirit." "Yes. The Holy Ghost is a person. What is the work or province of the Father?" "He created all things, and from Him all things proceed." "You speak of Him as the Creator. I desire to know what share He has in the redemption of sinners?" "He sent the Son." "Yes. What did the Son do?" "He died for us." "And what was the work of the Spirit?" "He applies Christ." The young man was thus plied with questions, drilled in the Shorter Catechism, and, after sundry exhortations, was told to resume his seat, which, says Hugh Miller, "I did so most willingly, for my legs were trembling beneath me."

Such catechising has formed no inconsiderable portion of the education of many a Scotch youth who became a famous Scotchman.

THE COVENANTER'S BIBLE.

WILLIAM HANNAH, the Covenanter, lived in the parish of Sundergarth, in Annandale. He was made a prisoner for his faith, and was faithful to the end. Besides his other retreats, he had, when under persecution, a hiding place in his own barn. When he was lying on one occasion among the straw reading his bible, which he always carried with him as his sweetest companion in his solitariness, the house was visited by a party of soldiers in search of him. In his haste to flee from the place, he left his bible among the straw, and fled to a distance. The troopers, in the course of their searching, entered the barn, every corner of which they pried into, turning everything upside down, and tossing about the straw that had so recently been the bed of him whom they were so eagerly seeking. According to their custom, they thrust their long swords down through the heaps of straw and hay that lay on the floor, with the view of stabbing any one who might happen to be concealed beneath. In this process, one of the men pushed his sword accidentally on the bible lying among the straw, by which means it received a deep cut, which, doubtless, its owner would have sustained if he had been in the same place.

The bible was afterwards found with the recent hack in it, and restored to Hannah, to whom it was more endeared than ever. It passed as a precious heirloom into the possession of his son William, who afterwards settled in Scarborough as a minister, and was uniformly used in the pulpit as the bible from which he preached. He held it in the greatest veneration for his father's sake, who had so often perused it, and derived from it much comfort in the days of his sufferings for conscience sake. When the Rev. Mr. Hannah retired from the ministry through infirmity, and returned to his native parish of Sundergarth, he brought his father's bible with him, and, after his death, it was retained in the possession of his friends as a relic too precious to be lost. This remarkable bible was printed in the year 1599, and was directly and indirectly the source of light, inspiration, and courage to many.

A CONVERSION IN AYR PRISON.

THERE have been many noted men in prison who have felt the power of the gospel both as a saving and sanctifying influence. Robert Fleming, in one of his best known works, records a case which clearly proves that it is the power of God unto salvation, even in the experience of the most degraded and criminal. He records the experience of a notorious criminal who had been sentenced to death in Ayr. He was so stupid and besotted, that those who knew him thought that he was beyond the pale of grace and the reach of hope. But while this man was in prison, the Lord wonderfully wrought on his heart. He began to think of his past life and the sinfulness of his heart. Then after much serious exercise and sore wrestling, a most kindly work of repentance followed, with great assurance of mercy. This continued for a time, and he was so rooted and grounded in the truth, that when he came to the stake, he could not cease crying out to the people under the sense of pardon, and the comforts of the presence and favour of God, "Oh, He is a great forgiver! He is a great forgiver!" And he added, "Now hath perfect love cast out all fear, I know God hath nothing against me, for Jesus Christ hath paid all; and those are free whom the Son makes free." His end was one of transport and joy, and by his death he exhibited the marvellous grace of God, raising him above the experience of other men who, not long before, seemed in some respects on a level with, if not below, the inferior animals of creation. Verily Christ can save to the uttermost all who come unto God by Him.

AN OLD SERMON RE-DELIVERED WITH EFFECT AT WHITEKIRK.

In the parish of Whitekirk, near Dunbar, during a terrible storm, a vessel, ladened with French goods, was dashed on the rocks, and totally wrecked. She soon broke up, and a great deal of the cargo was swept ashore by the waves, and was to be found strewn for miles along the coast. When the noise of this got abroad, many of the people in the neighbourhood assembled, and made free with the goods, removing them without scruple to their homes as if they had been their own. The parish minister, the Rev. William Paul, when he heard this, was sadly distressed, and determined to preach a sermon by way of improving the occasion and the character of his parishioners. Meantime, his father, the Rev. Dr. Paul, of Banchory-Devenick, on the banks of the Dee, about five miles above Aberdeen, heard of the occurrence, and the determination of his son to preach a sermon. He thereupon sent him word that he had a sermon, more than a hundred years of age, which was preached on a like occasion, by the celebrated Judge Hailes, the effect of which was, that all those who had stolen the goods, brought them back during the following week. This was not done in a concerted manner, but individually. Dr. Paul advised his son not to prepare a new sermon, but take the old one of Lord Hailes, and preach it to the people, telling them who the author was, and what effect it had on those who originally heard it.

The minister of Whitekirk adopted the suggestion given, and when Sabbath came round, a large congregation assembled to hear a discourse concerning the shipwreck, which had stirred the minds of the people in the neighbourhood so much. Lord Hailes' sermon was delivered with most marked impression. The circumstances were so much alike, that it fitted the whole case. And what was best of all, the like spiritual and moral effects followed the second as followed the first delivery. For early in the following week, many of those who had enriched themselves with portions of the cargo of the wrecked ship, quietly brought them back, and sought in this way to make some reparation for the evil they, perhaps, had thoughtlessly done. The effect of the whole proceedings on the parish was beneficial. Lord Hailes, though dead, yet spoke, and through the lips of another man his words were those of spirit and power.

M'PHAIL AND THE JUDGE.

In the middle of last century, the minister of Resolis was a man of peculiar methods and ways of doing good. His name was the Rev. Hector M'Phail, and he was well known throughout the whole of the north of Scotland. He never lost an opportunity of saying a good word for the Master, and he always managed to do it in such a way as to give no offence. An instance of this is given in the way he approached a Circuit Judge on one occasion. When riding in the company of a brother minister, the travellers were overtaken, near Inverness, by the equipage of the Lord of Justiciary, who was to preside in the Circuit Court to be held that day. Mr. M'Phail suggested to his brother minister that this might be a glorious opportunity of doing some spiritual good to an influential man of the world, and urged him to assist in improving the precious and unlooked for moment. His companion, however, being, most probably, one of those rule and plummet ministers, whose favourite Scripture maxim is, "Let everything be done decently and in order," was not carried away by his zeal beyond the bounds of propriety, and politely declined the invitation. But Mr. M'Phail had long learned to "be instant," not only "in season," but also "out of season;" so the willing propensities of the white pony were again put in requisition. Riding forward to the carriage, Mr. M'Phail respectfully addressed his Lordship, and, after a prefatory remark or two, reminded him that the proceedings in which the Court was to engage were emblematic of another judgment-seat, at which his Lordship must appear, not as a judge upon the bench, but as a panel at the bar, entreating him, at the same time, with respectful but affectionate earnestness, to weigh well the nature of his case, and to commit it in time into the hands of the Great Advocate with the Father, who can never be an unsuccessful pleader, because Himself the propitiation for our sins. His Lordship appeared impressed with the address which he had heard; thanked Mr. M'Phail most warmly for his ministerial faithfulness, and invited him to become his guest at the close of the Court.

THE GLASGOW INFIDEL'S DEATH-BED.

JOHN HASTIE lived in the East-end of Glasgow, and was the only son of a pious mother, who had become a widow when he was quite a lad. He was sent to be an apprentice to a weaver who was an infidel, and who did all he could to propagate his principles. John Hastie, to the sad grief of his mother, imbibed infidel notions, and after his marriage with his master's daughter, who too had cast off all religion, descended rapidly into recklessness in thought and conduct. In this condition he remained till his own child had approached the years of manhood. Then his health began to give way, and soon it appeared that consumption had fastened its grasp upon him. Having opportunities for meditation, his indifference was broken up, and, at last, he sent for a minister, who, however, failed to remove his unbelief. One of Dr. Chalmers' most valued elders, in his visits, discovered the dying weaver, and found that his case required the most skilful management. He, accordingly, brought Dr. Chalmers to his humble dwelling. The Doctor, by his sympathy, and simple-hearted piety, so similar to that of his mother's, whose reason her son's abandonment of God had overthrown, soon won the confidence of the dying man, and drew from him a history of his life, and especially of his unbelief. The Doctor presented the truth as it is in Jesus to the acceptance of the wretched sinner. Once each week for three months did he visit him, and laboured most assiduously to adapt the presentation of the truth to the perverted, disordered, guilty, and almost despairing mind of the weaver. The blessing of God manifestly rested upon those efforts. As the man drew nearer the grave, his minister became more and more satisfied that his soul had been renewed by the grace of God, and that he was rapidly preparing for heaven.

The interview which both felt would be the last on earth came. "Doctor," said he, lifting his Bible off the bed on which it lay, "will you take this book from me as a token of my inexpressible gratitude?" "No, sir," said Dr. Chalmers, after a moment's hesitation; "no, sir, that is far too precious a legacy to be put past your own son—give it to your boy." It was not likely that the Doctor's advice would be disregarded. "Give me a pen," said the dying man. His request was complied with. Gathering up his remaining strength of mind and body he wrote, on a blank leaf of the Bible, the following homely, but, from the circumstances in which they were written, most interesting lines:—

> "To thee, my son, I give this book,
>   In hopes thou wilt from it find
> A Father and a Comforter,
>   When I do leave thee here behind.
>
> "I hope that thou wilt firm believe
>   That Jesus Christ alone can save—
> He bled and suffered in our stead;
>   To save from death, Himself He gave.
>
> "A strong desire I now do crave
>   Of them to whom thy charge is given,
> To bring thee up to fear the Lord,
>   That we meet at last in heaven."

Having written these lines, he laid his head back on the pillow and expired.

A BOY'S FAITH AND LOVE.

In the West Highlands of Scotland there is a mountain gorge not less than twenty to thirty feet in width, and about two hundred feet in depth. Its rocky and all but perpendicular walls are bare of vegetation, save in their crevices, in which grow numerous wild flowers of rare beauty, and most difficult to get. A company of scientific tourists came to the place, and were desirous of obtaining specimens of these rare plants, but did not know how to reach them. A Highland boy had joined them, and it was thought that he might descend to where they were if he were asked. They at once offered him a handsome sum of money, if he would consent to be lowered down the cliff by a rope and gather a little basket of them. The temptation was great, for the boy's parents were poor, and money was scarce in that part of the country. He looked wistfully at the reward, but when he gazed at the yawning chasm, he shuddered, shrank back, and refused to let himself be lowered down. At last a happy thought struck him, by means of which he could run the risk with safety, and, at the same time, secure for his parents and family the reward. His heart grew strong, and his eyes sparkled with determination when he said,—"I will go, if my father will hold the rope." This was at once agreed to. The father was got. All things were arranged, and then, with unshrinking nerves, cheek unblanched, and heart firmly strung, he suffered his father to lower him into the abyss, and to suspend him there while he filled his little basket with the coveted wild flowers. When his mission was accomplished, he was cautiously lifted up by the strong arm of his father, and was congratulated on his daring exploit. It was a daring deed, but his faith in the love of a father's heart gave him courage and power to perform it, and to act the part of a true son and a little hero.

DR. CHALMERS AND THE DROVER.

Dr. Chalmers' power as a preacher was great, and it was felt both by the learned and the uncultured alike. No better instance could be given of how he affected the rudest minds than that recorded by one who was present and observed it. Dr. Chalmers was preaching in a country church in Tweeddale to a crowded congregation. One of the audience was a notorious character, a drover, who had much of the rather brutal look of what he worked in, with the knowing eye of a man of the city—a sort of Big Peter Bell.

"He had hardness in his eye,
He had hardness in his cheek."

He was a terror to all who knew him, and many were afraid when they saw him enter the church. Dr. Chalmers entered the pulpit, homely in his dress and gait, and having a great look about him, like a mountain among hills. He took for the subject of his discourse, "Death Reigns." He stated slowly, calmly, the simple meaning of the words, what death was, and how and why it reigned; then suddenly he started, and looked like a man who had seen a great sight, and was breathless to declare it; he told how death reigned everywhere, at all times, in all places; how all knew it, and would yet know more of it. After advancing proofs of the reign of Death, and shrieking, as if in despair, these words, "Death is a tremendous necessity!" He suddenly looked beyond, as if into some distant region, and cried out, "Behold a mightier!—who is this? He cometh from Edom, with dyed garments from Bozrah, glorious in his apparel, speaking in righteousness, travelling towards men in the greatness of his strength, mighty to save."

All present were astonished, hushed into awe, and impressed. So was the drover. He had sat down in the table-seat opposite the pulpit, was gazing up to the speaker at first in a state of stupid excitement. He seemed for a while restless, but never kept his eye from the preacher. At the close, he was completely broken down, weeping like a child, the tears running down his ruddy, coarse cheeks—his face opened out and smoothed like an infant's, and his whole body stirred with emotion. The strong man was bowed down by a greater than he, and, in his experience, the power and grandeur of sacred eloquence were exhibited. As that drover retired from that country church to his daily avocation, he would feel that life was much more real than he had hitherto thought it was, and he himself was a greater mystery to himself than ever, and more valuable to God who created him.

NO STRIFE IN HEAVEN.

The Session of the Scotch Kirk is composed of the elders, generally men of experience and influence, and the minister. Frequently matters of a serious character require to be discussed at the session meetings, and occasionally differences of opinion regarding them exist. At one of these meetings an elder had a somewhat serious dispute with the minister, and, on the part of the former, feeling ran high and hasty words were spoken. The minister felt wounded, but did not utter a word by way of retaliation. He felt broken-hearted and discouraged. When the meeting was over both went to their respective homes, but in very different frames of mind. When the elder appeared at the breakfast table next morning he looked ill at ease. His wife noticed this and said to him, "You look sad this morning, James, what's the matter wi' ye?" "Ah," he replied, "you would look sad too, if you had such a dream as I have had last night. I dreamed I had been at the Elders' meeting, and had said some severe things, and had grieved the minister; and when he went home I thought he died, and went to heaven; and when I got to the gates of heaven, out came the minister and put out his hands to take me in, saying, 'Come along, James, there's nae strife up here—I am happy to see ye. Come away.'" Immediately thereafter, the elder repaired to the Manse to beg the minister's pardon, but great was his astonishment to find that he had died during the night. This preyed so much on the elder's mind that his mind and body were affected, and, two weeks after, he also departed this life. "And I should not wonder," said he who related the incident, and who knew both persons, "if James met the minister at the gate of heaven, he would welcome him with outstretched hands, and say—'Come along, James, there's nae strife up here.'" And if there is to be no strife in heaven, why should there be any on earth?

HECTOR M'PHAIL AND THE KITCHEN MAID.

The Rev. Thomas M'Kenzie, Yester, gives a characteristic anecdote of Hector M'Phail. In the month of May, a few days before the meeting of the General Assembly in Edinburgh, to which, as a commissioner from the Presbytery of Chanonry, he was proceeding, he put up for the night at a comfortable inn on the Highland road. It was the invariable practice of Mr. M'Phail to hold family worship in every house he slept in, and to insist upon the attendance of every individual inmate. On this occasion he summoned, as usual, the family together for devotional purposes. When all had been seated, the Bible produced, and the group were waiting the commencement of the devotions, Mr. M'Phail looked around him and asked whether every inmate of the house were present. The landlord replied in the affirmative. "All?" again inquired the minister. "Yes," answered the host, "we are all here; there is a lassie in the kitchen, but we never think of asking her in, for she is so dirty that she is not fit to be seen." "Then call in the lassie," said Mr. M'Phail, laying down the Bible, which he had opened; "we will wait till she comes." The landlord apologised, the minister was peremptory. "The scullery maid had a soul, and a very precious one," he said; "if she was not in the habit of being summoned to family worship, all the greater need of joining them now." At length the host consented, the poor girl was taken in to join the circle, and evening worship proceeded. After devotions, Mr. M'Phail asked the girl the usual introductory question, "Who made you?" to which no answer came. "Do you know that you have a soul?" "No, I never heard that I had one. What is a soul?" was the reply. The minister further asked, "Do you ever pray?" The girl replied, "I don't know what you mean." "Well," said the minister, "I am going to Edinburgh, and I will bring you a little neckkerchief if you promise to say a prayer that I will teach you. It is very short, there are only four words in it—'*Lord show me* MYSELF,' and if you repeat this night and morning, I will not forget to bring you what I have promised." The little kitchen-maid was delighted; the promise was given, and Mr. M'Phail retired to rest, and next morning resumed his journey.

After his sojourn in Edinburgh, where Mr. M'Phail did not forget the Highland inn and its little menial, he retraced his steps homewards. He arrived at the inn late, and the man of God, ere he permitted supper to touch his lips, summoned the household around the family altar. Again, however, the little maid was absent, and again he inquired the cause. But it is now a different reason that withholds her. "Indeed, sir," replied the hostess, "she has been of little use since you were here; she has done nothing but sit and cry night and day, and now she is so weak and exhausted, that she cannot rise from her bed." "O, my good woman, let me see the girl immediately," exclaimed the minister, instantly divining the reason of her grief. Being conducted to a hole beneath the stairs, where the creature lay upon a straw bed, a picture of mental agony, the amiable man said, "Well, my child, here is the neckerchief I have brought you from Edinburgh. I hope you have done what you promised, and said the prayer I taught you." "O no, sir—no, I can never take your present," was the response of the girl. "A dear gift it has been to me; you taught me a prayer that God has answered in an awful way. He *has* shown me myself, and O what a sight it is! Minister, minister! what shall I do?" Mr. M'Phail entered into her case fully and sympathetically, and after a conversation regarding the gospel method of salvation, the interview was ended by recommending the use of another short and comprehensive prayer, "*Lord show me* THYSELF." This ultimately led the dark soul into the glorious light of God's dear Son, and for many years she lived not only a consistent character, but an eminently holy Christian.

GUTHRIE THE MARTYR'S LITTLE WILLIE.

JAMES GUTHRIE, the martyr, had a son called William, four or five years of age, when his father was executed.

He was so young, indeed, and, consequently, so ignorant of the dismal tragedy that was approaching, that James Lowe, the beadle, could scarcely keep him from playing on the streets the day of his father's execution. Guthrie, whose soul yearned over his boy, so soon to become an orphan, took him upon his knee, and gave him such advices as were suited to his capacity. He bade him to become serious—to become religious—and to be sure to devote himself to that honest and holy course in which his father had walked to the death. "Willie," he said, "they will tell you, and cast up to you, that your father was hanged, but think not shame of it, for it is upon a good cause." After the execution, the head was set up on the Nether Bow Port as a spectacle for the finger of scorn to point at. But among those who repaired thither, and looked up at the long grey hairs rustling in the wind, and the features embrowning and drying in the sun, one little boy was often seen gazing fixedly upon that countenance, with looks of love and terror—and still returning day after day, and hour after hour, as if there was for him a language in that silent head which none else could hear. And who could that child be but Guthrie's young son—the little "Willie" of the martyr's last affectionate counsels and cares? His love of playing in the streets was over now; a new occupation had absorbed him; and as he returned from these pilgrimages, we may conceive with what feelings his mother heard him when, on her anxious inquiry as to where he had been, the usual reply was, "I have been seeing my father's head." The dying admonitions of the departed parent, enforced by such a solemnizing spectacle, seemed to have sunk deep into William's heart; for it was observed that after his father's death, he spent much time in solitude, and was often employed in prayer. Resolving to walk in his father's steps, he directed his studies to the Church, and became a scholar of excellent promise; but he died in early youth, when he was finishing his studies with the view of entering the ministry.

INDEX.

Agnew, Sir Andrew, his loyalty to conviction, 85.
Alexander, Dr. W. L., on Dr. Chalmers, 107; rebuked by Richard Knill, 135.
Anderson, Sir James, the boy who became a captain, 295.
Anderson, Rev. Dr. William, and the extortioner, 48; and a Cameronian elder on reading sermons, 199; on ministers' stipends, 255; on the simplicity of faith, 258.
Andrew, St., and Scotland, 173.
Angels, Rabbi Duncan on, 82; Rev. James Robertson on, 82.
Animals—Professor John Wilson's love for, 90; St. Columba and his horse, 142.
Annan, Robt., the Christian swimmer; his courage, 360
Arbirlot—Dr. Guthrie's first parish, 194; three remarkable parishioners, 194; special providence at, 297.
Argyll, Duke of, trial and death, 221; on Mr. Darwin, 336.
Assembly, the General, on Foreign Missions in 1796, 184.

Blasphemer (see Swearer).
Bretchie, Captain, on seeing and believing, 365; and the old tar sweeping out darkness, 380.
Brougham, Lord, decision of character in early life, 196.
Brown, John, of Priesthill, his death, 122.
Brown, John, of Haddington, a herd laddie, 117; his Greek New Testament, 117.
Brown, John, on infant salvation, 134.
Brown, Dr. John (Rab and his

Friends), on John Brown of Haddington, 117; on children, 121; on Ebenezer Brown, 128; his early experiences, death, and burial of his mother, 189; the old Scottish believer, 245; on bad drink for a child, 323.
Brown, Rev. Ebenezer, in London, 54; sermon in Inverkeithing, 54; and the carters, 128.
Bruce, Rev. Robert, Christ's presence, 44; sermon at Leuchars, 182; his death, 182.
Bruce, King Robert, and the Spider, a lesson in perseverance, 212.
Buccleuch, Duke of, and the herd boy, 248.
Balmer, Dr., a boy theologian, 163.
Balmoral, a pedlar at, 26; dinner at, 171.
Barker, Joseph, Colonel Shaw, of Ayr, overcoming his unbelief, 185; discussion in Glasgow, 185.
Bass Rock, The; Peden, the prophet, 49; Rev. Thomas Hog healed in, 362.
Beaton, Archbishop, and Patrick Hamilton, 51; in consultation, 166.
Beattie, the Rev. Dr., teaching natural theology, 62; his church, Glasgow, 31.
Begg, Rev. Dr. James, how to treat opponents, 132; his father and the radicals, 348.
Bell, Sir Henry Glassford, a pretended miracle exposed, 383.
Bible, The, and the criminal, 40; to be used as a gun, 76; Robert Flockhart's knowledge of, 104; importance of knowing it when young. 306; proved by Scotchmen, 357; A Covenanter's, 359, a repentant infidel's, 304.

Buchanan, George, his truthfulness and humility, 274.
Burn, Major General Andrew, his dream, 253.
Burns, Robert, his wife and grave, 98; New Year's day reflections, 129; his humanity, 197; in Paisley, 265; on true manhood, 384.
Burns, Rev. William, and the repentant publican, 361.
Braxfield, Lord, on the Sabbath day, 38.
Brewster, Sir David, disgusted, his humility, 169.
Bruce, Michael, his paraphrases, 331.

Cameron, Richard, his sufferings and death, 217.
Campbell, Friar, and Patrick Hamilton's death, 52; his miserable death, 164.
Campbell, Mary, gift of tongues, 171; healed by miraculous power, 172.
Campbell, Rev. Donald, his wonderful dream, 364.
Campbell, Thomas, closing his life, 246.
Campbell, Rev. John, an old man's story, 306.
Campbell, Rev. Donald, his temptation by Satan, 328.
Carlyle, Thomas, his mother, 21; on the Seceder elder, 127; and Emerson, 294; in sorrow, 312.
Cargill, Donald, kept from suicide, 218; visited in prison by Professor Wodrow, 219.
Carrick, Mr. Robert, his benevolence stimulated, 375.
Carstares, William, torture and courage, 309.
Chalmers, Rev. Dr., a lost opportunity, 84; change in preaching, 104; and the old woman, 107; his daughter, 122; needed and unexpected encouragement, 141; on hyper-criticism, 145; in Glasgow, the Astronomical discourses, 167 a fruitful sermon, 191; his integrity, 232; and Tholuck, 233;
on a mistake of the intellect, 255; and the school girl, 314; at an infidel's bedside, 393; and the drover, 395.
Chambers, Dr. William, Josephus utilised, 20.
Church service, Rev. Ebenezer Brown on, 54; Ordinances relied on, 98.
Cockburn, Lord, on Brougham as a boy, 196.
Collins, Rev. Thomas, at Orkney, 225.
Columba, Saint, his horse, 142; receiving a lesson in charity, 183; and the robber, 269.
Conscience, scruples overcome, 33; power of, 59; true to, 373.
Courage—John Knox before Mary, 23; mail guard, 36; Dr. William Anderson, 48; William Carstares, 309; Robert Annan, 360.
Croumbie, John, anniversary of a deliverance, 231.
Coupar Justice—administered by Bailie John, 106.
Covenanters—Peden, 49, 210; tent preaching, 63; Welsh of Irongray, 109; Brown of Priesthill, 122; James Guthrie, 157; James Harkness, 229; Renwick, 250; William Hannah, 389.
Cowie of Huntly—on the Holy Spirit; his fiddle, 118.
Cowper, Bishop, vision and death, 102.

Darwin, Mr., and the Duke of Argyll on design in nature, 336.
Davidson, Andrew, the fisherman, his triumphant death, 324.
Decision, importance of, 228; illustrated, 262.
Dreams—a poor woman's, about Dr. Guthrie, 55; James Howie's, 153; Major-General Burn's, 253; Rev. Donald Campbell's, 364; an elder's, 397.
Delays dangerous—a lost opportunity, 84; a chieftain's, 111.
Disruption, described, 285; Lords Rutherford and Jeffrey on, 285; incidents connected with, 373.

INDEX. 403

Drummond, Professor Henry, a prevailing argument, 330.
Drummond, Provost, his benevolence, 341.
Duncan, Rabbi, on angels, 82; logic of salvation with Cæsar Malan, 114; his salvation syllogisms, 115.
Dundonald, Earl, and the minister, 78.
Dunn, Rev. Wm., of Cadder, his imprisonment, 149.
Dying hours—Samuel Rutherford's, 24; converted infidel's, 46; Patrick Hamilton's, 51; Rob Roy MacGregor's, 63; George Gilfillan's, 100; Willie Greig's, 103; a child's, 120; Brown's of Priesthill, 122; Sir Walter Scott's, 137; Hugh M'Kenzie's, 143; James Guthrie's, 157; Walter Mill's, 162; Robert Bruce's, 181: Bailie Wardlaw's, 202; Wigton martyrs', 211; Richard Cameron's, 217; Duke of Argyll's, 221; Perth martyrs', 224; Thomas Campbell's, 246; Renwick's, 250; Dr. Norman MacLeod's, 256; Hugh M'Kail's, 260; Edward Irving's, 282; young woman's in Dundee, 317; Dr. Thomas Guthrie's, 322; a fisherman's, 324; Edinburgh student's, 330; martyrs' at Glasgow, 334; John Knox's, 370; repentant infidel's, 393.

Eadie, Dr., sermon to shepherds, 81.
Edie, Robert, his conversion, Dr. Chalmers' sermon, 191.
Edwards, Thomas, exhibition in Aberdeen, his independence and industry, 53.
Erskine, Rev. Dr., moderating a call, 377; his faithfulness to duty, 377.
Erskine, Rev. Ebenezer—hearing the Word, 25; as a preacher, 155; and the murderer, 178; and the blasphemers, 268; his mother, 382.
Erskine, Ralph, as a preacher, 155;

his mother delivered from death, 382.
Erskine, Rev. Henry, deliverances experienced, 72.
Extortioner, The, reproved, by Dr. Wm. Anderson, 48.
Faith—Dr. Chalmers and the old woman, 107; and works, 206; old Scotch believer, 245; simplicity of, 258; healing by, 326; illustrated by Captain Brotchie, 380; a boy's, 394; a widow's, 386.
Ferguson, Rev. Dr., his hymn and its influence, 292.
Fletcher, Miss Eliza, and Marjory Smith, life through death, 192.
Flockhart, Robert, aptness in quoting the Bible, 164; important school lesson, 236.
Forsyth, Robert, his parents, education, as an advocate, 92.
Fraser, Rev. James, and his wife, 332.

Geddes, Jenny, her stool, 43; a second, and the Chartist, 368.
Gilfillan, Rev. George, preaching his funeral sermon, 100; his generosity, 130; on the religious influence of mountains, 311.
Glencairn, Lady, her life, 298; appointing a minister, 299.
God—men of St. Kilda cannot forget, 50; seeking for, 180; trust in, 359; swimming for the glory of, 360; no terms with, 361; never dies, 386.
Gospel, The influence of the, on criminals, 40; as expounded by Alexander Patrick, 83.
Gordon, Duke of, and the farmer, 266.
Grant, Mr. Hay Macdowell, self-righteousness exposed, 71; Wm. Gilbert brought to decision, 139.
Greig, Willie, a young disciple, his death, 103.
Guthrie, James, and the dying woman, 65; his courage and death, 157; his Wee Willie, 399.
Guthrie, Rev. Dr.—Gospel bells, 55; first parish and parishioners, 194; on drink and death at Blair-

gowrie, 197; "a beautiful field in Edinburgh," 226; a special Providence at Arbirlot, 297; Ragged School work, 315; death-bed, 322; the Irishman, 347.

Hailes, Lord, discovering hidden treasures, 17; the New Testament and the Fathers, 17; and an infidel, 358; his sermon re-delivered, 391.
Haddow, Lord, his spiritual change, 205.
Haldanes, The, their conversion, 74.
Hamilton, Patrick, at the stake, 51; burning of, 166.
Harkness, James, returning good for evil, 229.
Heaven, Dr. Morison when a boy on, 76; No strife in, 397.
Henry, Rev. Dr., and the wearisome minister, 252.
Heywood, Luke, his oath, with Hector M'Phail, and conversion, 159.
Hogg, James, on Adam Scott, shepherd, and his prayers, 151; on popular preachers, 275.
Hog, Rev. Thomas, healing by faith and prayer, 326; in the Bass Rock, 362; marvellous restoration to health, 363.
Honesty, Scotch, the upright Highlander, 34; the street Arab, 385.
Howie, James, of Lochgoin, his dreams, 153.
Hume, David, and the child, 96; and Principal Robertson on the light of Nature and Revelation, 204; his scepticism and grief, 291.
Huntly, a Christian pilgrim at, 69; George Cowie, 118; swearer reproved in, 367.

Infidel, The, and Mr. Alexander Paterson, 46; David Hume and the child, 96; repentant, in Glasgow, 393.
Irving, Edward, and the shoemaker, 148; the scoffer, 187; his dying hours, 282.

James, Rev. John Angell—Katie Lowrie in Perth, 95.
Jamieson, Rev. Dr.—the angry farmer, 101; a suggested text, 179.
Jamieson, Rev. John, his letters, his advice to his son, 126.

Kentigern, St., and the king, 338.
Kidston, Rev. Mr., giving an explanation, 249.
Kirriemuir, an awful providence at, 339.
Knox, John, and Queen Mary, 22; life by M'Crie, 156; his prayer for Scotland, 235; his vocation, 369; closing his life, 370.

Lawson, Rev. Dr.—The captious member, 177; giving a wise answer, 257.
Learmont, Thomas, his prophecy, 355.
Leighton, the Good Bishop, 28; and a poor widow, 28; anecdotes of, 70.
Liberty and Equality, Mr. Shirra on, 45.
Lindsay, Rev. William, and the shoemaker's apprentice, 354.
Livingstone, David, his modesty, 237.

M'Cheyne, Rev. R. M., and an old woman, 119; as a preacher, 220; on a lamb of Christ's flock, 244.
M'Crie, Rev. Dr., and the publisher, 75; declining praise, 113; and Dugald Stewart; his life of Knox, 156; his sincerity, 170.
Macdonald, Rev. Dr., the preaching cure, 349.
M'Gavin, Rev. Dr., and the climbing boy, 279; on a lily among thorns, 317.
M'George, the royal mail guard, 35; his kindness and death, 35.
Macgregor, Rob Roy, his religion and death, 66.
Mack, John, soldier and minister, 345; his mother, 346.
M'Kail, Hugh, his last hours, 260.

INDEX. 405

Mackay, Farquhar, power of conscience, 59.
Mackenzie, Hugh, Highland elder's assurance of salvation, 143.
M'Leod, Robert, his prayer, 37.

Macleod, Rev. Dr. N., on men of St. Kilda, 50; and a waif, 175; his first sermon before the Queen, 222; with an old man, 228; his last hours, 256; and the poor woman on decision, 262.
M'Leod, Rev. Dr. Alexander, on the wrong way, 73.
M'Phail, Rev. Hector, his faithful wife, 87; with a soldier at Fort-George, 159; and the judge, 392; and the kitchen maid, 398.
Mair, Rev. James, a character in his congregation, 247.
Margaret, Saint, and her Gospels, 378.
Martin, Rev. John, his trust in the Lord, 359.
Mary, Queen, and John Knox, 22.
Martyrs, the Wigton, 211; at Perth, 224; at Glasgow, 334.
Matheson, Duncan, in the Crimea, power of song, 108; finding out Christians, 152; his conversion, 352.
Melville, Andrew, and James the Sixth, 284.
Methodist, Mr. Alexander Patrick, 88; Rev. Thomas Collins, 225.
Mill, Walter, the last popish victim, 162.
Miller, Hugh, a prayer wonderfully answered, 353; publicly catechised, 387.
Milne, Rev. John, his earnestness and ways, 304.
Mistake, A, by a Perthshire, elder improved, 76.
Missions, Foreign, in the General Assembly of 1796, 184.
Modern Divinity, the Marrow of, 27; found by Boston, 27; written by Edward Fisher, 27.
Moderatism, its fascination and influence, 272.
Moffat, Rev. Dr., his first sermon to the heathen, 319.

Morison, Rev. Robert, and the Artist, 289.
Morison, Rev. Dr. Jas., on Heaven at school, 76.
Mother, influence of Carlyle's, 21; Dr. Balmer's, 163; a good son and a bad, 279; love for her child, 320; John Mack's, 345; of the Erskine's, 382.
Muir, Rev. Dr., his sermon concerning floating bethels, 308.

North, Brownlow, sudden awakening, 174; and the Colonel, 26; turning a letter to account, 234; his method of study, 270.

Og, Alister, his prayerfulness, 207; and the outdone thief, 208.

Paine, Thomas, on the Bible and Scotchmen, 357.
Paterson, Mr. Alexander, and the infidel, 46; his companion, Mr. Edie, 191; Dr. Chalmers' sermon, 191.
Paterson, Rev. John, preaching the word, 294.
Patrick, Mr. Alexander, dealing with souls, 88.
Paul, Rev. William, Re-delivering Lord Hailes' sermon, 391.
Peden the Prophet in the Bass Rock, 49; in the cleft of a rock, 210; his prevailing prayer, 379.
Penman, Rev. Richard, an awful providence at Kirriemuir, 339.
Perth, Rev. William Wilson, 67; martyrs at, 224.
Pollok, Robert, his first public sermon, 351; his self-possession, 351.
Prayer—Robt. M'Leod's, 37; Rev. Henry Erskine, for food, 72; wonderfully answered, 94; blasphemer's answered, 112; for children, 121; answered near Dunfermline, 146; Scott, the Shepherd's, 151; Rev. John Smith's answered, 335; wonderfully answered, 353; a kitchen maid's, 398.

Preaching — Covenant tent, 63; Dr. Eadie, to Shepherds, 81; Wishart, at Dundee, 91, 136; George Gilfillan, his own funeral sermon, 100; Dr. Chalmers' change in, 104; an old style, 213; seventy years ago, 277; Rev. John Pattison, 294; itinerating, 311.
Priestly cursing, its effects, 329.
Prodigal's, A, return, 31.
Providence — deliverance experienced, 72; a Scotch lady, 166; Peden's escape, 210; special at Arbirlot, 297; at Kirriemuir, 339.

Quakers — Persecutions in Aberdeenshire, 195.
Queen, The, and a pedlar, 26; dinner at Balmoral, 171; Dr. Macleod's first sermon before, 222.

Revival, an old time at Cambuslang, 79.
Ritchie, Rev. Dr., and the swearer, 264.
Ritchie, Rev. Dr. William, and his violin, 372.
Robertson, Principal, and David Hume, 204.
Robertson, the Rev. James, on Rabbi Duncan, 82; Robert Flockhart, 164.
Rutherford, Samuel, his last words, 24; and Archbishop Usher, 131.

Sabbath, Lord Braxfield on the, 38; Highland respect for, 132; Sir Andrew Agnew's bill on, 85; market, 203.
Sage, Rev. Æneas, as a muscular Christian, 214.
Salvation, proclaimed by the Rev. Robert Shirra, 19; the logic of, 114; infant, 134; assurance of, 143; imparting joy, 203; illustrated by Captain Brotchie, 380; experienced in Ayr prison, 390.
Self-Righteousness exposed, 71; of a fifty years' communicant in Edinburgh, 98.

St. Kilda, the men of, cannot forget God, 50.
Scott, Sir Walter, at Rome, journey home, last days, 137.
Shaw, Colonel, his discussion with Joseph Barker, and Christian charity, 185.
Shirra, Rev. Robert, sermon at Kinghorn, 18; on liberty and equality, 45.
Simple, Rev. John, his style of preaching, 213.
Simpleton's Theology, 61; love to Christ, 241; simple-minded answers, 346.
Simpson, Sir James Y., the beloved physician, his superstitious forefathers, 208.
Simson, Patrick, sermon before King James, 340.
Smith's, Rev. John, Blackhills, prayer answered, 335.
Song, sacred, its influence in the Crimea, 108; at Panmure House, 292; in New Orleans, 303; when a fisherman was drowning, 324.
Stanley, Montague, on the theatrical sun, 301.
Stewart, Rev., of Cromarty, and Hector Munro, 203.
Stirling, James, his taking the pledge, 57.
Sutherland, William, an honest executioner, 151.
Sun, desire to see, 68; the theatrical, 301.
Stuart, Rev. Dr., on joy and tears, 203.
Swearer reproved, 30; prayer answered, 112; reproved by Dr. Ritchie, 264; reproved in Huntly, 367.

Theology, a simpleton's, 61; natural, 62; discussion concerning, 111.
Thomson, Dr. Andrew, preaching a silent sermon, 343.
Tweed, good seed sown on its banks, 244.

Watterstone, Rev. Adam, scruples of conscience, 33.

Wardlaw, Rev. Dr. Ralph, and his father, 202; outer and inner man of, 281.
Wardlaw, Old Bailie, his assurance; his deathbed, 202.
Welsh, John, his influence in France, 287; his wife, 288.
Welsh, of Irongray—pursued by Claverhouse, 109.
Wilson, Rev. A. M.—an incident in Bathgate Parish School, 76.
Wilson, Rev. William, in a good cause; his daughter, 67; and the soldier, 240.
Wilson, Rev. Dr. J. H., acting death, 124; on Highland respect for the Sabbath, 132; at the Queen's table, Balmoral, 171.
Wilson, Professor John, his love for animals, 90; chastising a carter, 90.
Wishart, Geo., preaching in Dundee, 91; at Mauchline, 136.
Wodrow, Rev. Prof., and Donald Cargill, 218; measuring his grave, 275.
Works, Faith and, 206; justification by, 213.

THE END.

BELL AND BAIN, LIMITED, PRINTERS, MITCHELL STREET, GLASGOW.

www.ingramcontent.com/pod-product-compliance
Lightning Source LLC
Chambersburg PA
CBHW051244300426
44114CB00011B/883